# TEACHING
SECONDARY SCHOOL
# SOCIAL STUDIES

# TEACHING
## SECONDARY SCHOOL
# SOCIAL STUDIES

JAMES HIGH, Ph.D., Department of History, University of California, Santa Barbara

John Wiley & Sons, Inc., New York · London

Copyright © 1962 by John Wiley & Sons, Inc.

All Rights Reserved. This book or any part thereof must not be
reproduced in any form without the written permission of the
publisher.

Library of Congress Catalog Card Number: 62-10923
Printed in the United States of America

# Preface

This work grew out of twenty years' experience in teaching at all levels from grade seven through graduate seminars in American history. For the last seven years I have been associated directly with teacher training, teaching history, geography and social studies instructional procedures, as well as directing practice teachers, in three institutions: a junior college, a teachers' college and a university. The book is an attempt to give credit to and reaffirm faith in superior teaching practices, and at the same time to re-emphasize subject matter in the secondary schools.

During the last fifty years, professional education as a scholarly pursuit has furnished teachers with a highly developed and well-understood set of teaching techniques. Teaching methods are now better than they have ever been. Also, the subject matter, especially in social studies, has become so large that its very diversity and scope are sometimes staggering to persons approaching it as secondary teachers. I hope to start from the firm foundation of existing and applied knowledge in the art of teaching and proceed to formulation of a scholarly attitude in the selection of subject matter and its presentation from the various fields of the social sciences; from that basis samples of human knowledge are presented along with reference material which can be translated into teaching units and courses for junior and senior high school students. I feel that this approach should supplement the already existing volumes on the subject of teaching methodology.

I conceived the idea for the book as the result of direct and continued requests from students as to how to teach particular subjects in the social studies. The final outcome has been this book, founded on a threefold premise: (1) that there is a sufficiently large and important body of knowledge to be identified as social studies and that mastery of it is a responsibility of citizenship, (2) that teachers of this material must know it well, be aware of satisfactory teaching methodologies and like to teach and (3) that there is ample psychological evidence to support the claim that most persons are capable of learning the rudiments of their cultural heritage, to the end of preserving and improving it.

Social studies at the secondary level represent the reflection of integrated study of social science at a higher level of scholarship. It is the assumption here that the social sciences have a common goal which has almost been forgotten in concern with immediate problems of methodology. This common goal is the attempt to formulate vital generalizations concerning the nature of man and society. There are, of course, other functions of more practical use, such as teaching social studies, but as the end of teaching social studies in schools is to produce adequate citizenship, so is it the concern of the social sciences to produce the vital formulations upon which the social studies are based.

Such generalizations, if they are to possess validity, must be equally true whether the immediate discipline under consideration is psychology, anthropology, sociology, economics, geography, history or political science. Principles of human relationships are not suddenly altered as the student passes from the anthropology classroom into the psychology seminar, though to the bewildered student it must often seem that this is quite the case.

This textbook is intended to fill a dual role. First, it should be useful as a manual along with the upper division college course in social studies for the secondary school; second, it could serve some of the needs of social studies teachers in service, as a reference to current curricular practices, recent materials, and as an attempt to make a whole pattern out of the welter of human experience in the western world. It is my hope that there may be presented in one concise volume a guide to expression of the social studies, based on an orderly view of the fields of knowledge and with an educational philosophy derived from many sources old and new.

I cheerfully assume responsibility for the major organization, at least some of the research and all of the errors. I wish, on the other hand, to give grateful appreciation to the dozens of scholars, teachers and library workers who have helped, wittingly and unwittingly. It is impossible to mention them all, but it is always fitting to name a few.

Among my colleagues in departments of education and in the various social sciences at several institutions, almost all of them have contributed something. Professor Paul Woodring, now of the Ford Foundation but formerly at Western Washington College of Education, and Dean Lindley Stiles of the School of Education, University of Wisconsin, have been especially helpful. For assistance in specialized fields I am indebted to Professor Thomas Hunt, emeritus, Western Washington College of Education, and Professor Edward Ullmann, University of Washington, for their help in geography; Professor Frank J. Klingberg, emeritus, University of California, Los Angeles and Professor Giovanni Costigan, University of Washington, for insight into historical problems; Professor Norman Gabel (deceased), University of California, Santa Barbara and Professor Herbert C. Taylor, Western Washington College of Education, as the ones who led me into anthropology; Professors Fred Halterman and Jerzy Karcz, for helping me unravel the intricacies of economics; and Dean Charles Spaulding, professor of sociology, for encouragement.

A particular word of gratitude is due to three separate sets of individuals: first to my wife, a teacher of small children, and our two sons whose fresh and curious outlook have often been inspiring. The second group is composed of poets, represented in the person of Leonard Nathan, poet. In the third category there are the several unnamed stenographers who have typed and retyped the manuscript, patiently correcting errors. The last person in this string of typists is Mrs. Patricia Griffith, an original thinker.

In such an undertaking as this it is inevitable that countless individuals subtly and slowly—as Doctor Johnson said, "imperceptibly and by degrees"—become more or less influential in its outcome. It is impossible, eventually, even for the author to identify them personally. This group includes my former teachers, present colleagues, professional editors and all the authors of the books I have read. There is no way to assess their contributions. One can only be grateful for their knowledge and for their devotion to teaching.

JAMES HIGH

*Santa Barbara, California*
*January, 1962*

# Contents

part I
IDENTIFYING
THE SOCIAL STUDIES

# 1
# Definitions and goals of social studies

An examination of the concepts and values clustered around the term "citizenship," and of their condition in American social beliefs, reveals a critical inability on the part of traditional social philosophies to express and defend our heritage of privacy and freedom for individual citizens in modern communities.

The Tension of Citizenship
H. MARK ROELOFS, 1957

## 1. Studies of Human Relationships

The aim of social studies is to teach competent citizenship. Social studies teachers, therefore, must first know what citizenship is, what its components are, what its values can be in terms of Western civilization. Social studies teachers in the United States, as in any other country, are citizens of a particular nation. They must know what the values of that nation are, how they were derived, and why they are held.

Citizenship in the democratic Western world is a complicated matter. It consists of several interlapping parts and nurtures many variant values which sometimes conflict with one another. Every American, for example, is a part of the cultural and biological tradition of Western civilization, and to the extent that the East has intruded on the West, he is also a citizen of the whole world. Primarily the American is a nationalist, that is, he owes political allegiance to the United States without question, and he owes loyalty to his cultural state, but not exclusively. These loyalties do not conflict politically, but they very well may in terms of economics or of taste. At least, to bear the burden of citizenship and to enjoy its privileges, people must know about it— its character and its values.[1]

[1] Mark Roelofs, The Tension of Citizenship (Holt, Rinehart, and Winston, New

3

The protection of life, liberty and property embraces the chief values of democratic citizenship in the Western world. Basically all of the nations in the world accept these, but each has its own particular way of pursuing happiness which could be said to be the fulfillment of the original proposition. Life is just as sacred in Germany and England and Italy and France as it is in the United States, but it is protected in different ways in all of these places. The value is the same to each nation's people and therein no conflict arises, but at the same time, each of the nations mentioned has been at war with every other one of them. Under war conditions the value placed on life is strictly of a national nature. For instance, during World War II it was a matter of the German trying to kill the Englishman, or the American trying to kill the Italian. Here then is a definite conflict.

While a war might rage between Germany and the United States, with Americans proclaiming their belief in the superiority of democratic values over totalitarian forms, the Germans would invoke the same God to whom an American general or president prayed for success. In World War II both the Germans and the Americans fought for life, liberty and property, but for their own particular forms of each.

Another conflict of seemingly similar values exists during wartime, when belligerent nations often trade with each other through neutral nations while they are diligently attempting to destroy each other's productive potential at another level. During World War II, American industrial holdings in Germany were used by the Germans throughout the war and then returned to the American owners at the end of the conflict with little alteration in personnel or equipment.

Liberty may be held as a value in many different ways. It may mean complete individual choice as to mode of behavior regardless of the effects on anyone else; or, as in the United States, it may mean individual freedom of action so long as no one else is damaged. This concept is written into our constitution and is the fabric of our laws. Liberty may mean the right of a national social group to grant sanction to an oligarchic or totalitarian government. It may mean the jealously guarded right and obligation to fight every threat to nationalistic growth within one state. In every case liberty as a value held by citizens is of the same philosophic quality, but in each instance the manifestation of that value will take on regional or national characteristics.

---

York, 1957), preface, vii. Quotation at the head of this chapter by permission of the publisher.

In the matter of liberty as a value in Western civilization, representative self-government is the common expression of every state in the community of nations. The wellsprings of representative decision are in the long tradition from Babylon to the United Nations, and all people in the world partake of its flavor. In certain of the Western nations democratic processes are held in much higher esteem than in others. In the United States our representation is carefully regulated by law. In England this is also true, but in an entirely different manner. Our president is elected every four years and cannot be removed except for dire cause. The British prime minister is appointed by the ruler and has tenure only as long as he can command a majority in the House of Commons. No two systems could be more different, but they are both descended from the same ancestors and they are equally democratic ways of carrying on representative self-government. In Russia a representative assembly exists and there is a representative method of choosing a premier and cabinet, but there is no minority with rights of protest. Nonetheless, Russia has a representative self-governing system, although not democratic in our sense, and Russians hold liberty as a value. Theirs is the liberty not to be interfered with by other nations holding different views. Here liberty is a national value, not an individual one.

Government, since the end of the feudal period, has accepted the role of protector of property, public and private. Since the seventeenth century when John Locke so succinctly stated the proposition that government must basically have that quality, all successful governments have made protection of property a part of their traditional and constitutional frameworks. Property has the most easily discernible value of all. It can be priced in monetary terms, sometimes even equated with two other elements: property–money–life. This value system comes down to us rather directly through our Anglo-Saxon ancestry from the Germanic tribal belief in the value of a man in gold or property according to his rank. The idea has been more or less accepted, with ameliorating modifications, by all of Western civilization. Therefore, property, by convention, has a monetary value which can be recognized easily, and a man's worth is sometimes computed in property or money terms. Life insurance rates or disability compensation point this up. Property has both monetary and intangible value. We have fought wars and revolutions, at least partly for property's sake. Each nation and each group within a nation sets a different intangible value on property. A unique quality of the American form of social and political organization lies in the individual's right to assess his own acceptance of the non-monetary aspect of property value. Here, again, is a value which has easy universal acceptance while at the same time presenting facets of disagreement and conflict, not only on a national scale but even as to individuals.

All other philosophic considerations, not covered under the heading of life, liberty and property, may be classified as "the pursuit of happiness." We may call these things spiritual values. Religious belief and practice in the Western world tend to be Christian; at least most peoples in our world are monotheistic and speak of the same God even though they may call the deity by different names. Even the great pantheistic nations such as China and India are becoming more and more interested in some kind of faith that will relieve them of the burden of thousands of gods and devils. China seeks this in Communism and India pursues the ideal of passively achieved justice. The United States has gained a position which allows each person to choose his own spiritual values, his own mode of expressing or not expressing a religious faith.

Esthetic values (enjoyment of color, sound, texture, temperature or taste), intellectual values (enjoyment of ideas and the manipulation of knowledge) and moral values (individual dignity as the gauge of rightness and wrongness) are all part of the liberty to pursue happiness in the tradition of Western culture. All Western men have this tradition, but it is handled in many different ways. Each person does not hold every value, neither do all persons give equal weight to the ones they hold most dear. Tolerance is an intangible aid to the assessment of any value system in our society, and as such, must be included in the spiritual, esthetic and practical application of ethical democratic citizenship.

These are the guides to a selection of material for learning competent citizenship. The tradition of Western man and the particular experience of one branch of that tradition, the United States, form the reservoir of instructional material for the social studies. Citizenship can best be exercised on the basis of the most complete knowledge possible of Western man in his setting, past and present. The only limiting factors are the aptitude of the student and the availability of time.

### Social Studies Defined

Most simply stated, the social studies are the school mirror of the scholarly findings of the social sciences. Such data as social scientists may gather is integrated and simplified to appropriate levels of expression for children in all the grades. The persons who do this are the teachers of social studies. Curricular designation may be under the name of any one of the social sciences, often history, geography or economics. More often, particularly in the lower grades, this part of learning is called social living, or community life, or contemporary society, or social studies, or sometimes, especially by junior high school students, just "homeroom." [2]

Current educational definition is usually stated in terms of behavioral objectives of social studies instruction. In educational language these are designed to ". . . give a measure of knowledge for understanding contemporary society." [3] Michaelis says that the ". . . central function of the social studies is identical with the central purpose of education—the development of democratic citizenship." [4] Wesley's definition of social studies as ". . . those portions of the social sciences . . . selected for instructional purposes," [5] may be applied to include anything pertinent to the immediate purpose of learning and adapted to the level of comprehension of the student; in short, absorption of as much or as little of man's heritage as may be decided. If the desirable behavioral outcome is directly related to knowledge of the past and present, then Jefferson's advice to study liberal and practical arts, given to the youth of Virginia in the eighteenth century, was sound, and current educational theory would serve the same end.

Sometimes the behavioral outcomes are refined in statement and given as the curricular objectives, thus obscuring the basic relationship between knowledge and behavioral choice. It is assumed in such cases that the behavior patterns themselves can be taught as such, eliminating the need for choice. These might be to teach people in the United States to become loyal and patriotic Americans; to develop responsibility, concern for others, open-mindedness and cooperation; to gain respect for differences of opinion and to have regard for the rights of minorities yet abide by the decisions of majorities; to acquire and use the skills concerned with basic social functions of human

[2] Cf. Edgar B. Wesley, "The Social Studies," *Encyclopedia of Educational Research*, edited by W. S. Monroe (New York, 1950), p. 1214, which gives a tighter definition based almost exclusively on social sciences, following the ideas of Charles A. Beard in *Bulletin* 54 (Social Science Research Council, New York, 1946).

[3] Maurice P. Moffatt, *Social Studies Instruction* (Prentice-Hall, New York, 1954), p. 1. Quoted by permission of the publisher.

[4] John U. Michaelis, *Social Studies for Children in a Democracy* (Prentice-Hall, Englewood Cliffs, New Jersey, 1956), 2nd ed., p. 3. Quoted by permission of the publisher.

[5] Wesley, *loc. cit.*

living: production of goods and services, transportation and communication, conservation of resources, esthetic and religious expression, health, recreation and government; to develop habits of critical and creative thought, and how to act socially in consonance with sound decisions. In summary, Michaelis points out, using these as teaching aims, social studies should help people to act "courageously and with integrity . . . consistent with democratic ideals and processes." [6]

These are all worthy enough hopes, but one can only expect to achieve them as realities of behavior if students are taught and given an opportunity to learn the actual content of knowledge in the human heritage that will allow sound decisions. The proper aim of all education should be to enable people to make sound and worthy decisions. The subject content is what can be learned, and the decisions are the result of a mental process which can be taught only if there is something to submit to the process. Specific patterns of behavior can be taught, too, but they are not, in that way, the result of a thoughtful process.

Taking these objectives and definitions, a fundamental philosophy of education may be developed which will bridge the hiatus between ideals and actuality in the social studies classroom. Most simply stated, social studies comprises the broadest possible investigation of human relationships. This can be conducted in the classroom in a disciplined and professional manner if there is a philosophy of education, mastery of the definitions and goals of social studies and sufficient knowledge of materials and methods pertaining to the field.

### Education as a Profession in Relation to the Social Studies

Education, or the profession of teaching, is probably one of the oldest of all, but its exact status as a profession has not always been clear. Perhaps this is because of the wide variation in skills and knowledge which have been considered to be acceptable in various parts of the craft, and because teachers have never been organized into a cohesive group. All physicians consider themselves a part of their professional group as do all lawyers, but the university professor of astro-physics or of classical studies frequently dissociates himself completely from his brother teachers who preside over the primary grades in a village school. Usually he thinks of himself, not as a teacher, but as a physicist or as a classical scholar. It is probably true that most college and university professors identify themselves with

[6] Michaelis, op. cit., p. 12.

their subject matter specialities rather than with the teaching profession.

The elementary school teacher, on the other hand, thinks of himself as a teacher first and is more concerned with the skills necessary in the development of the child's understanding than with the subject matter itself. This is in part because the subject matter with which he deals is much simpler than is the teaching skill necessary for imparting the knowledge, and in part because the elementary school teacher has been greatly influenced by the pragmatic principles of John Dewey and others who hold that the process of learning is a matter of experiencing life and solving problems rather than mastering subject matter.

The secondary school teacher is halfway between these extremes, being possibly closer to the status of the college professor. His outlook must reflect a sharper attention to the knowledge content of his professional equipment. For example, a person teaching economics and business to high school seniors must command the scholarly knowledge of the discipline of economics, but at the same time, in order to achieve optimum success instructing the relatively unselected students in an American high school he must also have mastered the professional content of teaching as a vocation. He must be a teacher *and* an economist. In practical application this means that such a person will possibly have to have a baccalaureate degree in education and a master's degree in economics, or vice versa.

Education is different from all other professions in that it deals directly with all branches of knowledge, for it is obvious that the teacher must have a thorough knowledge of whatever subject or subjects he is to teach. It is not enough that he know that which the student is to learn, it is essential that he have a much broader and deeper knowledge in order that he may interpret the varied and complicated relationship of ideas.

The ideal teacher is both a scholar and a teacher. At all levels of the schools, teaching is important; the primary teacher needs to be every whit as skilful a teacher as the college professor. But scholarship becomes increasingly important in the more advanced levels of education.

It is possible to be a scholar without being a teacher. The teacher as a professional person must be more than a scholar. He should have professional skills of the highest order, skills which are probably at least as difficult to learn as any of the skills in the other professions.

Moreover, the development of these skills rests upon a deep understanding of several of the social sciences, most specifically upon psychology with concentration upon the psychology of learning and motivation. If the teacher does not understand the principles of learning, much effort will be wasted in ineffective activity. It seems reasonable to say that psychology is the basic science for all teachers.

In all areas of teaching, this homely truth cannot be overemphasized: no matter how well motivated the student, nor how gifted in technique the teacher, if the teacher does not possess superior knowledge of *that which he is to teach,* then both his and the students' time is wasted.

## 2. Social Sciences

Free inquiry and the pursuit of knowledge form the basic tenet of Western civilization. Learning has intrinsic value. Without much doubt, Western man has devoted a great share of his time during the last three or four thousand years to its pursuit. Such information as man has gained has been treated cumulatively and subjected to certain philosophic formulations. Accumulated knowledge is man's cultural heritage from which he takes his values and philosophies which in turn make possible further learning. Such formulations, for the most part, have been within rigid structures of assumed values, as Christianity, Platonism, Marxism, capitalism or the like. These have been called value systems or ethical arrangements, but in every case they must rest on some form of investigation, even though it be random experience or divine revelation. In other words, man must draw on some part of the cumulative information and wisdom of human experience. As Gautama the Buddha pointed out over twenty-five hundred years ago, man must know that which is needed to achieve peace and progress.

In our day it is more difficult to decide what this might be than it would have been in a time further into the past. There was less to know, for example, for a man of the Middle Ages when the ultimate human goal was a future life. The essentials were obedience and faith according to a simple formula of existence. It was even simpler in Buddha's time when the absence of physical reaction was considered to be the final acquisition of peaceful knowledge. Peace of mind was the highest form of "well-directed" thought or complete knowledge.

Now we recognize that all knowledge is too great for any one person to acquire. Further, it is often recognized that tight formulation of values and therefore objectives cannot be universally and dogmatically stated for everyone in all time. In a remarkable way this places a higher value on knowledge than ever before. If formulation of values is not eternal yet is based upon knowledge, any philosophy must be ever tentative—just as findings in natural science are always subject to change on the basis of new experimental results. This is the essence of critical thought. Hence, knowledge has an end in itself, but one which cannot be predicted nor controlled through a restrictive philosophy. Two things immediately accrue to this line of reasoning: man must seek knowledge cooperatively in order to overcome his individual limitations; and he must be willing to accept tentatively a flexible philosophy of values rather than a rigid ultimate code or final truth.

Even though knowledge represents the reward for the highest quest, simple accretion of unclassified information does little toward formulation and revision of guiding principles. If knowledge were dependent upon random and undirected accumulation of experience there would be little cultural growth. If man had to discover everything as he discovered the use of fire or tools, knowledge would grow very, very slowly. The earliest philosophers recorded and classified information to the end of making it into a cohesive and useful body of knowledge. The life effort of Aristotle, for example, was precisely that.

Since the seventeenth century much of the best intellect of the Western world has been directed in the pursuit of empirical demonstration of principles in physical and biological science. This brand of knowledge has gone to tremendously greater lengths than anyone could have dreamed to be possible even fifty years ago. The scientific method—observation, hypothesis, controlled recording of observation, tentative finding with new hypothetical statement and continued repetition of the process—has advanced the organization of natural and applied science in geometric progression. Classification, subclassification, and even greater specialization in subject matter have been the inevitable result.

It must be remembered that such science does not include all of knowledge. It is easy to confuse the readily cumulative, material knowledge of technology with the critical and continued evaluation of that technology in its impact on man in his society. Obviously, man cannot continue to expand material science if he does not survive. It is not so obvious, but equally true, that man must learn about and understand his social and humane achievements in order to survive. Man must not only expand his knowledge but he must make it work

for him in both material and non-material ways. This is the burden of
social science and the technique is critical thought.

## The Realm of Social Science

A little over one hundred years ago scholars in the field of human
relationships began to emerge in Europe and the United States. Auguste
Comte, father of sociology, gave the proposition that scientific control
could be exercised in the examination of man's non-physical environment and attributes. This would become, then, in the words of Stuart
Chase, "social science," or "the application of the scientific method to
the study of human relations." [7]

Social science is a generic term covering the scientific study of man,
singly or in groups, as regards his essentially non-physical characteristics. The term is no longer of much practical use except to designate
vaguely the whole field of endeavor which has become increasingly
specialized and interdependent upon the findings in the disciplines
of natural science and entirely new fields of investigation such as
psychology. There is a tendency on the part of everyone dealing with
human beings to call themselves social scientists. History, geography,
economics, statistics, jurisprudence and biochemistry are often classified as social science. On the other hand, geography, psychiatry, medicine, criminology and psychology have legitimate interest in the techniques and subject matter of such physical sciences as physics, chemistry and mathematics.

All this illustrates the value of knowledge, but further, it points up
the need for classification in order to formulate principles of human
guidance in the quest after acceptable well-directed activity in society.
The social sciences emerge as individual disciplines of investigation
having sufficient independent bodies of subject matter to warrant
specialization. At the same time each of these must contribute to and
stay in contact with the central social science theme. Charles Beard
stated this as ". . . a body of knowledge and thought pertaining to
human affairs as distinguished from sticks, stones, stars, and physical
objects." [8]

## Social Sciences Defined

It is worthwhile at this point to define some of the various component parts of the social sciences. Definitions are germane to under-

---

[7] Wilson Gee, *Social Science Research Methods* (Appleton-Century-Crofts, New
York, 1950), p. 3, citing Stuart Chase, *The Proper Study of Mankind: An Inquiry
into the Science of Human Relations* (Harper, New York, 1948), p. 5.

[8] *Ibid.*

standing, and they must be extended and based on the scientific investigations that stem from the very need for classification which gave them cause and rise.

In general the social sciences are those bodies of learning and study which recognize the simultaneous and mutual action of physical and non-physical stimuli which produce social reaction. Alexander Pope's much quoted truism gives the binding slogan and at the same time implies the necessary objectivity which requires scientific specialization and investigation:

> Know then thyself, presume not God to scan;
> The proper study of mankind is man.

It is obvious that the term social sciences may be stretched or squeezed to fit almost any conception of disciplined knowledge so long as it deals with people and utilizes a scientific method. Such is true, but for practical purposes there is a generally accepted group of scholarly pursuits which can be named and which is usually classified as the social sciences.

The basic group for curricular purposes almost invariably includes history, geography, political science, economics, anthropology and sociology. These represent man's fundamental needs: the human record, habitat, political structure, subsistence, human derivation and social organization. Human or cultural geography and psychology must be added to this list to account for the further human needs of occupance and personal adjustment, but both these latter fields of knowledge are about equally concerned with natural and social science. Sometimes the social sciences may be expanded to include social biology, penology, ethics, philosophy, jurisprudence and statistics.[9] With particular specialization the list could be expanded almost indefinitely, including such things as general semantics, linguistics and education. In the direction of the humanities, inclusion of rhetoric, logic and grammar (the medieval trivium) could be justified. For that matter, possibly history belongs as much to the humanities as to the social sciences.

In short, all knowledge interacts, but it must be classified for the sake of convenience and in order to expand it in orderly fashion. On one logical basis we can attempt to show an overall relationship of the major fields of knowledge, their relationship to the best known professions, and extensive descriptions of only a few of the most easily classifiable social sciences: psychology (man's mind), anthropology (man's ethos), geography (man's abode), economics (man's sub-

[9] *Ibid.*, pp. 34–35.

sistence), political science (man's order), sociology (man's associations) and history (man's story).

## The Social Sciences and the Physical Sciences

At first glance it might appear that the physical sciences, dealing as they do with inanimate things and forces, have little in common with the social sciences. It is true that the subject matters of the two fields are very different but the interaction between the two is of tremendous significance.

The splitting of the atom was accomplished by nuclear physicists. Such fission seemed to be strictly a problem for the physical scientists. When Einstein announced energy equalled mass times the square of velocity measured in the order of the speed of light: $E = mc^2$ (basic formula indicating the conversion of mass to energy), his discovery seemed to have little import for the social scientist. But when the bomb exploded over Hiroshima no political scientist, social psychologist or historian could well ignore its impact. The bomb was physical but its effects and the problems of its proper use and control were not matters for the physicist alone to decide.

Erosion is a physical process and its study falls within the realm of the physical sciences; but when the Missouri River, carrying waters from the snowfields of Montana, floods the farmlands of Nebraska and Iowa, the question of its control becomes of interest to the economist, the sociologist and the political scientist, and certainly in time to the historian.

There are numerous other examples, but these should be sufficient to demonstrate that the physical and social sciences are not independent of each other in their influence upon mankind.

## The Humanities and the Social Sciences

When the student leaves a social science class and moves into a class in literature he feels, at first, that he is in a different world. But as time passes he may discover that the two areas deal, each in its own way, with the same problems. For both are concerned with human experience. Truth is unitary. It is not really segmented, but it may be approached by different roads. In general it may be said that the social sciences deal with groups of people—group experience, if there really is such a thing—though a large portion of psychology, one of the social sciences, is concerned with the individual. Literature deals, more often, with individuals, but frequently, as in Tolstoy's *War and Peace*, the individual is presented against so large a background that the subject matter can be said to be society rather than the individual.

With the exception of certain aspects of psychology and history, the data of the social sciences are objective. They are arrived at by observation rather than by introspection. In literature the reverse is true, at least in large part. The great depression of the 1930's is an historical fact. As such, it is of concern not only to the historian but also to the economist, the sociologist, the social psychologist and to the political scientist; but the depression, or aspects of it, may be and have been the subject matter of literature, as in Steinbeck's *The Grapes of Wrath*. (This novel has been described as "realistic," a designation which must confuse the epistemologist for it will seem to him that any novel worth writing must present and interpret some aspect of reality.)

Is Steinbeck's interpretation of that depression more "true" or more "real" than the interpretation of the historian or of the social psychologist? To many a student of literature it will seem that it is. It deals with a much smaller portion of the depression and with only a few of the millions of people who were involved in it, but it presents the experience of those few more vividly and thus carries to the reader more impact, more emotion. The reader feels that he, too, has experienced the depression, a feeling not often gained from the reading of historical documents or textbooks in social psychology or economics. Some believe that this feeling and the accompanying insight constitute a higher reality. But in learning about the depression through such novels as those of Steinbeck one is faced with a serious difficulty. The reader may be led to believe that the small unit of experience dealt with by the novelist constitutes the totality. He may come to see only one aspect of the problem.

*The Grapes of Wrath* is an example of this point. The reader identifies himself with the "Okies." He understands them and sympathizes with them; but what about the police, the state officials, the long-time residents of California who also were caught in the depression and were struggling against it? Does the reader ever come to see the depression through their eyes? It seems unlikely.

It is possible that this is not so much a statement of the limitations of the novel as it is a criticism of Steinbeck as a novelist. For it is certainly possible for a novelist to present his material in such a way as to state both sides of a problem situation fairly. There are, however, many novelists and many literary critics who hold that a novel may be great literature without such presentation—that it may in some cases be better literature if the writer makes no such attempt.

Another example of a problem, or a series of problems, which has been dealt with (each in his way) by both the social scientist and by the novelist is the culture pattern and the social structure of a New

England village. The sociologist's approach is exemplified by Warner's *Yankee City* while the novelist's treatment of the same community may be found in Marquand's novels, particularly *Point of No Return.* There is certainly room for debate as to which approach gives the reader greater insight into the community, its people, and its social structure. Each supplements the other and each makes clear some things which the other does not.

### The Fine Arts in Relation to Social Studies

If the fine arts are considered as part of the humanities, then music, painting, sculpture and the interpretive dance form a segment of man's knowledge, and therefore enter the historical record. They are part of his total experience, and are of interest in any social study. If there is a relationship directly from social studies to social science, thence to natural science, then the fine arts owe much to biology, chemistry, physics, mathematics, history, psychology and other fields. At the same time such responsibility is mutual, and in teaching social studies to students the instructor can no more afford to overlook the contributions of great painters, sculptors, musicians and dancers than he can disregard the great physicists, historians, sociologists and philosophers.

The great Greek creator of the statue "Winged Victory" must have known much of anatomy, of physical balance, of the political impact of psychological stimuli, perhaps of economics or medicine. Who knows? Who is to judge between the degree of objectivity reached by that artist and the accuracy of Thucydides as an historian of ancient Greece? They were equally concerned with man and society, one speaking in words, the other in marble.

When Michelangelo chiseled out "The Boy David" he was living profoundly in his own time and drawing on the Christian knowledge of his heritage. He was indebted to a scientific understanding of at least rudimentary biology. Leonardo da Vinci painted portraits but he also designed a submarine and prepared a medical treatise on anatomy. Can he be called a lesser commentator on Renaissance life than the politician Machiavelli or the poet Aretino? As the rebirth of learning came north to Holland and Germany could it be said that Rembrandt van Rijn knew less of his society as he painted "The Merchants of the Cloth Guild" than did Martin Luther as he nailed his *Ninety-five Theses* to the church door? All knowledge is interrelated even as it must be classified in some manner in order to survive and serve civilization.

Terpsichorean art seems, at first glance, to be the most remote from science, from philosophy, from history or political science. Consider, however, Isadora Duncan, who brought neo-classical forms to the twentieth century. Her inspiration was the Golden Age of Greece, her audience was the modern world, and her stage was Western Europe. She was an artist in social interpretation and rhythm as she disported herself with Gabriel D'Annunzio, the Italian diplomat-soldier-artist-author. She knew of science, art and society. She spoke of them in movement, making sheep's eyes at George Bernard Shaw as he spoke of them in another art form, literature—prose, poetry, drama, political tract, letter and lampoon.

Japanese *Kabuki* players and *Nō* dramatists express the rigidly formal tradition of old *Yamato* just as their nine or thirteen syllable verse, or *uta*, does. Japanese social history without mention of the positional significance in their drama and ceremonies would be pointless. Similarly, southeast Asian and Indian ritual is completely intermixed with intricacies of the dance.

Borodin and Rimsky-Korsakov were medical students. Their *Prince Igor* lives as a social problem and commentary in the repertory of the ballet. Beethoven first admired Napoleon, then despised him. His musical comments on this were his third and fifth symphonies. *Eroica* states the faith of enlightened anti-revolutionary Europe in the towering progress of the great leader, Bonaparte. The *Fifth Symphony*, later on, is man's or society's *pathetique* and thundering denunciation of the tyrant, Bonaparte. Such examinations of social reaction are not the scientifically controlled experiments of modern measurement, but they are real; and at least, music has a mathematical structure.

Examples of human relationships in science, art and the humanities could go on indefinitely, but those that have been cited are more than enough to show the point. Knowledge, however classified, is the basic structure of culture. Social science is that part of cultural knowledge directly bearing on man's activities in any field; and the social studies offer a learning situation and insight into all knowledge.

### Philosophy and the Social Sciences

Originally the whole body of knowledge, as shown in Figure 1, was called philosophy. Later on, theology as the core of philosophy came to be known as "the queen of the sciences." Now, it is not generally thought of as either natural or social science, but rather as the scholarly body of information upon which rests the ministerial profession. Philosophy, in our time, has become highly specialized and centered severally in expressions such as philosophy of science, philosophy of

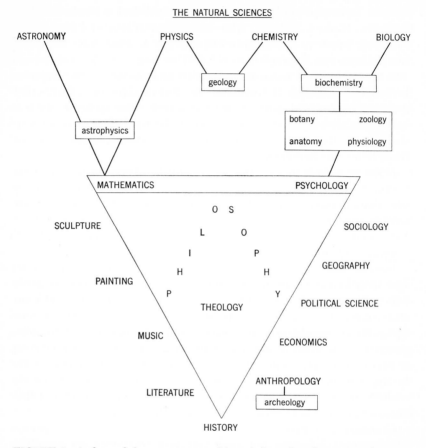

FIGURE 1. A chart of the organization of knowledge. This chart is simply meant to illustrate in another way the relationship and interaction of the various branches of knowledge as they are organized and named for purposes of study. Further, it shows graphically the unitary quality of knowledge and the historic concept of philosophy as a center of thought. In the middle ages, theology was called "queen of the sciences."

education, philosophy of history, or for that matter, even philosophy of engineering or of plumbing. For purposes of college teaching there are usually three main divisions: introduction to philosophy, logic and ethics. Thus the basic meaning of philosophy has come to be the name of a scholarly discipline equated with psychology, history or any of the other social sciences. The only relic of the old nomenclature is the name of the "highest academic award," Doctor of Philosophy; but ironically, this may be Doctor of Philosophy in philosophy just as it may be Doctor of Philosophy in English or chemistry or theology, not to mention Doctor of Education, or laws, or engineering, or musicology—without even the word philosophy!

By a simple act of truncation, despite the violence it will render to the body of knowledge, we will leave out any description of philosophy in this account of the social sciences and their relationship to the sciences, humanities and fine arts. Through such an act it becomes unnecessary to discuss esthetics, epistemology, eschatology and religion. This is an arbitrary deletion and in no way should it hinder the student from any amount of investigation in those fields. Perhaps the suggested reading lists at the ends of chapters may inspire him to a search for first causes or the nature of man's enjoyment and sorrow. Here we must fulfill the mandates of space and time.

### 3. History as the Central Theme

In order to understand what history is it is necessary to dwell on two definitions: culture and civilization, and then to conclude with an examination of man's view of his own story, that is, history. History carries the burden of human progress as it is passed down from generation to generation, from society to society. In the process of education in the United States of the twentieth century, the responsibility for the teaching of history is largely in the hands of social studies teachers. In any social studies course history is ordinarily the central theme, the cohesive element in instruction, just as it is in the general transmission of culture.

*Culture—the sum total of the attainments and activities of any specific period, race, or people including their implements, handicrafts, agriculture, economics, music, art, religious beliefs, traditions, language and story.*

Culture embraces the conception of man as organism in the developmental environment of the world subject to natural laws which govern all life. In modern scientific structures of knowledge it is necessary to make a distinction between the older view of civilization based on knowing how to write and leave records, and this more newly organized estimate of man's story as a unity from earliest times to the present. A culture, as compared to a civilization, might include thousands of years of development organic to the growth of man, and yet not include the knowledge of reading or writing (or for that matter, the development of any kind of record keeping). Technically such a phenomenon cannot be called civilization, but it may be called culture. The academic discipline most concerned with definitions of culture is anthropology. Since the nineteenth century, in order to study civilization and to divest such study of biased preconception, cultural considerations have become more and more important.

*Civilization—a culture possessing specialization of labor, social stratification, urbanization, technological and investigative tradition. With reference to this work, civilization might be deemed the sum total of modern man's intellectual, social and cultural progress.*

Former understanding of civilization was relatively easy. It included the historical record in writing—"the lie agreed upon" *—of Western man's struggle for political and social order, subsistence and technical advance. As the world expanded to include the Orient, knowledge eventually became broader and more specifically organized, so that at the present time the world is one unit in time and space; civilization as a concept became the complicated emergence of man as an organic part of life.

The very word, civilization, is not old. Boswell urged Dr. Johnson to insert the term in his lexicon in 1772, but Johnson preferred the older world "civility." This, like "urbanity," reflects the contempt of the townsman for the rustic or barbarian; it is an invidious term, although in a way justified by the fact that only where towns have grown up have men developed intricate civilizations. The arduous and dispersed tasks of the hunter, shepherd and peasant folk do not afford the leisure, or at least the varied human contacts, essential to the generation of new ideas and discoveries. But modern anthropologists have pointed out that peoples without cities, such as the tribes of Polynesia and the North American Indians, are really highly "civilized." They have subtle languages, ingenious art admirably suited to their conditions, developed institutions, social and political, as well as religious practices and confident myths, no better and no worse substantiated than many that prevail today among the nations of Europe. All these betoken and presuppose a vastly long development. Among English speaking people, the first to point this out clearly was E. B. Tylor who published *Primitive Culture* in 1871, the same year in which Darwin's *Descent of Man* appeared. These two books would alone have served, by different approaches, to give the word "civilization" a far more profound meaning than it had ever had before.

The way is now cleared for a new view of civilization which would not have been possible fifty or sixty years ago. Civilization is no longer

* Napoleon.

contrasted with "rusticity" or "savagery," but with man's purely animal heritage. It represents all of the other side of a dual human heritage: how man came to be more than purely animal.

Man inherits his animal characteristics: his form, necessity for food and shelter, sexual desire and prepotency. He keeps his civilization through memory and expansion of his collective intellect, or by way of knowledge. Most of what man does from his animal heritage he does not have to learn. He can eat, sleep, love and hate without knowledge. The elements of his heritage which set him apart from the other animals he must learn. This is civilization.

Civilization, is, in large part, the knowledge and record of itself. It seems now an imperative fact that all civilization, the total social and traditional heritage, would fall away immediately and completely should a thorough-going forgetfulness, an overwhelming and profound oblivion, overtake humanity. As Graham Wallas suggests, those least civilized would have a possible chance of surviving. It is only uncivilized man that might go on indefinitely. We are all by nature wild animals *plus;* and our taming weakens us for the ancient struggle in the forest, naked and barehanded.

We are all born uncivilized and would so remain through life if we were not immersed in civilization. There is a long time in which we may, according to the place where we are born, be molded into a well authenticated Papuan, Chinese or Parisian. We have no choice as to whether we will talk like a German, a Hottentot or a Russian. We learn to do in all things as those do among whom we are brought up. We cannot but learn their respective customs, scruples and ideas, for all these things are imposed before we have any choice or discretion. Children do as their elders learned to do when they were children, and this is carried on from generation to generation. It becomes inexorable law.

This accounts for many of the characteristics of civilization: its continuity, slowness of change, persistence of prejudice and tradition, universality of many values. It is generally considered that the majority of persons achieve the maximum in growth of knowledge and even intelligence by the age of thirteen or fourteen, since an overwhelming part of civilized knowledge is implanted during the childhood period of dependence.

It is the exceptional human mind which continues to grow beyond the point of physical maturity which accounts for the extension of knowledge and consequently civilization. E. L. Thorndike has amply shown that the *ability* to learn, non-representative of the average or normal, may continue in evidence to rather advanced ages. This constitutes a chief justification for secondary or advanced schooling.

The tremendous majority of men and women assimilate in childhood the common and familiar forms of civilization in the midst of which they find themselves, but hardly outrun them as life goes on. Perhaps one in a hundred may allow his opinions to be altered by assiduous reading, or take pains to cultivate his insight into art and literature and scientific discoveries.

Despite the great differentiation from other animals that man has been able to write into civilization, he still stumbles rather blindly in the clutches of infantile reliance on the past and on his fellow beings. He depends upon his mother and father, then upon society for the respectable elements of organized deceit which give him the courage to exist. He is still rather enslaved by the past than liberated by its knowledge. Reasons for this are becoming more apparent than ever before, and might be made the basis for a type of education, especially in childhood, which would greatly forward and direct a future advance of civilization.

*Race—major subdivision of mankind, either having or thought to have major common characteristics; sometimes used unscientifically to mean racial subdivision, nationality or even clan or family.*

One of the most vexing problems of definition centers about this short word, race; racism is a peculiar growth (phenomenon or disease, as you will) of the modern world. The ancient Greek had contempt for all barbarians—non-Greeks. This contempt was based upon cultural differences, not upon hair color, eye color or skin color. The ancient Roman took pride in his ability to say *civis Romanorum sum* and was prejudiced against those who could not claim Roman citizenship. Roman citizenship, however, depended upon enfranchisement and was not based upon skin color or shape of head.

Even in the seventeenth century a slave working in the Barbados was despised only as a slave, and black slaves, white slaves and a few Indian slaves all worked together. In the eighteenth century there dawned, and in the nineteenth century there flowered, a concept of Western European whites as a superior or master race. Usually a codicil was added that blonde, blue-eyed Nordic types were superior representatives of the so-called white race.

This curious view of divine or natural superiority of one race of mankind is a product of an historical happenstance. In the sixteenth, seventeenth and eighteenth centuries, Western Europe, by virtue of the industrial revolution and a resulting propensity for out-fighting, out-breeding and out-colonizing other peoples, became dominant over nearly all the known world. The prejudice which Europeans usually felt toward other peoples was cultural and religious, but gradually, since they were white and their subject peoples were not, it came to be associated with skin color. Thence, we develop the theory of the superior race.

Regardless of the outcome of any particular phase of man's development, his own view of that growth is what makes up history. It is significant to realize that in many disparate languages representing several independently developed cultures the words for history and story are synonymous. In French and Spanish, both based on Latin, *l'histoire* and *la historia* equate with both story and history, or man's story. German *geschichte* and Japanese *rekishi* have precisely the same meaning. Man's story, man's cultural memory is history, the transmitter of culture and thus of civilization. Whatever man's basic nature may be it has been colored and molded by his own view of it and by his own interpretation of what he has done. For good or evil the human group perpetuates itself in terms of its history, therefore it is inescapable that any study of human relationships must be bound by history and have that as its central theme.

## 4. Geography as the Coordinating Study

Geography has been traditionally an elementary school subject. Formerly this was universally true, but of late years, possibly resulting from the tendency to fuse many subjects into one social study, even elementary geography at the lowest level of sophistication—place name drill—has been neglected. Not at all meaning to be merely nostalgic, one regrets the passing of a systematic review in elementary school of the physical elements and place name knowledge traditionally assigned to geography.

Basic geography, when it appears in the curriculum at all, seems to fall usually in the junior high school, but relatively rarely as a separate subject. Judging from the junior high school social studies textbooks, geography now shows up, and will probably continue to increase, as a strong component of study, but ordinarily as a part of the specialized setting of a much more general theme in history or culture.[10]

As geography appears in the junior high school it is generally in

[10] Louis M. Vanaria, "Bibliography of Textbooks in the Social Studies, 1958–1959," *Social Education* (December, 1959), p. 384 ff., is the eleventh annual supplement to a bulletin published by the National Council for the Social Studies. These lists, incidentally, show an increase in elementary geography books, but none in high school texts.

support of a historical or social subject placed in a particular region. For example, in certain grades there may very well be inclusion of Latin American life as the year-long theme of social studies. In the course of this work students may become quite familiar with places, climate and economic production in Latin America—but not with the rest of the world. In junior high school there is usually no coverage of world history, and so consequently there is no examination of world geography. The most to be expected from an integrated or fusion approach to geographic study is treatment of those areas that make up the central theme of whatever course is under consideration.

As students enter high school it might be expected that the same fusion approach to history-geography-culture would be followed. The usual first course in high school social studies is world history; if this were accompanied by world geography, then there would be no need for this sort of comment. Such is not ordinarily the case. World history is a tremendous subject and it takes all of a teacher's ingenuity to get through it with a respectable feeling of "coverage" in one year. Usually, also, the teacher is not a geographer and he often feels reluctant to undertake a whole course in geography when he is supposed to be teaching history.

This is incidentally a commentary on the disparate characters of the two divisions of American education: elementary and secondary. High schools are inhabited, not by young children, but by people who are suddenly growing up, and their teachers are properly concerned that they learn as broadly and quickly as possible in the specialized fields of knowledge. It is expected that high school students come equipped with the fundamental skills needed to encounter the liberal arts subjects. In certain fields it has been recognized that this cannot always be true; in mathematics, for example, it has become a commonplace to offer elementary or remedial arithmetic in high school; writing, composition, spelling and grammar—even reading—are skills that are being given fundamental remedial attention in high school. Geography, an equally important skill, has not received the same recognition.

High school social studies teachers usually and quite properly teach history. Unfortunately there are not many high school geography teachers, and there are not many courses in geography in high schools. In a survey of 107 school systems made in 1953, only eight required geography and this was usually in grade nine (most often grade nine is in junior high school).[11] If more teachers were trained in geography,

[11] Emlyn Jones, "Analysis of Social Studies Requirements," *Social Education* (October, 1954), pp. 257–258.

then social studies teachers might properly and usually teach geography. If it is assumed that geography is essential in social studies, that it is primarily a social science, and that it is not exclusively an elementary school subject, then there are two sharp implications for general education. First, a respectable established place must be made for geographic study in secondary schools, and second, teacher training must take this into account. Neither thing has been adequately considered, say, in the terms that history occupies interest in the public school curricula and in the process of teacher training.

Possibly the first consideration is to establish the meaning and scope of geographic study. It is primarily a coordinating study, having practically no exclusive body of source materials, such as might be the case for nuclear physics or organic chemistry. On the other hand, geography is above all studied empirically, and therefore is a science insofar as methodology is concerned. No geographic formulation can be made without impeccable evidence. The meaning of geography is implicit in the relationships that nature bears to man, and it must be remembered that man is part of nature, both affecting and being affected by his environment. In fact man is part of his own environment. Geography cannot, therefore, arbitrarily exclude any part of the environment from its scope of study; the geographer cannot say "such and such a subject has no meaning for me; it is the field of the climatologist, the historian, the biologist." All knowledge relates to all other knowledge, and it all bears on man's occupance of the earth; therefore geography is both a social and a natural science, but fundamentally it is socially oriented because knowledge of man's setting is of no significance without man and it is not entirely subject to exact measurement. Geography must be viewed as an orderly and as nearly scientific as possible coordination of the fields of knowledge most pertinent to man's understanding of himself as a social being in a physical setting. Professor Hartshorne has perhaps stated the matter as thoughtfully and succinctly as anyone in America. He says that "geography is concerned to provide accurate, orderly, and rational description and interpretation of the variable character of the earth surface." [12]

Without quibbling about the exact limits that might be placed on geographic study, and there must be some in order to make possible any individual's mastery of the subject, it is obvious that it is not a discrete science such as geology, for example, at the same time neither is it a traditional social science such as sociology or political science,

[12] Richard Hartshorne, *Perspective on the Nature of Geography* (Rand, McNally, Chicago, 1959), p. 21.

dealing only with human relationships. Neither does geography partake of the humanistic artistry of good history, dealing as it does with man's image of himself. On the other hand, it is equally easy to see that geology, sociology, political science, history, have little meaning without reference to the nature of the environment on earth, and that the geographer cannot refuse to consider the findings and interpretations of any of those fields listed as well as many others. Geography is truly the bridge between natural and social science, and as such should certainly be included in general secondary education.

At the lower levels of education, geographic relationships are first represented by simple, worldwide place name knowledge. Small children are quite capable of and much interested in learning the designations of nations, cities, rivers, mountains and the like, along with their vital statistics and such items as production, governmental significance, climate, communication, activities, elevation, population, distances—all of the things that constitute the elements of geographic relationship. Next, the basic principles of the solar system, isostasy, the earth's declination, seasonal change, the effect of elevation on temperature, polar and mountain variations from mid-latitude plains, ocean currents, winds and weather—all of the relatively unchanging superficial environment can be of interest to young children if properly presented, and such knowledge can then form the basis for more complicated and sophisticated consideration of relationships at a secondary level of general education.

No subject of consequence can be learned completely and in all its ramifications in one passage over the material. A repetitive or spiral approach to social studies learning has long been a principle, with successive grade level offerings in the same subject. In United States history, for example, the usual experience of school children is to encounter the subject some three or four times between the third grade and graduation from high school, with the expectation of yet another survey during the first two collegiate years. It is therefore safe to assume that geography on a world scale cannot be mastered in only the elementary review possible before entry into high school. The junior high school fusion of geography into a total social study in some measure recognizes this principle, but such treatment is neither universal nor consistent.

From these things it may be inferred that geography could have, and should have, a place in secondary school social studies. It does have a place there, regardless of whether it is recognized in the curriculum or not, since geography is a study of relationships among environmental factors. Its neglect can only reflect a degree of ignorance, and high school teachers are far from being an ignorant lot. Good students and good teachers have always paid some attention to the elements of geography. It is only argued and advocated here that the obvious should be recognized, and that geography should be included in curricular offerings on the same grounds as other components of liberal, general education.

A second consideration of major importance after the acceptance of geography into the high school curriculum has to do with the way in which it is to be handled. Actual technique of instruction is one element of this consideration, but not the first one. Of first importance is the decision as to whether geography is to be handled as a discrete subject, allocated to a specific course in high school or as a fused part of other courses such as United States history, world history or general problems. There is a cogent argument for either method, and in either case basic educational philosophy is involved and teacher training has to be considered.

If, on the one hand, social studies teachers are well enough equipped to integrate the knowledge of geography and history so that the students are left with a rounded and full view of both subjects in their multiplex relationship, then the approach to human experience in its complete setting is infinitely preferable. It is, however, doubtful that most social studies teachers are expert in both geography and history, therefore it is probably best to teach them as separate subjects and hope for an integrated result in general education—much the same as it is hoped that students will develop a balanced knowledge of their roles in life through the study of English, mathematics, history, natural science and foreign languages.

If geography is to be incorporated into other social studies courses, then naturally the instructor will have to adopt a basically different philosophy from that of the specialist. He will also have to have a much broader specialized knowledge in order to be able to supply the necessary information at the appropriate points. He will first of all need to give up any rigid adherence to coverage of material specifically included in only one discipline, such as history. He must make room for the geographic study, and this means that some other subject will have to be replaced at least in part. Next, the instructor will have to develop techniques to allow him to incorporate geographic relationships. Just to indicate one such procedure, the history teacher can use several different kinds of maps to illustrate his lessons in history which may be accompanied by some introduction to the way in which maps are made, their specialized uses and general function in geographic study. Many student exercises are available to achieve familiarity with maps, such as problems to work out on outline maps, or particular embellishment of a large wall map with place name postmarks or other items obtained from the places in question.[13] The technique is unimportant so long as the objective is clear and the result is achieved.

Whether geographic study is to be pursued separately or in conjunction with some other subject it is necessary to decide what ought to be incorporated into the body of learning to be achieved. From the outset of geographic study, whether it be on a very restricted local level or of worldwide scope, there are two major categories to consider: physical and cultural. They are not mutually independent of each other, but for purposes of study they must be broken down into component parts or else the student is likely to be confused by their complexity. Starting with the lower grades the more purely physical elements are perhaps easiest to envisage, and as the student progresses through the grades and high school he may gradually advance to a position of understanding geography as a whole just as he is expected to do with history, or his language, or the general body of scientific knowledge that he must have in order to function usefully as a citizen.[14]

### 5. Suggested Further Reading

Aristotle, *Basic Works,* edited by Richard T. McKeon, is the first organized classification of knowledge in the Western world.

Plato, *Works* (Tudor, 1954), shows the first organized attempt in the background of Western society to define absolute truth and values.

Saint Augustine, *Basic Writings,* edited by Whiting J. Coates (Random House, New York), 2 vols., is the early medieval application of revealed truth to human affairs.

Auguste Comte, *Cours de philosophie positive,* translated by Harriet Martineau (London, 1893), 6 vols., 3rd ed., is the modern doctrinal version of the arrangement of knowledge according to natural principles.

Charles Darwin, *Descent of Man* (Appleton-Century-Crofts, New York, 1871), contains empirical evidence undermining the position of reliance on revealed truth relative to man's origin.

[13] See James K. Anthony, "Geography: Suggested Activities," *Social Education* (March, 1956), p. 115.

[14] This section on geography is substantially drawn from an article by the author, "Geography: Coordinating Element in Secondary Social Studies," *The Journal of Geography* (September, 1960), pp. 270–278.

John Dewey, *Democracy and Education* (Macmillan, New York, 1916), puts the doctrine of progress and the theories of Darwin and Spencer, together with a pragmatic philosophy, into the realm of education.

Will Durant, *The Story of Philosophy* (Garden City, New York, 1930), is a simple resumé of the principal philosophies of Western man.

Charles Frankel, *The Case for Modern Man* (Harper, New York, 1957), presents a synthesis of the thinking of four great modern philosophers who criticize the liberal position, and then a further analysis of the basic holdings of liberalism. This is an inclusive treatment of the matter of survival and its relationship to liberal learning and action.

Johann van Goethe, *Faust* (numerous editions), delves into the shadows of man's mind, and presents an eternal picture of man's search for the ultimate.

George Santayana, *The Last Puritan* (Scribner's, New York, 1936), is the memoir of a philosopher expressed as a novel. It embodies the theme of defeat for modern liberalism.

Herbert Spencer, *The Data of Ethics* (Rand, McNally, Chicago, 1879), presents a human or sociological application of the doctrines of Darwin. Spencer is usually associated with the doctrine of progress.

Paul Woodring, *A Fourth of a Nation* (McGraw-Hill, New York, 1957), is the first attempt in our time to synthesize a philosophy of education out of the classic thesis of liberal arts and the progressive antithesis of John Dewey's pragmatism. It transcends mere polemic.

Wilson Gee, *Research Methods in the Social Sciences* (Appleton-Century-Crofts, New York, 1950), analyzes the various definitions of and inclusions in the social sciences. Extensive treatment is accorded the different techniques used in expanding the knowledge of social science.

*The Social Sciences in Historical Study*, Bulletin 64 (Social Science Research Council, New York, 1954), presents a most interesting and timely attempt to point out the necessity for integration of the knowledge of the various social sciences.

# 2

# Growth of social studies
# in American schools

"... it would be well if they could be taught *every* *Thing* that
is useful, and *every* *Thing* that is ornamental; but Art is long, and
their Time is short. It is, therefore propos'd that they learn those
Things that are likely to be *most useful* and *most ornamental*."

BENJAMIN FRANKLIN, 1749

## 1. Curricular History of Social Studies in the United States

Social studies have not ordinarily been included in the general secondary curriculum for much more than half a century. It is possible,
among living men, to find those who can remember when history, as
the only representative of the social sciences was not even a standard
inclusion in the secondary course of study. History, if it was taught
during the nineteenth century, usually had merely a didactic purpose,
and it was likely to be a very dull subject.

Even now, on the part of a good many adults in this country, it is
quite common to recall history as the most boring thing in high school.
It is also a commonly held belief that history is good for students
because "history repeats itself," because "if you know the story of
the past you can guide the future," and that "people can profit by the
mistakes of the past." This is a moralistic relic of a pedagogical interpretation of history as "philosophy teaching by example," which was
common in the nineteenth century. Before 1890 there had been a
slowly growing tendency to teach national history and possibly classical
or even medieval history in such few high schools as existed, but along
with the rest of the curriculum this was a part of the chaotic and
unsystematic selection of subject matter which graced public high
schools.

Since the social sciences are little more than one hundred years

30

old their reflection as social studies could not have been found in secondary schools of that time. Auguste Comte (1798–1857), founder of sociology, lived into the middle of the nineteenth century. William James (1842–1910), whose name is associated with beginnings of psychology, died in the early twentieth century. Anthropology is even younger. Political economy, as the science of politics was called, came to life with Harriet Martineau (1802–1876) and John Stuart Mill (1806–1873). Economics first became a college subject of respectability in the twentieth century with the publication of Richard T. Ely's much read text, *Outlines of Economics*. Social scientists were just coming into their own at the turn of the twentieth century.

For that matter, the secondary school as a whole made but poor headway until the dawn of our century. When the high school emerged as a true part of public education in consonance with the contemporary growth of the social sciences, social studies became most important. Notwithstanding the obscurity of the origins of this term, at the present time most secondary schools devote up to one-third of their curricular time to subjects included in the category. History still remains as the nominal basis, with sociology, political science or social relationships as the next most important fields.

For present purposes the story of history as a part of the secondary curriculum can start at about 1890. Before that time there were occasional courses in United States history, civic organization, and political economy. The idea of "consecutiveness" was not applied. There was a great proliferation of subjects both academic and practical in the early 1890's. Hardly two schools offered the same things. Generally, in the upper grades of the grammar schools (roughly corresponding to the present elementary school) there was some attempt to teach United States history or government. This was largely oriented toward justification of what the United States had done, e.g., the Civil War, the Revolutionary War, the various constitutional amendments, and patriotic holidays. There was no apparent attempt, even sporadically, to include the study of man in his society or the nature of personality characteristics.

In 1890 the National Education Association appointed its "committee of ten" which constituted the beginnings of modern secondary education. Although this body was largely responsive to the requirements of higher education, its impetus has been felt strongly by the general education movement which has since taken place. In its turn this committee appointed, among nine such bodies, a "Conference of History, Civil Government, and Political Economy." These people met at

Madison, Wisconsin and drew up a general recommendation for a four year sequence in French, English, American and local history, including civil government.[1] There seems to have been a gain in history offerings after this, but rather indiscriminately divided between United States history and general history which was popular at the time.[2] The committee had advised against the latter on the grounds that it was too remote from present needs and too thinly concentrated in any one period. These results appear to bear out the generalization that current intellectual trends, whatever they happen to be, find their way into the school curriculum rather rapidly.

The American Historical Association, in 1899, appointed a Committee of Seven under the chairmanship of Andrew C. McLaughlin, an eminent historian, to consider the same problem. This committee studied current offerings in the American high schools and found little evidence of any well defined program of consecutive historical training. Further than that, according to Professor McLaughlin, "there was no recognized consensus of opinion in the country at large, not one generally accepted judgment, not even one well-known point of agreement, which could serve as a beginning for a consideration of the place of history in the high school curriculum. Such a statement cannot be made concerning any other subject commonly taught in the secondary schools." [3]

At this point the American Historical Association's Committee of Seven sutured to future curricular offerings of four year American high schools the following content of history, in lieu of social studies:

[1] United States Bureau of Education, *Report of the Committee on Secondary School Studies* (United States Government Printing Office, Washington, D.C., 1893), pp. 163, 174.

[2] During the Enlightenment in the eighteenth century the Encyclopedists had attempted to compile lexicons of universal knowledge in voluminous sets of books. In the next hundred years the influence permeated the historians' thinking, and by 1900 general or universal histories were available everywhere. A typical example was *The Great Events of Famous Historians*, edited by Charles F. Horne and Jno. Rudd ( 20 vols., The National Alumni, London and New York, 1906), which stated its purpose as "comprehensive and readable accounts of the world's history. . . ." As for the truly great American historians who wrote during the nineteenth century ( such as Francis Parkman, John Lothrop Motley and William Prescott), their work was more likely to be considered as *belles lettres* than as reasonable text material for students.

[3] *The Study of History in Schools,* Report to the American Historical Association by the Committee of Seven ( Macmillan, New York, 1909), p. 3.

Recommendation of Committee of Seven, 1899

First year:    Ancient and medieval history to 800, 814, or 843 A.D.
Second year: Later Medieval and modern European history
Third year:    English history
Fourth year: American history and civil government

Until the end of World War I this was the recognized pattern of secondary social studies, for better or worse.

The concept of educating "all the children of all the people" was expanded, beginning at about this time, to include most of the age group up to sixteen or seventeen. High school students graduating in 1900 numbered 94,883, having jumped from 43,731 in ten years. By 1940 this figure was to swell to 1,221,475.[4] In ten years more (or in 1950) 5,707,000 youngsters were in public high schools alone.[5] Presently there are about 8,000,000 students in our high schools, public and private, with the prospect of 10,000,000 only a few years away. Simple extrapolation of the activities of 15,000,000 babies born between 1945 and 1954 will bear this out.[6]

It is interesting to notice the relative influence of a learned society such as the American Historical Association at the beginning and at the end of this period. When the bulge of school attendance first hit at the start of the present century, schools, ever alert and sensitive to public pressure, turned naturally for advice to the scholarly reeves of knowledge, in this case the historians. These people, sensitive in their turn to college preparatory needs, designed a social studies curriculum that fitted these purposes. In 1900 high school graduates furnished about 75 per cent of their number to colleges and universities as candidates. A similar proportion held until World War I when it gradually gave way to social change. More and more people attended high school, and a lesser and lesser percentage of the graduates went on to college.

[4] *Statistical Abstract of the United States, 1949,* United States Department of Commerce (United States Government Printing Office, Washington, D.C., 1949), p. 120, from *Biennial Survey of Education,* Federal Security Agency, Office of Education.

[5] Arthur Bestor, *The Restoration of Learning* (Knopf, New York, 1955), comments on the facts of school enrollment and projection of school populations, but with an emphasis on reinstituting a more restrictive liberal arts program with very little provision for the below average.

[6] Philip D. Reed, "We're Betting You'll Be Prosperous," *American Magazine* (July, 1954), pp. 15 to 95.

At present only about twenty-five per cent of high school graduates attempt the baccalaureate course, although since World War II there has been a gradual increase. Notwithstanding the reduced percentage as compared to the beginning of the century, the positive number of persons in both high school and college is increasing steadily.

While the historians and other learned groups were concentrating on college preparation as the main objective of high school, John Dewey, William Heard Kilpatrick and others—the founders of the "new education"—were thinking of "education for the needs of life" as a prime goal of secondary education.[7] From this group a whole complex of social studies experts arose emphasizing methodology of teaching rather than liberal arts erudition. Social studies gradually became identified with the new academic study of professional education with its own professional organization, the National Council for the Social Studies which was originally an offshoot of the Association of School Administrators. History remained as the province of liberal arts-trained and specialized historians, but its public school use passed over into the hands of professional teachers—not historians. History as such is now not so much a school subject as it is a recorded body of knowledge that can be tapped for illustration of man's predicament in modern society. In any case, the American Historical Association is not now asked when a major curricular revision is contemplated. It is more in order, since World War I, to call upon such a body as the National Council for the Social Studies as a branch of the National Education Association.

The pressure of obligatory attendance in high school of nearly all of the age group in question, and the urgency of modern problems of technological growth (in geometric progression) have worked in the direction of entrenching those who adhered to the new professional education following World War I. Those representatives of liberal arts, academicians who formerly dominated the secondary curriculum with an eye to selective college preparation, have lost their dominant position.

Possibly up to one-half of American secondary students can in some measure master the traditional body of culture commonly composing the liberal arts content. This does not mean that these alone should have exclusive access to the classics, ancient and modern history and the like, but that those persons who show the ability to gain from an

[7] Irving E. Miller, *Education for the Needs of Life* (Macmillan, New York, 1923), *passim.* Dr. Miller was John Dewey's first doctoral student at the University of Chicago, and he reflects in fairly undiluted form the teachings of Dewey.

intellectually accelerated program should be encouraged in its pursuit. All students must have the opportunity to enjoy learning, and none should ever be denied this right. As children go on in school it becomes apparent that some can get more from those courses and subjects which are most immediately adaptable to adjustment to everyday living. Some students do not even find it advantageous to finish high school. These people must also be provided for, and of necessity their curriculum will be different. At first this was achieved by many schools in homogeneous ability groupings based on IQ, and the introduction of units of work corresponding in difficulty to the ability of the students.

With at least some of the above considerations in mind, in 1912, the National Education Association, by then dominant in the advisory capacity, appointed a Commission on the Reorganization of Secondary Education, of which a Committee on the Social Studies was a part. By 1916 this committee presented a program which reflected the growing importance of general education as well as the importance of the new junior high school. Their recommendations included:

Social Studies Curriculum, 1916

Grade 7    Geography, European history, civics

Grade 8    Geography, American history, civics

Grade 9    Political, economic, vocational studies; economic history and civics

Grade 10   European history since 1700

Grade 11   United States history

Grade 12   Problems of American democracy [8]

This program forms the basis of current modal offerings over the United States, but world history (never accorded national sanction by the historians) has tended to take the place of tenth grade European history. In addition, state or local history and geography have entered the curricula in many places.

During the middle period of the growth of social studies, from a tendency to legislate local requirements, and from educators' well meaning attempts to gear the school offerings to current needs certain abuses arose. Some school districts insisted upon units in regional history and local industries or institutions at several grade levels throughout elementary and secondary curricula. At the same time,

[8] Edwin R. Carr, "The Curriculum in History in the Secondary School," paper delivered before the American Historical Association, Pacific Coast Branch, Berkeley, California, December, 1955.

legislative requirements have not always specified a particular placement, and individual teachers have expanded what might appear to be the children's logical interest to concentrate on a limited and particularistic set of topics. Instead of broad knowledge of basic geographic, historic and political concepts this sometimes resulted in very narrow but detailed examination of a few special cases. In extreme cases it was possible for a child, remaining in one locality for the twelve years of his school attendance, to have studied the production of oranges and the growth of one harbor eight or ten times. This could only be done at the expense of other possibilities of learning, and certainly it would be a deadly bore to the child. In another instance, because of the lack of uniformity of grade placement of local history requirements, a student who moved three times during his four year high school career in a single state might be subjected to state history and government four times in succession. Certainly these are extreme examples, but such things did happen, for whatever reasons, and they contributed to a watering down of the curriculum which, after World War II, was more and more widely noticed and criticized by both educators and the public.

At the beginning of the twentieth century school officials and advisory groups felt that the secondary subjects should possess uniformity throughout the country, and further, that a desirable historical continuity was somehow related to this wish. As school enrollment increased so rapidly that both of these elements were lost, a vacuum filling elective tendency became apparent. At first, free elective choice of subjects was considered to be more democratic than a rigidly prescribed course. Only the college preparatory students tended to adhere to a specified sequence of solid social studies courses. Even this began to give way to the elective system during the 1930's. By 1940 some public high schools and junior high schools went to an extreme in attempting to introduce active democracy into the classroom and into the curriculum by adopting a nearly unregulated elective system. The whole trend of electives was encouraged during these middle years by the vagueness of social studies objectives and a child centered attempt to democratize education. If extremes were reached and abuses arose it may very well have been because the original objectives of educational reform at the beginning of the twentieth century were largely realized; improved techniques of instruction, better teaching materials, and above all, the mass handling of an unprecedented number of students were all achieved before World War II.

In the process of handling the astronomically increasing numbers of children in school, partly due to the very numbers, partly to the lack of homogeneity in their learning capacities and possibly as a result of the fluid and sometimes chaotic state of the curriculum arising from many causes, the new procedures and techniques in teaching were blamed for an apparent lack in subject achievement. Most often the actual failures to learn as much as in the "good old days" were non-existent, but in some cases schools did not meet the standards expected of them by their patrons. From this circumstance, fancied or real, arose something of a controversy which, since 1945, has been polarized between professional education and university academic specialization. The extremists on either side were always few in number, but rather vocal, and since World War II there has been an insistent attack on the curriculum of the high schools and on teacher training and certification. The attack has been rebutted, largely in statistical form and through the professional organizations of teachers and administrators.

Postwar society, responsive to the tremendous promise of technological development resulting from World War II, began to be more conscious of the necessity for universal proficiency in basic school subjects. The immediate result was increasing pressure on the curriculum for enhancement of the elementary subjects, the three R's. There has been an evident response in secondary schools to the growing pressure on the lower schools. More legislation of graduation requirements, more insistence on basic skills and better generalized statements of objectives have been steadily growing. Between 1950 and 1960 there seems to be emerging a new synthesis of educational thought which is producing a workable philosophy of education which in turn bids fair to produce a satisfactory curriculum to meet the tremendous task of educating the coming millions of school students.[9]

[9] Since 1950 a strenuous polemic has developed between two extreme positions in education, certain academicians tending to assess all blame for what they see as a failure in education to the uncritical pursuit of a philosophy of education stemming from the pragmatism of John Dewey. Arthur Bestor and Mortimer Smith are figures most often associated with this side of the controversy. Their Council for Basic Education supports a need to return to the liberal arts curriculum of the nineteenth century and strict attention to the standard disciplines of knowledge. In all fairness it must be mentioned that the new leader of CBE, Thomas Bledsoe, is much more moderate than Mortimer Smith. His present position is summarized in his own short statement in *School Management* (December, 1960, pp. 26–30, 65): "There never were any good, old days. . . . What we need is a good new day in which we will try to give adequate intellectual training to 80 or 85 percent of the students." Bestor and Smith's attack has been aimed at education and teachers in general and so it has been difficult to counter concisely. Public opinion

Although extremists in both parties to the philosophical polemic of the 1950's have claimed total sanction from the public, express democratic values and quote Jefferson *ad nauseam*, one fact is overlooked that Jefferson himself knew, namely: all people have the same political rights and the right to a means of livelihood, but all people do not have the same mental endowment—some persons are more mentally gifted than others, can learn more in the same length of time. There is need, therefore, for a diverse range of curricular offerings in modern secondary schools with ample allowance for a free choice but with reasonable guidance and counseling. Good schools and good educators have increasingly provided this since the beginning of the twentieth century.[10]

With continuing stress on these elements in the elementary schools the urgency will be transmitted to the secondary schools. As more and more of all children from five to eighteen remain in school such demands will become more and more important—not only to the schools and to children but to society as a whole.

Since 1916 most states have seen fit to legislate graduation requirements in various parts of the social studies. Among these it is significant that most states have a statutory ruling that all students in order to graduate from high school must have completed one year of United States history and government in grade eight and another in grade eleven. In addition to the two years of American history required there is often added another year of state or local history and government. Recently a fourth year requirement in some states has been added: world problems.

All this seems clearly to indicate several principles: (1) children will go to school and be offered certain things in social studies, (2) United States history is a core of social studies, (3) patriotism and other democratic values must be reflected in school curricula, (4) the American public is becoming aware of the place of the United States

---

has been stirred up, however, and certain legislative pressure has been placed on schools to reassess themselves. Out of the issue thus joined much thinking on the part of educators has emerged, and a few very fine books. I. B. Berkson, *The Ideal and the Community* (Harper, New York, 1958), is a new philosophy of education statement stemming from an extensive critique of John Dewey's influence. It is sound and balanced. Paul Woodring, *A Fourth of a Nation* (McGraw-Hill, New York, 1957), is one of the best current analyses of the possibility for a new synthesis of old and new currents of educational philosophy. Curriculum and teacher training are re-evaluated here. Both these men are professors of education, from whom one would expect a reasonable philosophy of education to come.

[10] James High, "Teaching: Stronghold of the Individualists," *Clearing House* (February, 1955), pp. 323–327.

in the world as indicated by the numerous offerings in world problems, and (5) our citizenry reserves the right to advise its public schools.

## 2. Present Modal Offerings

Grounded on these principles and in view of the historical development of the social studies curriculum thus far, it seems logical to generalize typical or desirable offerings for each of the grades in an eight year spread of secondary education. Grades 13 and 14 are included here in their role of high school continuation rather than as the first two baccalaureate years. In actuality those grades serve in both capacities in various localities, depending upon whether they are in a strictly junior college or part of the newer concept of the community college.[11]

Let us say then that the following choices may be subjectively considered to be "most useful and most ornamental . . . ," always remembering curricular sensitivity to popular need and cultural tradition. If the objectives of social studies are kept clearly in mind these suitable general subjects may be used as guides to reasonable choices to be made under differing local conditions.

A mere glance at fifty years of secondary school curricular history in the United States assures one that a large share of school time has been spent on social studies of one kind or another. This tendency certainly seems to be on the increase. It is a little more difficult to see any logical pattern of sequence in these offerings, or any definite relationship with principles of child growth. In the elementary school psychological and physical maturation have directed that studies be centered around the idea of an increasing and expanding outlook on the part of the child as he first emerges from his mother's dominance, then goes through the grades, always becoming aware of a larger and larger community. At first his studies are concerned with home, then the neighborhood and city. He examines the parts played by the various community and civic services and their employees, such as the fireman, the postman, the policeman. Next he is made aware of expanding technological ideas and devices. The history of local, state and national growth are presented to him. His contemporary neighbors in foreign lands become more real as the child learns of the geography of North and South America. He discovers some of the similarities and differences among modern people all over the world—how they earn their

[11] See James Abel Starrak, *The Community College in the United States* (Iowa State College Press, Ames, 1954).

livings, become educated, travel, and enjoy themselves. As the young-ster comes into the fifth or sixth grade he returns, in his social studies program, to the United States and learns of the specific application of technology and social growth in his own area. He may, at this point, be particularly concerned with finding out how his electrical, or water, or sanitation system works, how it is related to the common political experience of his community. If the elementary school happens to in-clude the seventh or eighth grades the final year will probably be spent on a review of United States history including an attempt to expand the child's knowledge of geography, politics, economics, and social organization. These last two years usually have inter-related programs of language arts and social studies.

Such a sequence is geared to the growth pattern of early childhood and merges into the capabilities of preadolescence. At the same time, using the central theme of American life, the whole pattern has some degree of familiarity to the American child, and on the whole, is probably conducive to achieving the objective of better citizenship and life adjustment. At the same time, with United States history coming at the end, a traditional patriotic and civic need is served. From the outset of American national growth public sentiment has dictated an emphasis upon certain values best illustrated by a study of national development. In some measure this need is outmoded now by the introduction of the junior high school which in large part has supplanted the last two years of elementary school, but on the other hand, if there is no concerted effort to provide a continuous and logi-cal pattern of social studies offerings in the secondary school much of the benefit of elementary school logicality is lost.

It is quite possible to conceive of six or eight years of secondary schooling as a unit added consecutively to the groundwork of the first six years of school experience, and to establish a social studies pro-gram which is equally synchronized with the characteristic rhythm of pre-adolescence and early adolescence. Simultaneously such a se-quence may contain enough flexibility to embrace the individual dif-ferences in these age groups which become more and more marked as the child becomes older. The aim of social studies is competent citi-zenship, the keynote is objective progress, and the vehicle is knowl-edge. These things must be tempered by recognition of the historical tradition of the secondary curriculum, which in turn, reflects social pressure and values. So with an eye to tradition, current practice, and future development we may justify the present selections in the light of history, psychology, and urgency.

Grades seven through nine, or the most common organization of junior high school, should contain social studies units designed to increase the preadolescent's rapidly expanding interest in technology and its social implications, followed by emphasis of the westward movement of great ideas from Europe in the early modern period and their further westward movement from colonial America into the wilderness and finally to the Pacific coast. The exploits of the men and women engaged in that dramatic sweep and swell of Western civilization will grip the minds and stir the emotional creativity of young people almost incalculably. The colorfully great personalities of our past, the mighty heroes of our history, can become indelible symbols in the knowledgeable imaginations of young citizens, thus serving both tradition and present need. As children arrive at age fourteen they seem to be best adapted to learning some of the facts concerning their nation in a closely integrated world, such as a comparison between the Spanish-American War, the first venture of the United States in military imperialism, and the Korean conflict when the United States upheld the principles of the United Nations' avowal against imperialism. Citizens of that age are able to be and certainly should be keenly sensitive to American participation in the affairs of the world. What happens at Suez or in Hungary is of moment to our citizens of all ages. Geographic concepts here are compelling and important.

The next logical step in satisfying expansive adolescent curiosity in regard to man's present status would appear to be a survey of Western civilization. If Egypt is now in the news and modern Britain is struggling for existence in a complex contemporary Europe, how did Egypt and England come to be what they are now? If the ordinary Briton and the ordinary American speak a common language and think along common lines concerning fundamental ideas, how did this come to be? The modern Egyptian, Turk, Greek, Italian, Briton, German, Hungarian, Canadian and American all share a common heritage of great ideas; even their languages have some common elements, at least in philosophic basis, despite the fact that three linguistic stocks are represented. In order for the attainment of intelligent citizenship in the Western world it is necessary for the young adolescent to learn of the growth and transmission of ideas from a cradle of civilization in Egypt through Greece and Rome to Germanic influences in France and Anglo-Saxon based England and on to the New World. Grades nine or ten have been selected for this subject through usage, and psychology corroborates the choice.

As human consciousness has become more global in this century gradual additions to the history of Western Europe have tended to transform that school course for the tenth grade into "world history." Often this has become an almost unlearnable and definitely unpalatable bite of erudition. Although adolescent minds are active and pliable the young bodies accompanying those minds are restless, and both have limits to their endurance.

Presently it seems most feasible to devote the tenth year to a survey acquaintance with the literature and the lasting ideas of Western Europe. Idealism, rationalism, scholasticism, humanism, Christianity, the Enlightenment, world discoveries, capitalism, the Reformation and counter-Reformation, popular revolution and the growth of democracy—all these things appear now to be the underlying elements of our current, dynamic, technological present world. The child of fifteen, in order to adapt to his adult role of citizenship must have the opportunity to gain at least a rudimentary knowledge of this sequence of currents and crosscurrents in Western man's evolution.

Grade eleven, usually with legislative sanction, has become the nearly universal choice for presentation of a final review of United States history and government. Very often with two or three required years of social studies in high school, students will, at this grade level, come in contact for the last time with any possibility of a formal presentation of the basic usable facts of history and government that every political citizen should know in order to perform his civic responsibilities. Constitutional forms and derivations, stressed at such an impressionable, formative age—just a few years before adulthood —seem to be more understandable than at an earlier age; and if left until the final year of high school very often the press of other affairs precludes full attention to such matters, and so for at least seventy-five per cent of high school graduates the eleventh grade is the "last chance." Of course, it would be well in every case if the great belletristic writing of American authors could be presented at the same time, although not necessarily in the same class.

The final high school year, so far as social studies are concerned, is mostly elective. It probably should be so. By this time the students are about to enter postadolescence. Many of them, within two or three years after the start of their senior year in high school, will be fathers and mothers, wage earners and housewives, with all the responsibilities of the adult world. For these people as well as for those who will go on to more advanced study it becomes important to select, at least tentatively, an occupation, and seriously to consider the immediate future with all its trials and problems. These problems are different for each individual, and therefore each person should have multiple opportunities for exploration of his capabilities and desires. A truly elective application at this point is psychologically and practically a necessity. Such elective procedure does not mean mere frittering of academic time. It should be with ample objective guidance, given by trained and intelligent people and with access to a well-balanced curriculum.

It is suggested here that a reasonable program for seniors would include opportunities for studying vocational and personal adjustment. It might contain much more, and it might very well embrace more than grade twelve, but the present suggestion is meant to be a minimum even for a small high school. A half-year in how to pick a career is certainly in order. Young men and women, even if they have definitely decided at the age of seventeen or eighteen what they will do for the rest of their lives, should by all means know what the other one hundred eighty million Americans do for a living. As a matter of fact most people have not the slightest idea of what they want to do for a permanent livelihood at the age of eighteen. They *must* assume this responsibility some time. What better way is available than on the basis of objective knowledge of the possibilities?

Corollary to the choice of profession or vocation is the necessity for understanding the emotional and physical underpinning of personality. Another half-year course in basic psychology seems to be imperative in such a curricular structure as has been sketched here. This course might include as a framework mental hygiene, or sufficient insight into one's own personality to meet society's demand that every person "remain sane." Such a course could also introduce students to the social effects of maladjustment in recognizable form, such as the psychopathic personality.[12]

As it has been noted, after the influence of curricular suggestions made at the turn of the century began to submerge in the rapid growth of the secondary school, elective choices became more prevalent than a prescribed sequence of courses. Elective additions to the basic offerings in social studies are to be welcomed if they have a purpose and if they contribute to the achievement of established goals in education. Sometimes this has not been the case. Without generally accepted objectives as a guide, electives have been added in aimless fashion with each new social pressure, attempting to bring consonance

[12] See Robert Mitchell Lindner, *Rebel Without a Cause* (Research Books, 1945), a case study of psychoanalysis of a criminal psychopath.

## SANTA BARBARA CITY SCHOOLS
## SANTA BARBARA, CALIFORNIA
### 1960 - 1961

The word "and" is used in some course titles to identify the two-semester courses. Examples are English 3 and 4, Latin 1 and 2, and Spanish 3 and 4. Students who enroll in any course so identified are expected to complete both semesters of the course.

A "dash" is used in some course titles to identify those courses which may be taken for one or more semesters. Examples are Color and Design 1-2, Mechanical Drawing 3-4, and Typing 1-2. Students who enroll in any course so identified may take both semesters but are not required to complete more than one semester.

Courses which are offered for one semester only have no semester numbers in the course titles. Examples are Creative Writing, Ancient History, and Penmanship and Spelling.

An asterisk (*) is used to identify the courses in which 10th grade students may enroll.

### REQUIRED COURSES

10th Grade

1. Physical Education or ROTC ........................................... one year
2. English ........................................................................ one year

11th Grade

1. Physical Education or ROTC ........................................... one year
2. English ........................................................................ one year
3. U.S. History ................................................................. one year

12th Grade

1. Physical Education or ROTC ........................................... one year
2. English ................................................................. one semester
3. American Government ............................................. one semester

### SCIENCE

1. A minimum of one year, 10 semester periods taken in 10, 11, or 12th year. Students who plan to go to college must take a laboratory science in either the junior or senior year.

### ELECTIVES

1. Seventy (70) semester periods (units) of credit.

### DIPLOMA REQUIREMENTS

To qualify for a diploma you must have earned:

|      | Academic credits | Non-academic credits | Citizenship credits | Total |
|------|------------------|----------------------|---------------------|-------|
| 10th | 120 | 30 | 18 | 168 |
| 11th | 120 | 30 | 18 | 168 |
| 12th | 125 | 30 | 18 | 173 |

FIGURE 1a. Comprehensive high school curriculum. The program reflects quite substantially what James Conant has found to be prevalent in the United States (*The American High School Today*, McGraw-Hill, New York, 1959).

AGRICULTURE
*General Agriculture 1-2
*Ornamental Hort. 1-2
*Ag. Animal Husbandry 1-2

ART
Advanced Composition 1-2
*Art Apperciation
*Arts and Crafts 1-2
*Ceramics 1-2
*Color and Design 1-2
*Commercial Art 1-2
*Freehand Drawing 1-2
*Leather 1-2
Painting

BUSINESS
Bookkeeping 1 and 2
Bookkeeping 3 and 4
*Business English (Spring)
*Business Exploration
Business Law
Business Machines
Merchandising 1 and 2
Office Practice
*Penmanship and Spelling
*Personal Typing
Shorthand 1 and 2
Shorthand 3 and 4
*Typing 1-2-3
Typing 4

DRIVER TRAINING (Students who
will be 16 during the semester and
do not have a driver's license are
eligible to enroll)

ENGLISH
*Creative Writing
*Newswriting
*English 3 and 4
English 5 and 6
(An English elective may be sub-
stituted for one semester of
either English 4, 5, or 6. Teacher
and counselor approval is re-
quired.)
English Literature 1 and 2
Types of Literature
Forge, (Prerequisite: Newswrit-
ing) Photography
O and G (by permission)
*Reading (May be repeated for
credit)

ORAL ENGLISH
*Broadcasting
Hi-Lights (Prerequisite: Broad-
casting)
*Public Speaking 1-2
*Theater Arts 1-2
Theater Arts 3-4 (Tryouts)
*Stagecraft 1-2

HOME ECONOMICS
  Child Care
  *Clothing 1-2
  Clothing 3-4
  Family Living (Boys and Girls)
  *Foods 1-2 (Boys and Girls)

INDUSTRIAL ARTS
  *Auto 1
  Auto 2 (permission)
  Auto Trade Trng. (permission)
  *Electronics 1-2
  Electronics 3-4
  Electronics 5-6
  *Graphic Arts 1-2
  *Graphic Arts (Adv)
  Mechanical Drawing 1-2
  Mechanical Drawing 3-4
  Mechanical Drawing 5-6
  *Metal Crafts 1-2
  *Metal Shop 1-2
  Metal Shop (Adv) (Sem)
  *Wood 1-2
  Wood (Adv) (Sem)

LANGUAGE
  *French 1 and 2
  'French 3 and 4
  French 5 and 6
  French 7 and 8
  *German 1 and 2
  German 3 and 4
  German 5 and 6
  *Latin 1 and 2

*Latin 3 and 4
Latin 5 and 6
Latin 7 and 8
*Spanish 1 and 2
*Spanish 3 and 4
Spanish 5 and 6
Spanish 7 and 8
*Practical Spanish 1 and 2

MATHEMATICS
  *Algebra-Geometry 1 and 2
  *Algebra-Geometry 3 and 4
  Intermediate Algebra (Fall)
  Advanced Algebra (Spring)
  *Basic Math 1-2
  *Basic Math 3-4
  *Basic Math 5-6
  *CPM 3 and 4
  Solid Geometry (Spring)
  Trigonometry (Fall)

MILITARY SCIENCE
  *Military Science 1 (1st yr.)
  Military Science 2 (2nd yr.)
  Military Science 3 (3rd yr.)
  *Special Military 2

MUSIC
- *A Cappella Chorus (Tryouts)
- *Band (Tryouts)
- Double Male Quartet
- *Girls' Ensemble
- Harmony
- Intermediate & Beginners' Band
- *Music Appreciation
- *Music Fundamentals (Fall)
- *Orchestra (Tryouts)
- *ROTC Band
- *Triple Trio (Tryouts)

PHYSICAL EDUCATION (BOYS)
- *Physical Ed 1 and 2
- **Physical Ed 3 and 4**
- Physical Ed 5 and 6
- *Physical Ed Indiv. Correct (placed by school physician)
- Instead of Phys. Ed class you may select from the following:
- *Basketball (Tryouts) Fall-Spring
- *Basket "B" (Fall)
- *Cross-Country (Fall)
- *Football (Tryouts) Fall-Spring
- *Football, Soph. (Fall)
- *Baseball (Spring)
- *Golf (Spring)
- *Swimming (Spring)
- *Tennis (Spring)
- *Track (Spring)

PHYSICAL EDUCATION (GIRLS)
- Advanced Dance
- Advanced Swimming
- Advanced Tennis
- GAA
- Golf-Sports (Spring)
- *Beginning Tennis
- *Beginning Modern Dance
- Sports
- Swimming

SCIENCE
- *Biology 1 and 2
- *Chemistry 1 and 2
- *Life Science 1 and 2
- Physical Science 1 and 2
- Physics 1-2
- Physiology

SOCIAL STUDIES
- American Government
- Ancient History (Spring)
- Elementary Sociology
- International Relations (Spring)
- Preparatory Psychology
- U.S. History 1 and 2
- *World Geography
- *World History 1 and 2

WORK EXPERIENCE EDUCATION
Arranged with the placement office and counselor.

between the modern school curriculum and the rapidly changing outlook of society. For example, after World War I when American citizens were acutely aware of the application of the "clear and present
danger" doctrine and the espionage laws, many courses in United
States government and citizenship appeared; or, during the Great Depression in the 1930's various courses in sociology or modern society
showed up always looking toward reform. Even such a course as applied ichthyology might become an academic euphemism for curricular sensitivity to the art of fly-casting.[13] These may all be sound offerings, but if they do not fit a reasonable, attainable pattern of social
learning they have little justification as electives in the social studies
program of the secondary school.

Rather, it would appear that in addition to a cohesive three year
pattern of social studies, there should be a supplemental elective program designed to fit the psychological needs of the whole secondary
range, but primarily applicable to the final year. These courses should
be designed to enhance the opportunities for knowledge growth of
those students who are precocious or specially talented in the direction of the social sciences, or, on the other hand, to exploit the meager
or retarded abilities of students who would otherwise fail with the
average of their age groups. One of the shames of our society is that
in the name of democracy backward students have been allowed to
suffer emotional shock while they were unwillingly retarding their
faster schoolmates simply by being subjected to class work which
they could neither comprehend nor appreciate. At the same time, an
even worse sin against society is being perpetrated if there is neglect
of the brighter than average (the talented or gifted student) who
often through boredom at the slow rate of average achievement may
turn his talents to gangsterism or simply lethargic withdrawal from
reality. The school owes both these youngsters, and particularly the
latter, a better chance than that suggested as the extreme in either
case. A thoughtfully organized program in social studies at all levels
of the secondary school might correct or preclude this neglect.[14]

Currently some experimentation has been carried out in an interesting aspect of the elective program: advanced placement in college

---

[13] Paul Woodring, *Let's Talk Sense about Our Schools* (McGraw-Hill, New
York, 1953), p. 116 ff.

[14] Robert F. DeHaan and Robert J. Havighurst, *Educating Gifted Children*
(University of Chicago Press, 1957), is a combination of theoretical examination
of the problem and practical suggestions for programs in both elementary and
secondary school.

curricula for specially gifted high school students. There are several different versions of advanced placement; some of them have an eye to shortening the whole period of school and college attendance by accelerating the program while others feel that it is simply a way of eliminating repetition from the bright student's courses of study so that he will have more time to devote to specialized or enrichment material during his school life. There are many different findings to date on the various outcomes of such programs, but very little concurrence as to the best methods to be employed. One point of agreement has emerged: the average grade achievement of high school students taking college courses in all of the schemes of advanced placement is higher than the average grade achievement of the regular college students in the same kind of courses. The answer is fairly simple; such students are simply much brighter than the average. In any case, the experimental spirit evinced by such thinking seems to be healthy and the movement certainly points up the desirability of cooperation between university faculties and the teaching staffs and administrations of high schools. It also illustrates the need for an elective system for advanced students. Good schools and good teachers have always known this.

Instead of further loading the courses of study with new offerings responding to the latest gadget inspired social pressure, or further amplification of the already overburdened "surveys of world civilization" with each week's current events, a different type of selection can be made in line with the principles outlined here.

Although the Western world has been the wellspring of our culture for the most part, at many different points the Orient has intruded into our lives. This became painfully apparent at the opening of World War II. As an elective for the student who has already mastered the appropriate core of Western knowledge a course in Far Eastern life might seem like an oasis in the dry ground of repetition. The same could be said of South and Central American life. In this case much of the influence has been reversed, that is, from the United States to the countries lying south of us, but certainly this in itself is worth knowing for the sake of being responsible citizens in a more and more unitary world. That every Latin American constitution is directly modeled after our own is a simple and intriguing fact which can be elaborated with bright secondary students from grades seven through twelve. The intricacies of the Pan-American Union should not remain mysterious to most high school graduates.

Finally, in the young adult of secondary school age, sometimes including grades from ten through fourteen, contemporary world problems as an organized course is beginning to enter the curricula. In certain cases such a course has been ordered by fiat or legislation as requisite to graduation from high school. In American universities and colleges (under the name of Modern Society) it shares with the history of civilization a major position in general education requirements. It is felt here that world problems should be an elective reserved for those capable of grasping the significance and scope of world affairs, and willing to ferret out the necessary knowledge of past and present to understand them. There is no prescription for a course of this kind because its tradition is too short, its application too scattered as yet. That it is valuable is quite certain, provided it does not degenerate into mere current happenings and future speculation.

The above sketch of possible present choices in social studies is not meant to be the last word. There is no such thing in an educational field as broad as ours, and in a society and time as fluid as ours. These suggestions are simply that—suggestions, based on some thoughtful consideration of psychological factors, of traditional practices, of expert opinion and of plainly subjective belief in the value of knowledge as a way to competent citizenship for all. We could decry the very values we hold if we were to enunciate curricular choices without countenancing the possibility of variations, and it must be remembered that statements made in textbooks are not likely to determine the curriculum in any marked degree. In the United States public opinion reflects in the school curriculum at least as much as professional guidance. A good teacher would deny his philosophy if he refused to alter his methods or choice of material when the circumstances demonstrate such need.

## 3. Possible Future Trends

Fifty years ago the family, the church, the place of employment of some children—all shared in teaching young people what they had to know in order to survive. Now, the school, through social pressure and because of the tremendous body of learning which must be covered, has assumed the greatest proportion of the burden. Natural science, social science, the humanities and professional education furnish the tools; American citizens pay the bill; and American youth, one-fourth of the nation, is the recipient.

Since this is a relatively new arrangement (only about fifty years old), there have been many nostrums put forth for accomplishment of the objectives. When the great wave of students swamped the secondary schools at about the time of World War I, the comfortably ensconced exponents of liberal education saw little cause for alarm. They thought it would be simply a matter of building more schools and training more teachers. In contrast to the present, their objectives were clear. As far as high school was concerned the masters and doctors of philosophy felt that students could either learn what was offered or they could fail to graduate. In opposite reaction to this philosophy of education there arose a movement which had something for everyone. The "whole child" was spoken of as a new discovery, and a new education emerged aiming to equip a bulging mass of school students with a means of coping with the enlarged prospects of a twentieth century democracy.

At first the objectives of the new education were fairly plain, growing out of pragmatism and designed to allow people to adapt to the fluctuating requirements of an expanding culture while at the same time preserving the values of democratic social organization. Recently there has been a move toward re-evaluation of lengthy and disparate statements of educational objectives and more emphasis on subject and thought content of curricula rather than on the efficacy of attitudinal and behavioral indoctrination.

Social studies grew during this time out of old-fashioned history into the medium for transmitting "objective values" representing democratic living. Vaguely idealistic goals of behavior, taught under such course names as social living or social learning, sometimes dominated whole curricula, but there has been enough neglect of basic knowledge to produce a nationwide criticism of all education; whether or not justified is not the point in question here.

In any case, the objective of education is now more clear than it has been for many years. It is most simply stated as the process of obtaining knowledge and mastering thought processes in order to be able to make worthy choices throughout life.[15] Education is not wholly a matter of mental training nor is it only a matter of adjustment to life situations; however, the greatest emphasis must be on mental development, on intellectual processes. The objectives of education in the United States must also embrace the realization that all persons are entitled to and have the obligation to pursue an education. Therefore

[15] Paul Woodring, A Fourth of a Nation (McGraw-Hill, New York, 1957), p. 112.

the techniques of presentation and the selection of materials must be
varied and broad. To educate "all the children of all the people" is a
noble aim, and an accomplishment difficult of attainment.

A basic principle adopted in meeting the problem has been to recognize individual differences in students; to take the student from
where he happens to be to a point somewhere along the continuum
to an objective. Child growth and development, as a result, is much
better understood than it was thirty or forty years ago. Testing and
measurement are on a much firmer footing; evaluation is now much
more scientific. These things came partly from the impetus provided
by the new professional education. In addition, a body of tested teaching techniques has been made available to add to the scholarly content of education.

Scholarly knowledge is responsible for the results of research which
have produced the literature on child psychology. Social and natural
science have been combined to refine the instruments of measurement
used to define and quantify intelligence, aptitude in special fields or
simple achievement of subject matter. Sociology, psychology, psychiatry, medicine, physics and anthropology have produced instruments
for school use, but seldom has the specific knowledge of these disciplines been introduced to teacher or student. It is necessary for secondary school social studies teachers to expand their acquaintance with
the sciences, social sciences and humanities as well as to master the
techniques of modern pedagogical practice.

The old areas of liberal arts knowledge still exist. They are bigger
than ever, in fact. Many new disciplines have been added since 1900,
and there is a much more complete and integrated whole than at any
time in the past. Students should have access to it.

Social studies at the secondary level represent the reflection of the
integrated social science results of study at a higher level of scholarship. It is the assumption here that the social sciences have a common
goal which has almost been forgotten in concern with immediate
problems and methodologies. This common goal is an attempt to
formulate generalizations or laws concerning the nature of man and
society. There are, of course, secondary functions of more practical
use, such as teaching social studies; but as the end of teaching social
studies in schools is to produce adequate citizenship, so is it the concern of the social sciences to produce the vital formulations upon
which the social studies are based.

With a tremendous body of supporting knowledge, including what
to teach and how to teach, the social studies teachers are now equipped

as never before to reach their goal. They can contribute significantly to the major purpose of education: developing the ability to make worthy choices. Social studies instruction can and must support American values derived in a knowledgeable way. Up to the present, Americans have put practically all of their children in school; now the results of that universal attendance can be improved qualitatively, really for the first time. Naturally it is impossible to make predictions with any assurance that it is to be anything more than a guess, but at least the best guess for the future of social studies is that its teaching will be both more widespread and better in quality than it has ever been in the past. Perhaps the names of subjects will change (just as social studies is a relatively new phrase) but the content will be basically the same and continually growing. Human relations and history set in a place, the world, will always be the subject matter regardless of the individual labels on separate courses of instruction.

### 4. Suggested Further Reading

HISTORY OF EDUCATION

R. Freeman Butts, *A Cultural History of Western Education* (McGraw-Hill, New York, 1955), presents a well synthesized account of the philosophic foundations and the chronological growth of education in the Western world. It is valuable for showing the background of American development, but it falls down in the treatment of recent trends.

Xenophon, *The Education of Cyrus,* translated by H. G. Dakyns (Everyman's Library, 1914), despite its emphasis on military glory, describes a process of education devoted to the purpose of learning as much as possible. Cyrus, Prince of Persia, is described as a man who has "set in his heart the threefold love of man, of knowledge, and of honour."

EDUCATIONAL PHILOSOPHY

Charles Kingsley, *Alton Locke* (Everyman's Library, 1928), is a nineteenth century appeal, in the form of a novel, to young men's interest in learning history in order to know the scientific way to cope with problems of politics and society.

Thomas Carlyle, *English and Other Critical Essays* (Everyman's Library, 1940), says that history must be learned since it "lies at the root of all science."

John Dewey, *Psychology* (1887), *The School and Society* (1915), *Democracy and Education* (1916), *Education Today* (1940), and *Problems of Men* (1946), all present, in highly complicated form, the background and basis for alteration of the old educational processes and curricular choices. Over such a span of time (sixty years) many changes would necessarily take place. Dewey changed during this time, and it is feared that he has been much misread.

Lord Percy of Newcastle, *The Heresy of Democracy* (Regnery, Chicago, 1955), maintains that mere teaching of democratic technique is the surest way to lose real democracy. Individual competence based on firm standards of value will alone serve the needs of present education.

W. R. Niblett, *Education: The Lost Dimension* (Sloane, New York, 1955), maintains that subjective values must play a large part in the philosophy of education which must emerge. Schools are not the child-centered havens from reality that the author feels has been the philosophic heart of educational practice in the immediate past.

## CURRICULAR CHOICES

Earl S. Johnson, *Theory and Practice of the Social Studies* (Macmillan, New York, 1956), shows a fine correlation of knowledge and teaching in the social sciences at an advanced level. This book presupposes a sound liberal arts background in high school plus the expected maturity of adults.

*The Future of the Social Studies,* edited by James A. Michener, proposals for an experimental social studies curriculum by the National Council for the Social Studies (Banta, Menasha, Wisconsin, 1939). Michener, subsequently author of *South Pacific* and *Return to Paradise,* attempted to prescribe a comprehensive and cohesive minimum of knowledge for grades I through XII in order to teach the technique of adapting to a radically changing society.

*Social Studies for Young Adolescents,* edited by Julian C. Aldrich, Curriculum Series Number VI, National Council for the Social Studies (Washington, D.C., 1951), is an attempt to form a basis for selecting material for the junior high school programs in social studies, but it is still centered in *current* child needs, paying little attention to the problem of preparing students for an adult life.

H. S. Jennings, *The Biologic Basis of Human Nature* (Norton, New York, 1930), or any other recent book on the same subject, gives ample reason for the various choices of curricular content in the social studies from the standpoint of human structure.

*Improving the Social Studies Curriculum,* edited by Ruth Ellsworth and Ole Sand, Twenty-Sixth Yearbook of the National Council for the Social Studies (Washington, D.C., 1955), contains a survey of all the recent literature concerning social studies curricula in the United States. It is a very important book as a reference to curriculum makers.

*Education in Great Britain* (British Information Services, New York, 1952), gives an outline of the national attitude toward education in England, Wales, and Scotland.

## 5. Suggested Activities for Further Study

1. Read three of the books in this chapter's reading list or notes and then prepare a thoughtful essay showing their relationship to a curriculum with which you are acquainted.

2. Make a critical comparison of the British and American systems of education in regard to the social studies programs of both. Are the aims of both the same?

3. Discuss the reasons why an American school should or should not spend a whole year on the study of western civilization.

4. What are the responsibilities of an artisan in our society toward the exercise of the franchise? What can the schools do to implement the discharge of that responsibility?

5. Find the most recent article or book on social studies curriculum and review it in relation to the philosophy expressed in this chapter.

6. Is United States history more important than European history to the American secondary student? Explain.

7. What place should geography take in the secondary social studies offerings?

8. Identify the educational philosophies of John Dewey, William James, William Heard Kilpatrick, Arthur Bestor, Paul Woodring, James A. Michener, Earl J. McGrath, Lord Percy of Newcastle, W. R. Niblett, Mortimer Adler.

9. What are the relative positions in the modern curriculum of English, French, Latin, history, geography, political science, anthropology, biochemistry, biography, mathematics? How much of each and under what name should they appear in the social studies program of any school?

# part II
# THE LEARNING
# PROCESS

# 3

# Social learning and the individual

We live under the shadow of a gigantic question mark. Who are we? Where do we come from? Whither are we bound?

*The Story of Mankind*
HENDRIK WILLEM VAN LOON, 1921

## 1. Objectives of Social Studies

American citizenship is not only national; it is participation in a complicated yet unified world. Nationalism is still the greatest single force in the association of nations, and United States citizenship demands first allegiance to our state. What the future holds in regard to this no one can tell. A closely knit world of national states is a fact, and for the future the best guess is closer articulation of those states. This, in turn, demands increasing knowledge of both our own ideals and the characteristics of the rest of the world. Without much doubt citizens' responsibilities are becoming more complex and extending over a wider base. A higher degree of sophistication is required than in any time when the United States was safely isolated between two oceans.

The current era in this country emphasizes general education and re-examination of educational objectives and philosophy. Scientists, humanists, historians and educators are striving to make sense of what is happening and of what has happened. The exigency of the moment, the terrors of the future, and the record of the past must be resolved into a tenet of action. No longer is it sufficient to rely on liberal verities of the past. Neither is it satisfactory to prepare for isolated democracy. We live in a highly cohesive and integrated world, yet one which is rent by diverse social patterns and political beliefs. In order to retain that physical cohesion, and at the same time to promote continuity in the preservation of established objective values, we must be aware—educators and laymen alike—of the need for continuing readjustment of content and technique in meeting school needs. These are the demands of citizenship. Definition, understanding and knowledge are needed time out of mind.

According to law in most states every person must devote eight to twelve years to study aimed at achieving a common body of knowledge at public expense. Citizenship is an American birthright. Adequate citizenship, therefore, becomes the first goal of education. This is not merely an understanding of politics. In view of the diverse yet unified character of the world it becomes much more complicated. Despite specialization as a necessity in operating the complex whole, a sense of the integrated nature of things must be a part of everyone's thinking. This is the essence of general education, not a method of thought or a catechism of platitudes concerning patriotism and the "American way," but as much knowledge as possible of world culture.

Social studies, clearly, becomes the core of study in any public school attempt at generalized education for citizenship. The social studies represent directly that body of knowledge ". . . suited to and needed by, youth for life in American society. It is the education that *all* persons ought to have within the limits of their capacity to receive it." [1] Evidence of this may be adduced from the demands of industry that its employees understand the relationship between business and democracy. It may be seen in the required offerings of about half of American colleges in courses about "modern society," the joint efforts of history, sociology, psychology and economics. Several leading universities are encouraging doctoral students to go into integrated social science fields. Patriotic and civic organizations seek to strengthen public school courses in citizenship. School social studies programs usually emphasize history and geography in this connection.

All deference is due the individual disciplines which are behind the social studies (social sciences and humanities). Without the contributions of history, geography, economics, political science, anthropology, sociology, psychology, ethics and jurisprudence—not to mention theology, general literature and the communication fields—no scientific social studies could be possible. It is sincerely hoped that the countless scholars representing these continue to pursue their diligent and creative efforts to widen the horizons of knowledge.

[1] William Albert Levi, *General Education in the Social Studies* (American Council on Education, Washington, D.C., 1948), p. 6.

Despite this, ". . . until economists, political scientists, sociologists, psychologists, historians, and moralists sit down at a common table and talk a common language appropriate to their common concern will a general education in social studies, or, indeed, any education in social studies worthy the name be a real possibility." [2] Since the "proper study of mankind is man," then society becomes the subject of the social sciences; critical social understanding is the general objective of social studies. Here is the central problem and province of social studies, and it follows, we believe, that the heart of study is history.

Learning social studies, like crossing a street, requires first a clear-cut immediate objective. The reason for crossing a street is usually simple: to get to the other side. Culturally it is easy to arrive at a full comprehension of the meaning of a roadway, even to the type of traffic it carries. Man usually knows how to walk, and the general rules of modern self-preservation. A simple motivation, therefore, and almost unthinking compliance with known principles of behavior make it possible for the adult to understand his objective and to achieve it in such a process as crossing a street. For the small child that may not be the case. In fact, it may be a very complex procedure simply because there is not any clear knowledge of the objective. The child may do it for adventure, for exercise, out of perverseness or wilful disobedience, for the sake of pointless curiosity, or to see more clearly and closely a dog or a pretty flower. In the last instance, he comes nearer to a full comprehension of his objective; he at least has established a motive. When this is joined by knowledge of technique, then the full process becomes a whole. The child may cross a street as full-facultied adults do, with safety and reason.

The chief purpose of the social studies is to achieve equipment for citizenship—citizenship in tomorrow's world which is only the inevitable extension of what is known now based on what has been known in all the yesterdays. Such a broad statement is tantamount to the child's desire to examine more closely a brilliantly colored blossom across the street.

To bring the analogy into focus, more detailed objectives must

[2] *Ibid.*, p. 11. Arthur F. Corey, "California Schools Do Educate: A Reaffirmation," *Atlantic* (December, 1958), pp. 63–66, quotes Paul Woodring, *A Fourth of a Nation* (McGraw-Hill, New York, 1957), as follows: "In a society of free men, the proper aim of education is to prepare the individual to make wise decisions. The educated man is the one who can choose between good and bad, between truth and falsehood, between the beautiful and ugly, between the worthwhile and the trivial." It would be difficult to find any essential disagreement with this aim of education except in a totalitarian state.

emerge along with means to achieve them. That is the purpose of this book. Right here it is necessary to state the conceptual goals of social studies in general terms, followed by definition at greater length.

Such a credo may be put in the form of hope for materialized concepts that the individual student will achieve, in a degree commensurate with his ability, by the time he graduates from high school. This would include adjustment and knowledge sufficient for:

A. *Social competence,* needed for living in a community, state and nation.

B. *Moral competence,* the ability to know and use an acceptable system of value judgment.

C. *Personal adjustment,* or sufficient psychological insight to permit self-approval and group participation.

D. *Global awareness,* man's place in a nation of the world based on understanding the physical environment, technological growth and cultural heritage.

E. *Political competence,* or the legal and moral responsibility to participate in the democratic process of electing civil officers and abiding by their decisions, as well as knowing the reasons for doing it.

F. *Skill and technical competence,* the measure of independence necessary to understand each individual's ultimate dependence on others. To gain this the person must have specific knowledge of history, geography, sociology, anthropology, psychology, political science, international relations, economics, business law and commercial technique sufficient to spare himself the embarrassment he might otherwise encounter. In addition, the terminal student in high school should have enough technical skill to allow him to adapt to a position in commerce or industry with a minimum of training.

### Defining the Objectives

A. Social competence might be broadly interpreted to include the whole goal of social studies instruction: adequate citizenship, or for that matter, of all education. Here, however, let it include only those areas of human intercourse outside political action, international understanding, technical skill and morality.

It is absurd to believe that such a status may be achieved without regard to the way in which one makes a living or the manner in which he makes his judgments. The individual at any age must make decisions, large and small, based on his ethical conceptions.

At adult ages he must make a living. But above and beyond these considerations he must live with other individuals. At birth he does not know this; he must learn it. Much of it he will learn (or not learn) in school.

Preschool life for the ordinary American ends before the age of six. The present attendance in kindergarten during the fifth year and an increasing tendency toward nursery schools may mean an even earlier introduction to social experiences.

Although home environment does not end at this point, there is certainly a marked transition from babyhood. Mothers' direct influence is sharply curtailed. It is not certain as to how much of a person's basic personality orientation comes in the first few years, but the aphorism "no sin before seven" is persistent. The schools, mostly public, have the major burden of responsibility for producing socially competent graduates twelve to fifteen years later. It is always hoped that parents will cooperate with schools and other social agencies, but our culture decrees that the primary job is public.

Most states have legal requirements for teaching elementary children basic minimum skills in reading, writing, arithmetic, grammar, local history and geography, and some sort of manners, morals or social adjustment. The latter concepts are usually, in the modern school, part of a program of actual democratic living in a group; the classroom itself is a real social situation in which young citizens must "get along." They begin to learn how to do this at the outset of the first environment outside the home—at school.

It remains for the secondary school to intellectualize these experiences and to produce a competently socialized individual during the six years of junior and senior high school. It is mostly the task of social studies in not more than one-fourth to one-third of the total curricular time, usually much less, to attempt these concomitant results along with instruction in their factual bases.

Throughout colonial times, indeed until the twentieth century, social competence insofar as it was required came out of the central family experience. The family was large, usually in a small community, and surrounded by an extended family. A group of ten or twelve brothers and sisters was like a society in microcosm in which to become used to the world from earliest memory. School attendance was not widespread, and served the principal purpose of supplying technical training, even though that might have been no more than the rudiments of reading, writing and arithmetic. Social understanding was no principal goal of schools. The family, in its relative self-sufficiency, furnished the precept and the principle. Buttressed by the church, family life set the pattern and tone of social integration. Now this is no longer true. Schools now act as a transition between the socially less important family unit and adult society. Schools in the immediate past have been tempted too far into this realm, but other social agencies are coming to their rescue. In any event, the family cannot any longer bear the whole responsibility, and the schools have at least that share of it directly to do with the mental and intellectual aspects of producing socialized beings.

About two million young adults emerge yearly from American high schools. American society assumes that they are prepared to accept its challenge. Despite the emphasis on science, on crisis, on the future—promise and terror alike—secondary school social studies must smooth the absorption into society for these individuals. About two-thirds of those who graduate from high school go no further in formal education.[2a]

Specifically, boys and girls from all ranks of society and at all levels of verbal ability must learn *in school* such things as how to spend wisely and budget income, analyze propaganda, live in good health, make home repairs, care for babies, realize the principles of successful marriage—even how to drive a car. A higher percentage of people than ever before vote in national elections, know about George Washington and Abraham Lincoln, can and do read the newspapers, earn more money, eat more meat, have indoor plumbing, own more automobiles and radios and listen to good music on the radio, television and phonograph records, both at home and in public. More people know about labor relations, politics, chemistry, nuclear physics, birth control, current literature—than in any generation in this country since its origin on the James River in 1607. Social studies not only cover a large proportion of this actual subject matter, but they are directly concerned with producing an awareness of all of it and an appreciation of learning as a whole.[3]

   [2a] Robert J. Havighurst, "The Coming Crisis in Selection for College Entrance," A Symposium of the American Educational Research Association (1960), p. 1: "Last Fall there were 827,000 new students enrolled for the first time in degree-credit courses in American Universities and colleges. This was the highest total in our history. Relative to the numbers of 18-year-olds, this was 41 per cent of the young men and 28 per cent of the young women reaching college age in 1959." Obviously the tendency is toward a greater proportion.

   [3] James High, "Teaching: Stronghold of the Individualists," *Clearing House* (February, 1955), pp. 323–327.

B. Moral competence is an extension of social adjustment which, in our culture, takes a peculiar turn. The United States is a Christian society stemming from Western Europe. It is identified by a system of morality derived from many sources but codified and symbolized by Christianity over a period of nearly two thousand years.

Our Bill of Rights, the first ten amendments to the constitution, states a system of ethics in practical terms that has set a pattern for democratic growth throughout the world since 1789. It is a political golden rule, but it also incorporates specific prohibition against sectarian domination or, for that matter, of any mutual interference between church and state. It is characteristic that no bishop was allowed to preside in America until after the Revolution was accomplished. Americans were always devout, but always jealous of their rights and privacy too. Until religious domination of political life was frustrated, the church could not come into its own.

Out of this particular set of circumstances our non-sectarian guarantees of liberty grew. Along with them arose respect for individual conscience and right so long as the individual did not interfere with society as a whole or with the same privileges of other persons.

Religious ethical forms are met by citizens at every turn. The flag salute includes "under God." Thrift, honesty and piety resting on the precept of the Scriptures are commonplace virtues. Public meetings are opened and closed with alternations of canonical and national ritual. People learn these things in school and should continue to do so.

In time past, moral decisions were made wittingly in intellectual Christian terms or in fear of supernatural retribution. Before the American Revolution, both home and school had the definite responsibility of inculcating rules of behavior rigidly squaring with Christian faith. A catechism of ultimate morality and personal behavior was part of the school curriculum.

Church membership is not now universal, and all children do not fall under the guidance of any organized force toward ethical and moral considerations. It remains for the school to give at least the intellectual basis for choice. Most states forbid sectarian treatment of religious topics, but at the same time our society must live by an essential moral code.

Beyond ethics as a working guide there are systems of value judgment. Behind the Bill of Rights there was the philosophy of Thomas Jefferson. Jeffersonianism and its contemporary opponents can be examined and understood in high school. The whole tradition of Western culture from which we have grown is studded with philosophers who considered the problems of arriving at values. Hammurabi, Plato, Aristotle, St. Augustine, St. Thomas Aquinas, Locke, Montesquieu, Voltaire, Darwin and Bertrand Russell in our own time—only to name a few—are available for understanding to the high school student. Equipped with the Bill of Rights as a handbook in democratic living, and even a rudimentary knowledge of the great philosophers of the Western world, modern young men and women can confidently face the crisis of tomorrow, and be ready to make the decisions which they will be called upon to make.

Moral decisions will be made consciously or unconsciously. If they are made in terms of understanding, one of the goals of social studies will have been met. If some critical judgment is attempted, a higher degree of skill in citizenship will have been reached.

C. Personal adjustment, in contradistinction to social adjustment, becomes the problem of "living with oneself." In the past, even the recent past, society expected little of its individual members in this regard except to remain within rather broad bounds of overt behavior. When a person slid over the boundary of "sanity" he was generally treated as a criminal. If not that, and his family had the means, he was incarcerated legally or informally to get him out of sight. At any rate, it was a problem of social repression, rather than personal responsibility to society. It was not a matter of citizenship to take any precautions against mental imbalance.

Since the advent of modern psychology, which is hardly older than William James or Sigmund Freud, the individual increasingly has assumed responsibility for his own adjustment. It is true that sometimes this involves adjustment to a norm that seems in retrospect to be quite abnormal. As one author has said, fifty million Frenchmen can be, and often have been, dead wrong. At the present time, nonetheless, each person, as an obligation of citizenship, must stay "sane." He must adjust not only to society but to a flexible recognition of his own place in it and to the life within himself. If he fails, he will find that his "adjusted" contemporaries will firmly and with scientific kindness either force him back to their reality or humanely restrict his rights of citizenship to the extent of protecting him from himself and society from him. He will be locked up.

Mental hygiene is as much a part of our lives as coffee for breakfast; therefore social studies, reflecting the discipline of psychology in the secondary school, falls heir to the job of giving boys and girls the basic tools of self-administered preventive therapy. Social science has given to education a most valuable tool, in this respect, in the form of disciplined organization of sociodrama and psychodrama, which makes possible a controlled classroom adaptation of the play acting propensity of children that may have gone to waste in an older time.

A current jest pictures the neurotic as one who builds castles in the air; the psychotic as one who lives in them; and the psychiatrist as the one who collects the rent. Such a thing can only suggest a general social recognition of individual responsibility for sanity. Each person must be his own psychotherapist within reasonable limits. In turn, general public education must allow the individual to have access to the necessary knowledge to make this possible.

D. Consider global awareness in this age of nuclear physics, of speeds exceeding that of sound, of international movement and tension. What man can sit in his chair and say, "I am a safely isolated American"? The world is small now, and getting smaller. Spatially it is as big as ever. Soon it will expand to include a ring of man-carrying satellites. Undoubtedly, if civilization survives at all, it will include the moon and perhaps unlimited reaches of outer space. But by the very means of expanded contact in larger orbits man has put himself operationally closer to every potential enemy. He has made his friends around the world more dependent on him, and he, in turn, on them. The earth is, in truth, only seconds large as measured in temporal terms. A radio wave goes from continent to continent with almost measureless speed. Rockets and aircraft are only comparatively slower. "Swift as an arrow" has no literal meaning now in reference to the origin of the saying.

Every man need not be a nuclear physicist or a jet pilot any more than all of Columbus's contemporaries had to be master mariners or every Greek as well versed in philosophy as Plato. Each person, however, must know that he is a small speck in a slightly larger nation on a shrinking planet. On December 7, 1941, approximately one hundred forty million United States citizens became painfully aware of the global character of a war that had been already in progress some two years. All have the need and society has means for each individual to learn these things. Education must perform this function.

A course in world problems during the last year of high school may be, for many a citizen, the chief source of information upon which to base his knowledge of the global nature of our society. To understand the present organization of the world it is not sufficient only to know even a great deal of the scientific progress of the last few years. It is also requisite to have a familiarity with the relationships of man and the universe, the world in which we live and the society of which that life is composed. We must know something of geography: how man has adapted himself to natural factors and these to him. A man must know how he and his ancestors came to earn a living (capitalistic enterprise is no mystery after a little study). He must be aware of the systems of order that civilization has produced —absolutism, limited monarchy and democracy; and the respective examples of these systems—the Egyptian empire, the Greek republic, the Anglo-Saxon kingdoms and the American state.

The province of social studies includes the knowledge and the key to understanding relationships that have made possible five thousand years of growth in developing order, subsistence, society, the land and the general story of all these. Political science, economics, sociology, geography and history can be brought to bear on the problem of understanding the present in terms of the past.

E. Political competence is an exceedingly important consideration. Every human being in American society, simply by virtue of chronological attainment of the twenty-first year (eighteen in Georgia), becomes not only a citizen but a voting citizen. He may, and has the moral obligation to, exercise the franchise.

How he does this is largely dependent upon two forces: how he was conditioned by preschool environment, and what he has learned in school. Therefore, and without much equivocation, the public schools have assumed responsibility for the major role in training future citizens in operational democracy. How well people understand what they are voting for, whether for one party or another, must be the result in no small measure of what they have learned in school (for most people, in secondary school or even in the last two years of high school). This is precisely why most of the states have legislative requirements for high school graduation which invariably include proficiency in United States history and government and basic knowledge of local and state government procedures.

It is not the desire of any legitimate social scientist to dictate the partisan politics of anyone. Far from it. It is, rather, desirable that each voter exert his legal voice in terms of awareness of a value system which he accepts willingly, in full knowledge of the political considerations at stake, and with the assurance that if he is on the winning side the losers will accept wholeheartedly the decision of the majority. On the other hand, each minority must also know that its rights are safeguarded.

This is the very heart of our democracy, and training for participation in it at any political level is directly within the purview of social studies. One of the specific objectives of secondary schooling as voiced by the American Political Science Association is ". . . to give the whole student group those civic skills and humane ideals requisite for responsible participation in the political and social life of a democracy." [4]

F. With respect to the matter of skill and technical competence, at least 60 per cent of high school graduates will, in the years to come, be finished with formal education. They will seek and find employment in American industry and commerce. They will perform the multitude of tasks that are set by modern technology as they have in the past. Naturally it is not, and never will become, the responsibility of secondary schools to produce a degree of competence in specific job skill to satisfy the demands of every employer. No high school could be expected to turn out persons of journeyman standing. It is expected, however, that two things materialize in the high school graduate.

First, approximately two-thirds of the graduates will enter the adult world at the age of eighteen or nineteen with no further expectation of going to school. They will embark on their careers with what equipment they have at that time. In view of the cost to society that same society may well expect that those graduates can be employed in the jobs necessary to the furtherance of our economy with a minimum of supervision and training.

It should be possible for an employer to take a high school graduate into his firm as a junior clerk, a stenographer, a beginner on the sales staff, a half-finished apprentice, and without actually losing money in the venture make that person into a competent journeyman or senior clerk in the course of time needed by the individual to reach physical and emotional maturity. In other words, within two or three years after graduation a person should be a competent economic unit in his community. Such is the quality of social studies in the modern secondary school that this should be a reality.

Second, every high school graduate, as he enters adult life, either

[4] *Goals for Political Science* (American Political Science Association, New York, 1951), xvii–xviii.

directly or by way of some further schooling, must be a competent consumer. He must know how to spend his money to the best advantage of himself and society. He must be aware of the principles of modern capitalism in order to do this. Further, he must know the political and social relationships with economics. As he must know the basis of the home and family, he must also know the fundamental realities of economic existence. A most evidently important function of high school social studies is apparent here.

The girls among high school graduates, even though they choose homemaking rather than industrial jobs, have an equal right to feel secure in enough knowledge to carry out their appointed tasks. Every girl who comes from the public schools and within two or three years becomes a wife and mother has a deep necessity to be versed in the skills of running a household, family management and socio-sexual relationships. In addition to the general social competence of all high school graduates she must have job skill equal in specialization to that of her husband.

Another responsibility for high school social studies exists in direct relation to the persistence of baccalaureate liberal arts. Every state supports colleges and universities at public expense, and therefore attendance at them becomes an optional part of American citizenship. Something over one-fourth of high school graduates have the prospect of four more years of academic study. These particular students must be prepared to succeed in the accelerated tempo of college work. Beyond the basic competency in citizenship they must also acquire enough introductory information in the standard disciplines of knowledge to progress through the more complicated offerings in college in order to achieve the bachelor's degree in four years. It is the obligation of secondary social studies teachers to see that the college preparatory students receive adequate training in history, geography, economics, sociology and psychology so that they can build on it in these categories of learning at a higher level.

If citizenship is the goal of education, then college educated citizens have a claim to knowledge appropriate to their calling. In view of the current trends more and more persons will go on to college and graduate. Society demands it.

Two things may well happen as a result of this demand. First, secondary school may extend to include the first two years of college, or grades thirteen and fourteen. This, in turn, may mean primarily an extension of the general qualification for citizenship as well as a tendency to subsidize the first two baccalaureate years. On the other hand, it may mean that the bachelor's degree will be conferred at the expiration of four years beyond grade fourteen. The promise of automation and specialized employment seem to indicate such a turn.

Second, American education may tend to develop two or more rather distinct channels entailing a choice somewhere along the line. It may be that vocational training will grow into a whole curriculum, or that baccalaureate preparatory teaching take a separate turn, or that general education be separated from the others. Several possibilities present themselves, more or less meritoriously, but none of them has been settled upon as a substitute for the current, general high school. In any case, it will be desirable from a democratic point of view that students choosing one path have the continued opportunity of shifting to another, preferably on the basis of achievement.

Regardless of whether or not separate ways be provided, of whether or not grade fourteen becomes the legal terminal point of compulsory education, it remains clear that secondary schools, however constituted, will and must continue to furnish preparatory courses for college so that appropriate students will be guided into higher learning.

## 2. Attitudes and Behavior

There is a good argument in favor of approaching the general objective of teaching students how to solve problems—any problems; and if there is a scientific method of problem solution it makes very little difference what its content may be (although there is almost universal agreement that it should be significant, just in case there may not be much transfer of method from one situation to the next). Another positive facet of studying varied social problems lies in the necessity it entails of bringing to bear findings from a number of the social sciences, thus cutting across traditional subject matter lines. It is conceivable, for example, that in studying race relations in the United States, material from sociology, demography, economics, psychology, political science and history might well be used. On the negative side it may be objected that the usual social studies teacher does not command sufficient knowledge of these various fields to be competent in the use of their data. It also may be argued that the students, not getting enough of any one field to appreciate its worth and dignity, may fall victim to the trap described in the cliche, "a little learning is a dangerous thing."

The chief objection to a total disregard of subject matter and its discipline, with too much emphasis on problem solving methodology, is that no pure method as such exists, that there is little transfer of learning from one problem to the next, even if they are quite similar. It seems probable that most learning situations present a pattern or *gestalt*, which may have many elements in common with some other pattern, but a rather different total impact on the learning process and on individual behavior. This is especially true if the objective set up in a course in problems is behavioral change in the students. It has been found that attitudes expressed in verbal or written form can be taught and learned (for testing purposes) fairly easily, but that behavior in accordance with attitudes as they are expressed is often not the case, and an altered expression of attitude seldom finds immediate expression in altered behavior.[5] For example, it would be relatively simple to instruct a high school group in the proper attitudes toward Negroes, by means of films or sheer indoctrination. Test results would show that the group had gained a desirable set of attitudes. The chances, however, of these attitudes, if they were much different from customary behavior, being translated into altered behavior toward a particular group of Negroes would be very slight. To say that one is tolerant of Negroes and has no prejudice is a far different matter from being tolerant and unprejudiced. Further, removal of prejudice against Negroes does not necessarily carry over to an automatic removal of prejudice against Indians, Jews, Orientals or anyone else.

Notwithstanding the disabilities and disadvantages, it may be assumed that high school social studies programs may very legitimately include courses in problems. Given this, no matter what the specific subject matter, whether it be a specified discipline such as psychology or government, or selected problems as such and drawing on the knowledge of a number of fields, a certain simply stated prob-

---

[5] Dean G. Epley, "A Survey of Human Relations Programs," *The Journal of Educational Sociology* (May, 1956), pp. 378–385; Philip Rothman, "Socio-Economic Status and the Values of Junior High School Students," *Ibid.* (November, 1954), pp. 126–130; E. Grant Youmans, "Social Factors in the Work Attitudes and Interests of Twelfth Grade Michigan Boys," *Ibid.*, pp. 35–48, shows that attitudes tend rather to follow interesting experiences in patterns of behavior. Warren Brown and J. Oscar Alers, "Attitudes of Whites and Nonwhites Toward Each Other," *Sociology and Social Research* (May–June, 1956), pp. 312–319. John H. Haefner, "Proposals for a Social Studies Curriculum," *Social Education* (May, 1960), pp. 200–204, is the most recent plea to change the social studies curriculum in terms of a realization that attitudes come as the result of positive knowledge of subject matter, not as the result of indoctrination.

lem solving method can be applied. This method is merely a practical application of the scientific method of investigation. The only differences lie in statement and application. Critical thinking, another variant of the scientific investigative principle, must also be encouraged; this implies a student-teacher criticism and evaluation of every step in the whole process of analyzing problems.

The most easily stated steps in handling any problem are:

1. Recognize and define a problem (critically assess its significance. Does it warrant a whole group's time and effort in terms of its cogency to the social needs of the group?).

2. Analyze the problem into its basic elements and form tentative hypotheses (tantamount to the second, or middle step in the scientific method of research).

3. Collect data on each part of the problem (test the hypothesis).

4. Evaluate the data (the same process as recasting the hypothesis in preparation for further investigation).

5. Organize and interpret the data.

6. Form a working conclusion (the third step in scientific method).

7. Verify conclusions by test and comparison.

8. Apply the conclusions to see if they will work (this is the essential difference between basic or pure research and applied research or problem solving. (A problem solved should produce a better social situation.) [6]

In view of the foregoing, a course in senior problems may emphasize political citizenship, personal and social adjustment, or some combination of those. These divide roughly into two further segments: personal and social adjustment on the one hand, and vocational exploration and adjustment (including college preparation) on the other.

### Mental Hygiene and Health

One of the first requirements of the human being is, in this age, to adjust to his group or to get along with others. The basic elements of this need must already have been mastered by the time the child is through high school, although never throughout life can the job be said to be finished. Conditions of society constantly change and so must the individual change along with society or he will not be happy or successful.

Therefore, individual, personal adjustment becomes the primary

[6] See I. James Quillen and Lavonne A. Hanna, *Education for Social Competence* (Scott, Foresman, Chicago, 1948), pp. 128–129.

factor in a general balance of social adjustment. The individual is the basic unit, the most important element in our society. He must be allowed to keep his dignity; but he must also allow this in all others; that is, he must respect society as it is expected to respect him. We can recognize the breakdown of this process and ideal only in the extreme cases, in the definable psychotic instances. Then we, as a society, segregate the offensive individual. It is considerably more difficult to prescribe prophylactic measures, to define "sanity," or specify desirable adjustment to a society which really is no more than the aggregate of individuals.

The importance of mental hygiene, or the business of staying sane, seems to be beyond question, and it further seems evident that if each individual is mentally hygienic, society will be the sum of all the adjusted individuals involved. In order to achieve any kind of understanding of what sanity may be, it is necesary to learn at least something about the whole field of psychology, or the science of human mental behavior. It is even necessary to try to learn about the extreme patterns of derangement or insanity in order to know what to avoid.

As a high school subject, then, rather than approaching separate problems of behavior in isolated cases, since there is available a well developed body of psychological knowledge, it would be valuable to teach a simple exploratory course in psychology with emphasis on the emotional factors in human behavior so far as they are known. This does not mean that college psychology should be mastered by the high school student, but only that such parts of well established principles in psychology as are applicable to the solution of high school students' basic problems in adjustment should be made available to them in orderly, disciplined form.

Psychology as a high school subject has been taught here and there since before the beginning of the twentieth century. It appears now in representative curricula of forty states, and is probably offered, under other course names such as problems, in all states. Only about ten per cent of courses dealing with psychology are actually called that, and at least two per cent of high school students take a substantial course in beginning psychology, while two per cent more get some experience in other courses. The subject rates very high among the students who take it.

Since a majority of high school psychology teachers are not primarily trained in psychology but in education or general social studies, most of the instruction is directly related to a textbook. Publishers recognize seven books as specifically written for the high school level, five of which contain the word psychology in the title. These books stress such topics as biological foundations, statistics, intelligence, personality, learning, mental hygiene, vocational and social adjustment. For example, Sorenson and Malm, *Psychology for Living*, devotes thirty-one per cent of its coverage to mental hygiene; T. L. Engle, *Psychology: Its Principles and Application*, gives twenty-two per cent to biological foundations of psychology; on the whole, personality and learning get the most overall coverage.

According to the author of the latter text, although "relatively few of the total number of high schools in the United States offer a course in psychology, the popularity as a field of instruction for the high school level is increasing. Psychology as a course for high school instruction is to be found in at least forty states and probably is taught in all states. In most high schools, it is taught as a one-semester elective in the senior year. . . . Educators, high school students, and the adult public, are favorable to the teaching of psychology in high school." [7]

Using psychology as the basic subject matter for a problems course, or at least part of a course, it is suggested that a variant of the problem solving method may be adopted. The difficulty which arises when highly individualized and personal problems are used, is the students' inability to generalize and make relationships between "experiences that are personal, immediate, and real to issues that are large, complex, and abstract." To avoid some of this difficulty the use of a case method has been outlined (this method has been utilized in legal training for over eighty years in this country). "The object is simply to relate personal decisions to general cultural decisions and in this way relate the abstract material in the social studies to the personal concerns of the student." [8]

The added elements involved in the case method of instruction are merely to furnish typical illustrative cases in brief written form for the students to read, and discussion of each case in a particular way relating it to the hypothetical generalization to be derived from any scientific method. In short, the case method is simply a particular representative documentation of an individual set of circumstances

---

[7] T. L. Engle and M. E. Bunch, "The Teaching of Psychology in High Schools," *The American Psychologist* (April, 1956), pp. 188–193; T. L. Engle, "High School Psychology," *Contemporary Psychology* (May, 1956), pp. 140–143, is a late survey of the textbooks available and an analysis of course content.

[8] Donald Oliver and Susan Baker, "The Case Method," *Social Education* (January, 1959), pp. 25–28, suggests the case method generally for all social studies.

illustrating a major finding. True, there will be innumerable grada-
tions of relationship involving many cases in their relationship to a
principle, but this in itself constitutes a strength inherent in the technique.

The case method requires certain steps, just as the problem solving
method does:
1. Select the problem to be illustrated.
2. Analyze and break down the problem into its component parts.
3. Gather evidence to expand knowledge of particular parts.
4. Select typical cases and present them to students in brief form.
5. Point out and discuss the aspects of the case which illustrate or
refute the generalizations in the hypothesis.
6. Integrate the learning from each case into practically applicable
situations in regard to the immediate, personal problem.

Incidentally, this method gives greater emphasis to the use of study
guides in the classroom. Each case as it is written up constitutes an
adequate study guide when coupled with the general rules of procedure.

As an example that might arise in a high school course in psychology
during the study of the emotional basis for some kinds of behavior,
two cases in point might be used: that of Napoleon in his rise to
power as dictator over the French people and with ultimate designs
on the role of world leader; and that of any prominent student. At
least some of Napoleon's personal motivation arose from his inordi-
nate bio-social need for dominance of other persons, an emotional
complex identifiably different from the average, but still representing
something in common with all human beings—the urge for power.
Napoleon's individual emotional manifestations in statement and
behavior were exaggerated enough to be apparent and sometimes
aberrant enough to be obviously dangerous. (It is noteworthy that in
mental institutions he is the person with whom extreme schizophrenics
often identify.) By comparing the case history of Napoleon with that
of any high school athlete, or dramatic student who has a leading role
in a play or the president of the student body, it may be pointed out
that there are similar emotional forces at work, but that they are not
exaggerated, and that common emotions connected with the general
desire for approval and positions of power and leadership are not bad
in themselves. Every individual has something of the will to dominate,
but this is a healthy, competitive force when understood and managed.
This generalization in psychological knowledge is illustrated in rela-

tion to immediate personal problems, and also in relation to enduring, international problems such as world conquest, world peace and the right of individuals to self-expression as long as it does not interfere unduly with the rights of others.

### 3. Suggested Further Reading

THEORY IN PSYCHOLOGY AND THE SOCIAL SCIENCES

C. W. Churchman, *Theory of Experimental Inference* (Macmillan, New York, 1948), describes a theory applicable to all social science research.

James B. Conant, *On Understanding Science* (Yale University, 1947), explains general scientific theory very well.

George Humphrey, *Thinking: An Introduction to Its Experimental Psychology* (Wiley, New York, 1951).

Aldous Huxley, *Words and Their Meaning* (Ward, Ritchie, Los Angeles, 1940), is a discussion by the great novelist of theoretical meanings of words and their actual use.

Earl S. Johnson, *Theory and Practice of the Social Studies* (Macmillan, New York, 1956), is an attempt to make available disparate theories for practical use.

F. S. C. Northrup, *The Logic of the Sciences and the Humanities* (Macmillan, New York, 1947).

*Readings in the History of Psychology,* edited by Wayne Dennis (Appleton-Century-Crofts, New York, 1948).

*Theoretical Foundations of Psychology,* edited by Harry Nelson (Van Nostrand, Princeton, New Jersey, 1951), is helpful in identifying the schools of thought.

PROBLEM SOLVING

Julian C. Aldrich, "Developing Critical Thinking," *Social Education* (March, 1948).

A. Alpert, *The Solving of Problem Situations by Preschool Children* (Teachers College, Columbia University, New York, 1928), emphasizes permissive growth.

R. F. Bales and F. L. Strodtbeck, "Phases in Group Problem-Solving," *Journal of Abnormal and Social Psychology,* **46** (1951), pp. 485–495.

K. Duncker, "On Problem Solving," *Psychological Monographs,* **45** (1945).

K. Duncker and L. Krechevsky, "On Solution-Achievement," *Psychological Review,* **46** (1949).

David Krech and Richard S. Crutchfield, *Theory and Problems of Social Psychology* (McGraw-Hill, New York, 1948).

Arthur W. Kornhauser, *How to Study* (University of Chicago, 1924, 1937, 1956), is a set of hints for high school and college students in regard to getting the most out of their efforts.

Kurt Lewin, *Field Theory in Social Science,* edited by Dorian Cartwright (Harper, New York, 1951), in which the subject is examined from all possible aspects.

# 4

# The ideal and the community

A right notion of the bearing of history on affairs, both for the statesman and for the citizen, could not be formed or formulated until men had grasped the idea of human development. This is the great transforming conception, which enables history to define her scope.

*The Idea of Progress*
J. B. BURY, 1903

## 1. Culture Conflicts

By nature men are free and equal in opportunity; but by mischance and bad choice man is sometimes denied this. United States citizens have privileges balanced by responsibilities which must be discharged in order to retain the benefits of the status of citizenship. In addition, as Jefferson and others have pointed out, eternal vigilance and jealous regard must be exercised in order to make the dualistic balance work, and to insure that the body politic will not "wickedness imbrace." We identify democracy with goodness as it represents our set of chosen values.[1]

The most easily recognized responsibilities of citizenship fall into two categories: civil and political. Each person has the compulsion to maintain law and order, to respect the property and personal rights of others and to defend his country against aggression. In this last part of his civil responsibility the citizen's activity merges with the political

[1] "Though none are Sav'd that Wickedness imbrace, Yet none are Damn'd that have Inherent Grace," *The Poetical Works of Edward Taylor* (1645–1729), edited by Thomas H. Johnson (Princeton University Press, 1943), represents the early American reliance on God, the only choice necessary being adherence to God's will. Now man must make his own choices.

field, since it is a political responsibility of government to furnish identification and direction in matters of defense. Political choice produces the President whose primary function, along with Congress and the Supreme Court, is to preserve the constitutional integrity of the nation, in other words, national security. The President's peculiar interest is in national defense, and therefore he becomes the citizens' agent and leader in the exercise of their privilege and duty to bear arms against enemies of the state.

As every person must do his part in the maintenance of law and order, he also is obligated to perform another simple function. He must vote. In order to choose the representatives of the people who form the deliberative, judicial and executive bodies making up the government at every level, the people are required to exercise the franchise, to vote for various persons to represent them. In turn, the political and administrative function is carried out by those chosen representatives who are responsible to the people again at the expiration of their terms of office. The laws which it is the responsibility of the citizen to uphold are made by the representatives of the citizens. The two categories of responsibility are mutually interactive.

Since choice is involved in both maintaining law and in selecting lawmakers, and since the principles governing the formation of regulatory procedures are in the historical tradition of the nation and in the written Constitution of the United States, it immediately becomes a further and most important responsibility on the part of each citizen to know as much as he can about both the history of the nation and the developmental body of constitutional law and tradition. Both the democratic principle of self-government and the factual narrative of how this principle has worked out during the course of about three hundred years are extremely important in equipping the citizen to appreciate, perpetuate, improve and use it.

So far only the aspect of responsibility has been mentioned, but it should appear obvious by now that the responsibilities are themselves privileges. The right to bear arms and the right to vote are not only rights guaranteed by the Constitution or responsibilities that must be borne in order to preserve democracy, they are also great privileges stemming from a long line of hard won struggles between men of good will and high intent against the forces of selfishness and the mischoice of men and societies that are always immanent. It must always be remembered that man is free, that he can make choices; but he also can make choices that will destroy him, and by nature he is free but not wise by the same means. He must guard his wisdom and increase it, or it will not serve to keep him free to make choices—either good or bad.

There is a subtle distinction between rights and privileges. Rights must be considered as natural accretions to the fact of existence, such as breathing and possessing appetite and the equipment for thought, for setting values. Privileges are those balances to responsibilities which accrue only as a direct result of man's assumption of civic and political duties according to a principle such as the democratic assumption that by nature "all men are created equal; that they are endowed by their Creator with certain inalienable rights; that among these are life, liberty and the pursuit of happiness." In the sense in which the Declaration of Independence speaks of rights one should read the word "ideals," which man can approach only through the exercise of responsibility, and for which the ethical tone was established by early Americans who set out to make subsequent development possible by the very fact of the Declaration and the Revolutionary War.

What we have come to think of as privileges in our political democracy is embodied in the Bill of Rights, the first ten amendments to the Constitution. In addition to the basic responsible rights mentioned above, there are listed specific guarantees of personal liberty such as freedom of speech and press, freedom of worship, freedom from cruel and unusual punishments, right to a jury trial and to *habeas corpus,* the right to free assembly; not to mention the great accretion of more recent privileges which have grown out of over a hundred seventy-five years of continued vigilance and activity in progressive reform—pure food and drug laws, the right of collective bargaining, direct election of senators and woman suffrage.

Generally speaking, our democracy is divided into three levels of activity and thought: social, economic and political. This triune division somewhat parallels the statement and implications of the Declaration of Independence. Life as a subject of interest to social organization must be protected not only by legal safeguards such as the Bill of Rights, but human life must be held in value—continuously reiterated as it has been in Western culture since Hammurabi's Code. The unique achievement of Anglo-Saxon society has been the gradual recognition of equality in the value of human life regardless of station and based upon existence rather than upon special accidents of birth or station. Such is the democratic substance of the right to life.

Liberty is a little more difficult of expression; it entails also a type of equality, a privilege to exercise collective political and ethical determination and to aspire to more material possessions as the result of individual effort; in other words, to live and let live. In a sense this is the constitutional form of the Epicurean compact in nature to refrain from destruction in order not to be destroyed, but it is more specific and less dependent on human good will and natural beneficence. Perversely, liberty is usually defined by prohibitions rather than by positive statements of what may be done. Privilege in this regard is what is left over after others' rights have been properly safeguarded. The Constitution, loosely construed, has turned out to be the basis for legal direction of liberty as the "best for the most," with the added attraction of protection for minority groups. Such balance is again preserved by a triadic formulation of government function into legislative, executive and judicial. The assumption is made that man is perfectible but not necessarily perfect, but that he can "wickedness imbrace," or on the other hand, choose to survive in a condition of liberty.

The "pursuit of happiness" is vague and subjective, and as a basis for law it cannot be made dependable. There is no major American court decision, just for that reason, which is based on the Declaration; rather, decisions are usually founded upon a portion of the Constitution which is much more firmly intrenched in property rights. The Lockean notion that government exists principally for the protection of property is, in the American tradition, really our definition of the "pursuit of happiness." In the last fifty years this has come more and more to mean public social reliance on "big government" as the arbiter, rather than guide and preceptor, of right and good in the relationship between the means of economic production and the consuming public, but such a tendency has always been based on the same democratic principles of choice and prohibition. Democratic political action has ever been the means toward satisfaction of the social interpretation of the Declaration of Independence with the Constitution as its legal bulwark.

In order to maintain the flexible and workable arrangement of responsibilities and privileges which go to make up our way of life and primary requisite is intelligent political action. Each citizen has the obligation and right to vote at public free elections; in order to exercise that franchise in the interest of making "good" choices, each citizen must know what he is doing. This falls into two parts: the structure and function of government, and the historical way in which this structure evolved.

Historically the resolution of culture conflicts has formed the basis of national self-awareness in this country. The United States has been called a "melting pot," and for very good reason. The various and different culture representations that have gone into the structure of the present American state have all brought something of value, but in every case these different cultural heritages have undergone changes while they have exerted their influence on the whole growth of a new society. In the process there have been (and still continue to be) a good many injustices and much heartache for individuals who have been caught in the culture conflicts so produced.

Perhaps the most widely known and most persistent culture conflict in the United States involves the Negro population. It has always been a minority, although now it is so large that it is difficult to think of

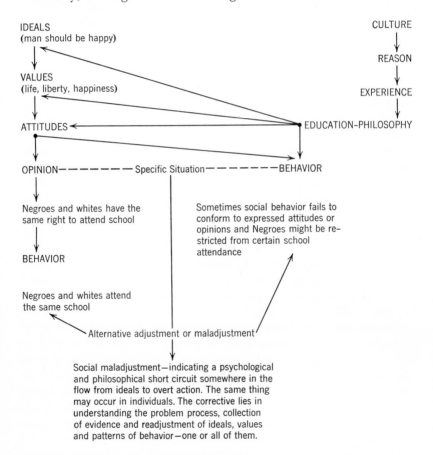

FIGURE 2. A social psychological basis for behavior.

the Negroes as being a minority. Also their introduction into our society was not with their consent. They came for the most part as slaves. Never really since the seventeenth century have Negroes achieved an unquestioned acceptance either as a minority or as mmbers of the total group except in individual cases. Progress has been made toward integrating this huge minority into our society in every way, but there is still a long way to go. Partial resolution of the conflict has been made on many successive occasions.

One of the outstanding obligations of education is to resolve this and other culture conflicts. Citizenship can only thus be encouraged in the sense that it has been suggested here. Good and bad choices will be made, and generally they will be made on cultural grounds unless education so alters the folk inheritance of prejudice and bewilderment that good choices, worthy choices, can be made.

### Some Important Definitions in Democratic Citizenship

Words form the basis of our semantic relationships. In addition to the words themselves there are complex psychological connotations with their roots in the social and cultural setting of the language. By reason of this, words or phrases often become symbols for institutionalized values and customs. Gradually the word may come to have three or more partly independent meanings and will be used indiscriminately for all of them. "Authority" is such a word. The derivation of authority is at the very heart of political democracy, therefore its possible meaning as a word and as a value symbol must be examined closely. Democracy, representative self-government, sovereignty, toleration, prejudice, objectivity, subjectivity—to name but a few—are all terms that have extreme symbol value. They must be used in the process of social communication in our time, therefore learn their meanings.

Knowledge, as a word, is one of the trickiest of all. It is equated in some dictionaries with science, from *scire,* the Latin term "to know." Then the definitions become vague and multifarious, using words to define themselves. Soon one becomes involved in the nature of gaining knowledge before the exact meaning of the word itself is isolated in its fog of implications. From "knowledge" it is a short step to "epistemology," or the nature of knowledge, thence to "eschatology," or the ultimate use of knowledge. At that point one is lost unless he is a theologian. It becomes apparent that knowledge is a word with double semantic significance; in a linguistic sense it has common meaning and also it is a symbol of value in direct relationship to the society in which it is used.

*Knowledge—information; learning; the cumulative culture of the human race; also actual or possible range of information.*

Knowledge as used here is almost synonymous with civilization. At least it is the backbone of civilization—its vehicle. Knowledge can also be used to include theories of knowledge, or epistemology: the exact nature of how man knows. For lack of a better category such studies have been included within the scope of the social sciences, but since ultimate causation and divine differentiation of man from animals is often interwoven into the discussions, it is preferable to exclude epistemology from the definition of knowledge. In the past, especially in Christian societies, original divine revelation of all knowledge has dominated much thinking.

Knowledge is here defined as empirically verifiable data. It is not the absolute truth. That "there is no God but Allah and Mohammed is his Prophet" is not a proposition susceptible to empirical proof, therefore it is a faith truth, not knowledge; however, information about its propagators is knowledge, constituting the bulk of Arabic history.

The obverse of this coin is that knowledge changes. Thirty years ago the atom was thought to be the smallest, the indivisible unit of matter. Today, based upon further investigation, we hold a different view. Each view is more or less a fragment of truth, but neither one nor both together necessarily constitute any unitary, absolute truth or ultimate knowledge. Further experimentation, further investigation, measurement and hypothesis change the nature of knowledge.

Faith, belief and taste, therefore, are not knowledge—though a study of them does constitute knowledge. The study of, and data concerning religion, the nature of the soul, eschatology (the divine ends of knowledge), or, for that matter, faith itself, all of these and related things contribute to knowledge. It is, therefore, clear that knowledge, however derived, cannot encompass all that which man feels, believes or "knows" on other than scientific grounds.

Further definition of terms and concepts could not exemplify more this attempted clarification of thought processes. It could only further illustrate, and would soon become compendious without discrimination. With such definition as has been done let the hope prevail that each student will do more of the same whenever he needs to. Behind each word is an idea, behind that is knowledge, still further back is truth. The half-life of undiscovered knowledge is reduced as the body of verifiable data becomes larger.

## 2. A Philosophy of Education

It is well enough to speak, along with Cardinal Newman, of the intrinsic value of knowledge, of learning merely for the sake of learning, of "art for art's sake." *Ars gratia artis* is even the trademark slogan of Metro-Goldwyn-Mayer Productions. It must have been seen by nearly every American many times. This concept has basic meaning for all of us, and we can be inspired by that idea. On the other hand, there must also be a practical, a pragmatic side to the application of knowledge, and therefore a more cogent reason for learning than mere delight in possession of information. Possibly this is the sage's notion of wisdom, or applied knowledge in the interest of mankind.

Acceptance of the concept of "bettering mankind" presupposes a human capacity for betterment and for progress in a genetic sense. This has been aptly illustrated by the tremendous strides in technology made possible by applying the findings of empirical science since 1900. Charles Darwin blazed the trail for almost unlimited progress in animal (and therefore human) genetics. Herbert Spencer linked the physical idea thus accepted with the hopeful outlook of such French revolutionaries as Condorcet, and opened the vista of a similarly unlimited objective in the non-biological affairs of men. Thomas Jefferson's notion of the equality of man changes from dream to potential reality if only man can learn what he must do. By the end of the nineteenth century man had realized his capacity to improve, to progress.

Education, in our time, instead of relying solely on revelation to establish unchanging truth and transcendent values, now seeks a continually growing ideal of perfection which recedes in direct proportion to the magnitude of human improvement. Intellectual, material and spiritual perfection can now be approached through a scientific encroachment on the undiscovered body of knowledge with a consequent readjustment and reformulation of values—none of which is ultimate, but which may become better with each deepening and spreading wave of learning.

Education, or the spread of knowledge, is no more an end in itself than is knowledge. It is simply the disseminating agent for bodies of disciplined and organized findings of science and folk lore. If the act of spreading knowledge, or the educative process, becomes self-contained, with only a mass of techniques devoted to the art of teaching constituting both the profession and the disciplined knowledge component, there is danger that scientific content will give way to a stereotyped reiteration of such things as "learn by doing," "uninhibited expression of experience" or "life adjustment." The Sophists of ancient Greece and their neo-Aristotelian descendants in the Middle Ages fell into the same trap and almost destroyed learning in the Western world on two previous occasions. If education has become a cliché-bound lexicon of double talk and orthodoxy it has betrayed the dream of Condorcet and Jefferson, it has denied the idea of progress conceived and nurtured by Darwin, Spencer and Bury, and it has parted realistic company with its great American exponent, John Dewey.

We do not think that such is the case. We like to think that it is still possible to maintain the ideal of democratic dissemination of knowledge. Underlying any support of public education there must be this goal. The earliest Americans in Massachusetts Bay legislated the idea of universal public free education. The beginnings were meager, it is true, but the germ was there, and its philosophic justification lies in the acceptance of man's improvability. The vehicle is education. The material is knowledge.

The American child and youth spends from eight to sixteen years of his life as a student in a school or college. During this period "getting an education" is his principal occupation. It is generally believed that this is desirable, even essential, that going to school will make him a better citizen, a more productive worker with a greatly increased earning power, and enrich his life in numerous intangible and spiritual ways. It is believed, too, that his social level as an adult will be, to a considerable extent, dependent upon the number of years of his school attendance. We believe these things even though we know that Abraham Lincoln attended school for only a few months and yet was an outstanding president, able to compose the *Gettysburg Address*. We know that Plato and Aristotle, although they received a considerable amount of what we call tutoring, never attended anything like a modern school or college. We know too, that even today there are numerous leaders in public life who had, at most, an elementary education, and, on the other hand, that many college graduates are not "good citizens" by contemporary standards, and many are not vocationally successful.

In all Western nations, and perhaps most conspicuously in the United States, education has become very highly institutionalized. This institutionalization began early in man's history but its rate of development has greatly increased during the past one hundred years. In colonial America a few colleges were available for the rare individuals able to afford them, but a college education was not considered really necessary even for those entering the learned professions. Either medicine or law could be learned by working a few years with someone practicing those arts. In some denominations ministers attended colleges especially set up for their training, but for the most part anyone could preach if he had received a "call." There were no public high schools and the few academies which were attended by boys only of what is now considered high school age were intended primarily as preparatory schools for colleges. Elementary education, although the idea was early put into law, was in reality a haphazard affair. Wealthy families hired tutors who might or might not be college graduates while poorer families either did not send their children to school at all or sent them for a few months each winter to a local schoolmaster who was paid a small fee for his services. John Adams obtained his first paid position as one of these.

Here was the beginning of the idea of progressive improvement through education, and also the beginning of the institution of free general education. Not only is free education now provided through high school, but in all of the states college education is available in state supported institutions. It is obvious that all this education is vastly expensive despite the fact that teachers' salaries are low compared to those of people in other professions. It is expensive to our economy, not only in the direct cost, but also in that it takes several million young men and women of working age out of the fields of productive work. A century ago it was not unusual for a boy to become self-supporting at sixteen or even fourteen; but now, if he goes through college, he must be supported in some measure by his parents or some one else until he is about twenty-five.

Such evidence illustrates the degree to which we have accepted the desirability and the necessity of education. We are willing to support it financially in a degree second only to war or national defense. We believe as a people, as members of the Western world community, that man's mind and therefore man's lot can be improved by education.

With this as a starting point it is only necessary to evolve the professional philosophic statement of educational aim. Reliance upon four principles is implicit: (1) civilization and its historical interpretation rest squarely upon knowledge; (2) knowledge and learning are primarily matters of the mind; (3) man's intellect and skill are subject to almost unlimited improvement or progress; (4) human values are flexible and not absolute and are attainable only through recognition of human dignity.

Based upon these principles a workable philosophy of education must be pointed toward the systematic acquisition of knowledge and skills that will push back the frontiers of learning for the sake of increasing knowledge, while at the same time it must support the accepted standards of moral behavior in our society as it is hoped that these standards or values will become better. Man's lot is to learn of his past while he strives to improve his future.

One more philosophic element must be considered in the practicum of teaching: individual differences in learning capacity. Learners range in ability from very high to very low, and it must never be assumed that all persons can learn exactly the same amount in just the same time with equivalent amounts of energy expended. This means in practice that nearly every class of students will operate more effectively if it is divided into convenient ability groups. As the student advances in the grades of study the grounds for grouping should gradually shift more and more to achievement instead of potential ability.

Practical curricular application of this philosophy dictates an elementary school procedure devoted primarily to learning "the three R's," the basic tools of communication—reading, writing, speech—the fundamental skills of understanding the material world of natural science, arithmetic and elementary physics, foundation indoctrination in morality, patriotism, spiritual tolerance and community living, as well as appreciation of the enrichment factors of life—literature, art, music. Varying degrees of specialization in all these fields is available to all in the degrees of their capacity. The secondary school pursuit of the body of human knowledge is still general in scope with additional and increasing opportunities for individual advancement. By the end of high school the student must have learned most of what will constitute his share of general knowledge, and in addition to this, most students will have added command of the basic skills necessary to vocational placement for life.

To these ends the high school reflects in adaptable form the scholarly, specialized bodies of knowledge. High school courses presented in departmentalized form usually bear the names of the disciplines reflected, such as physics, history, language, literature, or even more special classifications of learning such as algebra, geometry and the like. Even though such names exist to identify the parts of secondary education, the end of that education is not only mastery of its several parts; it is also the integration of those parts into an approximation of the unitary body of knowledge that supports modern civilization. Thus the professional equipment of the teacher must be a better organized integration of those bodies of learning plus the applied attributes of good teaching which in turn rest upon still more mastery of subject matter.

It is clear that a satisfactory philosophy of education for the secondary teacher, or for any teacher, must embrace a respect for and mastery of much knowledge, including at least one thorough specialization, and at the same time must recognize the integrated wholeness of knowledge and the need for skill in the professional aspects of passing on that knowledge.

Modern education demands that the best teaching, pointed toward progress, drive a philosophic course somewhere between faddish acceptance of catch-phrases like "democratic living," "experiential expression" and "free creativity," on the one side, and on the other side such equally misleading and hollow reiterations as "return to the liberal arts," "exclude frivolity from the curriculum" or "revive the three R's" (as though reading, writing and arithmetic were dead arts). The most practical way to do this is to assume that better behavior from citizens will accrue to a more extensive mastery of the elements of knowledge available, and then to present this material to students in school following a systematic arrangement by graded degrees of complexity from kindergarten through high school, making allowance for individual differences in capacity and taste by providing several levels of curricular diversity and difficulty.

In social studies at the secondary level these things become doubly important. Because of the vaguely defined lines separating the social sciences, and because of the variegated quality of human experience, social studies teachers in their role as social scientists have a heavy responsibility both to general knowledge and to specialization. On top of this it is necessary for them to be skilful representatives of the teaching art or else they will fail in the great aim of education: to help students to learn. As a contrast, it is certainly desirable for the high school teacher of physics to be aware of the social implications of his science, and it is necessary for him to have skill in presenting his material, but specifically his task is to know and present the organized content of physics to his students. The responsibility of the high school teacher of United States history includes presentation of the intellectual impact of the findings in physics, chemistry, politics—and everything else of significance that his students can understand.

In some sense the secondary social studies specialist must be a historian, social scientist, natural scientist and humanist all the while he is a professional teacher. It will be said that this is impossible, that there are no more Leonardos, that knowledge is too great. That is not true. To admit to inadequacy in the modern world is to accept defeat in man's quest for a better world, a better man. It is true that no man can expect to master all learning. Leonardo himself could not do that. It is also true, however, that any teacher capable of finishing a standard secondary training program can master enough of one discipline to give him competence and at the same time so increase his command of general knowledge that he is not completely ignorant of the rudiments of all the rest. Devotion to research, study and lifelong learning should become part of the mental equipment of every teacher of social studies along with his basic requirements for graduation. This process requires application based on a certain minimum of native ability, but it can be done. It will only be done by placing a philosophic value on knowledge at every level of achievement.

In summary, any acceptable philosophy of education means mastery of verifiable data, as it has since man emerged as a sentient being. This takes place as man learns of his heritage and uses this learning to further master the natural world to the end of making his life fuller and more knowledgeable. Man learns slowly but surely.

### 3. Suggested Further Reading

I. B. Berkson, *The Ideal and the Community* (Harper, New York, 1958), presents the latest available statement by a professor of education in regard to a new philosophy of education. The statement is based, still, on a pragmatic conception of ethics and politics. Cf. Paul Woodring, *A Fourth of a Nation* (McGraw-Hill, New York, 1957), which tends to be much more Platonic in tone.

Arthur Bestor, *The Restoration of Learning* (Knopf, New York, 1955), is, in the words of the subtitle, "a program for redeeming the unfulfilled promise of American education." It is different from the author's first book on the subject of education, *Educational Wastelands* (1953), which is purely polemical and not very useful.

Benjamin Franklin, *Autobiography,* edited by Max Farrand (University of California Press, 1949), is the most scholarly version of known texts of Franklin's inimitable exposition of American morality. It supersedes all previous editions.

Alexander Hamilton, John Jay, James Madison, *The Federalist* (any one of many editions), gives the basic arguments for establishing the constitution which has become the backbone of our national organization.

James High, "Teaching Citizenship: An Experiment in the World Problems Approach," *Washington Education* (February, 1956), is an attempt to translate the present necessity into understandable practice for the secondary school teacher training institution.

Wendell Johnson, *People in Quandaries* (Harper, New York, 1946), may give the reader an insight into the positive necessity for remaining "sane" which is often lacking. The therapeutic value of general semantics is well plumbed.

Albert William Levi, *General Education in the Social Studies* (American Council on Education, Washington, D.C., 1948), is the report on the Cooperative Study in General Education, 1939–1944.

Tamotsu Shilbutani, *Society and Personality* (Prentice-Hall, Englewood Cliffs, N.J., 1961), is a very recent and well-documented treatment of a social psychological interpretation of society as well as the resolution of culture conflicts.

*Social Science in General Education,* edited by Earl J. McGrath (William C. Brown, Dubuque, Iowa, 1948), is a recent survey of practices in American colleges in regard to the general education offerings in history and the social sciences. It is an attempt to assess the best available for practical adoption.

Lynn White, Jr., "The Changing Past," *Harper's* (October, 1954), is a most penetrating analysis of the human conception of history. It shows how the past is "altered" by the experience of the present.

*Philosophies of Education,* edited by Philip H. Phenix (Wiley, New York, 1961), is a symposium of divergent views on the purposes of education. Very stimulating.

# 5
# Skills in social studies learning

> Language implies more than learning to signal like a firefly or to talk like a parrot. It also includes how man can communicate across continents and down the ages through the impersonal and permanent record which we call writing.
>
> *The Loom of Language* *
> FREDERICK BODMER

## 1. Skills of Thought and Expression

Social studies learning is dependent upon a means of clear expression and the ability to understand what is expressed. Almost every form of perception can be employed and many types of symbolism can be used to present the material that is to be learned. The first and most important skill is reading because the bulk of perception is basically derived in this very broad field from printed prose. Corollary to reading is writing which serves two purposes in social studies. First, that which is to be read by the student must be written in clear and direct style with a rich vocabulary and extensive imagery. Second, the student himself, in order to supply the necessary reinforcing agency for his learning, must be able to write out his own ideas and formulations based on the original perception. Reading and writing, then, are the primary requisites to effective learning of social studies in all levels of school.

There are many more forms of communication, a symbolism that presents perceivable patterns of stimulus to mental activity for their comprehension. Pictures, maps, globes, exhibits (any form of *realia*,

---

* Quoted by permission of the publisher from Frederick Bodmer, *The Loom of Language* (Norton, New York, 1944), p. 33.

recordings of voices, music, rhythms), many combinations of sounds, room arrangement, facilities (the immediate physical environment), and the organization and structure of the material at hand and the thought processes behind the arrangement—all these things contribute to the fundamental purposes of social studies instruction and they represent a large assortment of skills that must be mastered in addition to the generalizations and facts typical of social studies curricula. In fact, without access to the basic skills of communication, learning of anything is haphazard and problematic; one never knows whether he has learned anything or not.

Although reading appears to be the fundamental skill, and it is usually the first one learned in school, orderly, clear and logical expression in writing is the most critical. It is in this process that the student can properly learn and clarify his thought processes. Writing is merely the formal arrangement of the thought process committed to paper. Thinking has a quality, when written down, of staring back at the writer. Oral verbalization is transitory. A mistaken concept or an opaque statement cannot be invoked against its utterer except through the exercise of someone's memory. When a thought is written down, however, it is irrevocably there to confront its author.

Behind any expression is the thought that gives rise to the statement. Language, written or oral, is merely the symbolic expression of a thought process and its results. Only if logical and critical thought is exercised is it possible to achieve any kind of reasonable expression in language. Therefore the most basic element of writing and speaking is critical and orderly thought. Organization of material and identification of priorities of importance in the material must be cultivated in any emphasis on the skills needed to understand social studies.

Skills have a dual meaning and purpose. First, one definition of skill has solely to do with method, with the process of learning. A skill is the wherewithal to gain an end; in social studies this is to learn the facts, generalizations and formulations of social relationships. The knowledge itself, in this sense, is not a skill; it is the result of the use of skills in its mastery. Second, there is another definition of skills favored by Charles Beard which classifies them as the "signs and instruments of power," as a "knowledge of how to acquire knowledge . . . a permanent possession which can be used throughout life." [1] In this regard one can speak of the skills necessary for lifelong participation in a democracy. The skill of citizenship is, in this way, the ability

[1] Charles A. Beard, *A Charter for the Social Sciences* (Scribner's, New York, 1932), p. 99.

to get along well and benefit from democratic social organization, or stated differently, the ability to use a total education in furthering one's life aims. This definition is very near to the whole purpose of education.

Such basic skills as reading and writing, then, have sharp significance to the social studies teacher and student. In order to learn about the human heritage it is necessary to read about it as well as to experience it in other ways. In order to carry out the more enduring functions of citizenship it is also necessary to read throughout a whole lifetime, but in a certain way, with a certain maturity of judgment which is a result of the total educational experience.

It might occur to some prospective social studies teachers that skills, or the way in which learning is to be achieved, are not their responsibility and province. It might be argued that reading, writing, reference techniques and so forth ought to be taught by others or at an earlier time. A moment's reflection should disabuse anyone of this notion, because skills have a great range of complexity. Some are simple—reading as a group of single skills is simple in essence—but it must be remembered that skill is also a matter of increasing complexity and the use of any skill is subject to almost continual improvement. Reading very simple primers is one thing, and reading and comprehending the more sophisticated matter which carries the burden of human experience is yet another. All of the skills used in learning need constant attention if only for the desirability of increasing their use. As one comprehends what skills really are, not only as the means to an end, it becomes apparent that new and more complex skills are needed at every stage of development. There is a double hierarchy of growth from simple to complex in any one skill, and a multiplicity of skills increasing in difficulty and complexity as the horizon of knowledge becomes ever broader. It is the responsibility of every social studies teacher to devote considerable time and effort to the matter of increasing his students' use of skills and to introduce them to new ones. If part of his work in this regard may be considered remedial, that also is his responsibility.[2]

Aside from the motor and social skills needed for achievement in social studies or any other subject (eye movement in reading, vocal organs in speech, getting along with one's neighbors) another group of skills exists which is of prime importance in a discussion of this kind. These are the more intellectual processes in learning, the com-

[2] See below, Chapter VIII, pp. 186–189 for a treatment of developmental reading in social studies instruction.

bination of single motor skills plus lucubration. Professor Beard has analyzed them into a concise statement:

1. Skill in methods of obtaining access to information
   a. Use of libraries and institutions
   b. Use of encyclopedias, handbooks, documents, sources, authorities and statistical collections
2. Skill in the sifting of materials and the discovery and determination of authentic evidence—in the use of primary sources
3. Skill in the observation and description of contemporary occurrences in the school and community
4. Skill in methods of handling information
   a. In analysis—breaking down large themes or masses of data into manageable units and penetrating to irreducible elements
   b. In synthesis—combining elements, drawing inferences and conclusions, and comparing with previous conclusions and inferences—logical and systematic organization
   c. In map and chart making and graphic presentation
5. Skill in memorizing results of study—with consciousness of application to new situations by exact reference and analogy
6. Skill in scientific method—inquiring spirit, patience, exactness, weighing evidence, tentative and precise conclusions [3]

In order to achieve an acceptable level of competency in the skills of social studies and citizenship, a definite program must be instituted. Most satisfactory is a system-wide attention to the problem, although the failure of a whole school system to organize a social studies skills program does not preclude attention on the part of one school or even one teacher to the principles by which desirable skills can be taught. The following is a list of eight principles designed to meet the skill objective stated above:

1. For the acquisition and improvement of skills, the learning activity must focus on skill development. Skill development will not take place by chance.

2. Experience designed to promote growth in skills must be meaningful to the learner. A certain skill must be accepted as important.

3. Experiences used in skill development must be geared to the maturation level of the learner. Just as a five-year-old cannot usually master a flowing script with a fountain pen, neither can a junior high school student be expected to achieve the same degree of skill in synthetic thought as a college professor.

[3] Charles A. Beard, *The Nature of the Social Sciences* (Scribner's, New York, 1934), p. 227, also cited in *Skills in Social Studies*, edited by Helen McCracken Carpenter, Twenty-Fourth Yearbook, National Council for the Social Studies (Washington, D.C., 1953), p. 11.

4. For the successful learning and retention of skills, repetitive practice is necessary. Reinforcement of learning is essential.

5. Skills should be developed in connection with on-going activities and not in isolation. Every social studies skill is, in the end, an integral part of the life equipment of the citizen.

6. Development of different skills should go on simultaneously. There is a gradual and steady growth of all of the parts in the process of education.

7. Evidence of skill development must be sought in changes in behavior. The whole purpose of education is to induce an improved behavior pattern.

8. Provision for the systematic development of skills must be made throughout the school program. This is merely to re-emphasize the idea that skills begin with mastery of simple, uncomplicated steps, and proceed to more complex and various patterns of activity. This principle is a summary of all the other seven.[4]

### 2. Formulation, Organization and References

In secondary social studies, beyond reading and writing, perhaps the skill needing first emphasis is getting to the heart of the matter: assigning significance to various items in proportion to their importance; how to formulate hypotheses to study; how to get at the basic elements, the irreducible parts of a problem. Such procedures present the urgent need for certain kinds of skill. Before a topic can be studied at all it must be given meaning. The important, large ideas surrounding a subject must be dissected out, and as the study progresses each subordinate part must be shown to have further components, some of which are more important than others. Organization of these elements either lends to their proper integral understanding, or else such understanding is frustrated and defeated by poor organization. The vehicle for organization of materials contributing to expansion of a first formulation is the outline. Skill in outlining can be learned. It cannot be learned without the students' being exposed to the idea. Outlining must be mastered at some stage of education and consistently improved thereafter. Social studies is a proper medium for this instruction, and the secondary level of education is at least one place where it can be taught or reinforced.

---

[4] Helen McCracken Carpenter and Alice W. Spieseke, "Skills Needed for Democratic Citizenship," in *Skills in the Social Studies*, pp. 12–14.

## Formulation

Both before and after the organization process (or outlining) begins, formulation as a skill must be invoked. The basic hypotheses are to be formulated in such a way that a challenge to further elucidation is implicit in the statement. It is not enough to say simply that "now we will learn about American government." There is no particular challenge in such a dictum. Rather, the student should formulate his initial questioning statement in a different way. "How has the Constitution been developed to take care of the altered political atmosphere from the eighteenth century to the present time? Why was it first established? What has taken place that has made it change? Has it actually changed?" This type of self-query invokes an imaginative plethora of speculation and thought that, once started, is hard to check. The objective is implicit: to find out about American government, and at the end of the study to incorporate the findings into an explicit and clear formulation that promises from the outset to possess vitality and meaning. American life as a continuous process with political significance reaching into the past and yet with present implications cannot be denied in such a formulation.

At the end of any unit or subsection of study students of social studies are required to intellectualize and put into words summarizing statements that can be remembered. The teacher can, of course, do this for his students, but if he does their skill will not thereby be improved. They may or may not learn the vital summaries handed to them. The chances are great that they will not learn them very well. At least they will not be real unless the student himself has reached a feeling of need for finding out answers to his own questions and then has developed sufficient skill to produce the answers. In this connection the basic skill of writing becomes an important adjunct to the mastery of the more complex skill of formulation based on carefully organized reference material.

## Organization

Organization, again, has two specific functions in connection with any social study. After the problem has been set, pursuing the example already stated, "How has the Constitution developed?," the question has to be dissected into its components in preparation for study. After the preliminary outline has been developed and the actual consultation of references begun, another process of outlining and organization has to take place.

To exemplify the first function of organization, in preparation for detailed study, the first question that arises is "What is the Constitution?" A standard simple form of outlining with headings and subheadings can be used, and the subject can be planned for further examination.

## WHAT IS THE CONSTITUTION?

I. The Constitution as a document
   A. Text of the document as it was written in 1787
      1. First ten amendments added as a condition of ratification
      2. Three principal parts
      3. Provision for amendment
      4. Terms of adoption
   B. Contrast with former constitutions
      1. Articles of Confederation
      2. Colonial charters
      3. Why did it have to be written anew? Why could not the first constitution have been revised?
II. Historical setting in which the Constitution appeared
   A. Radicals and conservatives during the Revolution
   B. The Declaration of Independence
   C. The Revolutionary War
      1. The Constitution as a result of the Revolution
      2. The Constitution as a reaction to the Revolution
   D. The first government of the United States under the Constitution
      1. Washington
      2. Jefferson and Hamilton
III. First major alterations of the Constitution
   A. Revolution of 1800
      1. Jefferson and Marshall
      2. Strict construction *versus* loose construction
   B. Supreme Court decisions and judicial review
   C. Executive authority expanded under the Constitution
      1. Purchase of Louisiana, 1803
      2. Jacksonian Democracy and federal authority, after 1828
IV. The Constitution as a guiding principle rather than a rigid document
   A. Changes in interpretation
      1. Executive power under Washington

    2. Executive power under Jackson
    3. Executive authority expanded under Lincoln during the Civil War
    4. Twentieth century expansion of executive power
      a. Woodrow Wilson; World War I
      b. Franklin Roosevelt; World War II
  B. Present expanded constitutional body of experience, precedent, law and the original documents
V. Important amendments to the Constitution and alterations in its spirit
  A. Fifth Amendment; rights of accused (limit on federal power)
  B. Fourteenth Amendment; due process of law clause (limit on state power)
  C. Nineteenth Amendment; woman suffrage
  D. Labor relations cases based on statute from 1890 to the present
    1. Sherman Anti-Trust Act
    2. Wagner Labor Relations Act
    3. Taft-Hartley Law
      a. Judicial acts—injunctions
      b. Balance between rights of minorities and the majority
VI. Present status of the Constitution
VII. Final summary and formulation of the finished problem with suggestions for further study

With such an outline the student can go to work on the next phase of the problem: elucidation of the various subtopics stemming from the original statement. Depending upon the time available for study and the ability and skill of the student any degree of detail may be added to the organization already itemized. In making such an outline obviously most students would need some help. A certain amount of information is needed before even a bare outline can emerge, but the questions and challenges to further study far outweigh the knowledge contained in the abbreviated statements of the case.

*Reference Material*

"Locating and gathering information at the junior high, senior high, and junior college levels is largely a process of strengthening, broadening and refining these skills that were learned in the primary and intermediate years. Acquaintance with additional resources and refinement of skills in information gathering, note-taking and checking facts should proceed simply and directly as needs develop." [5] The first place, usually, for the student to look in his quest for information is in his textbook. In the preliminary process of reducing the major problem to a working outline this is necessary. As unanswerable questions arise, as they will, such points should be noted for further search. When the first outline has been completed it will be apparent that much more needs to be learned in order to have anything like a complete picture. The very comprehensive nature of most textbooks, with emphasis on coverage of extensive material makes it necessary to truncate nearly every topic that is treated. Nonetheless the essence of the problem is usually explained, at least in enough detail so that a working outline can be constructed similar to the one given as an example.

In using a textbook, or for that matter, nearly any other book, it must be remembered by the student that the author of the book was aware of the principles and rules of good grammar, diction and organization. In most cases the topic sentences of paragraphs will stand out in the pages of reference books. The topic sentence is ordinarily, but not always, at the opening of the paragraph. In any case it sets the tone for the paragraph and usually will suffice for outlining purposes and for note taking. This phenomenon of the topic sentence is extremely useful to the secondary social studies student. First, he should be able to recognize it in his texts and other books. Second, he should be encouraged to use cogent topic sentences in his own writing. In fact, teachers should refuse to accept any consecutive prose compositions from their students that do not have an apparent outline in the form of topic sentences showing almost at a glance. Third, the topic sentence should be the basis for systematic note taking by students in most of their reference work.

The next step in developing information on a given topic after exhausting the textbook is to consult the library. Here the skills involved become a bit more complicated. Among younger students, the teacher and librarian should cooperate to make the job of finding suitable reference materials a little less monumental. This can be done by placing appropriate books and magazines on one or two tables so that the more advanced skill of searching bibliographies and the card catalog is not invoked at all. In many cases the mere act of looking through the index of one book beyond the text is enough for the limited experience of the student.

[5] Emma L. Bolzau *et al.*, "Locating and Gathering Information," *Skills in Social Studies*, p. 69.

As students become more adept in searching out information they can be expected to find their own titles as they are stored in the library. Basic tools for this task are the card catalog and the various bibliographic collections which all libraries have.

Taking the first Roman numeral item in the outline given, "The Constitution as a document," the text can usually be found in a standard textbook on United States history or government. The student can read it and satisfy a good deal of the requirement contained in the "A" section of the outline. The three principal provisions for separation of powers are implicit in the organization of the Constitution. The three parts are marked legislative, executive and judicial. The first ten amendments, or the Bill of Rights, is obvious, and usually there will be a note as to the human rights character of these amendments and the fact that they had to be included as part of the price of ratification. The "Bill of Rights" then becomes another point to note for further search. The provision for amendment of the document is also included in its text, as well as the terms of adoption and ratification.

At this point it may become desirable to go to the card catalog in the library and look up some of the books listed under such headings as "Constitution," "Bill of Rights," "executive," "judicial," "legislative" or words that have a similar or related meaning. Perhaps a dozen books will be unearthed. Not all of them will be appropriate, but it then becomes necessary to make choices based on skimming the tables of contents and the indexes of the books in question. Possibly some topic sentences will be seen that require taking a few notes.

Either concurrently or later the student should follow the same procedure in some encyclopedias or other general reference works such as *Compton's Pictured Encyclopedia, World Book Encyclopedia, Encyclopaedia Britannica, Encyclopedia of the Social Sciences, Dictionary of American History* or *Dictionary of American Biography*. Besides the information directly contained in such references there is usually a short list of relevant monographs, biographies and other books at the end of each article.

Under "B" in the outline, "Contrast with former constitutions," some textbooks may contain a copy of the Articles of Confederation, but very few would have reproductions of colonial charters. Some of the colonial charters, such as the Mayflower Compact, Fundamental Orders of Connecticut, and the Charter of the London Company of Virginia all contain points of interesting relationship to the spirit and form of modern American constitutional government, and no comprehensive understanding of the Constitution can be complete without a comparison with the parent documents. These and many other documents of significance in the development of United States government may be found in *Documents of American History,* edited by Henry Steele Commager (Appleton-Century-Crofts, New York, 1940, 2nd ed.). There are also a few collections of historical documents and source materials designed particularly for high school students which have been referred to elsewhere in this work.

As to the actual comparison of the Constitution and the Articles of Confederation, one of the first points of difference will be seen to be the comparatively great strengthening of central authority in the new Constitution. Another difference immediately perceivable is the manner of financing the state. Under the old organic law each state was supposed to contribute a share, but there was no means of enforcing any levy. The new Constitution changed this arrangement. Many other disparities are to be seen. At once the question arises as to why these things were no longer considered appropriate to the task of governing the United States. The enterprising student will soon ask the question, "What was the political complexion of the group that wanted the Constitution?" If a student has gone this far it should not be difficult for him to find a good many opinions and a great deal of fact concerning the political structure and attitudes of eighteenth century America. It might not be surprising to find out that there is still some degree of controversy over exactly why some Americans wanted a new constitution.[6]

Through the same process of search the student will soon find that the colonial charters of government granted certain rights to American colonists that have carried over to the present day. Representative self government in the New World stems directly from the efforts and charters of the first colonists from Britain. The colonists had the right and exercised it, of choosing their own representation, of rejecting laws and regulations that seemed to them counter to the New World current of free political expression. Such attitudes grew from beginnings in Virginia and Massachusetts to the mature expression of popular will that we know in the twentieth century.

Each step in the outline can be searched and studied with the aid of books, magazines and other materials until a vast body of infor-

[6] See Merrill Jensen, *The Articles of Confederation* (University of Wisconsin Press, 1940), for a discussion of a revisionist point of view concerning the adoption of the Constitution.

mation is amassed. At the conclusion of such study it should be mandatory that the student, having revised and expanded his outline to include all of the detail he has found, write out a concise formulation that can express the vital and meaningful knowledge that he has acquired.

It should be easily seen that the development and use of skills is thoroughly integrated into the total process of learning. There is no such thing as learning to use the library in a vacuum, no sense to writing unless there is something to write about. Skill in learning the material of social studies is tantamount to learning social studies. These two aspects of education are in truth really only one.

## Note Taking and Reference Cards

As a specific subordinate skill attached to reference searching, one device has been found to be very useful. Note cards or reference cards facilitate keeping a record of the works consulted and of the material gained from such search. Cards are not the only way in which references can be kept and systematized, but they furnish one method by which the ends of learning can be furthered. The real object is to get the material organized and into the mind of the student.

There are two kinds of note cards: bibliographical, and for the actual notes. The same size card should be used for both so they can be filed together and rearranged conveniently in any desirable sequence. Three inch by five inch or larger cards are suitable, because each note should be on a single topic or book, and usually only a very scanty notation of subject material is necessary in order to remind the reader later of what he has seen in a particular book.

A bibliographic card should be made for each separate book, pamphlet or article that is consulted or is to be used. Right at the outset of investigation, upon the first examination of a card catalog or bibliography, each separate item should be completely cited on a single card so that later it can be easily identified as a whole. As soon as the general theme of the book or article is known the card should be annotated briefly. At first, before one has looked at the work, this of course is impossible. Proper and complete bibliographic information should be put down on this card. It is important to remember this because at a later time, after many books have been handled, it is very easy to forget small details such as an author's initial, or the date of the book in question or even what the book was about. The general subject of investigation should appear in one corner of the card, and the same arrangement of data should be maintained on every card to facilitate filing and arrangement of the cards.

Jensen, Merrill Monroe                              Constitution
  *The New Nation: A History of the United*          and Articles
  *States During the Confederation, 1781–*           of Confederation
  *1789*
  (Knopf, New York, 1950)


Shows the positive operation of the Articles of Confederation as a constitution adequate to the majority conception of democracy in the eighteenth century.

FIGURE 3. A sample bibliographical note card.

For subsequent cards containing notes taken from the same book a different scheme of identification may be used. The bibliographic information, once recorded, need not be repeated on each card carrying notes from the same book. Some system of abbreviated identification may be used. The book needs to be identified positively as well as the general subject and the specific topic within that subject. The general subject, in the example, is the Constitution and the Articles of Confederation. Below this, as a subtopic, might be the eighteenth century concept of democracy as represented by the Articles of Confederation. A sample note taken from the book just mentioned could appear on a card as follows.

Jensen, *The New Nation*                     Confederation-democracy
  pp. 1 ff.



Eighteenth century Americans believe that political democracy was best achieved by decentralization and weakness of central government authority. The Articles of Confederation represented a majority view of the kind of document necessary to achieve this.

FIGURE 4. A sample note card.

Each topic and each work consulted as they are found from the original outline should be treated in the above fashion. After a number of notes have been garnered, then it becomes periodically necessary to review them and reorganize their sequence. Finally a new outline must be prepared, a topic sentence written for each paragraphed section, and then the oral presentation or written form of a report can be very easily accomplished. The result will be an organized and coherent account of illustrative material pertaining with accuracy to the outline which is really only the expansion and detailing of the first question asked.

This is a very brief introduction to the business of note taking and organization of research material. It is by no means complete, but it serves to illustrate the problem that exists in regard to individual investigation of any problem in the social studies. Obviously there are required several skills that do not "just grow." They must be taught, and the process is laborious and sometimes painful. It is necessarily a slow one, but a useful and indispensable adjunct to any successful pursuit of social study. Students in high school social studies ought to be introduced to the expanding skills of research as soon as they are able, some even while they are in elementary school can absorb a great deal of the knowledge of such skills if they only have the opportunity.[7]

The best test of how well students are learning the use of social studies skills is to assign to them definite projects to be studied and presented in written form. It is necessary to give instruction in the various steps to be used in the process. It is also necessary to be sure that the project assigned is within the capability of the student. Nothing is gained by setting up an impossible task except frustration for both teacher and student. Step by step deadlines should be announced for each phase in the preparation of a paper. Formulation of the topic, the preliminary outline, sample note and bibliographic cards, a tentative bibliography, an extended outline, and finally the completed paper; each of these steps should be made as a definite assignment to be completed by a certain date. At each stage of progress the teacher

[7] For further expansion of the description of research skills see Homer Carey Hockett, *The Critical Method in Historical Research and Writing* (Macmillan, New York, 1955, 3rd ed.). This book was written for the purpose of introducing graduate students to the art of writing history, but its principles and techniques are equally applicable in secondary teaching. For the most widely accepted standard forms of bibliographical and note citation, as well as all aspects of style, see *A Manual of Style* (University of Chicago Press), issued every three or four years since 1906.

will need to give specific instruction to individuals as it becomes necessary. At the end of the process, after the paper has been handed in and the teacher has read it, there is an important opportunity for the student to find out what he did that could have been done better. At this point he should be given a chance to revise his work or to do it over as it becomes desirable to alter his approach to the problem. He should be made aware of mistakes in skill technique and faulty interpretation or too scanty use of reference materials. It is in this way that the student acquires knowledge and skill in making that knowledge accurate and useful to him, not only in school but in his whole life to come. In this connection no student should be finally judged on less than his best effort. Social studies work is to be evaluated in a combination manner, that is, no total emphasis can be given solely to skill in technique on the one hand, or only to the subject content on the other hand. Both things go together inextricably, much in the same manner that skill in teaching cannot be divorced from the teacher's knowledge of the subject that he is supposed to teach. Ever so fine an idea, if couched in bad language and stated in a disorganized way, loses a great deal of its value and force. In fact, it can be questioned whether or not anything can be learned properly if it cannot be expressed clearly and in acceptable language.

### 3. Manipulating Materials

Critical thinking is perhaps the great goal of social studies instruction. "Who are the critical thinkers? In what matrix are they formed? At what age do they first appear? What is the responsibility of the school in fostering their development? The importance of these questions can be gauged by the fact that the success of a democracy is predicated, not upon an elite minority of critical thinkers, but upon a citizenry in which they constitute the rule rather than the exception." [8] Critical thinking is possibly the only kind of thought worthy of the name. As Boyd Bode has said of thinking, it ". . . may be defined more simply as the finding and testing of meanings." [9] In any case, it is to be achieved and encouraged wherever and whenever possible.

No one has really stated for all time exactly what the nature of thought processes is, but John Dewey came about as close as anyone

[8] Prudence Bostwick, "The Nature of Critical Thinking and Its Use in Problem Solving," *Skills in Social Studies*, p. 45.
[9] Boyd H. Bode, *How We Learn* (Heath, Boston, 1940), p. 251.

in his analysis of "states of thinking." From a perplexed and mis-understood situation to the clarification and formulation of ideas in a lucid manner, he pointed out five stages or steps. These are (1) state the exact nature of the problem to be solved, (2) make suggestions as to what might be done, (3) gather information as indicated by the suggestions, (4) check the original suggestions against the facts gathered, allowing for new suggestions or hypotheses, and finally, (5) test the suggestions by actual or imaginative action—merely another way of stating the steps in scientific methodology.[10]

The responsibility of the school, it would appear, is obvious in regard to using critical methods of thought in all of its instruction. The needs of the student and society as a whole are implicit. Skills of thought, as specific responsibilities of the citizen, must be taught in the social studies. As a support to the intellectual description and practice of the skills of critical thinking, contact with concrete objects is often very valuable. In the process of testing meanings, especially, direct experience with things sometimes brings the extra needed touch of reinforcement in order to learn a new thing, to make it one's own. As early as the seventeenth century in the history of modern development, pedagogical philosophers stressed the importance of handling *realia*. As critical thinking and other social studies skills are a continuing burden of responsibility in a social and political democracy, the school must do what it can to help realize a desirable result in their learning.

Projects done in social studies classes which have as part of their fulfillment the construction and manipulation of things are sometimes very worthwhile. For example, learning about global geography, the relationships among the planets and man, the physical principles upon which are based the very existence of our own earth, cannot be accomplished at all satisfactorily without the direct experience of handling a globe. Relief maps have a certain advantage over flat maps because of the very fact that another sensory organ is employed in their use—they can be felt. The curvature of the earth's surface and its complicated relief structure can be imagined much more clearly if a model of the unevenness can be touched. Shapes, sizes, colors, textures, smells and flavors all contribute something to sense perception and therefore to the total thinking and learning process.

One concrete example of how reinforcement of learning and addition to critical thinking might be achieved may be given in relation to a study of medieval history. In a ninth grade class in the history of

[10] John Dewey, *How We Think* (Heath, Boston, 1933, rev. ed.), p. 107.

civilization the teacher, at the beginning of the semester, assigned a choice of projects to each student to be completed in relation to some topic in world history. One student chose to undertake the construction of a model medieval castle. First he assembled a bibliography of mature and scholarly books on the subject of castles, their military and social functions, and of certain specific castles along the English-Welsh border. After building an outline on castles in general, he decided to study one particular structure, Kidwelly Castle in Wales. The reasons for such a choice were that the castle still stands in the twentieth century in fair repair, it was representative of the style and function of most castles in that part of England and it dates from the time of the Norman Conquest. In order to find out these things the student had to search diligently for material, obtaining books from a neighboring university library. The standard of achievement was held very high and exact accuracy was always a goal. After an outline and research had been completed it was a relatively simple matter to write an interesting and logical paper on this subject.

At this point the student was in a position to fulfill the original terms of the assignment. He built a scale model of Kidwelly Castle out of wood and plaster of Paris, painting and embellishing the final mounted model. Of course, he received a high mark on the work, and derived a sense of enjoyment and achievement that would be hard to duplicate. It was an exacting and painstaking job, but certainly worth the effort. He now knows more, and more deeply, about castles and their relationship to medieval and modern society than he had thought possible before he began.

One warning is necessary in connection with such a project as the one described above. It should never become an end in itself. The mastery of skills of construction, aside from the content of thought, is not the province of social studies. Skills in thought and the achievement of knowledge of social relations are always the goal, and so must be held above mere manipulative skill. A great deal of time can be wasted and no appreciable result obtained unless the project is a combination of both intellectual effort and direct experience. It must be remembered that in the time given to the building of a scale model castle a good many books could have been read.

[11] Model built by David High, ninth grade student in San Marcos High School, Santa Barbara, California, 1959. The chief reference used was G. T. Clark, *Medieval Military Architecture in England* (Mynan, London, 1884), 2 vols., which contains scale drawings of Kidwelly.

FIGURE 5. Model of a castle: Kidwelly Castle on the Welsh March, built in the 12th century.[11]

## Notebooks

Another kind of manipulative skill that can be used and constantly improved by students in social studies is the construction of various kinds of notebooks. Keeping notes is an old process, but it is subject to many new twists. First of all, it entails handling and manipulating a great many different kinds of material. A notebook may be used to keep the record of all learning materials. It may be the repository of research notes, class notes, reading lists, pictures, spontaneous drawings, tables or just plain doodles. Naturally, it has its most orderly and cogent purpose when it is devoted to a specific organization and recording of data and formulations concerning a particular topic. Several notebooks should be kept by every student, and enough care should be exercised in their preparation so that they will be proudly retained over many years.

For example, when the Constitution is studied, as it is in American schools many times, the child might prepare a notebook in extended fashion over the whole period of study. The Constitution can be dissected and reassembled in notebook form by a student, using his creative skill in embellishment and organization, and it is a fair bet that he will remember the provisions of the Constitution and its formation better than if he had only read about it.

One eighth grader decided to keep such a notebook. On the cover page he selected a passage with some inspirational quality. "Proclaim liberty throughout the land unto all the inhabitance thereof. . . ." He went on to each succeeding step of the adoption of the Constitution and its major provisions. Each page was devoted to one topic and embellished with original drawings or copies of cartoon and portraits, each appropriate to the meaning of the particular point being studied. Certain pages contained notes taken in class when the teacher explained things, and certain other pages were devoted to items of knowledge gained by independent study.

In connection with the Constitutional Convention in 1787, one page illustrated some of the personalities involved in the Great Compromise between the large states and the small states.

## Summary

The skills of social studies are so numerous and varied that it would become encyclopedic to list them all, and probably there would be disagreement as to what to include. It is sufficient to bear in mind a short list of major skills including almost innumerable subdivisions. There are skills of communication: reading, writing,

FIGURE 6. Facsimile page from an eighth grade student's social studies notebook.

speaking, listening and drawing; skills of thought: criticism, skepticism, discrimination and choice; skills of research: seeking references, using experience, organization, outlining and formulation; skills of construction and manipulation: handling maps, charts, tables and globes, making and using illustrative material such as notebooks, dioramas and models; and other skills of expression including drama, forensic discussions and the dance.

Further, it is always true that any given skill is subject to further perfection through practice. No skill "comes naturally"; they must all be learned. Social studies teachers must teach the necessary skills as the students' maturation levels make such learning appropriate.

Finally, social studies skills are inseparable from social studies content. In one sense wisdom is the skill of using knowledge.

**4. Suggested Activities for Further Study**

1. Select any one of the major skills used in social studies, such as reading, and analyze it into component parts. List and describe each of the single subordinate skill activities that taken together form the skill of reading.

2. Show how specific social studies skills which have essential usefulness in learning social studies in school may be carried over into everyday living throughout a lifetime. In other words, is there any real difference between social studies skills and the skills of citizenship?

3. What is your opinion of the different types of thought? Is there a basic difference between critical thinking and memorization, for example?

4. Devise a philosophy and means of incorporating a skill-training program with a total social studies curriculum in the whole secondary school.

5. What is the distinction between an intellectual skill and a mechanical one? Which is more important? Can the two be separated either for purposes of instruction or for permanent and general use?

6. List the skills most important to the study of a course in American government in the order of their priority of application. How much of any of them can be taught concurrently with American government?

**5. Suggested Further Reading**

CRITICAL THINKING

Julian C. Aldrich, "Problem Solving in Citizenship Education," *The Phi Delta Kappan* (December, 1951), pp. 194–195.

William A. Brownell, "Problem Solving," *The Psychology of Learning*, Forty-first Yearbook of the National Society for the Study of Education, Part II (Public School Publishing Company, Bloomington, Illinois, 1942), is a summary of research in the field.

Leonard Doob, *Public Opinion and Propaganda* (Holt, New York, 1948), is a classic in the study of propaganda and therefore useful in any consideration of critical thinking.

James I. Quillen and Lavonne Hanna, *Education for Social Competence* (Scott, Foresman, Chicago, 1949), Chapters 5 and 6.

## FOR GATHERING INFORMATION

J. Wayne Wrightstone, Dorothy Leggitt and Seerley Reid, *Basic Social Science Skills: Finding, Evaluating, and Using Information* (Holt, New York, 1944).

## LIBRARY SKILLS

Elizabeth Scripture and Margaret R. Greer, *Find It Yourself* (Wilson, New York, 1949), 3rd rev. ed., is a small pamphlet filled with practical suggestions.

## SPEAKING AND WRITING

Ethan A. Cross, *Teaching English in High Schools* (Macmillan, New York, 1950), Parts II and III discuss methods of developing oral and written English skills.

James H. McBurnery, *The Principles and Methods of Discussion* (Harper, New York, 1939).

## MAPS AND MAP READING, GRAPHIC PRESENTATION

David Greenhound, *Down to Earth* (Holiday House, New York, 1944), is very instructive.

Charles F. Hoban, Charles F. Hoban, Jr. and Samuel Zisman, *Visualizing the Curriculum* (Cordon, New York, 1937), has concrete suggestions as to how to use graphs and charts.

Daniel C. Knowlton, *Making History Graphic* (Scribner's, New York, 1925).

# part III
# PROCEDURES
# IN TEACHING
# SOCIAL STUDIES

# 6
# Professional equipment
# of the teacher

This pertains most of all to human nature, for we are all of us
drawn to the pursuit of knowledge; in which to excel we consider
excellent, whereas to mistake, to err, to be ignorant, to be de-
ceived, is both an evil and a disgrace.

Marcus Tullius Cicero, 46 b.c.

## 1. Responsibility to Knowledge: The Teacher

### General Qualifications

Every good teacher must have three separate qualifications. First,
he must know and like young people. Second, he must believe that
they can be taught, and he must make the necessary effort to learn
how best to accomplish that teaching. Third, he must master the
subject that he is going to teach. Without any one of these things
the teacher will not succeed; they work together in the preparation
of the teacher and in his professional life.

Since, most likely, persons entering the teaching field are somewhat gregarious by nature and have a rather strong sense of obligation
to social service, the first attribute is the most easily acquired, but
if it is absent—if a teacher does not genuinely like young people—
he had better choose some other vocation. A teacher must believe
in the capacity to learn and thereby to increase power for positive
social action. Any extensive acceptance of the principles of general
education and the advisability of mass instruction must be predicated
on the assumption of improvability of human behavior and the
educability of the individual. To believe this one must like people,
especially young people.

Something similar may be said concerning the teacher's obligation
to learn and use acceptable methods of instruction. It is necessary

117

to like what one is doing in order to do the best job; in teaching this means first to like the students, and second, to know and like the process by which we believe the students will become educated. Many persons over a good many years have been teachers. There have been outstanding teachers ever since the dawn of history. During the course of this time certain techniques of presentation and philosophies of education have evolved and have been tested by usage. At present there is a whole academic discipline devoted to professional study and training in the field of education and drawing heavily on findings from related fields in sociology and psychology. Teacher training institutions have organized many courses around the philosophy, history and methods of teaching which are required for teacher trainees. With the aid of whatever courses of instruction there are, it seems reasonable and requisite for teachers to master the content of a study of the history and philosophy of education, at least the fundamentals of psychology and its application in educational situations, and certain bodies of information concerning the methodology of teaching technique. In the case of such a specialized field as secondary social studies the last category requires further study of the particular procedures most successfully used in that field. In any event mastery of pedagogical methods is a relatively small part of the whole process of acquiring equipment to teach.

The major task of any prospective teacher, given competence in the two foregoing requirements, is thorough knowledge of the subject matter which the teacher will attempt to get his students to learn. It is futile to demand of the apprentice that in which the master is not adept. One author recently has warned new teachers to ". . . bear in mind that lack of subject preparation stands near the top of virtually every list of causes of teacher failure." [1] This certainly does not mean that every high school teacher must be a specialist scholar in some obscure branch of study; that is the function of doctors of philosophies in universities and laboratories. The teacher, however, must know, broadly and deeply, the field in which he teaches. He must also strive continually to strengthen and expand this knowledge in his discipline and also in others, especially as they impinge upon his own. For example, it is not enough to know that Thoreau and Emerson were figures in the Transcendental Movement in United States history and that this was a significant current in American cul-

---

[1] Raymond E. Schultz, *Student Teaching in the Secondary Schools: A Guide to Effective Practice* (Harcourt, Brace, and World, New York, 1959), p. 330. Quoted by permission of the publisher.

tural development; it is also needful to read what they said, to examine *Walden* and the *Essay on Man* and to attempt to decide critically and independently what their influences might have been. Such expansion of knowledge into supporting fields can, of course, only be started in preprofessional training during college. It is to be carried on for a lifetime, and in a very real sense no one ever knows "enough," that is, enough to cease learning.

Teachers, and particularly social studies teachers, should early get into the habit of "field study," that is, an application of a field theory to the process of learning, both for themselves and for their students. Each problem that comes up for investigation and learning is a field of inquiry which can be examined from many different points of view and by drawing upon the knowledge of many different disciplines. Diverse knowledge, narrowly applicable to a particular problem, is available through study at any time, not merely as part of the larger body of knowledge that makes up the whole disciplines of history, physics or anthropology; yet in the examination of any number of specific questions access to portions of the information in each of these fields might be appropriate. It is the moral and practical responsibility of the teacher to determine and learn that pertinent knowledge regardless of its discrete quality as part of a different discipline from his own specialization.[2]

Add to the above, in assessment of the teacher's responsibility to knowledge, a distinction between information or mere facts and conceptual use of that information to the end of wisdom and wise action, and one begins to visualize the position and role of the teacher as he is ideally drawn. Knowledge has a value in itself and mastery of information is the basic element in the foundation of conceptual knowledge, but though a concept be ever so highly intellectualized, until it is made into wisdom or the guide to wise and desirable social action it remains as only part of the teacher's equipment. There is a practical side to the acquisition of knowledge also, and for the teacher this is equally important with the purely academic and intellectual side.[3]

### Special Preparation for High School Teaching

Although what has been said above is generally true for all teachers it is doubly significant for secondary teachers. They must be morally

[2] Maurice P. Hunt and Lawrence E. Metcalf, *Teaching High School Social Studies* (Harper, New York, 1955), pp. 18–21.

[3] Edgar B. Wesley and Stanley P. Wronski, *Teaching Social Studies in High Schools* (Heath, Boston, 1958), 4th ed., pp. 221–222.

qualified for their vocation; they must be specially prepared in those aspects of sociology and psychology that apply to the age group with which they are to deal; and they must be particularly well prepared in the subject matter content of the high school courses and in the special methods of instruction peculiar to the high school. These attributes and special training may be summarized in the form of objectives for the high school teacher:

To maintain an attitude of intellectual curiosity in regard to knowledge for its own sake.

To expand one's own knowledge continuously in anticipation of the practical needs of life.

To help youth understand and state its own values as they relate to the culture.

To meet the emotional needs of adolescents.

To work effectively and intelligently with groups and individuals.

To assess constantly the effectiveness of teaching materials, and to seek and use fresh resources for instructional purposes.

To evaluate continually the methods and results of instruction.

It must be remembered that the American high school is the terminal educational facility for about three-fourths of the citizenry, and that during the years in high school people must learn the basic tools by which they are to appreciate and deepen their understanding of the past, of distant places and peoples, of the fundamental processes of production, trade, politics and social organization. The high school responsibility includes implanting in young minds a deeply rooted capacity for developing individual ethics, national morality and a sense of patriotic interest in the forces of nationalism that have positive potential for organization and maintenance of a better world.

There is little agreement as to who should be educated and as to how the secondary schools should be organized. There is, however, a set of facts which all secondary teachers must recognize. Approximately 85 per cent of the age group in question is in high school, no matter what the ability of any individual may be, and no matter how the high school is organized. As a median in thinking the high school has traditionally been considered to consist of four years, grades nine through twelve, but over half of American high schools are made up of some other combination of grade levels. Three years of junior high, grades seven through nine, and three years of high school, grades ten through twelve, is a popular combination, although there are various other arrangements, even including in some cases the first two college years or grades thirteen and fourteen. However it is done the responsibility of the teacher is the same.

Again, a good many observers are reluctant to admit that all children of high school age should be in high school. It has been said that only those who are capable of the highest level of academic achievement should be included in high school graduating classes. The facts are not in accord with this point of view, and it is now traditional to expect to encounter high school students of all degrees of intellectual capacity. From historical evidence of the growth of secondary education from about ten per cent of the age group in 1900 to 85 per cent in 1958, it is not likely that a reversal of tendency is about to take place. There is no common consensus of opinion as to how this is to be handled for the future, but in the meanwhile the new high school teacher must be prepared to meet a great diversity of ability in his students, and most importantly, he must be prepared to do the best he can for every student regardless of his capabilities. Each student in secondary school has the right to expect the best instruction that his teachers can give him.[4]

An interesting new trend is apparently in the course of developing in regard to the classification of students for instructional purposes: a system of two, three or four tracks or curricular patterns, each suited to an ability group with more or less common aptitudes and interests. Such a system is being adopted in an increasing number of high schools throughout the nation. The merits and disabilities of such a procedure are not pertinent to the discussion here, but regardless of what kind of ability grouping may exist the high school teacher must cope with it and in addition maintain a steadfast grasp on his objectives and responsibility to knowledge and to the needs of his students.

### The Teacher of Social Studies

Three outstanding elements characterize any profession. They are a special and extensive body of knowledge and skills beyond the ordinary acceptable level of baccalaureate training, a particular methodology peculiar to the exercise and application of the knowledge, and lastly, a certain set of personality traits specially adapted to the successful practice of the profession.

First of all, then, the social studies teacher must be a specialist in his field. The very breadth of the field might seem to preclude the

---

[4] See Jean D. Grambs, William J. Iverson and Franklin K. Patterson, *Modern Methods in Secondary Education* (Holt, Rinehart, and Winston, New York, 1958), pp. 12–30, for a recent statement of this idea.

concept of specialization, but upon reflection this will be seen not to be the case. Social studies, approaching the multiplex problems of human relationship from many points of view and with the scholarly aid of many social sciences, become a kind of total study of man in his setting, and therefore a specialty in the nature of complex generalization. One might call the social studies expert a specialist in general. In any case, the knowledge of subject matter must be very broad, and deep in some places. The social studies teacher is a specialist in the art of synthesis, putting the vital findings of separate social sciences along with the formulations of psychology and the theories of learning to make statements and produce concepts that can be learned at the various levels of many students. At first this might seem to be only the professional obligation of any teacher, but the social studies teacher has a special responsibility in this regard, in that psychology is a member of the social sciences in some respects, and as such it must be explored by the social studies teacher.

In becoming the generalist implied by the breadth of the social sciences, the social studies teacher must have a sharper specialization in one of the social sciences or in history, more specifically in one phase of a particular field. In other words, he must become a specialist in a narrower sense as well as in the general sense of social studies expert. This process in the training of a teacher involves, in all likelihood, the necessity of an undergraduate major in one of the social sciences in order to have adequate preparation for at least a limited amount of graduate study in the same field. For example, an aspiring teacher might take a major in history, enhance that undergraduate learning with several courses in geography, anthropology, economics or sociology, not to mention the near necessity for studying political science (at least to the extent of its evidence in American government). He might then participate in a seminar in history at the graduate level, including an examination of the principal sources and the major bibliography of history and an introduction to the actual process of research and the writing of history. It is almost axiomatic that no one can truly understand the main concepts and the principles of history without some experience, even though limited, in the step by step preparation of man's story as it appears to the average consumer of printed history. It is not necessary for the secondary social studies teacher to immerse himself completely in a fine point of undiscovered history, to become a specialist in only that, to the exclusion of awareness of the rest of learning. In fact it is not desirable at all to "learn more and more about less and less until one knows everything about nothing." Such activity may be specialization to a high degree, but it is not the specialization of the good social studies teacher.

The social studies teacher, nonetheless, must be a specialized generalist. He must know a considerable amount about a great deal, and he must know even more about at least one field in the social sciences. Anything less in the way of knowledge does not constitute a sufficient body of peculiar learning to warrant the professional label. Sound methods of instruction and a pleasing personality are indispensable to the social studies teacher, but they are worthless without the required knowledge.

Social studies have always been the "proper study of mankind," meaning the study of human relationships, and there is certainly nothing new about the interest man has in himself as a social being. Such studies have a special broad emphasis because they are clustered around problems of social behavior involving much diverse information drawn from many standard disciplines of knowledge. Information thus used loses its discrete character when brought to bear on problem solving. History and geography become reservoirs of knowledge that may be used to illustrate and illuminate problems in economic, political or social organization.

Thus two outstanding characteristics of social studies and the social studies teacher emerge at once. First, social studies is a recognizable separate field, distinct from any of its component mother disciplines, such as history, anthropology, geography, political science, sociology, economics or psychology. In addition to containing great slices of information out of the social sciences, social studies includes, as its reason for being, recognition of human situations in which choice must be exercised and in which social knowledge must be utilized in a practical fashion. The second aspect of the matter is the obvious implication that social studies is a school subject—a learning medium.

Teachers of social studies, as a very natural result of all these aspects of the field, must have two sets of professional qualifications. They must be adept at teaching, just as all secondary teachers, and in addition they must possess competence in a special field: social studies. In order to achieve such competence colleges have developed several patterns of preparatory training. Common to almost all of them is a requirement to develop a major in one of the social sciences, and, in addition, to explore three or more of the other social sciences as well as to integrate all of this background into a workable and recognizable body of *social studies* knowledge. At the risk of understatement of the case it may be said that social studies teachers have a very broad responsibility to knowledge and a rather rigorous course of study in order to be properly qualified to meet the demands of their particular specialization.

To summarize the distinctive qualities of the social studies teacher among all teachers, he must have:

The general attributes considered acceptable to the profession as a whole.

Specialization in one of the social sciences.

Comprehension of social studies as the study of human relations.

A peculiarly keen interest in and insight into public service.

Particular interest in leading youth into improved patterns of problem solving and the use of knowledge to wise ends.

The social studies teacher must have a sound understanding of the relationship between school and society. This, of course, is essential to all teachers, but for the social studies teacher it is doubly important because he is so often the spokesman for his school and the interpreter of society to his school. As a "specialist" in human relations he is called upon more often than many of his colleagues for public appearances and as a moderator of discussions of current and public interest.[5]

The biggest single problem of the social studies teacher is to know "enough," or to be able to determine what is enough. By definition he is in some degree master of history and of all of the social sciences. Obviously this is impossible, but at the same time the attempt is necessary. It is a truly difficult task and a continuing challenge to anyone who takes up the job of instructing in this broad and diversified field. Because of this, especially in the upper levels of secondary school, there is a tendency to separate courses of instruction into different classes in the different parts of social studies, that is, history, government, geography, economics, etc. Regardless of the curricular administration, however, the social studies teacher has a field of his own precisely because he is concerned above all with human relations. If these relations are given vital formulation by the respective social science fields, in social studies they are made available to students. Therefore social studies teachers are highly responsible and doubly specialized.

Another responsibility lies in recognition and acceptance of objec-

[5] See I. B. Berkson, *The Ideal and the Community* (Harper, New York, 1958), which is a piercing critique of the educational philosophy of John Dewey and William Kilpatrick and a new statement of ideal in philosophy for American public education. John Dewey, *The School and Society* (University of Chicago Press, 1915), is the standard account of the earlier pragmatism.

tivity as a continual criterion. The purpose and task of the students is to learn to attempt to solve problems, to apply knowledge to the end of wisdom, to make worthy choices among alternatives; it is not the aim of social studies to have teachers give ready made answers to these problems. The teacher's objective duty is not to select for the student, but to point out to him the choices which he may make himself and a method by which such choices may be made. The teacher's job is not to indoctrinate but to equip students to make decisions based on sound and objective knowledge.

Certainly this is not to say that social studies teachers cannot have opinions. On the contrary, they should have opinions—derived in an objective manner from a weighing of evidence. Teachers, just as anyone else, are citizens, with the same privileges and responsibilities. It is only that there is a higher degree of scrutiny of the actions of teachers—as public servants—and that they are charged, in school and out, with setting a precept and standard of behavior that can stand examination and be worthy of following by the impressionable youngsters who make up their student bodies. This is truly one of the mainstays of democracy: the right to personal opinions and the obligation to arrive at those opinions in an objective and knowledgeable manner. In a very real sense, high school social studies and its teachers form the core of democratic action in the United States.

### Academic Freedom and Controversial Issues

Academic freedom, in its most fundamental expression, is the right to investigate anything. By definition this is largely the purview of schools and scholars, and so academic freedom is most directly at stake in schools and colleges, although sometimes it is felt that only colleges and universities are concerned with the need for freedom to pursue truth, whatever its form. Public schools, especially secondary schools, and most particularly social studies are always concerned with controversial issues, and they definitely need a guarantee of freedom to do this objectively.

It is often felt that only teachers and professors are involved in academic freedom, but equally, and more importantly, the students in any school who hope to learn to evaluate human relationships must have academic freedom to learn. No matter how freely scholars can do research and teach about their findings, if students are restricted by culture or social sanction and prejudices, they cannot learn much beyond their preconceptions. In fact, one of the chief obstacles to academic freedom is the climate of opinion reflected in the attitudes and behavior of students who in turn draw their background from their cultural determinants. All of the society—students, professional people and laymen at large—must agree to the proposition that scholarship, learning, the schools and teachers have as a basic responsibility the right and obligation to push back the frontiers of knowledge into the wasteland of ignorance. This right must not only be allowed, its exercise must be obligated. Freedom of inquiry must be followed by free and objective instruction in the findings of social research to the end of making all citizens competent to arrive at worthy choices among as many alternatives as there are. If there are no alternatives, of course there is no ground for choice, and therefore no problem of academic freedom.

Academic freedom does not mean the right to indoctrinate. In matters of opinion there are always different points of view. Granted, some of them stem from prejudice or ignorance, but still there will be honest differences of opinion arrived at through objective means. An opinion, derived by any means, if made the sole content of teaching and set up as the *right* answer, constitutes indoctrination and cannot be countenanced under the guise of academic freedom. This does not admit of definition as freedom to pursue any investigation. Indoctrination may be assumed as the function of the state in supporting an ideology, as in Russia, or as a basic procedure in the armed forces of even the United States. There may be certain points of view that must attach to the successful functioning of an institution, but this consideration has nothing to do with academic freedom, nor is it reasonably allowable in a school. Schools are for the purpose of broadening the knowledge of students illimitably, so that they will be continually better equipped to choose among the multitudinous alternatives that will present themselves.

At this point it is necessary to make a distinction among three varieties of freedom, all of which we hold in value in the United States: academic, civic and personal. Academic freedom has to do with investigation and teaching objectively and reflectively. Civic freedom has to do with public philosophy and public policy. It may be very closely related to academic freedom. Indeed, it is impossible to envisage a truly free society without also accepting the need for freedom to investigate all of the possible body of knowledge and to teach about it. There may be, however, a high degree of strictly academic freedom without its having appreciable and immediate affect on public policy. The medieval university illustrates this in that medieval scholars studied and argued among themselves about all sorts of things, but publicly there was little effect on the universal curbs placed on unorthodoxy. Personal freedom is still another matter, involving the ways in which individuals are allowed or not allowed to follow their own whims in non-professional matters. It is not likely that a wastrel will be the most renowned scholar or the best teacher, but there have been examples of aberrant individuals who were most stimulating teachers and most productive scholars. Personal behavior is, on the whole, subject to certain regulation and restrictions, both in statute and by way of social suasion. Conformity to normally accepted patterns is usually implicit in any teacher's professional outlook. In other words, being a dope addict or an habitual drunkard might well exclude a person from the teaching profession, and this would not be an infringement of academic freedom, no matter how brilliant he was in his moments of lucidity.

In any discussion of freedom, academic or otherwise, there is always a relative comparison. There are certain customs and there is always a certain climate, varying greatly from time to time and place to place, but nonetheless, always there. These mores and the way in which they reflect social philosophy must be considered by the individual who aspires to the status of social studies teacher. The social studies teacher is perhaps in the public eye more than others because of the nature of his subject matter, dealing as it does with people and with the contemporary scene. He must discuss issues that are considered controversial (and, indeed, all issues are controversial, since an issue demands a choice) and therefore he must be doubly careful to pursue his investigations and teaching with objectivity. There are times and places that some subjects cannot be aired, and the social studies teacher must be sure that he is operating within the limits of good taste as well as in the pursuit of truth.

Despite the difficulties involved in presenting controversial matters in school or of investigating subjects surrounded by tension, teachers ought to be sure of enjoying academic freedom. In return for this right they should be willing to exercise good judgment, hold objectivity in high esteem and encourage reflective thought both in themselves and among their students.

Even though a majority of persons in a community favor reflective study of issues, there is something a vocal and well-organized minority which does not. Criticism by minorities, organized or not, is a well-established right in a democracy, and protection of academic freedom includes a valuing of minority opinion. Democracy, however, does not mean rule by a minority.[5a]

[5a] Maurice P. Hunt and Lawrence E. Metcalf, *Teaching High School Social Studies* (Harper, New York, 1955), p. 451, is part of a very good discussion of the problems of academic freedom in American schools. Quoted by permission of the publisher.

Many minorities have attempted to control, curtail or modify education in the United States, and sometimes they have succeeded. Reacting against this, at times, a majority or a coalition of minorities has operated to reduce obnoxious minority interference with academic freedom. The best defense, in a democracy, against minority tampering with the process of investigating controversial issues is a clear-cut majority view of what is wanted from the schools. Through the democratic procedure of assessment of the public philosophy and its subsequent incorporation into policy, an educational philosophy may become generally acceptable. Its purposes are to clear the way for the best possible general education and liberal broadening of the base for public decisions to be made by an enlightened citizenry. Academic freedom is implicit in such an arrangement, and part of the public schools' duty is the necessity to encourage reflective thought. Continued interest in the preservation of academic freedom throughout all ranks of society must stem originally from the schools' own discharge of the mandate given to them by their patrons. The process is endless and fraught with continued danger, thus making the schools continually alert to the need for eternal vigilance.

Specific threats to academic freedom most often appear in the form of restrictive oaths and the censorship of textbooks. Loyalty oaths, vaguely worded and reflecting minority interests which always have to be stated in negative terms against a poorly defined "enemy," constitute an eroding threat to vigorous investigators, because the oath, affirming nothing and attacking almost anything potentially, always stands as a deterrent to objectivity and therefore to truth. In the face of a loyalty oath, ominously clouding free discussion of ideas, scholarship will certainly dwindle. This, of course, is precisely what purveyors of oaths want, because they represent the feeling that their existence is predicated on a certain *status quo:* any change must be bad, therefore it is best to eliminate the possibility of change by reducing the possible choices of action. The loyalty oath is definitely the handmaiden of anti-intellectuality, which, in its turn, means the death of truly liberal education.

Textbook censorship is merely the extension of the vague loyalty oath into the realm of positive action. Any censorship, in the damaging sense of the word, is an imputation of the objectivity and good taste of teachers who are to use the textbooks. Again, the assumption is made that no choices are necessary, only indoctrination in the one "right" way. This is fundamentally undemocratic, and, of course, denies a basic element of academic freedom. Because of the same forces of cultural determination that make students sometimes suspicious of reflective thought, textbooks often have a tendency to become stereotyped, to avoid issues or conceal controversies. Publishers sometimes say that they cannot sell books that strike at sectional or class prejudices. Most insidiously this turns out to be a kind of censorship for which no one is responsible. Whereas official censorship of books can be countered through insistence on the right of academic freedom, the more subtle conformity and flaccidity of standardly accepted textbooks can only be changed or improved through the active scholarship and exercise of academic freedom by the members of the teaching profession.[5b]

Aside from recognition of the problem by every social studies teacher and his insistence on objectivity and scholarship, there are professional organizations which constantly scrutinize the profession and society for signs of resurgent attacks on academic freedom. No individual can do as much in combating the foes of intellectuality as can the combined efforts of the whole profession. The National Education Association, the National Council for the Social Studies and their state and local affiliates offer a nuclear point around which all teachers can combine to present a solid phalanx of objection in cases of infringement of academic freedom. In addition, there is the American Federation of Teachers, a union of professional teachers affiliated with the AFL-CIO, which is prepared to use the methods of organized labor to support the academic rights of its membership. All of these associations, at different times, have brought the teacher a greater voice against those who would suppress intellectual freedom.

## 2. Teaching Skill or Methodology

Methodology for the teacher is possibly more important than it is in some professions, but basically the teacher must depend on his knowledge, not merely on a "bag of tricks." The social studies teacher, beyond almost any other instructor, is responsible for a very wide range of knowledge and wisdom. He must not only command a specific discipline, but he must be versed in five or six others, and he must be a sensitive interpreter of his society and a good citizen. On top of all this he must command commensurate skill in the process of teach-

[5b] See Albert Alexander, "The Gray Flannel Cover on the American History Textbook," *Social Education* (January, 1960), pp. 11–14, which is a study of textbooks made in New York City exposing the mediocre conformity to standards of non-controversial character of the books available to students.

ing—of bringing to students the fruits of his knowledge and wisdom.

Professional competence is achieved by combining all of the attributes of professionalism, not merely underscoring how to teach or only knowledge of what to teach. It must involve bringing together a body of complex learning, generalization and detail, with a group of learners whose talents range over an entire spectrum of ability and interest. There are, of course, certain techniques and methods that will help accomplish the objectives of social studies education. They are not set patterns or skills that can be learned in college and directly applied without much thought in the subsequent teaching process. Rather, methodology, truly integrated into a teacher's professional competence, starts with knowing a body of subject matter, and combining that with a set of learning objectives and a growing proficiency in the actual skills of teaching.

The skill of teaching or methodology is based on three main things: verified knowledge about the learner and the learning process as it has evolved from the researches and reflection of psychologists and other clinicians, familiarity with a large part of the body of human knowledge making up the findings of social scientists and historians, and the cumulative experience of teachers over a number of years who have by trial and error eliminated or established specific patterns of instruction. It has been found, for example, mainly through experience, that no person ordinarily learns any set of facts and relationships by going over them only once. Therefore most important subjects taught in schools are treated several times in successive years, each time approaching the same vital generalizations and formulations by different means and with ever increasing complexity and refinement of consideration. Scientific psychology has borne out the teachers' pragmatic findings by producing the principle of reinforcement which, in its turn, has been incorporated into professional education and the school curriculum as a spiral or cyclic repetition of various subjects.

As an important example with inferences for the social studies teacher, American history is usually introduced in the elementary grades at a relatively low level of abstraction and with close attention to the elements of history that have familiar contemporary overtones. United States history is next encountered by students at the junior high school level, this time with more emphasis on a major theme such as the westward movement or the growth of democracy, and with the use of more abstract materials and more enrichment from other fields. In high school nearly every person undergoes more instruction in United States history. At this level the person is nearly adult and is assumedly capable of rather intricate reasoning processes. The purposes of reinforcement at this stage are usually served by stressing a political theme, democracy in its dynamic aspect of popular control and change. The history does not change, but the awareness of its significance becomes keener, the insights to be developed are more subtle and sophisticated although based on the same sources of information. A subsequent reinforcement of learning is likely to take place in college if the student goes that far, in what is generally known as a survey of United States history. If the student goes on to graduate study he may find that a whole lifetime can be devoted to continued expansion of knowledge and deeper understanding of the nuances of American history—and a continued reinforcement of the basic facts.

It may be seen that methodology in social studies instruction cannot be separated from knowledge of the subject, but that there are certain skills of presentation that can be worked out and cultivated which will achieve the goals of teaching. The following chapters will attempt to take up some specific samples of ways in which this can be done.

### Selecting the Best Method of Presentation

The first problem that presents itself to the preservice teacher trainee, after he has gained some mastery of his subject and some insight into the matter of the learning process and the nature of the learner, is the selection of methodology and its mastery. Although this is not the chief concern of experienced teachers, it looms as a large problem to the beginner, to the young man or woman just getting into the professional frame of mind. These are usually graduate students who have just finished a baccalaureate degree, and they generally feel quite confident of their knowledge of the subjects they have just studied. Now it occurs to them that their next big job is to find out how to teach these things to others, to younger students in junior and senior high school. Again, it must be warned that there is not any best method, no infallible way to pass on the learning that one has acquired. Each individual can undoubtedly remember his outstanding teachers, and upon careful analysis, if there was more than one, there was certainly more than one set of methods which those people employed. It is probably universally true that in every case of teaching a number of methods have been used, in infinite combination, variety being applied in accordance with the situation.

Any good method must include certain characteristics: introductory exploration and recapitulation of background (from the familiar to the new and more difficult), a satisfactory learning environment, common agreement and understanding with the students of the aims of study in concrete terms, available materials, search in the materials by the students and reflection on their findings, reporting of pertinent information, statement and explanation, formulation of problems or questions, reinforcement of learning, summary of learning and evaluation. The precise way in which these ingredients are combined is usually immaterial, at least theoretically. The simplest statement of the process may be graphically portrayed. It is a situation submitted to a process involving three entities and a continually expanding outlook. The learner exists in the form of the student. The body of knowledge is organized into subject courses. The teacher stands as the catalyst that precipitates the learning process. The methods of the teacher are completely incidental to the basic process which is learning and mastery of the subject matter, its details, concepts and formulations.

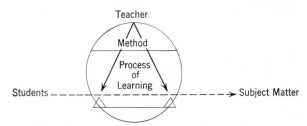

By repeating the figure in overlapping sequence and adding the dual expansion of process—evaluation and reflection—one achieves the symbolic representation of a spiraling reinforcement in which method is subordinate but subtly important as an extension of the teacher's catalytic function.

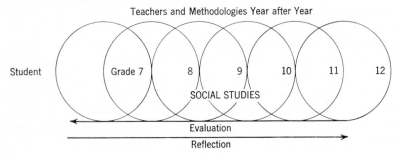

The best method for a given situation depends upon the material to be covered, resources available, student ability and educational aims. The teacher, in selecting methods, must be aware of and familiar with school policy and aims of the particular educational system and with the knowledge and potential of the students. It is fairly obvious that a single particular method, embracing only techniques useful with very young students, will not work every time in every age group to help the teacher perform the catalytic function which must be his primary position. Again, if a teacher fails to understand or appreciate the overall objectives of a school system he will undoubtedly find himself at odds with his colleagues and administration. For example, if a certain high school is essentially devoted to the purpose of preparing college entrants in the generally accepted liberal arts subjects, and if a particular teacher is not in sympathy with that aim, he will probably choose methods of instruction incompatible with the school's policy. On the other hand, the opposite might also be true.

Native ability in the students must of necessity have a bearing on the choice of appropriate methods. Techniques that will achieve the required motivating effect in dull students will not necessarily be of any use at all with accelerated children except to irritate them. Some people learn more easily and quickly than others, and therefore useful procedures in teaching various groups must take this into account. In classes that are unselected, that is, in which the range of ability is from bottom to top, there must be methodological choice considering this factor. In that case methods must be chosen which will have a common result on very disparate personalities. Experience is the surest guide to fortunate choice in the selection of a method for furthering the learning process once the teacher is equipped with sufficient knowledge to be sure himself of what he wants to teach.

### 3. The Professional Personality

Personality as an attribute of professionalism is the least tillable of the three components. Each individual possesses certain personality traits which are acquired in numerous and devious ways. At the point where a person chooses to be a teacher most of his personality has been formed. At least the characterological components have become deeply ingrained. Basically, he is not likely to change greatly thereafter. There are, however, some facets of personality that can be cultivated. The chief task of the prospective teacher in this regard is to examine and learn his own personality as it really is, and then to emphasize those aspects which have most positive bearing on his future occupation. He may find, and it will really be an advantage if he does, that his personality is disabling to his future success in teaching. There are personalities not at all adaptable to the profession, and any such should not try to become teachers at all.

The personality aspect of the teacher is related to the setting in which he expresses his profession. He is responsible for an attractive intellectual and physical environment both at school and in his private life. It is one of the ways in which the teacher can enhance his positive attributes. This translates itself into the way in which the school room is arranged and the way in which the personality of the teacher blends with his setting. If a person likes books, for example, they will probably be evident not only physically but in their effects as shown by diversity of interest, awareness of ideas and good taste.

Discipline and motivation lie very close together in this matter; increasing interest begets greater attention to more learning. The teacher unconsciously imparts this to the students. The teacher who accepts only perfect attention as satisfactory and inspires his students to work as nearly as possible to their capacities has very little trouble with problems of discipline. Part of this is exemplary and part of it is firmness; both are associated with basic personality.

There is no iron clad formula for assessing the exact content of the three components of prefessionalism in the social studies teacher. The relative admixture and composition of knowledge, personality and methodology is different with each individual. There are broad guides, as has been suggested, and there are numerous particular opinions as to what makes the best teacher, but no one has an exclusive claim to perfection. Herewith is presented a checklist, naming the various attributes that might add up to a good teacher of social studies. The neophyte might use this list as a guide to his own preparation, or it might be used by others to judge his progress.

### Social Studies Professional Checklist

| Knowledge of subject matter | Low | | | | High |
|---|---|---|---|---|---|
| Accuracy of fact | 1 | 2 | 3 | 4 | 5 |
| Specific subject of instruction | 1 | 2 | 3 | 4 | 5 |
| Associated facts and principles in: | | | | | |
|    Science | 1 | 2 | 3 | 4 | 5 |
|    Social sciences | 1 | 2 | 3 | 4 | 5 |
|    Humanities and arts | 1 | 2 | 3 | 4 | 5 |
| Conceptual understanding | 1 | 2 | 3 | 4 | 5 |

| | | | | |
|---|---|---|---|---|
| Current affairs | 1____ | 2____ | 3____ | 4____ 5 |
| Acceptable English usage | 1____ | 2____ | 3____ | 4____ 5 |
| Psychology (theory of learning, view of human nature) | 1____ | 2____ | 3____ | 4____ 5 |
| *Overall knowledge of subject:* | 1____ | 2____ | 3____ | 4____ 5 |

Methodology
Room management

| | | | | |
|---|---|---|---|---|
| Physical setting | 1____ | 2____ | 3____ | 4____ 5 |
| Discipline | 1____ | 2____ | 3____ | 4____ 5 |
| Techniques of instruction | 1____ | 2____ | 3____ | 4____ 5 |
| Motivation (recognition of individual differences, interest, intro. to topics) | 1____ | 2____ | 3____ | 4____ 5 |
| Organization | 1____ | 2____ | 3____ | 4____ 5 |
| Choice of material (suitable coverage, appropriate level and language) | 1____ | 2____ | 3____ | 4____ 5 |
| Variety of method | 1____ | 2____ | 3____ | 4____ 5 |
| Evaluation (self, students, program) | 1____ | 2____ | 3____ | 4____ 5 |
| *Overall use of methods:* | 1____ | 2____ | 3____ | 4____ 5 |

Personality

| | | | | |
|---|---|---|---|---|
| Grooming | 1____ | 2____ | 3____ | 4____ 5 |
| Cooperation (subordinates, colleagues, superiors) | 1____ | 2____ | 3____ | 4____ 5 |
| Intelligence (ability to adapt to a situation, insight, perception, sense of humor) | 1____ | 2____ | 3____ | 4____ 5 |
| Awareness of others' feelings | 1____ | 2____ | 3____ | 4____ 5 |
| Self-analysis (objectivity) | 1____ | 2____ | 3____ | 4____ 5 |
| Poise (dignity, pleasant outlook, firmness, balance) | 1____ | 2____ | 3____ | 4____ 5 |
| Enthusiasm (vivacity, liking for children, joy in teaching) | 1____ | 2____ | 3____ | 4____ 5 |
| *Overall personality:* | 1____ | 2____ | 3____ | 4____ 5 |

| | | | | |
|---|---|---|---|---|
| OVERALL APPRAISAL AS A TEACHER: | 1____ | 2____ | 3____ | 4____ 5 |

As there is no absolute way of specifying the exact ingredients of professional training, there is no single blueprint for achieving the status of professional social studies specialist. Many routes are open. There are, however, certain accepted practices found in most institutions which train secondary social studies teachers. In general, the first requirement is or ought to be an undergraduate liberal education with a major in one of the social sciences or history culminating in the bachelor's degree. This will usually insure a mimimum breadth of acquaintance with human knowledge and the heritage of Western man in particular.[6] In addition, there is usually a credential specification that the candidate acquire a year's work or more beyond the bachelor's degree, including a certain number and type of units in professional education. The national average requirement in professional education is something like fifteen semester units, usually including educational psychology, history or philosophy of education, teaching procedures and practice teaching. Often there are additional courses required in audio-visual education, tests and measurements, special applied psychology or educational sociology.[7]

It really makes very little difference how a desirable result in teacher preparation is achieved. The important consideration is that some kind of sensible balance be maintained between the two professional components that can be taught—content and method—and that appropriate personalities are chosen and cultivated for candidacy to the teaching profession.

### 4. Suggested Further Reading

There are, generally, three groups of textbooks available to teacher trainees in the social studies, including two distinct approaches.

First there are the older books stemming from the 1930's, many of which have been revised many times. The best known of these is Edgar Bruce Wesley and Stanley P. Wronski, *Teaching Social Studies in High Schools,* 4th ed. (Heath, Boston, 1958). A similar book but perhaps with more emphasis on the subject content of social studies is Arthur C. Bining and David H. Bining, *Teaching the Social Studies in Secondary Schools* (McGraw-Hill, New York, 1952), 3rd ed.; see particularly the chapter on "The Development of Methods of Teaching." Not revised since its first appearance is William C. Bagley and Thomas Alexander, *The Teacher*

---

[6] See Willis D. Moreland, "The Academic Preparation of Social Studies Teachers," *Social Education* (December, 1958), pp. 383–386, showing that a majority of institutions put more emphasis on breadth than on specialization in one discipline. As a comparison, dealing with social science requirements for the bachelor's degree in all fields, see Jennings B. Sanders, *Social Science Requirements for Bachelor's Degrees,* U.S. Department of Health, Education and Welfare, Office of Education (Washington, D.C., 1959), in which it may be seen that every college graduate can expect to take up to one-half as many courses in the social sciences as the social studies specialist.

[7] See *Requirements for Certification,* 17th edition, 1951–1953, compiled by Robert C. Woellner and M. Aurilla Wood (University of Chicago Press, 1952).

*of the Social Studies* (Scribner's, New York, 1937). I. James Quillen and Lavonne A. Hanna, *Education for Social Competence* (Scott, Foresman, Chicago, 1961, rev. ed.), is basically a report on the Stanford Social Education Investigation begun in 1939.

Among the newer books are: Maurice P. Hunt and Lawrence E. Metcalf, *Teaching High School Social Studies* (Harper, New York, 1955), which stresses the psychology of the biosocial approach and philosophy of the Dewey pragmatic school; Maurice P. Moffatt, *Social Studies Instruction* (Prentice-Hall, New York, 1954), which emphasizes attitudes and techniques of instruction; and Dorothy McClure Fraser and Edith West, *Social Studies in Secondary Schools* (Ronald Press, New York, 1961), new and up to date but not substantially different from some of the older books.

There are several books written from an entirely different direction of approach, with several authors attempting to illustrate various phases of social studies instruction and curriculum development, yet designed as textbooks. Among these, the most comprehensive is *Educating Citizens for Democracy: Curriculum and Instruction in Secondary Social Studies*, edited by Richard E. Gross and Leslie D. Zeleny (Oxford University Press, New York, 1958).

## THE SOCIAL STUDIES TEACHER

Jack Allen, "The Modern Social Studies Teacher," NEA *Journal* (November, 1952), and *The Teacher of the Social Studies*, edited by Jack Allen, Twenty-third Yearbook, National Council for the Social Studies (Washington, D.C., 1952).

Thomas A. Bailey, "The Obligation of the Teacher to Be a Scholar," *Social Education* (December, 1949).

William H. Cartwright, "Competencies Needed by Social Studies Teachers," *High School Journal* (October, 1956).

Earl S. Johnson, "The Social Studies Teacher as Therapist," *Chicago Schools Journal* (May–June, 1951).

Calvin W. Stillman, "Toward a Profession of Social Science Teaching," *Journal of General Education* (April, 1955).

## METHODOLOGY

Howard R. Anderson, "Trends in Teaching Social Studies," *School and Community* (February, 1951).

J. S. Caruthers, "Another Look at the Unit Approach," *Social Education* (January, 1957).

Mary E. Cunningham, "Junior Historians," *American Heritage* (September, 1949).

Stanley E. Dimond, "The Role of Generalization in Teaching the Social Studies," *Social Education* (May, 1958).

Arthur H. Doerr, "A Plea for Improved Writing in the Social Sciences," *Social Studies* (April, 1958).

Kenneth Evans, "The School and the Social Processes," *Social Education* (May, 1949).

Richard E. Gross and Frederick J. McDonald, "The Problem-Solving Approach," *Phi Delta Kappan* (March, 1958).

Jean F. Hamilton, "Creating a Learning Situation," *Social Education* (January, 1954).

S. H. Jones, "Generalizing in the Social Science Classroom," *Social Education* (December, 1957).

Curwen Stoddart and Charles H. Hession, "The Psychocultural Approach to Social Science," *Journal of Higher Education* (June, 1951).

PROFESSIONAL PERSONALITY

Gardner Murphy, *Personality, a Biosocial Approach to Origins and Structure* (Harper, New York, 1947), is a serious and scholarly work showing many findings in empirical study and much reflection on the problem of man's social and psychological organization.

Edwin R. Carr and Robert G. Risinger, "The Professional Growth of the Social Studies Teacher," *The Teacher of the Social Studies* (Washington, D.C., 1952).

Committee on Standards of Certification, National Council of Geography Teachers, "A Survey of the Academic and Professional Preparation of the Critic or Supervisor of Student Teaching in the Field of Geography," *Journal of Geography* (April, 1952).

Jonathan C. McClendon, "The Social Studies Teacher in School and Community," *The Teacher of the Social Studies*, Twenty-third Yearbook, National Council for the Social Studies (Washington, D.C., 1952).

Horace T. Morse, "Social Studies Teachers for College Programs of General Education," *The Teacher of the Social Studies*, Twenty-third Yearbook, National Council for the Social Studies (Washington, D.C., 1952).

Alice W. Spieseke, "The Preparation of Secondary School Social Studies Teachers," *The Teacher of the Social Studies*, Twenty-third Yearbook, National Council for the Social Studies (Washington, D.C., 1952).

Earl T. Willis, "Core Curriculum and Teacher Preparation in the Social Sciences," *Social Education* (February, 1953).

## 5. Suggested Activities for Further Study

1. Upon the basis of reflection and further reading attempt to assess the qualities of personality requisite to good social studies teaching. Make a checklist of the attributes you consider most desirable, then decide which of them, if any, can be cultivated. Try to summarize a statement of desirable personality and ways in which to achieve it.

2. As a check on the above exercise, interview a number of junior and senior high school students and ask them what they think the most desirable characteristics of their teachers are or ought to be.

3. Make a critical comparison and write a short essay on two such articles, representing two different points of view, as may be found in Jack Allen, "The Modern Social Studies Teacher," *NEA Journal* (November, 1952), and Cardinal Newman's view of the teacher in his essay on the university.

4. Read and review Xenophon, *The Education of Cyrus*, translated by H. G. Dakyns (Everyman's Library, 1914), and attempt to fit the personality

of the teacher who wanted to "set" in his student's "heart the threefold love of man, of knowledge, and of honour," into the pattern of modern criteria set up for social studies teachers.

5. Attempt to find some example of social studies teachers who have entered politics and have been elected to public office. What are some of the problems such a person might encounter?

# 7
# Techniques of presentation

Not a mother, not a father, will do so much, nor any other relative;
a well-directed mind will do us greater service. . . .

BUDDHA, 544 B.C.

## 1. Diversity and Unity of Methodology Aimed Toward Learning

The teacher teaches and the student learns—a mutual enterprise,
and there is no one correct way to do it. Every teacher learns about
educational philosophy, the psychology of learning, generalized and
specific techniques of teaching. It is, therefore, not the purpose here
to enter into a discussion of the best philosophical systems of pedagogical procedure. No teacher can learn one foolproof set of methods
before he enters the profession—nor afterward. Naturally, it is necessary to have a basic philosophy and as much information as possible
concerning specific ways of doing things. From these the individual
teacher will find out in time how to adapt his knowledge to the end
of furthering the knowledge of his students.

Among modern books on the subject, Gilbert Highet, in the *Art of
Teaching,* has managed to generalize an attitude out of a long teaching career. His book illustrates what each individual teacher must do
in the course of his time at teaching. Always holding the goal of increasing his students' understanding, he will take advantage of every
idea or method that seems applicable. What works for one teacher,
for one class, in one situation, will not necessarily be universally successful. The result is what counts.

Any list of specific methods attempting to be exhaustive would be a
veritable catalogue, and it would overlap every other such list but not
be in complete accord with any of them. In general, however, there
are three fairly distinct large categories of teaching technique, with
infinite variations, and each associated with a philosophy. (1) The
most traditional organization of material and method assumes essen-

140

tial passivity of the students, arranged in fixed position and responding only to the authority of the teacher. (2) Since 1900 a different view of learning and human nature has produced a reaction to the idea that the student is an "empty vessel" to be poured full of authoritarian wisdom. Whole systems of education have since been based on a thoroughgoing permissiveness, and students have been allowed to pursue their own way through or around bodies of knowledge. (3) Both extremes—authoritarianism and permissiveness—have also been combined to produce a true modern balance. Neither rigid control nor complete classroom and curricular anarchy is allowed to override good judgment and balance of teaching methods. In this type of teaching procedure there is an attempt to blend the best of the old and of the new.

Each of these general methodologies will emerge in identifiable form in direct proportion to the teacher's understanding and acceptance of a theory of learning. The behaviorist, for example, would be inclined to feel sympathy for some sort of activity program, and even though he only lectured to his class he would probably want them to exhibit some kind of activity to reinforce their learning. There are a good many different theories of learning, none of which is based on completely scientific findings in psychology; there is still much to find out concerning the actual process and nature of learning. No hard and fast rule, therefore, can be given as regards the best theory or the best methodology. If it is remembered that all of the theories and all of the methods have been shown to be useful in various situations, there will be less difficulty in choosing a particular tool for a particular task.

Key points should be kept in mind in selecting any technique. (1) Bio-social adaptation of the individual to his situation is a widely accepted psychological approach. (2) Multiple reinforcement of learning occupies the bulk of thinking in recent educational psychology.[1] (3) Reflection as an intellectual activity can be a learning and reinforcing device. (4) Bodily movement on the part of the student does not necessarily have anything to do with learning. A person can sit perfectly still and learn. (5) Students need to have a certain amount of control and security in knowing what their limits are, but they also need some degree of freedom, especially of thought. (6) Students need something to look at, something to do and at least some opportunity to express themselves.

[1] Gardner Murphy, *Historical Introduction to Modern Psychology* (Harcourt, Brace, New York, 1949), pp. 26 ff., 60, 105.

Most important, in keeping with the different kinds of social studies materials, is the need to diversify the attack on any given problem. This may be accomplished through choice of methods as well as by selection of materials. As tools for individual students to elucidate their learning situations, reflection, rationalism, authority, reason in its pure state, intuition and common sense, may be summoned to the task of solving a problem.[2] Numerous books on general teaching technique and procedure give detailed ways in which various specific approaches may be used.[3]

No matter which one or combination of methods is used, topical, chronological, question and answer, lecture, problem, project or laboratory, socialized or textbook, based on whatever theory of learning, it is necessary to provide both diversity and control. Assuming some degree of socialization of the classroom which is generally prevalent now, and an appropriate degree of student participation in the class activities, here are a few practical suggestions that may be depended upon in most cases.

### Diverse Materials and Objectives

Social studies as a school subject, so diverse in content, so wide in application, probably requires a basic textbook in order to keep both teacher and student directed continuously toward coverage of the specified material. It must not be assumed, however, simply because there is one basic text, that all pertinent information is contained therein. No maximum limit on learning should ever be set. For the able student no textbook will suffice. On the other hand, for those whose capacity falls below the average an ordinary textbook will seem much too difficult. For an average class, then, both simplified and enriched material must be provided in addition to a basic text.

One of the best ways to insure diversification of approach, to provide for reinforcement of basic skills, knowledge and generalizations, to take advantage of modern trends and to blend the best of the old

[2] Maurice P. Hunt and Lawrence E. Metcalf, *Teaching High School Social Studies* (Harper, New York, 1955), p. 53.

[3] Ernest R. Bayles, *Theory and Practice of Teaching* (Harper, New York, 1950), and Kimball Wiles, *Teaching for Better Schools* (Prentice-Hall, Englewood Cliffs, 1952), are outstanding in their explanations of student participation methods of teaching. Earl S. Johnson, *Theory and Practice of Social Studies* (Macmillan, New York, 1956), relates theory to practice specifically in the social studies. Edgar B. Wesley and Stanley P. Wronski, *Teaching Social Studies in High School* (Heath, Boston, 1958, 4th ed.), pp. 344–345, 349 ff., lists many social studies methods by name.

and traditional with the new and experimental, is to employ a unit approach. If a unit of socially significant learning is envisioned in the light of the objectives of social studies and with an evaluative scheme in mind, any or all possible methods may be employed to reach those objectives. Student interest becomes less of a problem and the principles of a field theory in study may be utilized. The modern unit of study is best adapted to the task of bringing to bear the widely different findings of the various social sciences to the specific solution of certain problems, always with the aid of the many particular methods available in social studies teaching.

## 2. Description of Combination Methods

### Unit Method

As one considers the possibilities of unit organization in a social studies field it becomes apparent that almost any logical arrangement of facts, concepts, activities and references might be possible. One widely accepted view of the unit of instruction is just this type of organization: a selection of a group of closely related topics as the basic intellectual core of the unit, such as the events surrounding the expansion of Europe at about the opening of the sixteenth century. These first level facts fall quickly into an outline, usually chronologically listed in a history course. Next, it is logical to develop a concomitant series of generalizations and higher level abstractions, or "facts" of a more sophisticated nature. A good unit would necessarily include all along the way, in the outline of facts and abstractions, specific references for the students' use in learning the needed background. Audio-visual reinforcement of the learning process might be in order, and the unit outline should include integrated use of such materials as they are indicated by the basic concepts to be illustrated. There is an almost unlimited range of activities that students may participate in which can be used to enrich and reinforce the various aspects of the unit of work. Each activity is represented by a special method of instruction, such as sociodrama, construction, outside reading, and so on. As an activity is chosen it should be entered in the general plan of attack on the unit in its proper place.

At the start of a unit there needs to be a special initiating activity of some kind. Again, the specific method to be employed is immaterial and the possibilities are very great. A lecture by the instructor or by a visiting specialist brought in from the outside, a film, a free discussion, a field trip—many, many different kinds of things are possible. As at the beginning, so at the end of a unit there should be a special emphasis on the matter of bringing the particular study to a close: a culminating activity such as a test, a play, an exhibit or a trip. The culmination of one unit can also be used to initiate the next one, especially in history, since there is a fundamental continuity in the experience of man as he builds his heritage. A field trip might be used in this way.

To help initiate a unit, bulletin board display of pictures taken from a magazine or obtained in the many ways available might help immeasurably in getting the students interested in the topic being presented. One of the simplest and most obvious ways of accomplishing this can be illustrated by means of Washington's birthday, a national holiday that usually requires some special attention in school. In February of any year, dozens of American magazines carry pictures of George Washington. It is a simple matter to cut out one of these, mount it on a colored paper background and post it on the bulletin board. In a way not possible by any number of words, the picture will call students' attention to the nation's first president. A bulletin board committee ought to be part of every teacher's class organization. At the same time, the teacher should keep part of the bulletin board reserved for the illustration of his program of study.

Arrangement of the furniture within a room is also important. A table moved to a central position and bearing a number of selected books and articles concerning the topic under study make it easy and attractive to begin reading. Variety in such display cannot help provoking some degree of interest. Even such a small thing as rearrangement of the desks or chairs tends to stimulate, if not interest, at least curiosity.

Since the social studies are concerned with the findings from a number of different scholarly fields, the unit method of instruction offers the opportunity to incorporate many different types of material into the examination of one certain topic. A generalization arises from the study of a group of facts, say, concerning the background of Atlantic exploration after 1492, exemplified by the apparent general fact that Europeans went out in search of new fields and thereby discovered great wealth in the New World. Such a generalization is easily verified by historical data. What might be left out of the students' deeper understanding of such an idea could be neglect of any examination of the economic principles that soon became involved. Banking, insurance and joint stock enterprise developed, following the discovery of new lands and resources. An expansion and inflation of the European economy set in which can be described rather simply at many different levels, but in order to understand and appreciate it fully, the student must examine the process of banking, the principles of insurance and the structure of corporate enterprise based on invested capital. The minute study of these matters is the purview of economics as one of the social sciences, but the social studies as the school outlet for those social sciences ought to take advantage of their learning. A course in history, administered in units of instruction, can readily incorporate enough of economic theory at such a point to stimulate interest and edify the students. Where this might be difficult to achieve in a straight textbook coverage of a social studies subject, if a unit method is used, then it is simple to insert the needed information and the appropriate references.

Thus unit organization of the materials and special methods of a social studies topic becomes a methodology in itself. It is more than a mere technique and is often called the unit approach rather than method. The primary requisite is a point of view that will allow the imaginative instructor to arrange and organize all available and pertinent information around a nuclear idea, and then select and provide references, aids and activities that will enable his students to master the basic material. A means of carrying out this method is to outline the information, list the learning materials and indicate the activities and special techniques to be used along with the objectives of study and the hoped for outcomes.[4]

## Socialized Recitation

One of the major long range aims of social studies is to bring students into a sense of awareness of their society and to stimulate in them a feeling of social responsibility. Man lives in societies, not as a lone being, either physically or intellectually. Therefore, social studies methodologists have attempted to develop various techniques for the purpose of socializing the classroom situation. Although the socialized recitation is labeled as a particular method, it is, as the unit method, more of a whole orientation to approach rather than a set method. This type of attack on the problem of learning in a group is characterized by many different combinations of separate techniques just as the unit approach is.

The identifying mark of the socialized recitation is its major re-

---

[4] See the recent framework statement of the California State Board of Education issued as *Report of the State Central Committee on Social Studies* (Sacramento, 1959), mimeo., for philosophical and curricular guidance in the selection of units.

liance on verbal communication rather than on reading and writing. All activities, however, might very well be used from time to time. As a basic structure in this approach there must be an outline of material to be covered, either in a textbook, a number of books or presented in some other fashion. As each part of the subject is covered, the students are presented with questions designed to stimulate the mental activity of the class and to produce some kind of answer. The answers may be written out in advance and read during class, or they may be produced in a discussion situation where the students may be required to "think on their feet."

Study guides become an important adjunct to this type of teaching. Each segment of learning is represented by a list of questions, passed out daily or at less frequent intervals. Study guides exist in a profusion of forms ranging from the printed and elaborate aids accompanying textbooks, to the simplest kind of statement prepared by the teacher and passed out or written on the blackboard. They are always characterized by a question element, and therefore fit very well into the socialized recitation approach.

It is obvious that this method can be almost identical to that described under the unit method, simply by the addition of study guides. The real difference would lie in the outlook and theory of the instructor. One concerned with information of a specified nature and believing that verbalization in a group is best will tend to rely on the socialized recitation with the aid of study guides. It may be generalized that both methods are more student-centered than some others, but the socialized recitation implies that the teacher is important as policy former, adjudicator of choice in setting problems for the students to work on, and that the curriculum is best established by a higher authority. Coverage of the topic is of greater importance than depth in this method.

STUDY GUIDES. In general there are three types of study guides that may prove especially useful in teaching social studies. The first type consists of individual and class project assignments, described in outline with appropriate suggestions as to source materials, time limits for completion of the various parts of the project and general methodology to be used. Second, there is the outline of a specified period of time in class, showing the main topics to be covered, the time to be consumed and the references to be used. Third, there is the bibliographical guide which may be separate from either of the above or attached to them. The bibliographical guide may be of any scope or length but it should always have two identifying marks: it should carefully specify the applicability of the selections, and it should give complete and accurate identification of the items.

Following are samples of study guides ranging from application in the eighth grade to the twelfth grade. They have been prepared and used by various student teachers in the University of California, Santa Barbara.

## BIBLIOGRAPHICAL RESEARCH GUIDE [5]
Eighth Grade Social Studies

Unit:       The Westward Movement
Directions: From the books listed below, select one which interests you.
            Read the book. Decide why the person about whom you chose
            to read is important in the Westward Movement of the United
            States. Which single event in his life do you consider the most
            exciting?

            Share what you have learned with the rest of the class by:
            (choose one)
            1. giving a short (3 to 5 minute) oral report.
            2. writing a two page report to include in your notebook.
            3. making a project which demonstrates clearly what you have
               learned.

            This assignment will be due in three weeks. By next class, decide
            on a book. By next week, decide how you want to present your
            findings.

### Reading List

   Each book listed below tells the story of an individual who played an
important role in the Westward Movement of the United States. (If you
would like to read a book which is not included in this list, please check
with me before you start your reading).

Baker, Nina, *Pike of Pike's Peak* (Harcourt, Brace, New York, 1953).

Brown, John Mason, *Daniel Boone: Opening of the Wilderness* (Random
   House, New York, 1952).

Beals, Carlton, *Stephen Austin, Father of Texas* (Whittelsey House, New
   York, 1958).

Daugherty, James H., *Daniel Boone* (Viking Press, New York, 1939).

Daugherty, James H., *Marcus and Narcissa Whitman, Pioneers of Oregon*
   (Viking Press, New York, 1953).

Eaton, Jeanette, *Narcissa Whitman* (Harcourt, Brace, New York, 1941).

Farnsworth, Frances, *Winged Moccasins: The Story of Sacajawea* (Julian
   Messner, 1954).

Garst, Doris S., *Buffalo Bill* (Julian Messner).

Garst, Doris S., *Kit Carson: Trail Blazer* (Julian Messner).

Garst, Doris S., *Bigfoot Wallace of the Texas Rangers* (Julian Messner,
   1951).

Garst, Doris S., *Chief Joseph of the Nez Perces* (Julian Messner, 1953).

Garst, Doris S., *Joe Meek, Man of the West* (Julian Messner, 1954).

Havighurst, Walter, *George Rogers Clark, Soldier in the West* (McGraw-
   Hill, New York, 1958).

James, B. R. and Marquis James, *Six Feet Six* [Sam Houston] (Bobbs-Merrill,
   Indianapolis, 1943).

   [5] Prepared by Dorothy Sherwin Collins, Santa Barbara, California, 1958.

Le Sueur, Meridel, *Chanticleer of the Wilderness Road, A Story of Davy Crockett* (Alfred A. Knopf, New York, 1951).

Seymour, F. W. S., *Meriwether Lewis, Trail-Blazer* (Appleton-Century, New York, 1937).

Wyatt, Edgar, *Cochise: Apache Warrior and Statesman* (Whittelsey House, New York, 1953).

**RESEARCH GUIDE** [6]
**Eighth Grade Social Studies**

Unit:      Discovering and Exploring a New World

Directions: Study the paragraph written below. From your reading in the textbook and in related sources, gather the information you may need to complete this assignment for your notebook. You may want to include charts and maps.

You are a young map maker living in Italy in 1490. In order to sell your world maps you must make them accurate and up-to-date. You are always anxious to learn the latest news about the explorers from Spain, Portugal, England, France and the Netherlands.

Describe your world map as it is in 1490. Tell all the changes you made on the map until you retired in 1545.

[6] Prepared by Dorothy Sherwin Collins, Santa Barbara, California, 1958.

**BIBLIOGRAPHICAL RESEARCH GUIDE** [7]
Eleventh Grade United States History

Unit 2:              The American Revolution and Founding of the Nation—The
                     U.S. Constitution
Directions:          Choose one of the following books to read. Prepare a five
                     minute oral report on one of the subtopics on page 3, using
                     material from the book you choose.
Time schedule:   Tuesday class will go to the library to select books. If you
                     have a book or report topic in mind, not on the list, discuss
                     it with me to see if we can arrange to include it. Thursday:
                     Hand in written statement including book, author, and topic.
                     Be sure the book you choose has adequate information on
                     your topic. *Two weeks from Friday:* Begin oral reports.
                     Talks will be given in the order they appear on the list. If
                     more than one chooses the same book, the reports may be
                     presented in the form of a panel discussion, if desired.

| *Books* | *Choose this book* |
| --- | --- |
| F. Morley, *The Power in the People,* New York, 1949. | If you like philosophy, want to delve into some of the philosophical aspects of our political system, like lots of quotes of interesting thoughts. |
| B. Rodick, *American Constitutional Custom,* New York, 1953. | If you like to know "why." Examines customs of the times which influenced the way our nation was founded. |
| Holcombe, *Our More Perfect Union,* Massachusetts, 1950. | If you like the challenge of a difficult book to gain a firm background in our Constitution and its development. |
| S. G. Brown, *We Hold These Truths,* New York, 1948. | If you like to get your information first hand. If you've ever wondered what Patrick Henry said just before he said, "Give me liberty or give me death." Selected documents of famous speeches, papers, etc. |
| B. Findlay, *Your Rugged Constitution,* Stanford, 1950. | If you like cartoons, illustrations, fun, worthwhile reading. Examines Constitution section by section and explains it. |
| C. B. Swisher, *The Growth of Constitutional Power in the United States,* Chicago, 1946. | If you are interested in the Supreme Court and would like to know the effect of court decisions on the Constitution. |

[7] Prepared by Gwen Landeck, Santa Barbara, California, 1958.

E. Walker, *Our National Constitution*, California, 1949.

If you want an interesting, illustrated book to strengthen your grasp of the things we've been covering.

E. Corwin, *John Marshall and the Constitution*, New Haven, 1919.

If you are interested in people and want to know more about a leading figure in American history.

## TOPICS FOR REPORTS [8]

Choose one of the sub-topics below (A–F) for your five minute oral report.

I. The Birth of the Constitution.
    A. The delegates to the Constitutional Convention.
    B. The Compromises made at the Constitutional Convention.
    C. The Ratification of the Constitution.
    D. *The Federalist Papers*—What they are and who wrote them.
II. The Constitution.
    A. The Duties of the President outlined in the Constitution.
    B. The Powers of Congress outlined in the Constitution.
    C. The Judicial Branch as outlined in the Constitution.
    D. The Separation of Powers as outlined in the Constitution.
    E. Checks and Balances envisioned in the Constitution.
    F. The "Elastic Clause."
    G. Amending the Constitution.
    H. The Bill of Rights.
III. The Constitution Today.
    A. How the Constitution keeps pace with the Twentieth Century.
    B. Amendments to the Constitution (Not including the first ten).
    C. The Constitution and Twentieth Century Civil Liberties.
    D. Segregation and the Constitution.
    E. The Commerce Clause.
    F. The Expansion of the President's Role.

[8] Prepared by Gwen Landeck, Santa Barbara, California, 1958.

### Multi-text or Research Method

A particular emphasis may be given to problem solving in the social studies. Based on a scientific methodology (described below) questions or hypotheses are developed in a class in order to have a problem to solve. Regardless of the techniques employed, the posing of problems will be at the center of the enterprise. As in the other combination methods proposed in these pages, this one depends upon the philosophical leanings of the instructor. If he is inclined to adherence to the biosocial interpretations in psychology and has a belief that students can be brought to recognize and understand their own best intellectual interests he will likely to attempt a problem solving approach based on hypotheses growing out of the students' own interests either felt or implanted. This particular turn of philosophy on the part of the teacher is adaptable to the use of a unit orientation using also a scientific problem solving technique.

After the general outline of material to be covered is established, usually from the basis of a curriculum guide furnished by the school district, units of instruction can be selected and reference material provided. In group discussion the specific problems for study can be evolved, based on the initiating activity. These problems are then broken down into cogent questions to be answered, after which the references are searched for illustrative material to solve the particular problem. Rather than being concerned only with a "right" answer discovered in a certain text between specified page numbers, the questions are open, first to discussion, then to a systematic research in all of the materials available in order for the students to find a tentative explanation. This, in turn, may give rise to further discussion and to further questions. There is rarely a total and final answer either in social or natural science. Findings are always to be held tentatively in keeping with true scientific attitude. This is the hallmark of scholarly outlook, of research, of seeking for the truth at any level.

One of the variants of a research and problem solving approach to social studies is known as the multi-text method. This is simply a descriptive name for the general method with extensive use being made of more than one text covering approximately the same field. Ordinarily, different texts in the same subject, say world history, are very much the same in basic factual content, but each one will vary in interpretation in the same degree that the personalities of the authors diverge from a standard pattern. Sometimes this is a great difference. If the teacher can select four or five texts with as many different philosophic points of view, he will then have a reservoir of research materials that can be made to illustrate a topic or problem in a variety of ways. In regard to a question of causal relationship in history this may become a very fruitful and thought provoking exercise for the students. As an example, causes of World War I are multiplex and subtle; they are not agreed upon by the many scholars who have worked in the field. Several texts may be found that will diverge so much in interpretation that even the basic identity of fact will be obscured. If the nuances of different opinion do not exceed the powers of perception of the students these differences can become the basis for a great deal of learning and constructive discussion.

### Core Programs

In many schools, especially in the lower secondary grades, there is a tendency to lump two or three subjects together under one teacher during one allocation of time. This is generally called "core." It is common to find, in the seventh and eighth grades, two periods a day given to social studies and language arts. Sometimes this is increased to three hours with health or some other aspect of natural science included. In some schools the device is simply an administrative measure to satisfy legal subject requirements and still keep the younger pupils under the control of one teacher during a major block of time in the school day. If this is true each subject is handled as a separate entity with no particular emphasis on a core of learning point of view.

In other cases the program embraces a philosophic attempt to integrate the subject matters of two or more disciplines into one learning experience. There are many versions of the core program, and almost as many definitions of what it should be. There is very little professional agreement as to what it really is.

There are, however, some common elements in all such programs. First, they all have social studies as the real "core" of learning. In nearly every instance the objectives include primarily the intention of broadening the students' knowledge and understanding of human behavior and experience in some of its multiphase manifestations. Second, there is usually an emphasis upon learning by experience. Purely academic achievement is ordinarily only a part of the attempt, with considerable attention to social adjustment. Third, language arts and communication are necessarily involved as part of the subject material on the ground that proper expression is implicit in understanding anything else.

It is, therefore, absolutely necessary for any social studies teacher, involved in such an endeavor, to be aware of more than his already overburdened background of knowledge. He must, as a minimum, command some degree of competence in history, geography, sociology, psychology, economics, anthropology and political science, as well as English grammar, composition and literature, and certainly the rudiments of speech.

To teach a core program successfully with an integrated approach a teacher must also be able to view, study and present a subject as a unit, yet be able to dissect it into all of the different disciplines which it represents. In short, the teacher must himself express that integrated personality which he hopes to induce in his students. Unfortunately there is no short cut to mastery of enough different disciplines of knowledge. Success is possible, but it requires tremendous effort and ability.[9]

## Motivation

Teachers are continually searching for devices to get students to learn. Motivation seems to be a problem that is never wholly solved. In the matter of scholarly achievement it would appear that the use of the language of mature scholarship is appropriate even though the level of performance might fall far short of the expectations of a professional. To use the term "research" with secondary students is a tactful way of letting them feel a sense of responsibility to objective scientific ideals. It must always be remembered that interest is directly proportional to knowledge; the more the students know, the more they will want to know. That is a psychological axiom which is not exploited enough by teachers. Students can be junior scholars at the secondary or any other level, but they must be told of the possibility. By letting them into the "mysteries" of scholarship—its language—the more likely they are to have respect for and desire to emulate those who possess knowledge.[10]

[9] See Irene S. Taub, "Ten Years with the Core Curriculum," *Social Education* (February, 1955), pp. 66–70, says, "There is just no doubt that the requirements of the core program increase the demands on the ability, time, training and experience of the professional staff. It is an arduous program." The author said, however, that despite the difficulties the core program is worth attempting. Morris Gall, "The Historical Novel in Twelfth-Year Core," *Ibid.*, pp. 75–79, gives a different impression. His experience with social studies–English taught to exceptional children with the aid of study guides seems to be highly successful and rewarding.

[10] Lawrence M. Fried, "Children Enjoy Research," *Social Education* (October, 1954), pp. 255–256. S. P. McCutcheon, "Why Should They Do It? A Technique of Student Motivation," *Social Education* (January, 1938), pp. 11–13, talks about increasing interest by knowing more.

Good teaching in any field is not simply a matter of knowing a number of tricks. Any number of devices or specific techniques will be insufficient unless the teacher is interested, full of his subject and dedicated to making this interest and content contagious to his students. Above all, he must know *what* he is teaching. He can only learn *how* to present it after he has achieved confident success himself in the content.

## Scientific Method

Regardless of the teaching methodology adopted or of the set of specific techniques and devices that each teacher will develop, there is a general method of thought and procedure which may be adapted to any teaching save sheer authoritarianism. One of the most important objectives of all education is to teach and cultivate a scientic method and attitude toward investigation. No subject is better suited to this than the social studies. Research is the heart of scientific examination, and in social studies there are almost limitless opportunities to make hypotheses which can be corroborated or rejected by available evidence. At any grade level in any of the fields of the social studies there are questions which concern every citizen. As a case in point, a twelfth grade class in sociology examining social adjustment, might scientifically study the evidence concerning the American family and the institution of marriage. To these people the question of when and whom to marry is of great interest. They might, as a class, hypothecate the most appropriate age for both boys and girls to begin married life. At this point each individual could then, to the best of his ability, be required to gather as much statistical information as he could on the subject. Next, they might be asked to get representative expert opinion, both from printed sources and from interviews with professional experts. At last, in a panel discussion they could present their evidence. It would be possible to derive a tentative conclusion which could be compared with the original hypothesis. In such a procedure there would have been reading for a specific purpose, analysis of statistics, interviewing, organization of information, and presentation as well as a gain in knowledge about a certain subject. The result should form a better basis for future decision in an important matter (marriage) than mere chance which would have to be the alternative of the ignorant. This type of study illustrates the scientific method as used in scholarly investigation. It cultivates knowledge and assesses the range of probability, and at the same time demonstrates a point of view. The process consists of hypothesis, research, tentative conclusion, followed by comparison of findings and hypothesis again. The hypothesis is either corroborated, modified or rejected. In any case, new hypotheses are suggested for futher research. The process is infinite.

Scientific methodology is dependent upon a point of view rather than upon difficulty of the subject. This attitude must be primarily a seeking for truth, at whatever level of sophistication. The discovery of a third grader concerning the type of food and shelter enjoyed by a local tribe of Indians is true knowledge to him equally with the more advanced understanding of the quality of resistance to the Stamp Act achieved by the eighth grader; truth about current practices in American marriages and family life arrived at by young adults in the last year of high school, if discovered and corroborated objectively, is exactly the same in essence as new contributions to man's total knowledge made by mature scholars and expressed in learned language in weighty monographs. The attitude brought to investigative study, the objectivity of research, the discerning use of source materials, the critical analysis of ideas and evidence are all attributes of learning. They may be present at any age in any learning situation. It is a sacred trust and duty of the social studies teacher to cultivate this attitude in himself and in his students.[11]

### The Social Studies Laboratory

Although not a certain method of instruction, such as the unit method or the socialized recitation, the particular setting and equipment used in the process of instruction has an unmistakable effect on the way in which learning takes place. Just as the peculiarity of the teacher's mental orientation bears on the specific learning process, so does the setting in which it takes place. Truly, the great teacher can teach anywhere, but he will be more effective, get more and better results, if the situation in which he finds himself is physically conducive to the task. Teaching social studies needs some equipment: books, maps, pictures and other audio-visual aids. It seems a simple truism that if the teacher has an interesting and important body of knowledge and a satisfactory method of presenting it, he also ought to have a pleasant, adaptable and well equipped place in which to practice his art.

[11] See Stanley E. Dimond, "The Role of Generalization in Teaching the Social Studies," *Social Education* (May, 1958), pp. 232–234, and Richard E. Gross and Frederick J. McDonald, "The Problem-Solving Approach," *Phi Delta Kappan* (March, 1958), pp. 259–265, for further examination of the method of arriving at generalizations through a scientific study of source materials.

An ideal might be to have each classroom set up and equipped with all of the necessary paraphernalia, with its own library, maps, globes and other aids. Financially this is usually impossible, although a certain minimum set of tools might be expected in every room. Beyond this, though, there are almost innumerable other items of equipment that could be procured for assistance in meeting the aims of the social studies.

The social studies laboratory or library or workroom, as it is variously known, is a highly desirable addition to any secondary school in which the teachers use a diverse methodology and go beyond the simple use of one textbook and a rigid curricular pattern. Such a room or building might be of any size. It should have a few basic essentials: good lighting and ventilation, adequate bookcases and other storage facilities, table and chairs to accommodate the students and teachers who are to work in it. As social studies classrooms and officers are usually arranged in secondary schools, in a departmental grouping, the laboratory ought to be central to this cluster of rooms and easy of access. Ideally such a center should have a full-time attendant, not necessarily a teacher, but someone who might be responsible for the security of materials and who might act as a secretary to the various persons using the facility.

As to the contents of such a laboratory, there is no formula other than the needs of teachers and classes as they encounter the problems posed by a study of social relations. First in consideration, necessarily, will be the books to be placed in this central position. Beyond the textbooks found in all classrooms, whether a single book for each student, or a multi-text collection, the laboratory library should be built around two basic groups of books. There should be fundamental and authoritative reference works such as encyclopedias, atlases, multi-volume or cooperative histories, geographies and other social science works. This group should include outstanding and detailed biographies of important personages, such as Sandburg's *Abraham Lincoln* and Freeman's *George Washington*. It should embrace printed collections of source material for history, economics, sociology and anthropology, American government and political theory. There should be books on all of the subjects of interest to the student and teacher of social studies, including pertinent monographs as they become useful. It is very unlikely that any school suddenly will appropriate the money to equip such a room and buy even the basic collections of books at one time. This sort of thing must grow over a long period. The second group of printed materials should include the periodicals of interest and usefulness in teaching social studies. The range here is even wider than in the field of books. There are numerous periodicals devoted to the field, in all degrees of difficulty and interest. No attempt can be made to enumerate them, but certain outstanding examples come readily to mind. *American Heritage*, a semimonthly journal, written in lively style with illustrations, devoted to American history, is probably the best magazine of history for secondary schools that has yet appeared in English. A daily newspaper, for example the *New York Times*, is really almost indispensable to the proper education of young people in the social studies. What better way is there to get maximal use out of it than to place it in the social studies laboratory? The *Congressional Record* would be useful. It is voluminous and much of it is quite unreadable, but it is the most complete record of day by day events publicly transpiring in the congress of the United States. One cannot believe that students can approach understanding the complexity and breadth of congressional activity without some experience with the record of those happenings. All kinds of pamphlet documents of government and industry, some edited and some not, are available on every hand. Whereas such things might not be used very much in a regular classroom situation, in the social studies laboratory they could be collected and filed by everyone concerned and used as the occasion arose. As an example, the United States Government Printing Office issued for the Department of Labor a little paper book, *Apprenticeship Past and Present*, priced at ten cents, but containing information not readily found elsewhere. There is a welter of commercially printed or foundation sponsored booklets, very cheap or free of charge, and extremely valuable. Some samples: *The Story of Tea* (American Education Press), *Rubber* (Wesleyan University and The Firestone Tire & Rubber Company), *Japan, Free World Ally* (Department of State) and countless others. As materials for source problem discussion these kinds of publications—"fugitive" materials—are unmatched.[12]

Supplementing the literary material to be used in social studies there is a great range of audio-visual material. Most important, even essential, to visual aid in social studies is the great variety of maps that is presently in existence. Every classroom should have some maps of its own, but a central collection, ever expanding, of the more specialized maps and charts of the social sciences should be kept in the

---

[12] See Derk Bodde, *China's Cultural Tradition* (Rinehart, New York, 1957), one of a series of illustrative pamphlets on enduring problems in world civilization. The Amherst Series (Heath, Boston), does a similar thing for United States history.

laboratory for use there or to be borrowed by classes. Relief maps and globes of various types are frequently useful but too expensive to be duplicated for every room.

Other audio-visual materials, including the equipment to use them, might be stored in the laboratory and coordinated in their use by the attendant. Films, slides, pictures, records, tapes and three-dimensional exhibits find their most frequent use if they are easily found and are actually located near the point of use. In this way it is also possible for the individual teachers to share their own materials that might otherwise be used only occasionally and by only one person.

The social studies laboratory, especially if it has a full-time attendant, might also serve as a headquarters for coordinating the use of another aid to teaching—difficult to classify, but really in the audio-visual category—the resource speaker drawn from the community, the lawyer, politician, scientist or other specialist who might be invited from time to time to visit a particular class or the whole student body and give a lecture or demonstration. If each teacher has the independent responsibility of procuring such services he is either likely not to do it at all or to start a run on some certain person's time that may be embarrassing. If the social studies laboratory maintained a list of willing and competent resource persons and if there was a scheme for equitably distributing the burden on such persons, then the most effective use of their services could be made.

The social studies laboratory, then, can become a combination center of storage, use and coordination of the diverse materials and activities of the social studies, so diverse itself. The laboratory may be a museum, workshop and library, always having the characteristic of producing that dynamic, sparking interaction among physical things and students. It is a place where ideas can come to life and be illustrated with activities and artifacts that will help to make the ideological experience more lasting and pervasive in the lives of students as they continue on into the future.[13]

Using the basic principle just described, every teacher can emulate

---

[13] See James W. Baldwin, "Teaching the Social Studies in Units by the Laboratory Method," *Social Studies* (February, 1949), pp. 58–63; Arthur C. Bining and David H. Bining, "The Laboratory and the Laboratory Method," in *Teaching the Social Studies in Secondary Schools* (McGraw-Hill, New York, 1952), 3rd ed., Chapter VIII; Maurice P. Moffatt, "The Classroom—A Learning Laboratory," in *Social Studies Instruction* (Prentice-Hall, New York, 1950), Chapter IX, for various other descriptions of the social studies laboratory. For some empirical findings on the actual beneficial results in using this methodology see Erwin H. Sasman, "Do Laboratory and Field Experiences Change Behavior?" *Phi Delta Kappan* (March, 1958), pp. 265–267. His answer is "yes."

FIGURE 7. A social studies laboratory under the direction of Joe Blake at La Colina Junior High School, Santa Barbara, California.

the idea even if the expensive equipment and special quarters and attendant are not available. Just a simple book shelf or table at the rear of the room can be the same order of nucleus for the activities of the social studies laboratory. The students themselves can serve the functions of attendant. After all, it is not primarily the equipment one has that can be stored and catalogued, but rather, the idea, the point of view is the important thing.

## 3. Other Methods and Procedures

Methods, procedures and techniques are all terms that may be used almost interchangeably in describing how teaching is to be done. Methodology may be thought of as a generic term to cover the whole range of activities in which teachers participate while working toward the end of getting students to gain access to the body of knowledge and the plethora of skills which support civilization. Certain general methods of approaching the problem in social studies have been outlined above. Now, as each of the methods treated includes a number of special procedures, it is necessary to attempt to catalogue and arrange those procedures and describe them in more detail. It is possible to derive from a methodology specific techniques by means of which the teacher furthers his total methodological aim.

In the unit method, for example, it may be observed that there is a great variety of separate procedures, each of which will probably not be used in every unit, but which must be mastered in order to use them when it is appropriate. These techniques, by name, can be listed and described. It is not anticipated that any sound and diversified methodology will employ only one of them for every occasion. Exclusive reliance on only one device, one procedure, will surely become deadly for student and teacher alike, although this has been done many times in the past and probably will be done again and again in the future.

### Single Procedures which Could Be Used as the Basic Approach to Social Studies

| Method | Principal Goal of Method |
|---|---|
| Single textbook | Coverage of a specified content |
| Lecture | Authoritative generalization |
| Question and answer | Clarification of points covered |
| Source | Critical judgment |
| Problem | Progressive problem solution |
| Project | Learning by experience |
| Directed study | Planned mental growth |
| Tutorial | Individual guidance |

These are some of the single methods which could be used to facilitate the learning of students in social studies. Each one could also be used as part of a unit organization and orientation, or with the aid of the social studies laboratory. With any one of them a particular bent of the teacher might also be employed, such as a biographical approach to the selection of material to illustrate the various topics under consideration, or a geographic approach emphasizing the setting for events and circumstances of social relationships. There might be many alternative modifications of any of the above procedures used as the main vehicle of attack on a body of knowledge.

Short description of the procedures listed is worthwhile here, but first, it must be noticed that the list falls into three separate categories. The first three methods are dependent upon a source of authority outside any pupil influence, a textbook or the teacher being paramount. The next three are more concerned with the objective of pupil growth in experience and critical judgment based on his own psychological and social needs, therefore there will be considerably less emphasis on coverage of a specified body of material, although no less total learning might be required. Objectives other than purely academic might very well occupy the most important place. The last two methods are mainly concerned with the individual student's ability to master, as independently as possible, all of the ramifications of a sequential body of information as well as to develop his critical ability in a maximum fashion.[13a]

### Analyses of Various Methods

SINGLE TEXTBOOK METHOD. This is perhaps the most widely used basic approach to social studies today, and also perhaps the least desirable because of its lack of variety and flexibility. Fortunately, if one textbook only is used, one or more other major techniques will probably also be employed from time to time. For example, in conjunction with a standard textbook divided up into chapters or units of work, most enterprising teachers will at least use some kind of a study guide, and they will test the progress of information mastery periodically. In fact, a good many textbooks have accompanying material to serve this purpose—study outline or workbook and standardized test items. The unrelieved use of a single textbook is the easiest method to learn and to follow, but it is also the least interesting, and therefore we would surmise the least effective.

LECTURE METHOD. In common with the single textbook method, lecturing is based on traditional authority, and it is a time-honored device for imparting knowledge. Of late years lecturing as the only means of instruction has been much maligned. It has been assumed that students' interest span is too short to allow the maximum value to be received from the lecture. It has been further assumed that aural learning is not sufficiently reinforced to make a lasting impression. Altogether, the lecture method for secondary students has fallen into very ill repute, although it is the principal form of instruction employed in most colleges and universities where it is seldom criticized at all.

On the other hand, the lecture, under the name of informative talk or explanation, is a perfectly valid and useful means of giving students information and a point of view peculiar to the lecturer. The method itself should not be condemned. The culprit is the bad

---

[13a] Cf. Edgar B. Wesley and Stanley P. Wronski, *Teaching Social Studies in High Schools* (Heath, Boston, 1958), 4th ed., pp. 344–346.

lecturer or unsuitable topic. People flock by thousands and annually pay a great deal of money to hear good lectures or talks. The adjectives used to describe them are often such words as inspiring, interesting, fascinating, dynamic, informative, exciting. School and college lectures often receive the same kind of praise, but sometimes, and rightly, lectures are called didactic, dull, bigoted or even stupid. This type of lecture ought never to occur. Good lectures are important, in teaching and for entertainment.

New insights concerning the lecture method have recently been achieved in the light of which this method appears to have much more of a place in teaching than has been the general opinion of educational authorities. As a single methodology, as the only way in which information is passed from the instructor to the students, lecturing should still be treated with suspicion, but as a technique of description, of explanation and clarification, the lecture has a unique place. It is indispensable, and not as a means of getting the professor's notes into the notes of the students without adumbration on the part of either party. If the lecture method is useful and effective with young college students, then it must also be with the same students only a year or two before they enter college—if it is used correctly.[14]

Lectures are best when confined to a supporting role, devoted to introductory and explanatory uses. An optimum length of time to devote to any one lecture is possibly in the order of twenty minutes to half an hour, followed or preceded by some other activity. An interesting aphorism persists out of a kind of folk wisdom, attributed to a seasoned bishop introducing a young curate to his new post. His sage advice was said to have been: "Always remember that there are no souls saved after the first twenty minutes." Of course, no such stricture need be placed on a special visitor who might deliver an hour long lecture on a particular occasion.

Lecturing is a high art, and its successful performance depends upon the teacher's extent and depth of knowledge, his awareness of human factors of interest and motivation, upon a dramatic sense and above all upon the need for a logical philosophical position—a need to know what he is doing. "Just anybody" cannot lecture satisfactorily. The lecturer must be prepared in a full sense. He must have a great reserve of background knowledge from which to draw as it is needed. As John Stuart Mill once said, he must be "full of

---

[14] Thomas F. Stovall, "Lecture vs. Discussion," *Social Education* (January, 1956), pp. 10–13, indicates that the amount of learning in both situations is the same, but that discussion produces better results in critical thinking.

his subject." He must have something to say that is to the point, and when he has said it he must know how to quit talking. Organization and emphasis are essential to the good lecture. Mere argumentation, without an opponent, is usually to little purpose. Demolition of a straw man may be good demagogical procedure, but it is not proper pedagogy. The lecture is primarily designed to impart reinforcement of key ideas and facts and to place them in a context of thought, to present a philosophical whole out of a number of related fragments of information that can be obtained piecemeal by other means but not put together sensibly without the mature judgment and wisdom of a good teacher. Lecture subjects also must be considered. Some topics simply do not lend themselves to lecture treatment. For example, the facts and statements in the American Constitution can be read and learned independently from a common text by any number of persons. On the other hand, certain subjects cannot be understood without considerable help by any students in a high school group. To continue the example of the Constitution, although the actual text of the document can be learned, the content of peripheral meaning, the context in which the organic law of the United States operates, may be very difficult of comprehension, even a closed realm, unless some explanation is given. This kind of explanation is often best done in a short lecture.

PROBLEM OR PROJECT METHOD. The next group of methodologies mentioned above has one common denominator. They all employ a problem formula by which some kind of solution can be reached. The emphasis is on the process and not on the subject; the manner in which man affects his environment through rational patterns of behavior derived by observation, criticism and reflection, seems most important here.

What has been described as a unit method of instruction may or may not have such a major objective, but in any case a problem or project approach is easily incorporated into the unit structure of study. As a whole method of teaching, with no attention at all to coverage, the study of one problem after another, always with the stress on method and process, might not achieve the job of rounding out a balanced education. On the other hand, without some rather pointed instruction and experience in the matter of problem solving, of scientific methodology applied to social situations, no education can be said to be complete. As with the other single methods presented here, this one is best suited to supplementary use along with many others.

THE CASE METHOD. In the same general category of methods dealing with process and problems the case method has been a specialized example for a long time. The legal profession since Roman times has used a case method of study in the preparation of its practitioners. It is a good method insofar as any single procedure can accomplish the training task, but it is too narrow an approach for the whole purpose of social studies. The case method, however, is often fruitful and interesting as a variant to illustrate a hypothesis or generalization. Individual cases, in this way, finally can come to represent valid examples of a principle that usually will apply in similar situations. The pitfall seems to be that there might be a mistake in the case chosen with disastrous results.[15] The case method may be worked into a longer single project method by means of expanding the study of a certain case, for example, the particular social organization of a single town might be the case, and subsequent study of the setting and people might be the project.[16]

SOURCE METHOD. The method of instruction primarily involving source problems falls into the same classification as the project or other problem methods, but with one distinction. The materials of instruction, best suited to historical study, are of a source character. That is, they are original materials of historical evidence that could be used to write history as it is generally known to students. A problem in source analysis might involve different interpretations of a given document, or actual doubt as to its authenticity, or it might be concerned with the significance of a particular source in a certain way. For example, such a source document as Captain John Smith's account of the founding of Virginia could be selected as the basic material of instruction for a topic using the source problem approach. First of all, the authenticity of the story has been established, i.e., the account that Smith wrote is known to have been written by him at the time he said it was, before 1610; it is truly the record of what Smith thought he did and saw. The problem involved as regards a high school class in early American history would be to assess the significance of the founding of Virginia in relation to the whole history of the colonies and the United States, to evaluate the part that Captain Smith played in the early venture, to decide whether or not his assertions of importance of the place of Virginia stand up

[15] See Donald Culver and Susan Baker, "The Case Method," *Social Education* (January, 1959), pp. 25–28, for suggested applicability in social studies.

[16] *Near Home*, 25 min., sound, blk. and wh. film, International Film Bureau (1946), shows such a project being worked out in an English classroom.

by comparison to other foundation attempts. A comparative study of this document and, say, other similar ones—those of William Bradford of Plymouth after 1620 and Father White of Maryland in the years immediately following 1632—could be used. Two things could be expected to emerge from this type of source problem analysis in a high school class: first, a detailed knowledge of a limited period in certain places would be bound to develop; second, it might be expected that a great deal of concomitant learning would take place in the methodology of history writing itself and in the matter of problem solving and critical evaluation, reflection.[17] It will be seen, then, that this group of methods is primarily devoted to the increase of skill in thinking and the process of achieving answers or solutions to problems, and only in a secondary way to the mastery of a large sequential body of information.

SUPERVISED STUDY. The two final methods are unique and possibly the best of all for achieving the maximum in learning and coverage of material. The uniqueness lies in their placing the teacher in a passive role and the student in the position of greatest possible intellectual activity. In these methods the student is expected to gain his skill, knowledge and insights through the process of absorbing and thinking about the material assigned. There is little emphasis given to the teacher's activity other than as a potential adviser and as someone to offer encouragement and coordination to the students' efforts.

Using supervised study, again, as in all of the other methodologies, is probably best suited to supplementing a varied program, but it might be used all alone. The procedure in its simplest form is to assign a certain topic, included in a certain number of pages in a single common textbook. After this the students read the passages indicated while the teacher patrols the room, helping with word meanings and difficult interpretation on an individual basis. The procedure may be embellished by all sorts of additions, as passing out a study guide with questions to answer either orally or in writing

[17] See Ralph Adams Brown and Marian R. Brown, "Jameson's *Original Narratives*," *Social Education* (February, 1959), pp. 59–60, lists an easily accessible collection of source materials for American history in the 19 volume collection generally known as the Original Narrative Series, and outlines a method of using them, including the simple process of duplicating these documents as mimeographed handout study guides. For the topics suggested above see *Narratives of Early Virginia*, edited by L. G. Tyler (1907); *Narratives of Early Maryland*, edited by C. C. Hall (1910); *Bradford's History of Plymouth Plantation*, edited by W. T. Davis (1908).

at a subsequent class meeting. In the case where supervised study may be incorporated into a unit method, the students may be allotted a short study period in class in order to get started in the process of answering questions, gathering data or writing reports. In any instance of supervised study the role of teacher is not active in an authoritarian sense, but rather of availability for help and individual consultation. This method is singularly valuable in teaching retarded students when the rate of advance is very slow and the differential in individual capability is great.[18]

Perhaps the greatest value of supervised study is the opportunity offered to increase the use of social studies skills. The use of maps, encyclopedias, dictionaries and the like is essential to maximum learning in the field, and each of these requires a certain skill which must be taught and learned. A period of study under the direct supervision of a teacher is optimum opportunity to get practice in the handling of such materials. The same may be said of writing, possibly the most important skill after reading in acquiring knowledge in social studies. One's own writing must be studied in the light of and modeled after the writing of others. Instead of the old fashioned three R's, we may think of Reading, Writing and History.[19]

TUTORIAL METHOD. Only a word can be devoted to this very best of all methods for teaching critical thinking, skills and a body of knowledge. In the first place it is largely impossible to use in American public schools because of the first requirement, time for the undivided attention of the instructor to the needs of a single student. The essence of this method is a face to face association between one student and one teacher for the purpose of furthering the education of the student. The oldest tradition of the tutorial method is in the universities of Oxford and Cambridge where it is still practiced.

Certain aspects of the tutorial situation can be incorporated into American public school social studies instruction, although as a general method it is not feasible except for the very rich. All teachers in high schools are usually willing to devote a limited amount of individual time to students after regular school hours, especially

[18] See Arthur C. Bining and David H. Bining, "Supervised Study," in *Teaching the Social Studies in Secondary Schools* (McGraw-Hill, New York, 1952), Chap. VI.

[19] Arthur H. Doerr, "A Plea for Improved Writing in the Social Sciences," *Social Studies* (April, 1958), pp. 127–135. See *Skills in Social Studies*, edited by Helen McCracken Carpenter, Twenty-fourth Yearbook of the National Council for the Social Studies (Washington, D.C., 1953), Chap. XIII.

those who show outstanding promise and are willing to put almost unlimited effort into their work.

The tutorial method involves the assignment, in agreement with the student, of a topic for investigation, along with suggestions as to where materials may be found. After this the student is expected to study on his own for a specified time (one week or more), write a paper using his best critical ability, report and read the paper to his tutor who in turn will dissect, discuss and argue with the position expressed in the paper, and make further assignment to rewrite the paper and repeat the process until a satisfactory result has been achieved. Obviously it requires a highly learned tutor, an intelligent and greatly motivated student and the time to bring them together under attractive circumstances.[20]

### Specific Supporting Procedures

GROUP DISCUSSION. Based on the work of twentieth century social scientists in the fields of sociology and psychology, such, for example, as Kurt Lewin, a new awareness has recently arisen of the peculiar values of discussion in groups, particularly small groups. The optimally efficient size of a small group could be somewhere in the order of eight to twelve persons.[20a] The arrangement of this group in a circular pattern in some peculiar and not entirely understood manner also affects the way in which the participants react to each other. A circle of seated discussants seems to allow a freedom of expression and an interaction that cannot be achieved in any other way. The two known reasons for this are (1) that in a circle where everyone more or less faces everyone else there is no physical indication of difference in status; there is an immediate elimination in this situation of the dominating position of the teacher "over" the group, and (2) that the eye span of the participants covers the whole group at once; this is impossible in any other seating arrangement. The first results of such arrangement are usually diffuse and lack the orderly efficiency of authoritarian organization, but within a very short time efficient handling of problems usually emerges, and leader-

---

[20] Gilbert Highet, *The Art of Teaching* (Knopf, New York, 1950), pp. 107–116, contains the best concise and entertaining description of the tutorial method as it was applied to his own education at Oxford.

[20a] "While it is a fruitless task to try to define a small group in terms of numbers, we may suppose that approximately 20 persons represents the upper limit of small group size, with two being the lower limit." (Michael S. Olmstead, *The Small Group*, Random House, New York, 1959, pp. 22–23).

ship will exert itself as a quick result of the easy alignment of sub-groups and personality axes which become apparent in a small group but would never show up in a larger assembly dominated by one person appointed to the job. Application in everyday adult life is obvious. Training, therefore, in group processes is one of the obligations of the social studies teacher. Using the small group discussion technique as a part of a methodology of instruction is not only in order and useful as a teaching tool, it is also a supplementary method of achieving some of the peripheral social goals of education—how to get the most out of human relations.[21]

Discussion for the purpose of evolving problems for a whole class to work on during the opening phases of a unit is best suited to activities of the whole group. Initial discussion should be held in the larger group with the teacher as moderator and director. After a hypothesis or a list of questions to answer has been set up, after the objective of the unit is well understood by all the students, and after enough information has been absorbed to point a direction in which investigation should go, the small group technique is often a useful device. An ordinary class of thirty or forty can be divided into four groups or committees. These committees can be given certain problems. For example, out of a list of twelve large questions three might be assigned to each of the four groups. Their objective would be to set up a work program for the purpose of finding material and learning its application to the solution of the questions. The various steps in the assigned responsibility are clear. First, decide what to look for, then, where to search, and third, to outline a report that will make it unnecessary for the other groups to repeat the same job for themselves. The small group should meet, select temporary leadership (a hallmark of the small group is its revolving leadership) and attack the problem. In the ordinary course of events in normal school work there will be some kind of deadline, but undue pressure for completion of tasks by small groups tends to disrupt the unique and dynamic quality of the operation.

One may wonder how four separate groups can function in the compass of one room without creating too much disturbance for anyone to get anything done. Ideally, each group should have a separate

[21] *Understanding How Groups Work*, Leadership Pamphlet Number 11, Adult Education Association of the United States (Chicago, 1956), especially p. 5. See also Kurt Lewin, *Field Theory in Social Science* (Harper, New York, 1951), p. 188 ff., and in general for a discussion of the theory that a group has similar dynamic qualities to a magnetic field.

conference room, but amazingly, it is possible to have several groups
going in discussion at one time in various parts of the same room.
The small clusters of interest seem to offer a more attractive pull on
the attention of students than is exerted in a negative way by the dis-
tractions. The key to group efficiency and effectiveness is the organization, the orientation of the furniture. It is most desirable to achieve
circular positioning, or second best, to have the people concerned
seated around a table (the warning here is that the person sitting on
the smallest side of any rectangle will preponderantly gain leadership
by this very fact). In any case, the group is left to commence its
function on its own. First a leader must be selected. Some previous
instruction in the necessity for this and in the mechanics of doing it
will expedite the group's deliberations. Next, the group decisions must
be made and recorded by some member of the group. If the committee first decides what it is to do, there will be little difficulty in
getting the job done. Incidentally, a small group situation seems to
make this fact clear in a way that no other process can achieve so well,
although it is sometimes a slow procedure. At the expiration of the
first committee meeting it is a good idea to have a general reporting
to the whole class by the various sub-groups. In certain cases only one
meeting is necessary, and for each succeeding problem it is interesting
to compose the groups in a different way. Surprising elements of leadership and imaginative capacity are uncovered in this fashion.[22]

Small group discussions are a little more difficult to handle than
some other forms of class procedure, but the results are rewarding.
Stimulation of interest and its consequent expansion of learning on
the part of the students is very gratifying. In actuality, the small group
method, in common with many other supporting methods, is not as
difficult to institute as it is unfamiliar. The real difficulty for the
teacher lies in his need to overcome an initial reluctance to attempt
something new, to inject some variety into his program of methodology. Procedures courses in college offer an ideal chance to practice
this method.

ROLE PLAYING. Group discussion is an invitation to use another
method of participating reinforcement of learning: playing out roles
as they appear to the students in spontaneous relation to the subject

[22] Cf. Mark F. Emerson, "Discussion Versus Argument," *Social Education* (December, 1952), p. 382, which discusses a technique of oral interchange in the
whole group. In the small group, even with student leadership, the problem of
prejudicial argument rarely arises to cause difficulty.

content under discussion. There is a play-acting urge, very strong in small children, which, if not allowed to flourish, will gradually die out of the conscious behavior patterns of adults. In the secondary age groups the urge is still strong enough to be taken advantage of in a learning situation. Akin to the therapeutic group procedure of psychodrama or the more easily handled sociodrama technique, role playing may become a very useful device in the social studies classroom. In connection with some episode in history, as an instance, the execution of the Open Door Policy in China at the beginning of the twentieth century, a dramatic situation may be set up in the classroom and various roles assigned without warning to members of the class. One might be given the role of the secretary of state, John Hay, another the role of the Dowager Empress of China, another the character of the President, and so on. With a small group of persons representing key figures in the real historical drama of the United States' arbitration of China's political and economic future, a classroom can become charged with the imaginative reconstruction of facts and their interpretation based on individual students' feelings and emotional outlook on the problem at hand. As each person is faced with the factual situation, only partly understood, he is called upon to act out and verbalize what he would have done had he been the historic personage whose role is being assumed. This requires an immediate kind of spontaneity and imaginative thought rarely called up by any other classroom procedure.

As in the case of group dynamics something unique happens to the participant, something that is difficult to explain simply, but something that has a particular value to the student involved. Perhaps it is mainly the actual involvement itself that is important here; the feeling that one is truly part of the past, inside the process of influencing one's own cultural heritage, is, at least, intriguing. Role playing is not a method that can stand constant repetition, nor can it be the primary technique in a total methodology, but as a support and to offer variety, it is worthwhile.

DRAMATIC READING OR PLAY. For the beginner, and still based on the play-acting proclivity of youth, there is a modification of role playing which may be easier to use. In the same situation as indicated above, the Open Door episode, a special reference on the subject may be used and followed verbatim by the students selected to dramatize the topic. From such a book as Foster Rhea Dulles, *America's Rise to World Power, 1890–1954* (Harper, New York, 1955), in the New

American Nation Series, may be taken descriptive passages which various students can then read to the rest of the class from a small group position at the front of the room. Perhaps at the close of this dramatic reading presentation, the same persons could be asked to assume the parts of some of the historic participants and play their roles to the extent of stating what they themselves would have done in the circumstances just described.

SOCIODRAMA. This particular method is best applied in the culminating stages of a unit of work and is perhaps most effective with younger students. At least, it will be better accepted by the majority of junior high school students than by the older people in the senior high school. In either case sociodrama is rather complicated in application and should be studied as a special methodological subject by the teacher.[23]

PANEL DISCUSSION. Dramatic in presentation and yet involving several students in the subject matter of their study, the panel discussion is a good illustrative or culminating activity for most social studies units. At the end of a particular period of group study on a given subject a reinforcing presentation of the salient points of that study is always desirable. The panel discussion offers a means for doing this. Especially interesting is this kind of presentation when the topic is controversial with two or more legitimate positions of honest difference of opinion.

The panel of commentators on a problem of current interest is commonplace on modern radio and television. The same pattern can be followed in the classroom. Several students can be allowed to prepare materials for presentation on various aspects of a problem and then give them orally in two or three minute reports as they are seated at a table before the class. After this, questions from the floor or from other members of the panel may be answered or discussed. Sometimes the repartee may become as lively and heated as it does on adult panels in civic meetings.

FIELD TRIPS. One type of panel discussion very important in American local government is the periodic meeting of city councils or county boards of supervisors. On these panels there are members whose political, economic and civic responsibilities are very real and very great. The discussions are often extremely heated and have far-reaching implications for the whole community in which they take place.

---

[23] Refer to Chapter VIII, "Materials of Instruction," under Non-Literary Aids in Teaching. See also *How to Use Sociodrama*, National Council for the Social Studies, How to Do It Series, No. 20 (Washington, D.C.).

What better way for students to learn the use and techniques of panel discussion than by a visit to a local city council meeting?

It may be inconvenient and time consuming for a teacher to arrange a field trip with his class, but on certain occasions this is one of the most rewarding ways of furthering the learning in social studies. Field trips ought to be used sparingly, they must fit into a specific need in learning, and they must be prepared for. The class must be motivated to make the most of the experience; they must know what they are going to look for, what it means to them as citizens and as students. Afterward the experience must be exploited and followed up with discussion and explanation of what actually was observed. Otherwise the field trip may be nothing but a vacation from a few hours of school.

Field trips for teacher trainees are essential to their proper introduction to the art and profession of teaching. Every social studies methods class should have the chance to observe experienced teachers practicing their skill.

The mechanics for arranging a field trip vary with school districts, but there is usually some office or individual who coordinates such activities. It is always necessary to get official sanction from the place to be visited, from the school authorities and from the parents of the individual students.

DEBATE. The debate may serve the same function as the panel discussion or other dramatic performance, but it has a special set of rules and a formal organization that make it relatively easy to master as a teaching method, but which also limit its application. The greatest advantage of the debate is its value in teaching the skills of organizing and using logical thought processes, and of calculated coolness in argumentation. Its weakness lies in the fact that only a few persons at a time can take active part in the debate itself. Most of the class must be passive and act in the role of listeners.

Debate is basically a competitive game, and as such there are certain rules to be followed. It is not absolutely necessary to follow the rules to the letter, but if the convention is to be changed then the name of the method will also have to be changed. It is best, therefore, to retain the traditional formal organization if the method is to be used in the social studies. The rules are simple: the two participating teams shall consist of two or three speakers, with the same number on each team. Each team shall have two or more constructive presentations and one or more rebuttals, but each team shall have the same number of the same length for each type. The affirmative side has the first constructive speech, then alternating with the negative side. The negative team has the first rebuttal speech. The affirmative side must make its definitions of terms to be used before the debate begins, and the negative then must agree or show cause why it cannot. Later there can be no objection to definitions as they are used.

The purpose of debate is to argue the desirability of adoption of a certain plan or policy or argue the morality of a past performance. The concomitant purpose is to give students experience in the organization and presentation of material in a logical and orderly fashion. The above rules apply to the setting for such an exercise. In addition there is the rule that the use of such a phrase as "ought to be" used by the affirmative does not refer to feasibility. The negative cannot expect to hold the affirmative debaters responsible for actual workability of a plan or policy in the light of law or history. The essence of the exercise is to practice logicality both affirmatively and negatively. Of course, there is another paramount rule based on the principle that he who asserts must prove. The affirmative, therefore, must prove its proposal for the edification of the listeners.[24]

As applied to social studies instruction the debate should be confined to areas of thought and knowledge that have or have had meaning for large parts of the society because, beyond the use of debate as a method, there is always the high purpose of social studies to learn about human relationships. The debate, or any other technique, has no place in an instructional program unless it contributes to this purpose.

A problem might arise in a social studies class as to the rightness or wrongness of a present policy, such as the value of capital punishment. This is a favored example and type of subject for debate. In setting up an affirmative and a negative the laws of the particular states must be consulted. They vary in this matter a great deal. In a state where there is capital punishment the affirmative would have to take the stand that it should be abolished: Resolved that capital punishment be abolished in the state of _____. The burden of proof must lie with the affirmative. Those advocating change must justify that change.

Outcome of such a debate, if it is a successful teaching aid, should be a general class advance in knowledge concerning the whole problem of penal practice, capital punishment in particular, and in the state concerned specifically. The resultant changes in attitude on the

[24] See George McCoy Musgrave, *Competitive Debate* (Wilson, New York, 1946), rev. ed., p. 9 ff., for a concise but complete analysis of the techniques of debate.

parts of individuals toward the rightness or wrongness of such punishment is unimportant in the learning process—they may be very important socially, but the objective is to learn and to get practice in organized thought and presentation. It is not to influence people emotionally, although this may happen too.

The essence of a successful debate presentation is organization and outlining. The steps are the same as in any outlining procedure. First, material is gathered, then arranged into categories. Next the main points have to be selected out and given precedence in the outline. Under each main heading the subordinate points and illustrations group themselves rather easily. The actual presentation based on the outline and divided up among the debaters in each case must have an introduction, an orderly transition from one point to the next and at the end a summation of the outstanding features of the proposal and the ways in which it is to be effected. The negative, speaking alternatively with the affirmative, must do its best to refute the argument for change and support the existing situation. Outlining and organization for both teams are exactly the same in method, but, of course, very different in content and outlook. Mere assertion of right, it must be remembered, is neither logical nor convincing. There must be evidence obviously supporting the assertion before it can have any weight.

BIOGRAPHICAL METHOD. Biography, particularly in the field of history, may be used in two general ways in the social studies. It is possible, but not highly probable that a teacher might either teach a course in historical biography as such, or the lives of great men. It would be more usual to use biographical material to illustrate movements and problems of the past or to assign biographies as supplementary reading to students in history courses.

In either case, biographies, such as those published in the Landmark Series or the Real Series, are very valuable. The seventh grader, as an example, who finds difficulty in mastering material concerning the United States in the modern world, may very well be able and willing to read a book on Thomas Edison and his struggles to get the world to accept electric lights. Such a book might even delve into nuclear power in the present world, and if it is couched in fourth or fifth grade language it may reach its mark. In the opposite case, a seventh grader with superior learning ability and advanced reading skill will gain greatly enriched knowledge from reading the life of Winston Churchill or Franklin Roosevelt, or any of the other great men and women in our age—*in addition to his regular textbook.* An enhanced result will have been achieved in both instances.[25]

WRITTEN REPORTS. By encouraging or requiring formal reports on the reading just described a teacher can incidentally add to learning in concurrent fields of study, such as English and logical thought. The better students may write their reports, maintaining a notebook file of the finished products over the course of a year or more for the sake of comparison. This may be a relatively independent activity on the part of the pupil. As for the less mature child, he may be allowed to present some of his findings in an oral report or as a contribution to a class discussion working toward a general conclusion.

ORAL REPORTS. Not only for the less talented child, but as a specific technique used by almost all teachers regardless of the general methodology favored, or of the composition of the class, the oral report is valuable to the student and convenient to administer by the teacher. In social studies a large part of successful learning depends on how well the student can verbalize his findings: put thoughts into words both written and oral, and express concisely the essence of what he has found out. The oral report of each student allows the group to share in each individual effort and it also allows the teacher an opportunity of recording progress for each student.

This method, limited as it is, could hardly constitute a whole program of teaching based on each child's telling the others what he has discovered. On the other hand, it is almost indispensable as a means of reinforcing certain types of learning. First, it gives the student making the report a chance to formulate and say certain vital things about the subject he is studying. This is one kind of individual reinforcement. Second, the rest of the class listening to a report gain aural reinforcement of things they themselves have met in their reading. Third, there is always the possible enrichments of everyone's knowledge through the individuality and resourcefulness of the reporting person.

It would be difficult and unwise to specify exactly what should go into an oral report, but there are some general principles that might guide the use of the method. Reports should, on a particular subject and at a particular time in the course of study, be centered around one generally known theme. All of the students, if they are working on a general subject, know something about all aspects of the subject,

---

[25] See John A. Garraty, "The Power of the Biographer," *Social Education* (November, 1955), pp. 295–298; also his *The Nature of Biography* (Knopf, New York, 1957), for a fuller explanation of the same theme.

but as individuals make special efforts to expand knowledge or interpretation of various parts of the topic they may fruitfully give oral reports. Each report should be rather short in most cases. From three to five minutes is ordinarily ample time for a student to make his points. If the project assumes greater proportions it falls into another category, the illustrative and discursive talk or lecture.

Each oral report by a student should be an exercise in the basic social studies skills. There should be a specific objective, an outline and careful organization. Skills of speech and other language factors must be given attention on the grounds that proper communication is best achieved within the framework of the conventions of our language.

As an example, one way in which oral reports can be used to good effect is to make them the chief vehicle of reporting a class's findings in problems of local government. State government normally supplies a variety of services to the citizens, such as labor management, police protection, mental institutions, etc. Each of these activities falls under the leadership of a department or bureau, and each department has some kind of legal basis and history. Each member of a class can be assigned the problem of learning about one specific phase of such government service with the intention of reporting orally to the rest of the class. Since some of the state government functions are more important or more extensive than others there is considerable variability in the difficulty of the topics. This offers a particularly good opportunity for the teacher to take into consideration the variable quality of his students' abilities. The more difficult topics should be given to the abler students.[26]

### Summary

As has been pointed out on several occasions, methodology is a diverse accumulation and application of special techniques and devices for the accomplishment in a school situation of learning results. The teacher and the students are all involved in the process of learning–teaching which is, in its turn, the conception, acceptance and achievements of knowledge of mastery, partly as an end in itself and partly for future pragmatic purposes. The teacher has the responsibility of furthering the whole process. This is done by means of a vehicle, a paraphernalia called methodology. It makes absolutely no difference what the method is so long as it achieves the best result. The best re-

---

[26] See *How to Use Oral Reports*, How to Do It Series (National Council for the Social Studies, Washington, D.C., 1954).

sult has been found to accrue from the use of a diversity of methods and combinations thereof.

### 4. Suggested Activities for Further Study

1. Work out a study guide including a topic assignment and a bibliography suitable for research in a given grade and subject.
2. Make an annotated list of books on teaching methodology which might be offered to a beginning teacher as a minimum guide in his first year.
3. Make a comparative review of Gilbert Highet, *The Art of Teaching* and Henry Harap, *Social Living in the Curriculum.*
4. What should a social studies teacher know about psychology?

### 5. Suggested Further Reading

GENERAL METHODOLOGY

*Education for Democratic Citizenship,* edited by Ryland W. Crary, National Council for the Social Studies Yearbook (Washington, D.C., 1951).

Henry Harap, *Social Living in the Curriculum* (George Peabody College for Teachers, Nashville, Tennessee, 1952), is a study of the core program in grades one through twelve.

Gilbert Highet, *The Art of Teaching* (Knopf, New York, 1950), is a sharp, anecdotal review of a philosophy of education in action. The book expresses the author's attention to and concern with knowledge, despite its avowed intention to tell "how to teach."

*Improving the Social Studies Curriculum,* edited by Ruth Ellsworth and Ole Sand, National Council for the Social Studies Yearbook (Washington, D.C., 1955).

Earl S. Johnson, *Theory and Practice of Social Studies* (Macmillan, New York, 1956), treats methodology from high school and college points of view, with an emphasis on theory.

Maurice Moffatt, *Social Studies Instruction* (Prentice-Hall, Englewood Cliffs, New Jersey, 1950, 1954, 1955), is a reasonably comprehensive presentation of standard methodologies in teaching social studies. Maurice P. Hunt and Lawrence E. Metcalf, *Teaching High School Social Studies* (Harper, New York, 1955), reflects the subtitle statement of its orientation, *Problems in Reflective Thinking and Social Understanding.* It is the only book in the field with this particular stress on the value of reflection as an aid to critical examination of material by students.

*Social Studies for Young Adolescents,* edited by Julian C. Aldrich, Curriculum Series, Programs for Grades Seven, Eight, and Nine, National Council for the Social Studies (Washington, D.C., 1951), implies certain methods although it is primarily concerned with curricular content.

Ruth Tooze and Beatrice Perham Krone, *Literature and Music as Resources for Social Studies* (Prentice-Hall, Englewood Cliffs, New Jersey, 1955), deals mostly with lower grades, but the idea of integrating the arts with social studies is not handled as well elsewhere.

## SPECIAL TOPICS

How to Do It Series, National Council for the Social Studies, is a series of small pamphlets costing 25 cents each, devoted to specific handling of certain methods in the social studies. The individual titles are:

No.  1, *How to Use a Motion Picture*
No.  3, *How to Use Local History*
No.  4, *How to Use a Bulletin Board*
No.  5, *How to Use Daily Newspapers*
No.  6, *How to Use Group Discussions*
No.  8, *How to Use Recordings*
No. 10, *How to Use Oral Reports*
No. 11, *How to Locate Useful Government Publications*
No. 12, *How to Conduct a Field Trip*
No. 13, *How to Utilize Community Resources*
No. 14, *How to Handle Controversial Issues*
No. 15, *How to Introduce Maps and Globes*
No. 16, *How to Use Multiple Books*
No. 18, *How to Plan for Student Teaching*
No. 19, *How to Study a Class*
No. 20, *How to Use Sociodrama*

The single most useful periodical in developing methodology is *Social Education*, published eight times a year by the National Council for the Social Studies, 1201 Sixteenth Street, N.W., Washington 6, D.C. Every issue contains at least one article devoted to a special methodology of instruction in the social studies.

In the particular field of group discussion and leadership, help is available from the findings of sociology. The Leadership Pamphlets of the Adult Education Association of the United States of America, 743 North Wabash Avenue, Chicago 11, Illinois, include such titles as *Understanding How Groups Work*, *Training Group Leaders*, and *How to Lead Discussions*.

# 8

# Materials of instruction

The general objects . . . are to provide an education adapted to the years, to the capacity, and the condition of every one, and directed to their freedom and happiness.

THOMAS JEFFERSON, 1784

## 1. Critical Thought and Reflection

The long range objective of social studies instruction is competent citizenship which is composed of knowledge, tolerant attitudes and acceptable behavior. The shorter range vehicle for achieving the greater aim is an organized sequence of specific information and certain techniques, coupled with the hope that more acceptable patterns of behavior will emerge along the way. This short range program may be a course in history, geography of the world, a study of the family in America, basic economics or any of the other diverse subjects which may present themselves. In any case, there will be a body of related information and a number of skills to master.

Critical thought is a great part of adequate citizenship. Its achievement depends partly upon intelligence, but mostly upon mastery of knowledge and a technique. A way in which to think, deductive-inductive reasoning which we call a scientific method, is quite essential and can be learned as a technique if accompanied by an attitude of willingness. It is, however, absolutely necessary to have a body of information about which to think, critically or otherwise. In general, it is reasonable to expect that critical attitudes of thought will develop if knowledge is gained by the method of scientific examination which has made possible the extension of civilization to the present time. In other words, gaining the objective of competent citizenship, with its element of critical thought, will be more likely to accrue with the acquisition of knowledge concerning the growth of that society in which citizenship is a birthright and in which the methodology itself grew.

Classroom application of scientific methodology may be likened to laboratory or library research which is conducted by independent scholars in order to advance the horizons of human knowledge. In every class, whether it be in seventh grade geography, fourteenth grade United States history, or in an advanced graduate seminar, students should have a problem, a hypothesis, a question to answer tentatively. Even in the primary grades children set up questions, seek information and draw a conclusion which leads to a further set of questions. It must be borne in mind that the answers are not absolute, that they are always tentative, and that they are subject to revision or rejection. As students progress in years and maturity their terminology becomes more complicated, and they can accept more sophisticated problems. A tenth-grade class in world history might undertake to elucidate and illustrate such a problem as religious faith in the Middle Ages, doing research in rather difficult books and documents, to arrive at a satisfying conclusion about that phase of Western cultural growth. As the same person approached the problem as a freshman in college each individual aspect of the project might be quite different and much more difficult. For example, a student might pose the proposition that Martin Luther revolted from the church partly for non-religious reasons; then he would have to examine psychological findings, economic studies and the philosophic content of Luther's mind as well as the contemporary historical record. His study might even grow into a graduate school problem with detailed research in the original documents and manuscripts which appeared at the time of Luther's posting of his Ninety-five Theses. In each case a conclusion is reached which is not a final truth. Each tentative conclusion gives rise to a new hypothesis to be examined and documented. In this way is each person's knowledge increased and therefore society's total understanding is expanded.

As the choice of material is governed by the objectives—both long and short range—so must each objective have a standard of evaluation. The subject matter can be tested in various ways. The techniques used can be judged in most cases. Mastery of facts concerning the church in the Middle Ages may be tested objectively and compared with other students' success in the same venture. Reading, writing and manipulating other materials can be evaluated more subjectively with emphasis on improvement of individual skill. Critical thought and application of scientific methodology are more difficult of measurement; but if a value is placed upon suspension of judgment in the inductive process, the very tentativeness of findings is a ground for evaluation. In short, evaluation without ultimate judgment, on the part of both teacher and student, is the logical growth from application of scientific methodology, with the hope that critical thinking will develop thereby.

## Reflective Thinking

Facts are available in many different levels of abstraction. In a social studies subject such as history there are two broad categories of "fact" which sometimes seem to have very little in common even though the two types might be associated with the same circumstance. First there are the simple, objective facts that can be recorded and re-examined later by an historian. An example might be the minute description of the Battle of Gettysburg as the step by step reconstruction of that historic three days could be achieved from looking at the field orders, the troop lists and disposition of forces. Such data are undeniably "fact" as it occurred. They tell a story, the record of what took place at Gettysburg, the physical outcome of the battle, who won and who lost, the individual units that participated, even to the extent of assessing heroism or the lack of it. This is one type of fact, incontrovertible recorded fact. With only this kind of fact, however, history is nothing but a journal of events. It tells us nothing about human nature and experience, about man's emotional structure and his advances and retrogressions. Nothing is hinted as to why people fought the Battle of Gettysburg.

Another kind of "fact" must be adduced in some fashion in order to assess the importance of the record as it can be discovered objectively. Every objective appearance has a subjective side, an emotional context attached to human intelligence, and this set of "facts" is both more difficult to find and less easily recognized than are the mere factual recordings of events. In connection with the Battle of Gettysburg, for example, why did two armies meet here in the first place? Again, it is simple to trace the journal of events in a military fashion that led up to the great battle in Pennsylvania, but that is not enough. There was the matter of states' rights, slavery, westward expansion, and above all, of human passions. Such facts, no less than the record of actual events on the battle field, can only be arrived at through a process of reflection. The historian must simply sit down and think about the facts at the first level that he can find and verify. He must consider other bodies of first level facts, such as the findings of psychologists in regard to human behavior, the cogitations of philosophers on the nature of man, on the empirical studies of government made by political scientists and others. Through the process of thoughtful rearrangements of all these patterns of facts, reflection, the historical scholar or secondary student can arrive at a higher level of factual abstraction concerning the single battle of the Civil War with which he started. Such questions might emerge, for example, as, "Would Pickett have conducted his heroic and useless charge as he did if he had not believed in slavery, in the innate subordination of one race to another?" Perhaps there is no answer, at least none that is completely satisfactory, but the exact record of the charge has nothing in it even remotely related to Pickett's attitude toward Negroes, yet he must have had one, and by thinking about it the student will also undoubtedly emerge with a richer and more complete understanding of what really took place, except that it will be at a more complicated, higher level of reasoning and abstraction.

Reflection is the only completely unique and original tool of scholarship that man has. No other creature can do it, just as no other creature can take advantage of the past experience of its kind. Reflective thought concentrated on the record of the human past results in wisdom for the exercise of human choice in the future. After reflecting, man does not always make the best choices, but without it any good choice would be totally accidental.

## 2. Choosing Literary Materials

*Reading*

In addition to setting up objectives, methodology and evaluative procedures, a most important element in the choice of materials must be recognized in the ability and interest level of the students. It is necessary to find reading matter within the capability of the student and at the same time appealing to his sense of dignity as a member of an age group. Further, students in any given class may range in reading ability as much as eight grades. In an eighth grade, for instance, it will be common to find persons with fourth grade and twelfth grade capabilities. It is, therefore, immediately imperative that learning materials be furnished with that much variation in difficulty. At the same time, the twelve-year-old with a reading capacity of an eight-year-old brother or sister yet has the same interests on a psychological basis as most other twelve-year-olds. His books, therefore, must be as interesting to him as more difficult ones are to other children. There are several series of publications

which attempt to take care of this situation, such as Landmark Books
(Random House). These provide topics and treatments appealing
to boys and girls of preadolescent and adolescent ages, but skilfully
graded for vocabulary difficulty ranging from fourth grade to adult.
Such books are primarily for the purpose of supplementing social
studies courses through expansion of limited subjects; there is, however, a growing tendency on the part of book publishers to apply
the principle of graded vocabulary to basic textbooks. There are
now a few available through the high school level. In any case, it is
important to have material appropriate to the students' abilities. It
does no good to set up worthwhile objectives, use good evaluative
techniques, and then provide only material which is either too difficult or too trivial for the children to bother with.

### Outside Reading

Educated persons read for pleasure and for the purpose of increasing
their knowledge and appreciation of things throughout their lives.
The whole process and experience of learning to read should merely
be an introduction to a lifelong habit. Much of the enjoyment in
reading is a matter of habitual skill in the technique of reading. If
it is easy, the habit is easy to cultivate. Reading can be easy for
nearly anyone if two things take place at an early age; if the introduction to the skill of reading is pleasant and thorough there will be
little pain connected with it, and if interest is engendered in the
reading material at the outset and at the level of psychological
readiness appropriate to the age level there will be little doubt that
reading will soon become a habit.

The function of the school in regard to reading is primarily to
get the student started. After he leaves school the student will not
have any further assignments in reading. If he reads it will be solely
because he wants to. His motivation will have to be self generating
from that time on. While he is in school the student may be urged,
or even forced, to read certain things, but the school's function will
not have been successfully fulfilled if the student does not continue
to read thereafter on his own initiative. This means that some sort
of self perpetuating motivation has to be incorporated into the process of teaching reading.

Social studies as a school subject has possibly the best opportunity
among all of the subjects to encourage and motivate students to
embark on a continuous experience of reading in diversified fields.
Every social study has a great many associated areas of investigation,

and practically all of them are reflected in some kind of belletristic literature such as novels, biographies, travelogues and dramatic productions. History, in particular, is most adaptable to illustration by means of novels and biographies, not to mention plays either read or performed. Every history course should be accompanied by reference to a list of supplementary books which can be assigned or suggested to students.

For the more willing and able students mere suggestion of titles to read outside of school is often sufficient. It probably should be the practice of teachers who suggest books on these grounds to keep some kind of record of achievement as it is reported. Perhaps two or three class periods a semester could be devoted to writing book reports or reviews for this purpose. The weight given to the grade in overall evaluation of a student's work in history should probably not be very great in proportion to the regular tests and other performance, but it should not be neglected, merely placed on a voluntary basis.

Where there are average or lower than average students the motivation to read outside of the regular text materials is a little harder to achieve. In this event the teacher will possibly have to make direct assignments and devote specified periods of class time to evaluation of the work. It is usually not good practice to require students to do the reporting on outside reading at home and turn it in as finished papers. There is too much temptation to copy others' work or to get someone else to do the job. It is better to have the students do their reading at home, take notes and appear in class prepared to write a short essay on the book in question under the supervision of the teacher.

Certain criteria stand as tested necessities in the assignment of outside reading and its evaluation. First of all, certain specified books should be listed from which the students can choose. The list submitted to them should be large enough so there will be some actual choice, the books must be readily available and they must have cogency and pertinency to the subjects under consideration in the class. Obviously it is essential that the teacher be familiar with the contents of the books recommended to the students. On the other hand, the selection should not be so large nor so indiscriminate that the students cannot tell the significance of each book or that they become frustrated at its very diversity and bulk. Being faced by too wide a choice is as bad as having no choice at all. In fact, the result in reading is likely to be about the same—nothing. An optimum kind of reading list supplementing a course in high school history might be about fifty books, divided between novels and biographies with a sprinkling of specialized monographs or special subject titles. Each book should be annotated briefly to indicate its pertinence to the field of investigation. The comment does not have to be long; in fact, it can be only a few words and still tell the needed information. Bibliographic information concerning each book should be complete and properly styled. These considerations are important for several reasons. Much of the information given in any school subject is only peripheral to the real purposes of instruction, but it should always be accurate and thorough, because a great deal of the outcome of educational effort is dependent upon the concomitant learning that takes place by way of the teacher's example or in the almost unconsciously gained attitudes implicit in any learning situation. Rather than a slipshod and indiscriminate listing of books, out of alphabetic order and without benefit of any identifying comment, it is much better to present an orderly list, executed in precise style and accompanied by a fruitful word or two. The hope of inculcating a desire to read throughout life will be much nearer fruition. An example:

Booker T. Washington, *Up from Slavery* (Doubleday, Page, Garden City, 1900), is the account, by a former slave, of the problems of Negroes after the Civil War. Aside from its value as a biography it points up a very important problem which is by no means solved even today.

### Teaching Reading in the Social Studies

How much time to spend on developmental reading in classes other than language arts is a moot question. Some maintain that reading instruction is the specific responsibility of elementary teachers in the time allotted for the purpose. Others feel that reading instruction is a continuing obligation in all grades and in all subjects. Something in between is probably the optimum treatment of the subject. Obviously, if children fail to learn sufficient reading skill in the elementary grades, and this skill is given mandatory attendance in high school, some attention must be given to repairing these disabilities. Since the basic skill needed to learn social studies material is reading ability it seems logical to devote some time to reading instruction. This amount of time must be balanced against the objectives of the particular social studies class, and geared to the general level of ability in the class. It would be absurd to overlook the basic intention of a course in United States history in order to attempt to raise the level of reading ability without regard to the facts and interpretations of our national history. It would be equally ridiculous to attempt to make students read American history couched in language and syntax of which they were ignorant. The text might as well be in Arabic if the students cannot read it in English.

It is therefore desirable for every social studies teacher to become acquainted with procedures designed to increase reading effectiveness. At least as a diagnostic device, it should be determined what the students' reading ability is in order to choose sensibly their reference materials. Further, it is probably desirable to devote a minimum of time to actual instruction and review of reading techniques, using the materials of instruction for the social studies objectives.

The following are some excerpts from a scheme of reading instruction, based on psychological findings and put into extensive practice in the high schools of Modesto, California.

## SOME BASIC PRINCIPLES AND SUGGESTIONS

1. Basic reading skills need to be taught at every level—first grade through college graduate level. There are new developmental skills to be taught as well as those skills the students have failed to learn or forgotten from an earlier period.
2. Students should always be given a purpose for reading—a purpose in terms of information or appreciation and another purpose in terms of skill.
3. If material is not at the student's instructional level, i.e., too easy or too difficult, little value is gained from reading instruction. Here is an easy way to tell if the material is correct for a particular student.
   a. Have him read aloud a few lines containing 100 words. He must accurately pronounce 95 per cent (not miss over 5) or the material is too difficult for him to gain maximum value from it.
   b. In checking comprehension by both factual and inferential questions, if the student consistently misses 25 per cent or more of the questions, get easier material. If he consistently gets 95–100 per cent correct, move him up to more challenging reading.
4. In assigning books for independent or recreational reading, the student must be able to pronounce 99 per cent of the common words (proper and place names excepted). He must comprehend

90 per cent based on factual and inferential questions. A person's independent reading level is usually 1 to 3 years below instructional level.

5. Most skills of reading can be developed in the natural setting of reading a short story, a section of a novel, or a chapter in a social studies book. By following a directed reading program in planning the reading assignment, these skills may be developed in all classes.

## DIRECTED READING ACTIVITIES

I. The development of readiness (orientation, preparation, motivation), 2–6 minutes.
   A. Attempt to interest the group in the particular story. Read the author's name and title of the story. Give background information. Read introduction to the story.
   B. Encourage students in discussion to share their background of information as geographical setting, customs, etc. Use illustrations, maps, charts, etc.
   C. Develop accurate concepts needed for the particular selection. Develop the relationship of the selection to the total unit of instruction or the previous reading.
   D. Give suggestions on how to read the story.
   E. Introduce the new reading vocabulary with an attempt to stimulate interest (three or four words only).
   F. Give a motive for reading. Use a motive question to give purpose to the reading.
II. Guiding the first silent reading (always done before oral reading), 10–20 minutes.
   A. Have students read silently as soon as you have given them the motive question.
   B. At least once a week they should be timed on silent reading and be informed of their rate (words per minute) and percentage of comprehension.
   C. As the student finishes reading he records the time elapsed and proceeds to answer questions.
   D. Types of questions.
      1. To stimulate interest and discussion. (Do you think . . . ?)
      2. To get facts.
      3. To get inferences. (Reading between the lines.)
      4. To develop working concepts. (What is the difference between . . . ?)

5. To relate previous experience.
6. To get the main idea.
7. To develop vocabulary and word recognition.
8. To develop organization and sequence.
9. To promote versatility. (Skimming, rapid reading, study skills.)
10. To provide for wider reading. (Reference books.)
11. To encourage use of dictionary. (Pronunciation and meaning.)

E. As a student finishes his questions he does independent reading until the entire class is finished.[1]

### Textbooks

The content of social studies instruction should be chosen in view of the objectives and the abilities of the students. It is usually impossible, therefore, to find all the necessary material for a given course within one book. This is especially true in the lower grades, whereas in the later grades of high school and the beginning years of college, subjects become more specialized and the student body a little more selected for aptitude, and a single text is likely to fulfill more of the purposes. Despite the inability of one book to encompass all the needs, it is usually desirable to have a central textbook and then to supplement its use with individualized selections from other sources. As Merrill F. Hartshorn of the National Council for the Social Studies has pointed out, ". . . the textbook is the single common denominator most frequently found in the classrooms not only in the United States but throughout the world." He continues:

A casual glance at instructional materials published in 1954 reveals many outward changes in appearance as compared with materials prepared in the past. Textbook format, type, illustrations, maps, and types of materials that the teacher may use in the classroom, have all contributed to the improvement and enrichment of this valuable aid to teaching. In addition, the content of social studies textbooks has been broadened. For example, the old history textbooks emphasized military and political history. Today history textbooks include also economic, social and cultural history, and introduce some of the geographic concepts that help to explain the course of history. Great efforts have also been expended to improve the accuracy and fairness of the content of textbooks.[2]

[1] Roger Chapman, "Teaching a Reading Lesson at the High School Level," mimeographed, n.d., Modesto City Schools, Modesto, California.

[2] Merrill F. Hartshorn, "The Improvement of Instructional Materials," in *Approaches to an Understanding of World Affairs*, edited by Howard E. Anderson, *op. cit.*, p. 441.

Alice W. Spieseke, "Bibliography of Textbooks in the Social Studies, 1955–1956," *Social Education* (December, 1956), again gave her annual choice of important books in each of the representative fields of social studies. These suggestions should prove useful to teachers, although if a textbook is to be chosen, it should be done on individual grounds arrived at by the teacher in view of his knowledge of the field and his own particular needs. Like all teaching materials, textbooks are constantly being revised and usually improved. "The more the teacher knows and understands such efforts, and the more the teacher helps contribute to such efforts, the more likely we are to achieve the overall objective of a stable world order."[3] This statement applies equally to all the materials that students and teachers use in the process of education. Authors and publishers are likely to be sensitive to the changing requirements of classroom use, and they are usually grateful for suggestions coming directly from teachers who will instruct from their books.

### Advanced Placement

In some American high schools, particularly in the senior year, honors courses have been set up for the unusually able and gifted students. These courses are designed for those students who know they will go to college and who have completed all of the graduation requirements a year before their contemporaries. They must be of very high caliber and have obtained grades of outstanding quality. It goes without saying that their teachers must also be of very high ability and achievement. In such classes there is practically no limit to the type and amount of reading that can be expected. An introductory college text can often be used with a class of this kind, and it can be expected that each student will read up to ten or more other books in addition. Individual conferences between teacher and student are necessary here to guide and supervise the supplementary reading which often takes precedence over class work or the basic text.

Sometimes, and increasingly, these people are assigned to advanced placement in college either while they are still in high school or upon an accelerated graduation. In any case, the idea is not basically to shorten the total period of schooling, but to eliminate elementary repetition and boring fundamental drill for the few students who can master the ordinary basic subjects much more readily than the average. There is certainly no reason for a student who has really

---

[3] Hartshorn, *loc. cit.*

mastered United States history in the eleventh grade to repeat it in the fourteenth. He may much better devote that extra year to pursuit of some more sophisticated body of learning.

There are age group characteristics of learning ability and of interest, but there are also individual differences which transcend these. Each student must be provided with materials appropriate to his accepted objective, and suitable to his capacity. An important psychological truism is often overlooked: interest grows in direct proportion to knowledge concerning a particular subject. As an example, given an adolescent boy's interest in baseball as an earmark of his age and life in American society, it grows in great bounds the more he learns about baseball and as he becomes more skilful at the game. This is true of all persons at all ages in every pursuit unless some traumatic experience intervenes. Familiarity does not breed contempt; it engenders interest.

In summary, then, it is necessary to know where to go, how to tell when you arrive, to strive for a spirit of inquiry, to be aware of individual differences, to know the common characteristics of students, and to appreciate the findings of psychology in regard to learning. If these things are kept in mind it matters little what the specific elements of knowledge happen to be so long as they are part of the human heritage of which we must learn in order to survive as civilized beings.

### 3. Non-Literary Aids in Teaching

Present day American life is becoming less and less dependent upon reading as a skill necessary to keep up with events, to make a living, and to relax. People look at television, listen to the radio, and they are assaulted daily in every possible place by signs, sounds, shapes and colors in every conceivable form of advertising device. News is purveyed by voice and picture. *Life*, *Look* and other newsmagazines give their messages in pictures. *Holiday* or the *National Geographic Magazine* take their subscribers around the world by means of technically perfect photography. Plastic and pictorial art have been bent to purposes of merchandizing, propaganda and news commentary. Much knowledge and necessary technical information is given to a public that might otherwise not be able to read it.

Education cannot overlook the possibilities offered in this obvious state of affairs. According to one observer the average American teenager, in 1954, viewed television seventeen hours a week, using some thirty million privately owned sets.[4] Nearly every station has some educational programs, and there are a number of stations owned and operated by universities and other non-profit organizations specifically for the purpose of broadcasting programs designed to further the learning of Americans. It would be simple enough to assign as homework some of the programs that might be watched by students anyhow. Teachers can take that much advantage of an existing situation.

It is a more complicated matter to consider the whole possibility of strictly educational television exploitation, such as a closed circuit system in a given school or group of schools by which means a single presentation might be made under controlled circumstances to a widely dispersed and numerous audience. There are outstanding examples of this already, both by commerical stations and by educational institutions, and there is little doubt that future use will be much greater.

In any case, students learn things by means of all the senses and by utilizing many different skills—not merely by reading alone, although reading must still remain the chief medium of social studies instruction. Our society is "sense-minded," and children will learn something of the "toughness of facts" by firsthand physical experience with some of them.[5] It is, therefore, only reasonable that educational practice take advantage of the multitude of audio-visual and other materials that exist outside the traditional literary expression of knowledge to be found in books.

### Films, Filmstrips and Slides

Perhaps educational films come to mind first in any summary of audio-visual aids to learning. Nearly every school has at least one film projector, and many business enterprises are anxious to furnish free or very cheap films for schools' use. In nearly every case such films have a particular point of view or product to sell. Much caution must be exercised in the use of such material. Of course, in addition to interested attempts to indoctrinate, there are sound and dependable sources of educational film supply.

It would be ridiculous to attempt to make an all-inclusive list of

---

[4] Philip L. Groissier, "Educational Television," *Social Education* (January, 1955). In 1961, privately owned T.V. sets numbered 45,000,000, and one may assume the same proportionate use.

[5] Earl S. Johnson, "Field Trips and the Development of Intellectual Skills," *Social Education* (March, 1956), p. 121.

the film producers and distributors, even in a book devoted to audio-visual purposes. To keep up to date one must consult the current edition and semi-annual supplements of the *Educational Film Guide* (H. W. Wilson), and for sponsored and commercial films, *Educators Guide to Free Films* (Educators Progress Service, Randolph, Wisconsin). Here only the simplest indication is given of some of the best known sources:

Coronet Films, Coronet Building, Chicago 1, Illinois.
Disney Productions, 2400 West Alameda Avenue, Burbank, California.
Educational Film Library Association, 345 East 46th Street, New York 17.
Encyclopaedia Britannica Films, Incorporated, 1150 Wilmette Avenue, Wilmette, Illinois.
McGraw-Hill Book Company, Text-Film Department, 330 West 42nd Street, New York 36.
Ohio State University, Teaching Aids Laboratory, Columbus 10, Ohio.
United Nations, Film and Visual Information Division, New York 17.
Young America Films, Incorporated, 18 East 41st Street, New York 17.

There are many, many more agencies that produce and distribute useful films, including most of the information services of foreign nations having representation in the United States. This list is basic since these organizations have a wide distribution and a broad coverage in subject matter applicable to the social studies.

Films from any source, when used in classrooms, should first of all have a definite purpose. A film should not be used unless it can do the instructional job better than any other method. The use of any piece of audio-visual material should always have a distinct and unique purpose, and it should always contribute to the achievement of the general objective of the particular instruction.

Before showing a film to a class the instructor should view it privately first, and then decide whether or not to use it. It is well to make some kind of written evaluation of each previewed film and file it for future reference.

Much the same thing may be said for use of filmstrips and slides as for moving films, except that it is more likely that the teacher will be able to make some of his own slides reflecting his own experiences. In this age nearly everyone has a camera. Nearly every teacher, especially during summers, takes some kind of a trip. What is simpler than taking snapshots of interest on a trip? Or, for that matter, right in one's own neighborhood there are illustrations of all kinds which if pictured could be used as classroom aids to instruction. A series of twenty or thirty color transparencies showing the beauties of Glacier National Park or the wildlife in Yellowstone Park or the majesty of

Niagara Falls will illustrate Rocky Mountain geography, animal life in the temperate zone, or the production of water power in economy, respectively. These things will probably be better documented in this way than by any amount of talking about the same things. Any teacher can acquire a 35 millimeter camera, load it with color film, snap the shutter judiciously, and have in his possession a set of twenty or thirty-six ready-mounted color slides when he returns from a summer excursion. In addition to this possibility, at every popular resort in the United States and many places abroad ready-made color slides are available at cheap prices. In fact, you do not even need to go to the place in order to get the slides. Simply write for them.

Eastman Kodak Company in Rochester, New York, maintains a most complete research laboratory devoted to the needs of educational photography, both amateur and professional. They publish many books and pamphlets on the various aspects of the problem. Naturally, they want to sell photographic equipment, but they also want it to be used educationally in the most effective way. Amateur photography as a learning medium should be used extensively in social studies teaching.[6]

When filmstrips or slides, obtained from commercial sources, are used, critical evaluation should be made exactly as for films, including a preview by the teacher. All pictures are more effectively used if the instructor has firsthand experience or research knowledge of their context. The viewers of slides and films will learn better if the instructor illustrates the many relationships that exist among subjects associated with what is being shown. A follow-up lesson should always accompany the use of slides and films.

Out of almost any collection of snapshots there will be some which warrant enlargement and can be used to illustrate a fact or concept pertinent to the objectives of social studies instruction. This perhaps is the most neglected reservoir of visual teaching material. How many times, in driving along past a large industrial plant, has one been struck by the stark beauty of functional design of the chimneys, towers, tanks and arrangement of the equipment used in the production of the multifarious American industrial output? How simple it would be to stop and take a picture of it. How useful to have that picture enlarged, mounted and placed on the bulletin board of the seventh grade class which is learning about American industry! But how many times is it done?

[6] *How to Make Good Pictures*, Eastman Kodak Company (Rochester, New York, 1949), is a non-technical handbook on photography.

Professionally made study prints, photographic or otherwise, are available in many forms from many suppliers. Usually the best ones are large mounted reproductions from magazines, books or specially prepared series of pictures illustrating the growth of a particular institution or product. *Life* magazine often runs illustrative pictures concerning a particular topic, such as medieval life, then the typically illustrative prints are mounted and numbered in sequence and sold at a nominal price in sets.[7] Sometimes business enterprises, associations of manufacturers or industries, foreign governments, chambers of commerce, labor unions or other organizations furnish such sequences *gratis* as their contributions to educational progress.[8]

The easiest way for teachers to procure needed pictures for social studies is to cut them out of the numerous illustrated magazines which are typical of American life at the present time. The most prolific sources of useful pictures are *National Geographic Magazine* and *Life* magazine. With circulations running into the millions each year, these magazines are easily available, and if the schools have not universally accepted the value of visual impact on the human mind, at least American magazines have understood it. With hardly an exception picture magazines have proved successful in the past twenty years. Why not take advantage of the same principle in education? Allow judiciously selected pictures from any source to be "silent partners" in the classroom. Flat pictures, in color and black and white, photographs or drawings, are by far the best visual aids that can be procured. They are also the easiest to get.

### Charts, Maps and Globes

Wall or desk charts, really only flat pictures of another kind, exist in every conceivable form. They may range from simple homemade bar graphs in black and white or color to complicated panoramic depiction of the course of world civilization. This latter "time line" chart is sometimes twenty feet long and may become a semi-permanent mural around the top of a classroom. Every newsmagazine is illustrated profusely with large and small bar, line or symbolic graphs

[7] Life-Time Education Service, 9 Rockefeller Plaza, New York 20. See Edgar Dale, *Audio-Visual Methods in Teaching*, revised edition (Dryden Press, New York, 1954), pp. 399–401, for a rather complete listing of picture sources.

[8] Before World War II the Japanese Tourist Service produced and distributed huge colored pictures of Japanese life at no cost in order to help convince Americans of the invincible quality of their national strength. At the present time similar efforts are being made by various other national governments and private enterprises.

visually demonstrating the various trends in American and world economics, social organization and politics. The pie-shaped figure representing a certain amount of money, such as tax revenues for a state or nation, is most familiar to the average citizen. The pie is cut into wedges of varying sizes to indicate the relative expenditures or sources of tax money. Such illustrations of all sorts of social concepts may be made in the classroom or procured from commercial suppliers. The National Association of Manufacturers is most happy to supply teachers with many different varieties. Nearly every government agency prepares some sort of graph for distribution. Foreign governments find this an easy way of presenting some of their information to Americans, and many businesses use the graph both in their own enterprises and for attempting to influence the public in various ways. Teachers of social studies should find graphs and charts, either commercially or otherwise available, extremely useful in presenting technical information with a numerical content.

Since charts and graphs should be as simple as possible they may be made extemporaneously with chalk on a blackboard just about as effectively as any other way. Teachers and students should always bear in mind the possibility of illustrating facts with simple chalk diagrams and charts. A series of octagonal boxes enclosing names or titles, arranged schematically and connected by lines of "responsibility," may be drawn on the chalkboard in the course of an explanation of tables of governmental organization or business structure. This would then become a chart which might be of only temporary value or which might be copied by students for future use. The possibilities of symbolic representation in graphic form are unlimited.

The definition of maps is given by Webster as "representation (usually on a flat surface) of the surface of the earth or of some part of it, showing relative size and position, according to a scale or projection or position represented." In other words, a map is a symbolic picture or chart, reduced in scale to a size that enables a usable view, accurately depicted, of a much larger area. If pictures are the most important of the visual aids, then maps, as a special category of pictures, are the most useful. Geography, although encompassing much more than symbolized pictures of the earth and its regions, is dependent primarily upon maps to record its findings. It would seem absurd to attempt to teach geography without maps. It would be just as meaningless to attempt to teach history or sociology or economics within them. Everything that happens to man—

and this is the content of social studies—happens to him in space and time. It is, therefore, necessary to locate the earth in the universe, regions on earth, and specific places in various areas as well as in relative time: geography and history. Both of these tasks are best done with the extensive help of maps of all kinds.

PHYSICAL MAPS. These range from simple outlines of land and water to more complicated depictions of altitude, temperature, vegetation, soils, precipitation and relief. They may sometimes be combined with other graphic data such as isothermic lines or bar graphs of climate or economic production. One of the most important types of physical maps is the simple outline map without place names, to be filled in as part of the learning exercises in a social studies class.

COMMERCIAL OR ECONOMIC MAPS. Such maps often show only one specific item such as the coffee growing areas of Brazil or the distribution of salmon in the oceans of the world. They may be pictorialized and exaggerated to show in a colorful way the special attractions of a region such as a travel map of Mexico showing the desirable places for tourists to stop. Sometimes "good natured maps" of a region are prepared to indicate the folklore background or the entertainment possibilities of an area.

POLITICAL MAPS. This is the most familiar form of map used by students. They simply indicate the political subdivisions of the mapped area. Political maps can vary from world coverage to the smallest subdivision: the town or village. They often appear as combination political-physical maps, doing the work of two specialized maps at one time. Every history textbook has them; they appear regularly in newspapers and magazines; they form the bulk of the contents of atlases.

SPECIAL PURPOSE MAPS. Basically, political maps can be prepared in almost unlimited variation for the specific purpose of showing one thing. Population distribution may be shown, for example, on a political outline map of the United States by the simple process of attaching a shaded or color key and then shading or coloring the states in relationship to a series of graduated densities of population. Some maps might have only a decorative purpose; sometimes very effective murals are treated in this manner. Others, such as those of the Pacific Ocean Area drawn by Miguel Covarrubias, combine the utmost accuracy of geographic detail with outstanding artistry, and at the same time serve a special purpose. They form a series of great value, each map treating a certain aspect of the region. One deals with the racial derivation and customs of peoples of the Pacific basin. Another depicts the aquatic life. Still another stresses the flora and fauna of the land areas, and so on.

Two recent developments in map use have appeared. Transparent maps, photographed or drawn on acetate, are available. These are chiefly for decoration and commercial display of a permanent nature. Now that plastic materials have become so plentiful and versatile, as might be expected, many maps are made of different plastics. These materials lend themselves to relatively indestructible yet fairly pliable relief map making. One of the chief drawbacks of flat maps has been their very flatness; relief cannot be shown except by some sort of convention such as shading or contour lines. Now it is possible to get relatively cheap relief maps made of plastic which has been molded over a raised pattern. They are lightweight and easy to handle, yet they show surface relief in its proper perspective.[9]

The atlas, or bound collection of maps and other data, is best used by the individual student. Atlases are of many types, in addition to the many different kinds of maps which they might include. One of the most valuable of special purpose atlases is a collection of physical, political and economic maps covering a region in various historical phases of its development. The best such historical atlas is Shepherd's (Barnes and Noble); but C. S. Hammond has made available inexpensive paper bound editions of some of the most important historical-geographical information.

The most obvious disability of any flat map is its failure to show the global character of the world. On a small part of the world this is relatively unimportant, but even the very best flat map projection contains some distortion. The only possible way to avoid this is to show the map of the world on a globe which is the same shape as the earth itself, but scaled down in size. Globes may be of any size and devoted to any of the special purposes of flat maps. Globes alone cannot serve all of the purposes of maps because of the size of the earth, but children should have the early and continued experience of seeing and *feeling* a globe with the map of the world on it.

Another related use of a "globe" is achieved in the planetariums which have been set up in various places. In effect the viewer stands inside the globe and looks up at the heavenly bodies which are placed in scaled perspective on the transparent surface of a huge globe. Smaller planetariums or solariums are sometimes used as models to be viewed from the outside to show the same relationship.

[9] Plastic relief maps from Areo Service Corporation, Relief Model Division, 236 East Courtland Street, Philadelphia 20.

## Other Three-Dimensional Exhibits

For purposes of attraction some times advertisements or other displays combine flat pictures with "raised" elements such as three-dimensional letters to make them stand out. This can be done effectively in school usage to make a bulletin board more attractive or to mark a special place in the school or classroom. Very often it is possible to have the students prepare exhibits of their own group work in a three-dimensional fashion. One of the best ways to do this is by means of a combination of a map and various articles, such as items of agricultural produce or pictures of places or persons. The map may be mounted on a central part of the bulletin board with the various items of display arranged around it and fastened to the wall. Each item then can be attached with colored yarn or ribbon to a pin stuck into the map in the appropriate place. This technique is especially useful in the study of the products of a region.

Among the possibilities for three-dimensional display the diorama is possibly the most interesting. Here, some sort of background is needed such as a box open at the top and front. Inside the box will be placed a model of the setting to be used, and figures of people, animals and other articles to illustrate the subject under study. Children like to prepare these displays for several reasons. There is opportunity for exercise of artistic taste in arrangement of color and design; there is the physical outlet for energy in constructing the various elements of a diorama; several different senses are brought into play in the process of learning. A diorama of an Indian village or the model of an ancient city of Greece, prepared by students and based on their knowledge of the time and place under consideration, will certainly reinforce their appreciation and make them more likely to retain a permanent impression of the matter studied. It need only be remembered that one of the most popular parts of any museum is the section devoted to large and professionally constructed dioramas. Another variation of the same thing can be seen in any aquarium where the chief figures are alive, or in any show window where the "actors" are mannequins displaying mutely the wares of merchandise.

## Models

A good share of children's toys are miniature simulations of larger, real machines used in everyday life, or semi-realistic models of people or animals: dolls. Every girl has either had or wished she had a collection of dolls wearing different costumes. Every boy has done the same with models of cars, ships, aircraft or other vehicles. The hobby shop merchandise devoted to these purposes is prodigious. One of the strongest selling points of toy trains is that they are exact reproductions in miniature appearance of the real thing.

At the Smithsonian Museum in Washington, D.C. there is an extensive exhibit of American historic costumes displayed on models of famous men and women. Martha Washington's inauguration gown may be seen there along with the other First Ladies' finery. In the same building may be seen Charles Lindbergh's airplane, The Spirit of St. Louis, as well as many other famous "firsts." It is not suggested that every student can go to Washington or that any classroom could contain a full sized aircraft or a collection of historic mannequins. It is possible, however, to introduce models of these items, either commercially procured or constructed by teacher and students.

Certain industrial companies are willing to supply models of their plants to schools as contributions to education. Many of the oil companies have miniature refineries or oil fields in the form of kits which they will distribute to teachers at no cost. Of course, they have a commercial interest in such largesse, but at the same time American students should know all they can learn about the processes of industry which make their country great.

### Sound

Recorded sound is available in many forms for classroom use. Music, voice, sounds of industry, animal and human calls, bird calls and jungle drums may be found on disk records, tapes, wires and sound tracks for moving films or filmstrips. Hundreds of radio and television stations throughout the world assault the ears of listeners twenty-four hours a day with all sorts of sounds. Nearly every home in America has one or more devices for reproducing sounds in some way: record players, radios, television sets, tape or wire recorders; sound is prevalent everywhere.

It is typical of this age with its exponential growth of technology that sound recordings are an essential part of it. By recording a song it may be sold and heard almost simultaneously and an unlimited number of times. In this way the voice of Enrico Caruso may be recalled and enjoyed long after the great tenor died. Very rapidly sound recording is becoming an important part of the historical record, especially of the mid-twentieth century. Such programs as those of Edward R. Murrow, "Hear It Now" and "See It Now," on radio and television, are also available on records, and they may be used in any of these forms to great advantage in American history classes from grade eight to grade fourteen.[10]

Special events, such as the national political conventions, are broadcast over radio and television, and even if a school does not regularly use or possess the necessary receiving equipment it may be rented or borrowed for such an occasion. Even a student-owned portable set is sufficient for the purpose. There are regularly broadcast programs for school use during school hours such as the Standard Symphony Hour. Others, like Walt Disney's science programs, are scheduled during the evenings, and they may be used as homework assignments when applicable. *Radio and TV Guide* gives specific information on programs in various sections of the country.

Ordinarily, it is preferable to use sound material which has been recorded, because it can then be fitted into the program of social studies according to the needs of the class rather than to suit the convenience of a scheduled presentation. It is possible, too, under those circumstances, to select just that part of a given selection which is needed. Like all other audio-visual aids, sound should be used when it can best do the job required.

One of the most convenient methods of obtaining sound recordings for the classroom is to "pirate" desirable selections from radio or television by means of a tape recorder. This is legitimate as long as no commercial benefit is derived for anyone. It is a simple matter to attach the recording mechanism to the two outlets on the speaker of a radio set, turn on the tape recorder and get a perfect reproduction of the program for as much as two hours of unbroken time. Afterward one can edit out all undesirable matter, and use the remainder to further achievement of an educational objective in school.

## Drama

Dramatic play is one of childhood's first and most lasting means of imaginative expression. It is the most common thing in the world to see children playing that they are cowboys or Indians or even horses ridden by cowboys. Nearly every facet of a small child's life is "played" into reality for him. Play is the normal way in which children begin to objectify their serious experiences. They play at keeping house with dolls and miniature household utensils. They play with blocks in great schemes of construction. Their "castles in the air" come down to earth this way. If a child can play his dreams into reality while he is grow-

[10] Edward R. Murrow and Fred W. Friendly, "I Can Hear It Now," recorded on Columbia Masterworks, Set mm800.

ing up the chances are reduced of his ever having to pay rent to a psychiatrist for attempting to live in those dream castles.

The organized drama of the professional or amateur stage is merely the formalization of childhood's dramatic play. Drama, since the time of Sophocles and Aeschylus, has been considered to carry a high degree of emotional outlet for both performers and spectators. Shakespeare's plays were written and performed for an audience keenly aware of the cathartic value. Drama is a part of human existence from earliest childhood to oldest age; it has been a part of the civilizing process from earliest times.

Lately the preventive therapeutic nature of spontaneous dramatic activity has been recognized and named. Psychodrama is used in individual psychiatric treatment sometimes to allow the patient to "act out" his subconsciously threatening aggressions in a harmless way. Sociodrama is, or was, the group counterpart of psychodrama for group therapy. It is now considered to be a harmless and useful tool for classroom expression of learning in still another way—by acting it out. The only essential difference from old-fashioned dramatic acting lies in the necessarily spontaneous nature of this dramatic play.[11]

Sociodrama, or dramatic play, may be thought of as the relatively unstudied activity accompanying the process of objectifying some body of learning by the process of oral expression. It is felt that such bodily expression, along with vocal repetition of an idea, will reinforce the impact of the information and provide one more method of sense perception. It is true that younger children are more willing to participate in this sort of thing, but even adults will take to role-playing when they get used to the idea. As a matter of fact, all persons play various roles all their lives. Sociodrama is simply an adaptation of natural impulses to a controlled situation.

Sometimes after a spontaneous acting out of a certain episode has taken place it may become desirable to record the performance, polish it into a dramatic presentation, and give it as a play to some sort of audience. This, however, ceases to be dramatic play. It has become drama in the older sense. Sociodrama is only the first step.

### Conclusion

Anything that can be used and that will further the aim of instruction is a legitimate aid to teaching. The primary goal of education is

---

[11] Arthur Katona, "Sociodrama," *Social Education* (January, 1955); *Psychodrama and Sociodrama in American Education*, edited by Robert Bartlett Haas (Beacon House, New York, 1949), develops and illustrates the theme in a very complete manner.

to teach students that which society requires them to know. The bulk of social studies' part of this responsibility is in literary form, in books and magazines, but there is a great deal of this knowledge which becomes clearer if its learning can be reinforced through some other medium as well as the printed word. Any device that can help achieve clarity and a lasting impression should be used—pictures, maps, globes, models, sound or drama. All are available and all may be useful.

Where do these teaching aids come from? The answer is the same as for their use: wherever they can be procured. If a certain device cannot be obtained ready-made, and it is worth having, then make it, preferably with the aid of the students. If that is too much trouble then probably it would not serve its purpose anyhow. *Guide to Free Curriculum Materials,* published annually in both elementary and secondary editions by Educators Progress Service, Randolph, Wisconsin, offers many possibilities. *Social Education* carries many articles concerning such things, for example, Dorothy W. Furman, "Free and Inexpensive Teaching Aids," in the issue of October, 1956, p. 279, tells where two very useful wall charts may be obtained which will illustrate presidential elections and party politics in the United States.[12] The *National Education Association Journal* has a regular feature listing recent issues of audio-visual material. Professor William H. Hartley, *A Guide to Audio-Visual Materials for Elementary School Social Studies* (Rambler Press, Brooklyn, 1950), has presented an exhaustive listing by category and subject of materials most useful to junior high school students. *A Directory of 2660 16mm Film Libraries,* Bulletin 1953, No. 7, United States Department of Health, Education and Welfare, Office of Education (United States Government Printing Office, Washington, D.C., 1953), was up to date at that time. The teacher's ingenuity and diligence can supplement this list indefinitely.

### 4. Suggested Further Reading

CRITICAL THOUGHT

Three books suggest themselves as a basis for introduction to the problem of critical thinking. There may be many ways of getting at the core of the matter, but the method chosen will probably differ a great deal with various individuals. This is only one way. Bertrand Russell, *Freedom versus Organization* (Norton, New York, 1934), is a brilliant analysis of national organization in the modern interdependent world—total organization precludes freedom, therefore eliminates critical thinking. Mark Roelofs, *The Tension of Citizenship: Private Man and Public Duty* (Rinehart, New York, 1957), is another philosophic examination of organized man and the individual's duty to that organization. In a sense it brings

[12] American Education Publications, 11 West 42nd Street, New York 36, N.Y.

Earl Russell's comments up to date. Karl A. Menninger, *Man Against Himself* (New York, 1938), is a scheme of critical evaluation by himself of any man—especially the teacher of social studies.

## TEACHING CRITICAL THINKING

Julian C. Aldrich, "Developing Critical Thinking," *Social Education* (March, 1948).

Howard R. Anderson, editor, *Teaching Critical Thinking in the Social Studies*, Thirteenth Yearbook, National Council for the Social Studies (Washington, D.C., 1942).

Edward Darling, "Twelve-Year Olds Can Think Critically," *Social Education* (February, 1945).

Malcolm Provus, "Teaching Critical Thinking Through History," *School Review* (October, 1955).

Richard E. Thursfield, "Developing the Ability to Think Reasonably," *The Study and Teaching of American History*, Seventeenth Yearbook, National Council for the Social Studies (Washington, D.C., 1946).

## SELECTING MATERIALS

*Accent on Teaching*, edited by Sydney J. French (Harper, New York, 1954), presents the opinions of twenty-four academicians on the subject of teaching. Each of them is very concerned with preserving the sacred academic tradition while at the same time serving the only real function of schools, teaching.

*Approaches to an Understanding of World Affairs*, edited by Howard R. Anderson, National Council for the Social Studies (Washington, D.C., 1954), presents several views by as many experts on social studies curriculum in the choice of materials and their use. It is centered on world affairs, but not to the exclusion of other ideas.

Hoyland Bettinger, *Television Techniques* (Harper, New York, 1955), is an interesting explanation of the ways in which television producers obtain their desired effects. Teaching can learn much from other fields.

Arthur H. Doerr, "Drama in the Classroom," *Social Studies* (December, 1956), p. 301, shows how a college teacher can use dramatic techniques to further his teaching process.

Margaretta Faisler, *Key to the Past* (Service Center for Teachers of History, American Historical Association, Washington, D.C., 1958), is an annotated listing of historical materials. The range extends over the whole of nonfiction literature.

James High, "History in General Education," *Social Education* (February, 1957), stresses an integrated approach to teaching at any level.

S. P. McCutcheon, "A Guide to Content in the Social Studies," *Social Education* (May, 1956), makes a few specific suggestions that are consonant with good teaching practice.

Alice A. Spieseke, "Bibliography of Textbooks in the Social Studies, 1955–1956," *Social Education* (December, 1956), is a sample of the annual supplement to the list of appropriate texts at all grades.

## FILM

*Near Home,* 25 minute, sound, blk. and wh. film, International Film Bureau (1946), shows a social studies project being worked out in an English classroom. It could be viewed with profit by every teacher.

## AUDIO–VISUAL

Edgar Dale, *Audio-Visual Methods in Teaching* (Dryden Press, New York, 1954), is the most comprehensive listing of techniques, materials and sources of supply.

Robert DeKiefer and Lee W. Cochran, *A Manual of Audio-Visual Techniques* (Prentice-Hall, Englewood Cliffs, 1955), is designed as a workbook to supplement any standard text on audio-visual education.

Alice M. Eikenberry, "Audio-Visual Materials for Teacher Education in the Social Studies," *Social Education* (January, 1955), presents some ideas that the teacher may use himself to increase his proficiency.

There are three periodicals which are of special importance to the social studies teacher in connection with audio-visual matters:

*Social Education,* National Council for the Social Studies, 1201 Sixteenth Street, N.W., Washington, D.C. Published monthly.

*Social Studies,* McKinley Publishing Company, 809–811 North 19th Street, Philadelphia, Pennsylvania. Published monthly.

*The Clearing House,* Fairleigh Dickenson University, Teaneck, New Jersey. Published monthly.

The most important producers of educational films in the United States are:

Encyclopaedia Britannica Films, Inc., 1150 Wilmette Avenue, Wilmette, Illinois.

Coronet Films, Coronet Building, Chicago 1, Illinois.

McGraw-Hill Book Company, Text-Film Department, 330 West 42nd Street, New York 18, now operated mainly to furnish college level material. Young America Films, Inc., 18 East 41st Street, New York 17, now owned by McGraw-Hill, supplies the lower graded material.

A complete listing of films is available in *Educational Film Guide* (Wilson). To keep up to date, consult:

*Educational Screen,* 2000 Lincoln Park West Building, Chicago 14, for educational films.

*Business Screen,* 7064 Sheridan Road, Chicago 26, for industrially produced films and filmstrips.

*Teaching Tools,* California Audio-Visual Education Association, 6327 Santa Monica Blvd., Los Angeles 38, for all sorts of teacher tested supplementary material and ideas.

For filmstrips and slides, outstanding sources of supply are:

Life-Time Educational Service, 9 Rockefeller Plaza, New York 20.

Ohio State University, Teaching Aids Laboratory, College Road Annex, Columbus 10, Ohio.

## 5. Suggested Activities for Further Study

1. Define the two terms, "critical thought" and "reflective thought" in a short paper.
2. Select an idea, such as slavery in American history, and after establishing the basic facts involved—origin, distribution, extent of trade, etc.—reflect on the whole problem and develop at least two or more statements of the problem of slavery in America at different levels of abstraction. Attempt to define the abstract "facts" involved and try to determine what might be an appropriate level of abstraction for an eleventh grade.
3. Design an audio-visual support program for eleventh grade United States history. Check personally on the materials included and determine how they will fit into the whole objective and support it.
4. Make a list of appropriate activities incorporating non-literary aids to learning of a body of selected material in a social studies course. Try to get beyond the mere use of illustrative films or pictures keyed to a particular bit of printed material such as one would find in a textbook. Rather, assume that certain people have a minimal skill in reading and therefore must learn most of what they are to know from sense perception without reading.
5. Take three well-known books often used in high school social studies, read them and attempt to guess their vocabulary difficulty in terms of grade level placement. Take the same three books and apply some standard measurement device such as the *Lewrenz Vocabulary Formula* (Los Angeles City Schools) which will give a precise grade placement figure. Observe the discrepancies in the two methods (subjective and objective), and try to determine why such discrepancy exists (if it does).

part IV
# APPLICATION OF METHODS AND THEORY

# 9
# Teaching United States history

These are the researches of Herodotus of Halicarnassus, which he publishes, in the hope of thereby preserving from decay the remembrances of what men have done. . . .

*History*
HERODOTUS, Athens, 449 B.C.

## 1. Introduction to Teaching History or the Story of the Past

Man's cultural heritage pervades our lives almost from birth. Its formal organization and presentation in school courses becomes the core of the social studies curriculum. Approximately three-fourths of high school social studies teaching time is devoted to history: United States history, hemispheric study and world history. Every state has some sort of legal requirement for the study of American history and government at some point in the student's school career.

History is the story of what men and women have done, of what they have left for others to enjoy and suffer. People have made fantastic blunders and noble contributions, but regardless of the quality of human activity it has given us a legacy of civilization, not always fine and noble but on the whole there has been progress both material and moral. Man's outlook is basically hopeful and there has been some justification for this. As students look at history, if they are guided in the true spirit of criticism and imbued with the necessity to look for the truth, they cannot help being inspired by the heroic proportions of their ancestors' struggle for existence and a better life. Such is the study of history as it was introduced to the ancient Greek world by Herodotus.

After about a million years of human struggle out of the fog and ignorance of primeval antiquity during which time man's history was in the hands of the gods (Clio became the muse of history) Herodotus gave the story of humanity back to man; thus rightly being called the "father of history." He did this in a very simple way, in a manner that we sometimes take for granted and therefore overlook; he simply observed people and wrote about what they did and thought. For the first time history was more than a mere symbolic record. Man was made aware of his heritage. He introduced humanism into the chronicles of war, degradation and the mysterious ways of Providence. He endowed men historically with freedom of will to make choices and to mold the course of events in which they were caught up. Herodotus delineated real people, perhaps not "exactly as they were," but in the spirit of inquiry and curiosity that has marked the Greeks as forever ours of the modern world.

Social studies teachers in American high schools have a tremendous responsiblity in making their students aware of the past as it applies to present-day life. Every American is a citizen of the United States, but he also shares in the heritage of the whole Western world. He must know about it in order to share it knowingly, wisely and patriotically. If students do not learn their history, dire results take place as was shown by the attitudes developed among the Chinese captors of many American soldiers during the Korean conflict. The following is an excerpt from reports of various Chinese Communist officials engaged in the unpleasant "brainwashing" campaign of that war.

Based upon our observations of American soldiers and their officers captured in this War for the Liberation of Korea from Capitalist-Imperialist Aggression, the following facts are evident:

The American soldier has weak loyalty to his family, his community, his country, his religion and to his fellow-soldier. His concepts of right and wrong are hazy and ill-formed. Opportunism is easy for him. By himself he feels frightened and insecure. He underestimates his own worth, his own strength, and his ability to survive. He is ignorant of social values, social tensions and conflicts. There is little knowledge or understanding even among U.S. university graduates of American political history and philosophy, the federal state and community organizations, state and civil rights freedoms, safeguards, checks and balances and how these things operate within his own system.

He is insular and provincial with little or no idea of the problems and the aims of what he contemptuously describes as foreigners and their countries. He has an unrealistic concept of America's internal invincibility. This is his most vulnerable weakness. He fails to appreciate the meaning of and the necessity for military or any form of organization or discipline. Most often he clearly feels that his military service is a kind of hateful and unavoidable servitude to be tolerated as briefly as possible and then escaped from as rapidly as possible with as little investment as possible.

Continuing to a logical conclusion the Chinese Communist author could not avoid the obvious: "Based upon these facts about the imperialist United States aggressors the re-education and reindoctrination program for American prisoners proceeds as planned."

It is, therefore, tremendously important that students in school—before they face the possibility of attempted "brainwashing"—learn the fascinating story of their past, that they learn not only about the hopeful outlook of man and his aspiring goodness, about their own particular myths and beliefs, but that they learn also about the degradation, misery and mistakes of the past. History is not one unbroken story of human success; it is the tale of progress which includes retrogression, errors and some meanness of spirit. If we are to survive we must know of our past and we must develop a toughness of moral and mental fiber. This, too, can be augmented through the study of history.

A corollary to the quest for knowledge in the past is the cultivation of humane values: honesty of mind, loyalty to person and nation, patriotism; not blind obedience to unilateral jingoism, but enlightened, knowledgeable patriotism based on real appreciation of one's culture. An individual's rights are directly proportional to respect for the rights of every other individual, and above all, these rights must be protected continuously. Protection of rights is not necessarily a fight against enemy aggression, although that is always a threat. Rights and privileges must be kept alive despite the selfishness of other contemporaries within the state; they must be improved and used or they will disintegrate. We must work at the problem of knowing ourselves culturally. We must study history, "thereby preserving from decay the remembrance of what men have done."

## 2. Teaching United States History

The most commonly taught course in social studies is United States or general American history. It often appears in elementary school, in junior high and again in high school. Many phases of United States history show up with varying emphasis in different schools and at different levels; no single course can possibly cover all of the available history, nor could all of the nuances of historical interpretation be understood by every level of student. Schools and teachers usually have to choose certain topics out of the whole narrative for treatment in a given grade. Textbooks tend to treat a certain standard group of topics, not always in the same way, and they all vary a great deal in the amount and type of detail which makes up the remainder of the book.

Secondary teachers usually try to cover a minimum of the centrally important topics in United States history, but they are ordinarily free to select the way in which this is done and illustrative detail to be included. For example, almost any high school history class will deal with the colonial foundations, the American Revolution, the Constitution, development of party structure, the westward movement, Manifest Destiny and the Mexican War, the Civil War and Reconstruction, industrialization, imperialism, domestic reform, World War I, the depression and the New Deal, World War II and the postwar prosperity with its global implications. These subjects might also form the basic outline of most textbooks in United States history at any level. Obviously any one of them could be expanded to include enough material to fill a whole semester. On the other hand, all of them must be touched upon in the course of almost any history class. It is necessary, therefore, to select the amount and kind of detail very carefully which is to illustrate the main points. Rather than coverage of a great mass of undifferentiated detail, it is far better to concentrate in depth on a few broad points, making sure that the students gain a real knowledge of the philosophic content and interpretation of facts that can be mastered in a reasonable length of time. While doing that it is also necessary to go into enough different facts in chronological order to impress the basic continuity that exists in history, not only within one nation but in the whole world over the whole course of time that man has kept records. Skill, experience and knowledge are needed.

As a preliminary exercise for the prospective teacher in helping him select subject matter, and later as a student activity, preparation of time lines or charts of comparative chronology will usually prove useful. The students or teacher, or both together, can devise any number of different ways to show graphically the passage of time punctuated by the various events and personalities which have been recognized as highlights in the panorama of history. One especially useful variant of this device is the international time scale with parallel columns of events and dates, one column for each of several regions or nations, such as Europe, Asia and America. As an example of one entry:

| Europe | Asia | America |
|--------|------|---------|
| Revolutions in Germany and France 1848 | Tai P'ing Rebellion in China 1850 | Mexican War 1846–1848 |

A basic reference for this sort of chart is *An Encyclopedia of World History*, edited by William Langer (Houghton, Mifflin, Boston, 1948).

Although only one of the many topics of study in United States history, the westward movement has been of continuing interest for many years. It cannot constitute the whole of our history, but a good many historians have emphasized the place of the West in American history far beyond any other force. A study of the West and man's tendency in our civilization to move westward will prove fruitful and fascinating to the teacher and to students. This is particularly true at the eighth grade level, usual junior high school placement of American history.

## 3. The Westward Movement

> Westward the course of empire takes its way;
>     The four first acts already past,
> A fifth shall close the drama with the day;
>     Time's noblest offspring is the last.
>
>     *On the Prospect of Planting Arts and Learning in America*
>     BISHOP GEORGE BERKELEY, c. 1725

### Old World Beginnings

Out of the Old World came the New. It was a westward-moving process from the Cradles of Civilization to the shores of the Pacific Ocean by way of Western Europe, the British Isles and the great Atlantic Migration, across the American continent with "Manifest Destiny" and on over to the Philippines to take up the "White Man's Burden." Always there was a frontier of space.

Americans usually want to know what they are, where they came from, how they became what they are. Adolescent curiosity blends with adult responsibility and childish carelessness in the United States, but every citizen should attempt to find out what he possesses that typifies him and sets him off from other people in the world. We are American in the United States as typically and surely as we are descended from every nationality and race on earth. We have two things which make us what we are.

We have (1) a Western European cultural background, and (2) we

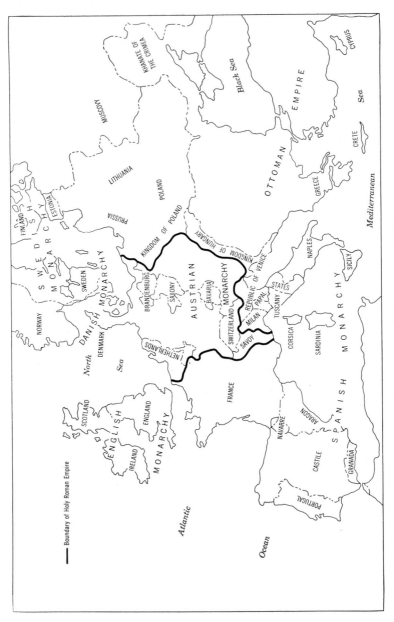

FIGURE 8. Map of Europe c. A.D. 1560.

have a unique national history even though it is a short one. The simplest unifying force in that history is its westward orientation and impetus. In a survey of United States history the frontier theme has validity in many ways: it is dramatic, true, personal, vivid and therefore appealing. It is simply understood to say that our European forebears looked westward across the Atlantic and wanted to get away from the fettering strictures of an old weary world that had run its course. It is logical to follow this explanation with a description of those same ancestors leaving the Old World to come to a new frontier wilderness, bringing with them those values which they held high—freedom, rule of law and energetic pursuit of an ideal. As each successive frontier was met and conquered, the old ideas and people became less and less recognizable as fugitives from Europe. As the English and other settlers crossed the mountains and plains of America they gradually emerged as a distinct breed of men and women, Americans.

But still they brought along through the generations the essence of Western culture—the language, laws, customs of Europe, the Middle Ages, Rome, Greece and the ancient Middle East. These things were molded and squeezed into a new conception and a new life, but the seed which flourished in the wilderness was originally transplanted from abroad.

When the New World was discovered the Old World had lately emerged from the complex somnolence of the Middle Ages. The Renaissance, that equally incomprehensible upsurge of individuality and energy, had already reached its height. In fact, the Renaissance was responsible in great measure for the discovery. Europe was cast in a particular pattern of strife that brought affluence and opportunity to many persons in high places, and misery and pain to many, many more in lowly positions. National states with strong tyrannical rulers appeared. The ancient Church underwent world-shaking moral and spiritual disastrophism. The Protestant middle classes were born in northern Europe. Southern Europe and the Near East went back to sleep. The farthest western nation of Europe spawned a pirate's covey of mariners who wrested the seas' control from Spain. Spain slumped into lethargic fear enhanced by the Inquisition and too much gold, too much land. The Dutch "Beggars of the Sea" roamed the Atlantic and the Pacific, picking up the crumbs of precious trade and loot that the earlier Spaniards and Portuguese could no longer protect.

Out of all this came factional national states over the face of Europe, and a social and religious atmosphere in England that made it possible, and almost inevitable, for a certain group of Englishmen to take advantage of the explorations and conquests of John Cabot and Sir Walter Raleigh. Middle class Puritans followed lower class Pilgrims and aristocratic Virginians to North America. Out of this forbidding and bounteous land they forged a state, at the same time old and new, free and trammeled, expansive and petty.

The land filled up in two hundred and fifty years, but the westward movement continued. It still goes on. The center of population in the United States continues its march in the direction of the Pacific coast. In 1950 it was at Olney, Illinois. By the 1960 census it had crossed Illinois, and it is now established at Meridian Township, Clay County, Illinois, about fifty miles east of St. Louis, Missouri.

There is no longer a frontier of space, but for Americans there is a boundless frontier in the realms of thought, science and technology. We are still a westward moving culture with a frontier mentality. The story of how we achieved that sort of mentality is the story of American history, of all the things Americans have done and left undone.

In order to start any kind of orderly understanding of the westward progression of American civilization across our continent, it is necessary to have some knowledge of the Western European background from which we came. Since the explorations and discoveries of Europeans from the tenth to the sixteenth centuries have cogency and interest in regard to the study of American history, they should be known to our citizens.

John Bartlet Brebner, in *The Explorers of North America* (Anchor Books, Garden City, New York, 1955), offers a concise and thrilling account of explorations from Columbus to Lewis and Clark. This book goes far toward explaining why explorations took place, and hence why there was an American settlement of those areas explored.

Charles E. Nowell, in the introduction to *The Great Discoveries and the First Colonial Empires* (Cornell University Press, Ithaca, New York, 1954), quoted Seneca at the opening of the Christian era:

> Our descendants will one day know many things that are hidden from us, for some knowledge is reserved for future generations, when all memory of us will be gone. . . . The world would be small indeed if there existed no possibility of new discoveries. . . . A moment will come when all that has been concealed will surge to light as the result of time and prolonged study. There will be a time when our ignorance will startle our descendants, because all these things will appear perfectly clear to them (from *Naturalium Questionum*).

This paragraph gives the point of departure from the known current of Graeco-Roman civilization which swelled and spread through the rise and decline of European feudalism, the decay of the universal Church, to the rise of nationalism, the Protestant Reformation, and the Age of Exploration. It gives the clue to final rejection of the ego-centric and therefore restricted notion of the universe centering on man in his own circumscribed orbit; and it shows the spark which ultimately drove the semi-literate frontiersmen over the Appalachian crests into the Ohio Valley seventeen hundred years later.

In the same series of short books, The Development of Western Civilization, other scholars, under the auspices of Cornell University, have covered other aspects of the growth, the background culture which produced the later American expansion. They are: Solomon Katz, *The Decline of Rome* (1955); Sidney Painter, *The Feudal Monarchies* (1951); Marshall W. Baldwin, *The Medieval Church* (1953); E. Harrison Harbison, *The Age of Reformation* (1955).

Richard Henry Tawney, *Religion and the Rise of Capitalism* (Harcourt, Brace, 1926; Mentor, 1953), gives a concise statement of the relationship among the factors of European development, religion, capitalism and nationalism, which made possible the westward growth.

D. W. Brogan, in *The American Character* (Knopf, New York, 1944), delineates and brings up to date the typically American emergence presently representing the outgrowth of twenty centuries of movement from east to west through Western civilization.

Carlton J. H. Hayes, in a trenchant essay, "The American Frontier— Frontier of What?," *American Historical Review* (January, 1946), summed up the background of American westernism in a paragraph:

> We used to know that we were Europeans as well as Americans, that we were not Indians or a people miraculously sprung from virgin forests like the primitive Germans described by Tacitus, but modern Europeans living in America on a frontier of Europe. All our original white ancestors on this continent knew they came from Europe. They and their sons and grandsons knew they had ties with Englishmen, Spaniards, Portuguese, Hollanders, or Frenchmen, as the case might be, not only on this side of the ocean but on the other. And generation after generation of their descendants on this side, no matter on what segment of the frontier they chanced to be, and no matter how intent on clearing new lands, were concerned and found themselves participants in all the successive major wars of Europe from the sixteenth century to the twentieth. . . . From the first, moreover, it has been known or knowable, if latterly obscured, that our language, our religion, our culture are rooted in Europe, that our ideals of liberty and constitutional government are a heritage of Europe.

Our frontier, our West, is truly an extension of the frontier of civilization carrying with it the whole heritage of Western man.

## 4. "The West"

Literally a direction, more broadly and adequately speaking a region, the West as a concept in American history is much more than either: it is a set of conditions obtaining and constantly changing in the land beyond the settled East. It is distinct from the Wesward Movement since the latter term indicates a process. The West is the *raison d'etre* of the Westward Movement. It is more than the frontier, since the frontier, or zone of the edge of settlement, was a local phenomenon. The West was the sum total, at any given time, of the various zones of advance: the impermanent activities of explorers, traders, and cattle rangers, the frontier of settlement, and finally the conditions existing between the frontier and the East, where the rigors of pioneering were partly overcome and the comforts of life had in part penetrated. The West included the whole series stretched in a rough grada-tion from the definitely established region where people had achieved satis-faction with their mode of life, out to the spaces known only by the reports of transient visitors.

The West everywhere presented (1) relatively unfettered political and social conditions, and (2) powerful forces to be overcome. Into it came people with well-defined ideas of life. The result was that original ideals and mores were modified both by the freedom and by the resistant nature of the primitive environment. At first the West forced the pioneer to put a portion of his civilization aside. Wisely he adjusted himself to the situation. But as rapidly as possible he introduced what he had held in abeyance, and always with alterations due to his new surroundings and experiences. This modified culture in turn affected the East, and its leaven continually helped to make the whole people different from the older East of Europe.[1a]

"United States Westward" is a major theme for the study of Ameri-can history; it may be a unit of study in a review of the whole of our national history or it may be the year-long center of interest as is often the case in grades seven or eight. In either situation, one or more units may be constructed around such topics as "Winning the Colonial West," "Reproducing a Culture," "Beyond the Mississippi," "The War of 1812 in the West—North and South," "A Deluge of People," "The West Becomes the Middle West," "The Permanent Indian Frontier," "The Attraction of Mexico and the Texas Revolution," "Manifest Des-tiny," "Sectional Difficulties in an Area Claiming National Status," "Overland to the Pacific," "The Civil War: Sectional Test by Fire," or the "Last Frontier."

### The Last Frontier

Suppose the last title is selected for a unit of study in United States history. "The Last Frontier," including treatment of the trapper's

---

[1a] John Carl Parish, "The West," in *The Persistence of the Westward Movement and Other Essays* (University of California Press, Berkeley and Los Angeles, 1943), pp. 183–184.

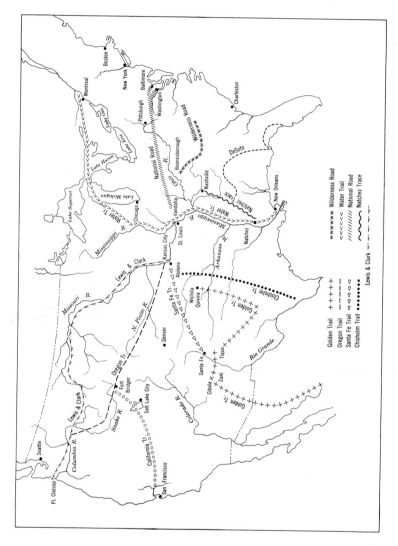

FIGURE 9. Map of the United States: "Trails West."

frontier, the mineral frontier, the age of cattle raising and final settling of the far West, covers a period roughly from the Civil War to about 1890 when the census showed that all parts of the United States had more than three persons per square mile, at least in terms of each state. The entire United States was organized into states or territories by the end of the Civil War, but great reaches of the country still qualified as frontier. In the course of thirty years this condition had passed and a new era was introduced. Of course, there has been a thread of continuity in American history, in all history, and this thread so far as the United States is concerned is most easily traced in political terms, but there have been interludes and there have been other activities than strictly political ones. The westward movement is one of these. It is persistent and it has old beginnings, but the so-called last frontier presents a recapitulation of the essence of frontier life and the movement westward of American civilization. It is encompassed in a relatively short time and it is often obscured by the concurrent and overlapping surges of economic change and political shift. As a unit in secondary school it is important to review and bring back to mind some of the principles and ideals represented by man's quest for the sun—the West.

As has been pointed out, organization of social studies into units is for the purpose of achieving learning goals in various ways, for the purpose of drawing from the organized knowledge of many social science disciplines. Because of this it is essential for the teacher to consider a good many aspects of the problem. Above all, it is necessary for the teacher to know the material to be covered. This consideration is always paramount. Next, it is just as important to know what the learning goals are, both in long range behavioral terms and in the shorter more specific sense. Long range objectives involve philosophy of education, the point of view of the particular school district and the quality of the students. In addition, a philosophy of history must also be invoked. Regardless of what the particular hoped for behavioral outcomes of any curriculum may be, the study of history as part of that curriculum can do certain things. There are many views of history that have been held in the past; it may be thought of as teaching philosophy by example, as merely a record of the past, as a partial revelation of the future, or only as a pointless accumulation of data indicating what some men have done. None of these phrases really covers an adequate philosophy of history, but each of them indicates some of the value or lack of value in the study of history. Most pointedly, history is the record, although only a partial one, of what man thinks he has done. It is the available story of man's culture, his heritage of cumulative memory. As such it cannot prescribe behavior that will avoid errors in the future although it may be possible to gain something in this field. History points out some improvement in man's behavior and certainly in his physical lot, but by no means can it be taken to imply that human society only becomes better merely with the passage of time. History is many things and serves many purposes; it is not all things and does not serve every moral purpose. Nonetheless, the value of history, if not the purpose, is in its revelation of a human course toward perfection. Not the least value it evokes is simply interest in one's heritage, the part of one's ancestors during crucial times in the expansion of the nation; the "Last Frontier" in the American West is such a period in historical study. Whatever the view of history and of the long range effects on students who study it, such views must be established and assessed for each unit or topic to be studied.

More easily stated are the short range objectives or immediate goals to be achieved at each stage of investigation. In the case of the "Last Frontier" these are best stated as gaining familiarity with the late nineteenth century contribution to the present state of American affairs. From this point it should be a simple matter to set up specific learning goals and situations to achieve the purpose. In this, as in any unit, there will appear two parallel columns of statements: subject matter and activities. The teacher should prepare himself, prior to presenting each unit, by making an outline of the material he hopes to cover and a list of appropriate activities for achieving that coverage. Activities for this unit might be text reading, discussion for the purpose of evolving questions to answer, oral and written reports, debate or panel discussion.

THE SETTLING OF THE WEST. By the end of the Civil War the entire United States was organized into states or territories. Statehood achieved by the new western territories included Nevada 1864, Nebraska 1867, Colorado 1876, Washington, Montana, North and South Dakota 1889, Wyoming and Idaho 1890, Utah 1896, Oklahoma 1907, New Mexico and Arizona 1912. The frontier was officially eliminated by the census of 1890, and the whole country was populated at a rate of more than three persons per square mile.

The western country included a mineral empire with its "frontier" beginning with the gold rush of '49 in California, and continuing with nearly half a century of "gold fever" in the West. Gold was discovered in Nevada in 1859, followed by gold and silver strikes during the 1860's in Idaho, Montana and Wyoming. Montana, during the next two decades became famous for copper as well as gold. William Andrews Clark, Helena banker and copper king and Marcus Daly, founder of the Butte smelters, contended politically and used the techniques of frontier survival to take out the rich ores.

Death Valley Scotty, last of the frontier miners, lived into the 1950's in a multi-million dollar palace near the scene of gold discovery in the preceding century. Ghost towns in the West and more money in the whole nation was the net result of the mining frontier.

Frontier, at least in the popular mind, means cattle. Before the Civil War and since early Spanish days wild cattle roamed the western plains. With the coming of the railroads it was easier to get cattle to market, and this resulted in the "long drive" northward from Texas and Mexico which actually made the cattle fatter and more marketable. This process began in 1866. During the next twenty-five years thousands of head were sent to the railheads in the northern West. Abilene, Dodge City and Cheyenne grew as typical lawless frontier towns, cow towns. The northern plains soon became centers of improving cattle breeds. Imported English bulls increased the weight and style of beef stock, and the longhorns became fewer.

The cowboy became a legendary American figure during this time when cattle roamed the plains marked only by an intricate system of brands to identify their ownership. Wars broke out between cattle men and farmers because the farmers tried to fence in their holdings. Packing houses grew into a major industry. Swift, Armour and Cudahy rose out of the decline of the open range and the improvement of beef cattle and transportation.

Barbed wire was invented in 1874 and very soon completely spoiled the open range system. As cattle became bigger and tamer they were harder to control out in the open, and in only a few years after the heyday of the romantic cattle frontier, beef raising turned into a farming procedure. The frontier of cattle was finished by 1890.

Aided by the Homestead Act of 1862, along with pre-emption and land sales by the land grant railways, settled farmers gradually filled up the West in the next frontier phase. The last great transcontinental railway was the Great Northern, built by Jim Hill in the 1880's and 1890's. It was not a land grant road, and the company had to create its own need and market as it went along. As the rails crept west, wholesale importations of immigrants, mostly Scandinavians, were brought by the railroad to the frontier of its advance. As the land became settled across the top tier of states the frontier moved rapidly westward, but each successive wave of settlement created the familiar frontier setting. Its only distinguishing feature was the speed with which it advanced.

Lack of water was the great problem of the plains. The West was first called the Great American Desert, and dry farming was only a partial success. The Mormons developed irrigation. After 1890 conservation and water supply became the political adhesive of the West. Theodore Roosevelt and Gifford Pinchot are the names that stand out in the growth of national conservation and the establishment of national forests after 1905.

The frontier quickly became more important in retrospect than it ever had been in reality, and as the West filled up all sorts of panaceas arose to cure the miserable conditions. Brawling, hard conditions and economic depressions prompted much political action. The senate was the most important because of the small population, making the western proportion of the house of representatives smaller than that of the older sections. Most westerners were economically motivated, so they felt direct political action could repair their failures to realize dreams of wealth. The West was agricultural and in debt, therefore most of the political movements were in the nature of attempts at reform.

The Granger movement was organized in 1867 as the Patrons of Husbandry by a clerk in the Department of Agriculture. With the panic of 1873 its numbers swelled to over a million and a half members. The movement coincided with a wave of popular sentiment against railroads, and thereby the railroads became the symbol of western exploitation. Grangers went into political action as small independent groups, usually against some railroad activity. Railroads retaliated by foreclosing land mortgages and displacing pre-emptioners—such was the immediate cause of the outlawry of the James brothers. The Interstate Commerce Act of 1887 was the most important result of this dual development of railroads and the Grangers. The Grangers probably had little to do with it except to focus popular attention on the railroads.

The greenback movement followed the height of the Grangers. It was based on a simple realization that more paper money meant easier credit and therefore was good for debtors. The few theorists who were associated with the movement recognized it for what it was, an attempt to organize western political support for a managed currency to prevent the tremendous fluctuations in the supply and price of paper money. As a political party the Greenbackers ran candidates for the presidency in 1876 and 1880, Peter Cooper and James B. Weaver. In 1884 they joined another grievance group, the Anti-Monopoly Party.

During the 1880's the Populists were the most threatening of all the western panacea parties. They attempted to join farmers and wage workers, but suffered a basic failure in the project. They polled, however, over a million votes in 1892. In the campaign of 1896 a majority of Populists defected to the standard of William Jennings Bryan, "boy orator of the Platte," with his "Cross of Gold Speech" at the Democratic convention. The ultimate result of the western reform movements was to enforce a measure of progressive legislation on the old parties. Woman suffrage, direct primaries, direct election of senators, use of the initiative, referendum and recall were all promoted mainly by the West rather than by the more conservative East.

### The West of Fiction

As the really dirty and uncouth frontier moved away from the East, it became the theme of fiction, usually highly romanticized. Pioneers themselves did not read, and if they did they would not want to read about themselves. A market had to be developed in back of the frontier, and a romantic version of the frontier had to be manufactured. The West furnished a projective device for the Americans in its wake, through fictionalized versions. Plays and wild west shows became popular in the early part of the twentieth century—Buffalo Bill, Wild Bill Hickok, Calamity Jane, etc. In 1910 moving pictures began to adapt western themes in fictionalized forms. Tom Mix, Hoot Gibson, Harry Carey and William S. Hart became the national heroes of American childhood. None of them was old enough to have been a frontiersman, and most of them came from the East.

Some western realism has crept into the literature of the West. Hamlin Garland, *Main Travelled Roads* (1891); E. W. Howe, *The Story of a Country Town* (1883); Frank Norris, *The Octopus* (1910); Willa Cather, *My Antonia* (1918); Ole Rolvaag, *Giants in the Earth* (1927) are among the best. These books are characterized by less romantic blood and thunder, but with considerably more accuracy than their romantic counterparts.

Historical interest in the West as a section was slow to start. Francis Parkman was probably the first, but he was mainly interested in the West as a scene of struggle between the great European titans, England and France, for the possession of the New World. His one truly western book was the *Oregon Trail*. Theodore Roosevelt's *Winning of the West* (written during 1889–1896), was the first significant western history. Frederick Jackson Turner in 1893, at the annual meeting of the American Historical Association, revolutionized western history by producing his famous frontier hypothesis. He claimed that ". . . the existence of an area of free land, its continuous recession, and the advance of American settlement westward, explain American development." He continued: ". . . from the time the mountains rose between the pioneer and the seaboard, a new order of Americanism arose." Frontier meant to him "the meeting point between savagery and civilization." Democracy came not from the Mayflower but "from the forest." The frontier was "a safety valve of abundant resources open to him who would take it."

Turner's thesis was novel and challenging. It has provoked more historical research than any other idea concerning American history. Its overall soundness is now very much in question and even discredited, but Turner's influence is undeniable, and out of that interest has evolved a tremendous body of information about the West.

The frontier clearly attracted some people and not others. The economically successful easterner seldom moved west. The migrant must have been economically, socially, or emotionally unhappy, and in addition he must have been superior in energy and initiative to break home ties and start a new life in the wilderness. In intelligence he probably represented a cross section of American life, but in aggressiveness he was above average—which implied holdup men as well as solid, substantial, law-abiding citizens. Basically these men and women were choosing between trying their fortunes in the West or in the factories of the growing eastern cities.

Western life was supportable only to people who were basically optimistic. Men moved west because they were hopeful of the future, and that hope sustained them throughout life. . . . Neither optimism nor exaggeration can be labeled exclusively western, but the West gave them a favorable environment.[1]

## 5. Approaches to American History in the Classroom

Out of all this has grown a stronger American nationalism, a deeper patriotism, while at the same time giving to the American state a typical and peculiar mythology and symbol of hardihood. Americans now know—they probably always did—that such tales as those of James P. Beckwourth are tall, even among generally tall stories (he claimed to have run at top speed ninety-five miles in one day in order

[1] Robert Riegel, *America Moves West* (Holt, Rinehart and Winston, New York, 1956), 3rd ed., p. 624. Quoted by permission of the publisher.

to escape the Indians); that Indians sometimes indulged in other activities than to burn, scalp and torture white people; that frontier life was generally nothing but hard work and filthy poverty; that Buffalo Bill was a delightful fraud, but still, there is a romantic uniqueness in the knowledge that only America has had a West. It was not as wild as we like to think it was. It was not the sole determinant of the American character. It did, however, leave its imprint on current American life, and in many intangible ways there is still a West, although it may be in the American imagination.

The immediate purpose in any school situation, beyond the overall hope that students may become good citizens and contributing members of their society, is to learn the material presented in class. Therefore each activity must be shown to lend itself to the task of learning. Usually history, in any given unit, is presented in chronological sequence. For all students there must be a basic minimum requirement of coverage, not necessarily geared to the lowest common denominator of intelligence, willingness and interest in the class, but capable of mastery by the average student. Such coverage is usually best established in terms of a basic text or a certain group of pages in a textbook. (Incidentally, nearly every secondary textbook in United States history has a substantial section on the West and the westward movement.) In a short unit a teacher may make such a basic text assignment either at the beginning of the unit or by increments throughout the unit. The fundamental text assignment should carry all of the main elements of information to be covered in the whole unit at the average level of the class. It should embody the specific objectives of the unit of study. This data is ordinarily stated in the table of contents of the textbook. If it is not clearly put, the teacher should reproduce a concise outline to be covered, and distribute it to the class at the beginning of the unit.

In addition to the basic text assignment, to make a unit adaptable to a wider range of ability and interest, a multi-text method may also be employed. Several other textbooks of varying degrees of difficulty may be assigned as supplementary or alternate reading. In the case of the very slow learner it may be advisable to assign a much simpler version of the story to be covered, and this may be all that can be expected of certain students. It may even be that the teacher himself will have to prepare an extremely simplified two or three page synopsis of the main points in the unit for such students. A teacher-made digest of the essential facts could take the form of a study guide in place of the printed text. On the other hand, average and better students will probably want to read other views of the same material covered by the general text or they may want to expand the detail suggested in their texts by reading biographies or even monographs on certain selected topics. The best students may be required to compare in writing the varying points of view and philosophies of history of different authors concerning the last American frontier. In instances where homogeneous grouping of students is practiced the problem is much reduced, but it is always present in some degree because no two persons are exactly alike in ability, interest or diligence. In any case it is well to supply students with more than one version of the same period in history if it is at all possible.[2]

As it was pointed out in the preceding chapter, in order to get the greatest value from the use of the multi-text method it is necessary to formulate questions with the class that need to be answered. Then the members of the class can independently search through the various books at their disposal for answers and illustrations that will clarify the questions. The basic process is akin to the scientist's method of proceeding in a controlled experiment. There are three recurring steps, as in any application of the scientific method, consisting of hypothesis (the question), search for material (answers to the question), and tentative conclusion (corroboration or refutation of the hypothesis). The principal difference in classroom application lies in the fact that there are many simultaneous questions and that the persons carrying out the search for illustrative material have many different levels of ability. Another difference that always plagues the student of history and the social sciences is that no human behavior, the chief subject material of those studies, is amenable to exact assessment or measurement as is often the case in natural sciences. The safeguard here is to stress the tentative character of findings, and to point out that any data are always subject to revision when new evidence is brought to bear on the problem.

Assuming a certain topic or unit of work such as the "Last Frontier," a class can evolve a set of questions with which to start. A class period or two should be devoted to formulating questions and discussing objectives. At this point two distinctly separate procedures may be in order: the lecture, accompanied by an outline on the blackboard, and a class participation in discussion to formulate and agree upon questions. The introduction to a unit may well have a lasting effect upon the way in which subsequent learning takes place. The initiating activity often sets the tone for accomplishment throughout the unit.

[2] See book lists at the end of chapter for some suggested titles.

At the outset of any attack on the body of knowledge making up a unit of work it is necessary to set up an initiating activity of some kind. The Last Frontier has intrinsic interest implied in the very title. No television viewer has long escaped a romanticized production of some phase of the cattle frontier. The figures of Matt Dillon and Calamity Jane and Wyatt Earp are considerably more familiar to children now than are Thomas Jefferson and George Washington and Abraham Lincoln. This may be unfortunate, but it is true, and it can be made to prove useful in the introduction of the "Last Frontier." Our generalized concept of the West is not at all in line with the real picture of the West as it actually was. Now the West is highly stereotyped and romanticized; the dirt does not show, and the villain always gets his just desserts while the hero prevails. At the same time, there is a false Robin Hood character given to every bad man of the Old West. Vigilante justice is shorn of its brutality and only the salutary results are left. Obviously the West, or any other time and place, has been inhabited by real people primarily concerned with making a living and working out their salvation as the environment allowed. The American West was no exception; it is only that the frontier idea has had a certain persistence in American thought, and it is interesting. The basic problem of the teacher is to show this difference between the real and the romanticized. Not much more than the mention of the frontier or the West is necessary to evoke the interest of almost any high school student. A short introductory lecture by the teacher on the subject of the romanticized West can very well serve to motivate students to a more thorough study of the subject. As one example, perhaps the most flagrant idealizing of a prairie badman, the dramatic story of the life and death of Billy the Kid and the subsequent myth that grew up around him could serve as a beginning.[3] The facts contrast sharply with the character of the popularized figure.

As the final result of a widespread and concentrated manhunt culminating years of terror perpetrated by Billy the Kid in the Southwest, Sheriff Pat Garrett, in 1881, shot Billy the Kid in an ambush. The whole West was vastly relieved momentarily to be rid of a lawless menace. However, in a very short time the romanticizing process set in, and Billy became confused in retrospect with the rapidly growing modern image of the West. On the other hand, nothing is remembered of the man who killed him except the name. The mixed emotions of the frontier are expressed in questionable literary form by a bit of doggerel:

[3] Other possibilities are suggested in the bibliography at the end of the chapter.

> Billy was a bad man,
> And carried a big gun,
> He was always after greasers,
> And kept 'em on the run.
>
> But one day he met a man
> Who was a whole lot badder
> And now he's dead,
> But we ain't none the sadder.

The bad men of the West included in their number many outright criminals who would have been outside the law anywhere, but the typical ones were the peculiar product of the advancing frontier. They were the circumstantial failures of the West. The Daltons, Youngers and the James' were of this type. Their careers gave rise to the western myth of chivalry and a quick gun which is still popular.

> Poor Jesse left a wife to mourn all her life,
> His children three were brave,
> But the dirty little coward that shot Mr. Howard,
> He laid Jesse James in his grave.

Included in the introductory lecture should be some description of the cultural setting and the physical environment—poor communication facilities, climate, means of agricultural livelihood including the ubiquitous feud between cattle herders and dirt farmers or "nesters," paucity of schools, frontier religion and the various ethnic traditions extended over from Europe. One of the best ways of illustrating the intangible cultural atmosphere of the West is by means of the songs and poetry that grew up in a folk manner. It might be useful to contrast an actual song used by cowboys to lull cattle to sleep on the open range, such at "Bury Me Not on the Lone Prairie," with Bing Crosby's rendition of "A Lone Cow Hand from the Rio Grand'." Exhibition of artifacts of the Old West is interesting; an old Colt .45 contrasts dramatically with a modern military .45 automatic pistol. Always using the theme of contrast between the real frontier and the modern dramatized version of the West, the teacher may set an intriguing scene to investigate. Students usually respond to truth, especially if it is dramatic.

The next step after introducing a unit is to evolve specific questions to be answered by the students in the course of studying the whole subject. These questions, of course, are suggested by the topic itself, by the mimeographed materials passed out by the teacher and by the things that the teacher might say. It is, however, important that the questions to be posed come from the students themselves, that enough interest be engendered in the students' minds so they will think about the problems presented and attempt to formulate questions which will further pull them into the subject. It is not desirable for the teacher to phrase and present certain stereotyped questions. If such questions are going to be used, then there is no need for the employment of a multi-text unit method of instruction. Much of the value of a unit approach is to get the students to evaluate critically the material at hand and to formulate their own vital propositions which they may in turn try to explain and amplify.

The teacher can avoid a diffusion of effort and disorganization of the questions that will arise by employing two techniques: first, he must have very clearly in mind a concise outline of what he expects his students to learn. This function can be assured by the preparation of a detailed plan, an outline of material, and by the use of a shorter, less detailed study guide for the use of the students. Second, the teacher should emphasize that there are certain generic guides to formulating questions based on common human behavior. Who, what, when, how and why, are key words and ideas to be considered in every subject. What kind of people came to the West? Who were they individually? What was their former environment? What setting did they find in the West? Why did they come? What did they do when they arrived? These questions are neither specific nor stereotyped in an obnoxious way. They all should lead to reflection on the part of the students and the emergence of specific, answerable questions concerning certain people and places and activities. The teacher should not hesitate to ask this sort of provocative question. The kind of question for the teacher to avoid asking might be, "Who was the greatest plainsman, and why did he come west?" In the first place it is unanswerable, and if it is answered, even erroneously, the statement can only be limited and perhaps meaningless. This would be an example of the stereotyped question, and it might be meant to evoke the stereotyped answer, "Buffalo Bill. Because he wanted to kill buffalo." Not much would be gained. Since children are largely concerned with themselves and with the present, questions about the past that have current meaning are most likely to emerge. For example, what might have happened in the days of the last frontier if there had been a Federal Bureau of Investigation, and Billy the Kid had found himself at the top of the list of the nation's ten most wanted men? What could the F.B.I. have done (more or differently) than the frontier posses, town marshals and local sheriffs? What differences would have been marked had there been available some of the modern crime detection procedures so familiar now to everyone, such as fingerprinting, high speed transmission of photographs and the many forms of chemical analysis used by criminologists? On the side of character evaluation, taking into account the generalized contemporary knowledge of psychology, what is the difference, if any, between a criminal of the type of Billy the Kid in a frontier setting and any modern gangster in Chicago or Los Angeles?

Questions of an entirely different quality might emerge. For instance, why did people apparently lose their balance and judgment to the extent of engaging in the gold rushes of the nineteenth century, especially the ones to ephemeral regions in the remote north and in the deserts of America? Or, in political terms, what elements were involved in the sometimes titanic struggles to gain statehood that went on in some of the western states? How did the process of gaining statehood in Washington compare with that of California, or more recently of Hawaii?

Questions will arise about any circumstance that can be used to exploit the abilities and energy of all of the students. After the class has agreed on a list of questions they should be reproduced in some fashion. They could be permanently written on the blackboard or on mimeographed sheets, or on a poster to be hung on the wall. The important point is that the questions be asked and accepted by the students as guides to their study.

Problem solving of this nature, paralleling a scientific method, follows the traditional three steps: hypothesis, data collection and evaluation, and conclusion with reformulation of new hypotheses. The questions plus the introductory outline constitute the "hypothesis." The next step is to search out the necessary data to frame answers to the questions, or illustration of the "hypothesis."

One of the most important considerations in applying the multi-text unit method is to keep in mind and to keep in the minds of the students that the problem under study has an open end, that no final answer is ever really available, that rather than an answer to a question there is only illustration of the problem in its various and unfolding aspects. Because of this point of view the possibilities in question framing are practically illimitable. As the work proceeds, in direct proportion to the interest, diligence and ability of the students, question after question will present itself for some kind of consideration. The teacher must meet this contingency with an open mind and willingness to consider and work on an ever expanding list of questions to be answered. An argument may be advanced that if all questions are continuously accepted as part of the work to be covered the work will never end. This is true to an extent, but one of the desirable outcomes of any teaching is to create a lasting interest in study, further individual study, of the topics. If a unit is not fully "completed" it is only another comment on the dynamic and continuing quality of true learning.

A device for controlling and organizing the various questions as well as for encouraging the "open end" character of the method is to prepare a chart or place on the blackboard all of the questions under the headings suggested above, that is, who, what, when, where and why. In this way, at any given point in time after the unit begins, there will be grounds for culminating generalizations in several categories, and if findings are always held to be tentative no harm is done by terminating study of a given unit before all of the material is exhausted. It merely leaves a residue of work to be done at some future time either as individuals or as members of some other class or group.

For most classes and for most average students the important body of material is encompassed in whatever textbook is available. Perhaps for everyone the initial assignment should be a specified group of pages in a common book in order to insure a universal minimum background of knowledge concerning the basic facts. Such a page assignment might very well accompany the outline of material previously placed on the board or distributed to the students.

As in all assignments, this one should be specific, with a certain reference and with a deadline date for completion along with a promise that it will be evaluated at a particular future date. It is important to tell children, as nearly as possible, exactly what is expected of them.

In addition, in order to put into practice the multi-text method and to take advantage of the known individual differences of the students, at the beginning of the actual assignment period in question, particular students, either singly or in groups, should be made responsible for answering certain of the class derived questions which make up the expanded "hypothesis." Specific dates and methods of reporting this information must be set up. A member of the class can be entrusted with recording the schedule of performance thus established. Naturally, the teacher will check on this performance, and the schedule should be posted.

As to the means of making reports, there are several possibilities which may be used. Many different kinds of reports may be combined in one unit, but it is probably less confusing to use one at a time.

That is, for the first round of answering questions, a series of two or three minute oral reports might be employed, giving each child in the class a chance to stand and deliver his findings to the whole group. The alternative of short written exercises, either prepared in class from notes or as homework, may be assigned. This method is less spontaneous and has the initial disadvantage of taking up quite a lot of time in reading the reports. Perhaps the first attack on a newly opened subject should be oral in order to invite discussion and further formulation of questions or of rephrasing the old ones.

As the discussion proceeds, after a few days it will become apparent that some of the questions posed at the outset need to be recast and made to assume more significance while others may be so easy to answer that they no longer need to be considered. For example, the mere existence of barbed wire might seem to be insignificant, especially in reference to the frontier. But with only a little preliminary investigation it becomes clear that without the invention of barbed wire and its widespread use as a cheap fencing material the great West might have gone on for years as an open ranging area for semi-wild cattle. The pattern of the "Last Frontier" would have been entirely different. Barbed wire, therefore, becomes a factor of major importance in any assessment of the West. Such a question as that concerning barbed wire, then, must be expanded and explored in all its ramifications.

As the hypothesis is refined and tentative findings are recorded in a study of the West, such a topic as barbed wire and its significance can be developed into a point of major emphasis. Topics of this degree of importance might be assigned to committees as the nuclei around which projects of various kinds may be organized. Depending on the skill of the students involved and the importance of the subject there are many ways of illustrating and reinforcing the learning process. One committee might be assigned the problem of writing an epic poem on the life of Jesse James or Wild Bill Hickok. Another might be given the task of reconstructing a gold mining camp such as could be found at Virginia City on the Comstock Lode in the 1870's. Still another could organize a panel discussion on the merits of Federal law enforcement in the territories as opposed to the system of local marshals and sheriffs. Tombstone, Arizona, largely under the control of federal marshals, contrasts nicely with Deadwood, South Dakota or Cheyenne, Wyoming.

As an alternative to the various types of presentation just suggested, each child or each committee, depending upon their skill, could be required to present a term paper or research report on a given topic. In this case it is necessary to spend some time explaining precisely how to go about the task. Each topic must be outlined and the outline checked by the teacher to insure its appropriateness and completeness. Next the students must take notes on their reading in some prescribed form satisfactory to the teacher. Finally, the finished written report must be prepared in an acceptable form with proper annotation, heading and style.[4]

After a week or two of semi-independent study of the "Last Frontier," most of the students will have acquired a general fund of information on the subject and will have achieved opinions on the controversial aspects of the problem. It is then time to consider the matter of bringing the unit to a close with an appropriate reinforcement of the most important elements of knowledge. There are two general types of culminating activity, one largely devoted to evaluation of the individual achievement, and the other mostly concerned with a capsulized presentation of high points in the study. Both forms can and should be used whenever possible. The latter probably has the greater reinforcing value and therefore should come first, followed by a test to determine the factual residue after study of a problem for a period of time. The whole grade for a unit should not be based on a single examination, so it is necessary to conduct short quizzes along the way and to record grades for each of the component performances or recitations—such as the reports, papers, panels, etc. Students should know the ways in which they are being judged and when such formal judgments are to take place.

One of the best ways to imprint memory of an important phase of history on students' minds is by means of a formal debate. At the end of study of a period in history at least two things usually emerge: first, there is often recognition of a core or central problem that has been illustrated but not definitively answered, and second, a certain group of students with superior ability and interest ordinarily becomes evident. These two circumstances can be put together to pinpoint for the rest of the class the most important elements of the study that has been in progress for several weeks. The topic of interest and importance can be presented as a formal debate, a climaxing performance, just prior to the final unit examination.[5]

[4] Note taking and outlining are treated elsewhere, see Chapter 5.
[5] See Chapter 8 for description of the debate technique.

The "Last Frontier" as a unit topic has, of course, many ramifications and much romantic detail, but the outstanding impression that tends to remain after studying the frontier is either a negative or positive reaction to the inevitability of the process of history. Did the frontier really exist as something different from any other experience? Has it actually disappeared? Was there something unique about American frontier mentality? What does it have to do with the technological revolutions of the late nineteenth and twentieth centuries? By choosing the most highly motivated and thoughtful students in a class, and after establishing a single resolution for debate, it is possible to present an hour-long program in formal arguments and rebuttals that can have a decided reinforcing result on the learning of a whole group.

As an example of a subject to discuss, consider the idea that the American frontier was typically the result of circumstance and personality, that the frontier experience was inevitable. Such a topic could be debated profitably. Another phrasing of the same topic might be: the American frontier produced and fostered democracy. This is, in effect, the hypothesis of Frederick Jackson Turner and it has been debated for over fifty years in the historical literature of the West.

### Many Other Methods Are Available

The above remarks are only suggestions for treatment of one of the topics of United States history, and only a few of the specific techniques of instruction available have been given. The possibilities are certainly too numerous to encompass in any one chapter of a book, and they are also too multitudinous to incorporate into the curriculum of a single year in any high school. Each teacher must evolve his own particular set of methods and the school must develop its own special curriculum.

Such suggestions as are made here only serve to illustrate one set of possibilities. Every period in history has high points and personalities that may be exploited by teacher and students to further the aim of education and the aim of historical study, to illuminate the past and thereby gain knowledge of man's cultural heritage that makes him different from all other beings on earth.

A fruitful exercise for any prospective teacher would be to select a period from United States history and develop it into a unit of instruction. Decide what constitutes proper objectives, long and short range, select the learning materials that will satisfy the goals, develop an outline and choose teaching methodologies that will motivate the students, gain and keep their interest and help them to learn the facts and formulations which have bearing on American life.

### Ideas Are Important

No matter what the content or the period of history involved, there is always a sure guide to the significant, the meaningful, and therefore to material which will be interesting. Ideas of men as they have affected the lives of other men are the only "real" facts of history. It is obvious, then, that ideas and their results, their circulation, must be the keynotes of any subject selected for historical consideration in the classroom.[6] "The Law in the Mind and the Thought in the Thing Determine the Method," may be taken as aphoristic statement of the whole problem of selecting, interpreting and teaching any phase of history. To illustrate, the Battle of Gettysburg, fought in 1863, was a diffuse and diverse struggle between two opposing forces, North and South. The troops were commanded by certain officers and there were certain numbers of killed and wounded on both sides. The outcome was assessed in purely military terms as a very costly victory for the North. Thousands of small incidents took place on the days of the great battle. Many personalities came into relief from time to time, and all of these facts could have been recorded and subsequent histories written about them. Many books and articles have been constructed out of the factual materials remaining from that episode. There was, however, a residue of affective results from the Battle of Gettysburg that had had little to do with the actual happenings of those days, recorded action by action. The independent facts of the battle could have been entirely different and the total resultant impact on American life would have been exactly the same. On the other hand, if the victors, the North, had espoused the ideas of the South, or some other ideology than the one they had, the total result would have been diametrically different than it truly was. Had that been the case, the minute, single events of the episode—the facts—could have been precisely the same as they actually were, but what a difference in the overall impact of ideas on men!

It is clear, then, that in history there are two kinds of facts; one set of facts can be recorded concisely and are subject to easy sense perception and intellectualization. The facts, exactly as they happened, may be said to form the basic body of historical source material, how-

[6] See William H. Mace, *Method in History* (Rand, McNally, Chicago, 1914), 2nd edition, Preface and Chapter I. This book is something of a classic although it is old and not generally read by modern students of pedagogy.

ever recorded or discovered. These "facts" have consequence and meaning only when considered in the light of the other sort of "facts," the ideas behind men's actions, and when interpreted, arranged and selected into an ideological pattern. Authors of history books do this, some, of course, better than others; so also must every teacher of history, and it is doubly important in the social studies instruction of secondary schools.

## 6. Suggested Activities for Further Study

1. Select a western theme for study of your local community, and then prepare a selected bibliography from local resources which could be used with an eighth grade class.
2. Work out a dramatization of some western figure based on his biography. As an example, the life of Jim Bridger is very important in relation to the nineteenth century migration of people over the Rocky Mountains. From the story of his life construct a short play that could be used to culminate an eighth grade unit on the Mountain Men.
3. Develop a satisfactory supplementary unit of study on state and local government, such as a secondary teacher in California would have to do in order to meet the state requirement.
4. Prepare a chronological table of the political campaigns up to the Civil War, showing the major parties, candidates and issues.
5. Outline a coordinated program of English literature and composition to accompany the study of the American frontier. This is the sort of requirement that was originally envisaged in the core or integrated program which has been adopted in many schools in the form of an allocation of two hours daily for social studies.
6. Canvass the currently available phonograph recordings, and develop a list of annotated recordings to illustrate the advance of the frontier from the Revolutionary War to the end of the frontier in 1890.

## 7. Teacher References on the Western Theme

GENERAL AND BACKGROUND

Robert E. Riegel, *America Moves West* (Holt, Rinehart and Winston, New York, 1956), is a fairly simple text built around the straightforward story of Americans filling up a continent. Essential emphasis is given to the chronological period between the adoption of the constitution and the closing of the frontier in 1890.

Ray Allen Billington, *Westward Expansion* (Macmillan, New York, 1949), presents a more detailed and somewhat longer account of the same process of westward movement of the American people. This book contains much anecdotal material and derives its interpretation from a diversity of sources.

Max Savelle, *A Short History of American Civilization* (Dryden, New York, 1957), especially chaps. 13, 15, 16, 17, 18, 19 and 22, illustrate non-political aspects of the sections of America.

*The American Nation,* edited by Albert Bushnell Hart (Harper, New York, 1904–1918), 28 vols.; vol. 4, E. G. Bourne, *England in America, 1580–1652;* vol. 7, Reuben Gold Thwaites, *France in America, 1497–1763;* vol. 14, *Rise of the New West, 1819–1829* by Frederick Jackson Turner, are all applicable.

Ray Allen Billington, *The Far Western Frontier, 1830–1860,* in New American Nation Series (Harper, New York, 1956), is the latest synthesis of the later frontier.

John Bartlet Brebner, *The Explorers of North America* (Anchor, Garden City, New York, 1955), is a good survey of the important explorations upon which the westward movement from Europe to America was made.

Charles E. Nowell, *The Great Discoveries and the First Colonial Empires* (Cornell University Press, Ithaca, New York, 1954), stresses the immediate result of exploration in the establishment of Western civilization in the New World empires of the 16th, 17th and 18th centuries. This is one of a series of in-expensive original books sponsored by Cornell University in an effort to make easily available the story of our cultural heritage extending from ancient times into the present.

Charles Raymond Beazley, *Dawn of Modern Geography* (Oxford Press, London, 1904–1906), 3 vols. (reprinted by Peter Smith, New York, 1949), is an old book, and a great one. It has the word geography in the title, but this is not the end of the idea presented. It is the first modern treatment on a large scale of the interrelationship of social processes in an adequate historical interpretation of man in the present world.

Frederick Jackson Turner, *The Frontier in American History* (Holt, New York, 1921), gives the basic ideas involved in the author's thesis concerning the outstanding significance of the frontier in American growth. It is around this book that the tremendous activity on the part of American historians has grown as they have tried to depict the story of the West. See Riegel, *op. cit.,* chapter 40.

John Carl Parish, *The Persistence of the Westward Movement* (University of California Press, Berkeley, 1943), is a small group of essays sharply illus-trating the persistent quality of the westward orientation of the American people even into the present day. The center of American population has consistently moved toward the Pacific coast from the first census to the last.

## ATLASES AND STATISTICS

*Hammond's American History Atlas* (Hammond, New York, 1954), is an inexpen-sive paper bound abridgement of historical and statistical data principally expressed in map form. Also useful for junior and senior high school students.

Thomas Pownall, *Topographical Description of the Dominion of the United States of America,* edited by Lois Mulkearn (University of Pittsburgh, 1949), was first published by the author at the time of the American Revolution in an attempt to get the British people to understand their American enemy. Pownall had been a colonial governor in the New World, and was a Member of Parliament at the outbreak of war.

*Historical Statistics of the United States, 1789–1945* (United States Government Printing Office, Washington, D.C., 1949), presents comparative tabulations of useful quantitative data concerning (among many other things) the westward movement.

## THE AMERICAN COLONIES AND REVOLUTION

Marshall Smelser, *American Colonial and Revolutionary History*, College Outline Series, No. 71 (Barnes and Noble, New York, 1950, 1952), contains a useful brief outline of the period, and most valuable bibliographical material.

*Great Britain and the Illinois Country, 1763–1774*, edited by Charles E. Carter and Clarence W. Alvord (American Historical Association, Washington, D.C., 1910), a collection of essays, shows the basic Anglo-Saxon quality of the American frontiersman.

Archer Butler Hulbert, *Historic Highways of America* (Clark, Cleveland, 1902–1905), 16 vols., especially *Braddock's Road* (1903), traces and documents the idea of natural roads to the West, from ancient animal use to the present.

Theodore Roosevelt, *The Winning of the West, Standard Library Edition* (Putnam, New York, 1889–1896), 4 vols., vol. 1 deals with the typically American aspects of the frontier.

Clark Wissler, *Indians of the United States* (Doubleday, New York, 1940), in chaps. 7–11, describes the Indian barrier to white advance into the West.

Lawrence Henry Gipson, *Great War for the Empire* (Knopf, New York, 1946–1949), vol. 1, *The Years of Defeat, 1754–1757* and vol. 2, *The Victorious Years, 1758–1760*, gives a detailed description of the military and political strife between Britain and France which finally ended in British supremacy after 1763.

Biographies of the men who pushed the Anglo-American frontier over the Appalachians and over the plains in the late eighteenth and nineteenth centuries offer delightful highlighting of the story. The drama of the frontier is heightened by the individual conquests of rugged and devoted men. In the remaining selections biography plays a major part.

## EIGHTEENTH CENTURY

Thomas Boyd, *Simon Girty* (Minton, New York, 1928), Indian fighter; Kenneth Bailey, *Thomas Cresap, Maryland Frontiersman* (Christopher Publishing House, Boston, 1944), describes a fabulous man who lived ninety years, facing westward with courage and spirit; H. A. Bruce, *Daniel Boone and the Wilderness Road* (Appleton, New York, 1902), illustrates the adventurous life of a great trail blazer; C. S. Driver, *John Sevier* (University of North Carolina Press, 1932), depicts "Nollichucky Jack," land speculator and pioneer in Tennessee; A. T. Volwiler, *George Croghan and the Westward Movement, 1741–1782* (Arthur H. Clark, Cleveland, 1926), is the life of a great Pennsylvanian, in tune with his time and devoted to the expansion of America; J. A. James, *The Life of George Rogers Clark* (University of Chicago Press, 1928), dramatizes the moving spirit in the settlement of the Ohio country; F. E. Wilson, *Arthur St. Clair* (Garrett, Richmond, Virginia, 1944), a great governor of Ohio Territory; Thomas Boyd, *Mad Anthony Wayne* (Scribner's, New York, 1929), further illustrates the reduction of the Ohio Valley to the uses of the Americans.

## THE JACKSONIAN WEST

Thomas P. Abernethy, *From Frontier to Plantation in Tennessee* (University of North Carolina Press, 1932), shows how the settled farmer came to be a democratic force in the West.

John Spencer Bassett, *The Life of Andrew Jackson* (Doubleday, New York, 1911), 2 vols., is a definitive work on Jackson himself, while Arthur Maier Schlesigner, Jr., *The Age of Jackson* (Little, Brown, Boston, 1945), relates the figure of Jackson to the political developments of the time.

Harriet Martineau, *Society in America* (London, 1837), presents an English view of the brawling West.

Richard M. Dorson, *Davy Crockett: American Comic Legend* (New York, 1939), puts a popular myth in its proper perspective.

Walter Blair and Franklin J. Meine, *Mike Fink: King of Mississippi Keelboatmen* (Holt, New York, 1933), paints the true picture of this colorful representative of a phase of the free West; Archer Butler Hulbert, *Paths of Inland Commerce* (Yale University Press, 1920), is a careful documentation of the part played by commerce in the expansion of democracy and the West; Mark Twain, *Life on the Mississippi,* is the great novelist's serious and factual account of the setting of his boyhood.

## MANIFEST DESTINY AND SECTIONALISM

*Journals of Lewis and Clark,* edited by Bernard De Voto (Houghton Mifflin, Boston, 1953), is a readable one volume condensation of the explorers' own record. It tells of the beginning of the process of "filling up" a continent. Also suitable for students.

Bernard De Voto, *The Course of Empire* (Houghton Mifflin, Boston, 1952), is an overall view of the western settlement.

*The Life and Adventures of James P. Beckwourth,* edited by Bernard De Voto (Knopf, New York, 1931), is a contemporary romanticized version of life on the plains just before the Civil War. Specializes in the tall tales of the West. A small paper bound excerpt is available under the editorship of Joseph Arnold Foster, Claremont College, 1950). This is one of several such selections illustrating various phases of western growth.

Frances Ann Kemble, *Journal of a Residence on a Georgian Plantation 1838–1839* (New York, 1863), is based on the letters written by the famous English actress while she was the wife of Pierce Butler living in Georgia. Selections edited by Joseph Arnold Foster (Claremont College, 1951).

Peter Cartwright, *Autobiography of Peter Cartwright, the Backwoods Preacher* (New York, 1856), illustrates vigorously the life of a minister in the frontier of Tennessee and Kentucky in the first quarter of the nineteenth century. Selections edited by Joseph Arnold Foster (Claremont College, 1950). These three books illustrate the sectional quality of the frontier growth shortly after it passes from the hunter-trapper phase.

J. D. Wade, *Augustus Baldwin Longstreet* (Macmillan, New York, 1924), tells of the times and life of the author of *Georgia Scenes,* the southern frontier.

*Religion on the Frontier,* edited by William Warren Sweet (Holt, New York,

1931), vol. 1, *Baptists, 1783–1830* (1931), is a collection of source material on the activities of that sect.

H. P. Beers, *Western Military Frontier, 1815–1846* (The Author, 52 Sunshine Road, Upper Darby, Pennsylvania, 1935), describes the nationalizing force of the army on the frontier and the West.

Lewis E. Atherton, *The Pioneer Merchant in Mid-America* (University of Missouri Press, 1939), concerns the problems of finance and banking for the merchantile interests of the West.

The Mexican struggle for independence and final statehood in the United States has produced a tremendous literature, both belletristic and factual. It would be impossible to encompass the whole field in a book full of titles. The controversies are legion and their reflection in books and artices is voluminous. Without entering into any more than a minimum of controversy it is an opinion that the following books will give a basic understanding of the problem: E. C. Barker, *The Life of Stephen F. Austin* (Cokesbury Press, Nashville, 1926); *Mexico and Texas, 1821–1835* (Southwest Press, Dallas, 1928); Marquis James, *The Raven* (Grosset and Dunlap, New York, 1956), 2nd ed., The Life of Sam Houston; J. D. P. Fuller, *The Movement for the Acquisition of All Mexico 1846–1848* (Johns Hopkins University Press, Baltimore, 1936); A. K. Weinberg, *Manifest Destiny* (Johns Hopkins University Press, Baltimore, 1935); Brainerd Dyer, *Zachary Taylor* (Louisiana State University Press, Baton Rouge, 1946); all sketch in various aspects of the Mexican War and the events leading up to it.

## THE LATER FRONTIER

Mark Twain, *Roughing It* (1872), contains personalized anecdotes of the West. Many students like these selections.

M. R. Werner, *Brigham Young* (Harcourt, Brace, New York, 1925), is the life of the mighty founder of Salt Lake City and the State of Deseret.

Louis Howland, *Stephen A. Douglas* (Scribner's, New York, 1920), tells of the personality who promoted western railroads, popular sovereignty, and sectional democracy in the West.

R. M. Robbins, *Our Landed Heritage* (Princeton University Press, 1942) recites the dreary tale of how American public lands were distributed without much profit to the nation.

Oswald Garrison Villard, *John Brown* (Houghton Mifflin, Boston, 1910), is the stark story of a madman who reflected a nation's madness.

Robert Glass Cleland, *Cattle on a Thousand Hills* (Henry E. Huntington Library, San Marino, California, 1941), among other things about California, tells of the impact of Anglo-Saxon culture on the leisurely ways of the Spaniards and the Mexicans. It is mainly about Southern California.

*The Journals of Francis Parkman*, edited by Mason Wade (New York, 1947), tells of the Oregon Trail and all that it implied to the West.

Fred Albert Shannon, *The Farmer's Last Frontier: Agriculture, 1860–1887* (1945), is a good survey of farming in the frontier West, and its relationship to the Populist movement.

John D. Hicks, *The Populist Revolt* (1931), examines the whole Populist movement toward American reform.

Theodore Saloutos and John D. Hicks, *Agricultural Discontent in the Middle West, 1900–1939* (University of Wisconsin Press, 1951), brings up to date the aftermath of the 19th century Populist movement.

Oscar O. Winther, *Via Western Express and Stagecoach* (Stanford University Press, 1945), tells of the competition for the western travel market.

Agnes C. Laut, *The Romance of the Rails* (McBride, New York, 1928), 2 vols., surveys western railroad development.

The Pacific Northwest, as a particular region in the greater West, offers a special opportunity to observe the economic relationship between expansion and the sources of financial support in the East:

James B. Hedges, *Henry Villard and the Railways of the Northwest* (Yale University Press, 1930); Henrietta M. Larson, *Jay Cooke, Private Banker* (Harvard University Press, 1936), concerns the financier of the Panic of 1876; J. G. Pyle, *The Life of James J. Hill* (Doubleday, New York, 1917), 2 vols.; Ernest Howard, *Wall Street Fifty Years after Erie* (Stratford, Boston, 1923); all give details of the growth.

Dorothy Johansen and Charles Gates, *Empire of the Columbia* (Harper, New York, 1957), is the newest general account of the Northwest, with a section on railroads.

R. C. Overton, *Burlington West* (Harvard University Press, 1941), shows how transportation came of age in the West.

Walter P. Webb, *The Great Plains* (Ginn, Boston, 1931), is a controversial book on the Southwest plains, but it also shows how the whole West became one, and then part of the United States.

The Granger Movement, the Populist Revolt, financial reform of the railroads and business, as well as the general move toward reform involving the whole nation, all played a special part in western development. A permanent imprint was made on American life which became apparent in the opening years of the twentieth century:

William Jennings Bryan, *The First Battle* (1896), the boy orator from the West preaches reform; Solon J. Buck, *The Granger Movement* (Harvard University Press, 1913), and *The American Crusade* (Yale University Press, 1920), Chronicles of America Series; C. McArthur Destler, *American Radicalism, 1865–1901* (Connecticut College Bookshop, New London, 1946), surveys the result; Frederick E. Haynes, *Third Party Movements since the Civil War* (1916), and *James Baird Weaver* (Iowa State Historical Society, 1919), show how a new party failed, but also how it influenced the old parties.

It is interesting to notice how similar forces affected Canada during the same period of time: Howard A. Fleming, *Canada's Arctic Outlet: A History of the Hudson Bay Railroad* (University of California Press, 1957), gives an exemplary study.

## SOCIAL BASIS FOR THE ROMANTIC AND FICTIONAL GROWTH IN AMERICAN HISTORY

Allan Nevins, *Emergence of Modern America* (Macmillan, New York, 1927), History of American Life Series, v. 8, pp. 235–251, sketches the emergence of the saga of the West; *Half Horse Half Alligator,* edited by Walter Blair and Franklin J. Meine (University of Chicago Press, 1956), traces the growth of the Mike Fink legend, with contemporary sources from 1823 to the present; William F. Cody, *An Autobiography of Buffalo Bill* (Cosmopolitan Bookshop, New York, 1920), illustrates the folklore basis of the cowboy myth as it was perpetuated by a late comer on into the twentieth century; *The American Songbag,* compiled by Carl Sandburg (Harcourt, Brace, New York, 1930), represents one collection of folk poetry and songs which illustrate the social ramifications of the West; Sigmund Spaeth, *Weep Some More, My Lady* (Doubleday, New York, 1927), describes American music in the West; J. A. Lomax, *Cowboy Songs, and Other Frontier Ballads* (1922), and *Songs of the Cattle Trail and Cow Camp* (Macmillan, New York, 1919), are collections of songs actually used in the social setting of the West. See especially Tooze and Krone, *Literature and Music as Resources for Social Studies* (Prentice-Hall, Englewood Cliffs, N.J., 1956), pp. 50–70.

Romantic aspects of the Far West in post-Civil War days that can be supported factually are illustrated by the following books on persons and institutions; the great gunmen of the West were few in number, and about equally divided between law breaking and law enforcement, and both groups contributed to the basis for the western myth of the fast draw and sudden death which has become such a real yet fictional part of our lives:

H. Birney, *Vigilantes* (Penn Publishers, Philadelphia, 1929), traces this legal substitute; Emmett Dalton, *When the Daltons Rode* (Doubleday, New York, 1931), is the story of professional bad men who countered the amateur vigilantes; *Pat F. Garrett's Authentic Life of Billy the Kid,* edited by M. G. Fulton (Macmillan, New York, 1927), is by the man who killed the famous Southwest bandit; M. A. Otero, *The Real Billy the Kid* (Wilson, New York, 1936), deglamorizes the badman; Emerson Hough, *Story of the Outlaw* (1905), is an attempt to explain and illustrate the typical badman of the West; J. B. Gillett, *Six Years with the Texas Rangers,* edited by Milo M. Quaife (Yale University Press, 1925), illustrates one experience with a particular antidote applied to the curse of the western outlaw; Walter P. Webb, *The Texas Rangers* (Houghton Mifflin, Boston, 1935), describes the famous law enforcement organization; F. J. Wilstach, Wild Bill Hickok, *The Prince of Pistoleers* (Doubleday, New York, 1926), he cleaned up Deadwood at the end of an era; D. Aikman, *Calamity Jane, and the Lady Wildcats* (Blue Ribbon Books, Toronto, 1940), shows that not only men could shoot and cause trouble; S. N. Lake, *Wyatt Earp* (Houghton Mifflin, Boston, 1931), is the story of the famous law man of Dodge City who kept order by the threat of his gun, actually killing only one man.

As the frontier passed, its romantic aspects became fictionalized and symbolized in the American mind as something that never really existed. At about the turn of the twentieth century this process came to its height, and shortly thereafter serious interpretation of its causes began. The following books make an effort to analyze the metamorphosis of the real West into a symbolic, fictional West: Bernard De Voto, *Mark Twain's America* (Little, Brown, Boston, 1935); William S. Hart, *My Life East and West* (Houghton Mifflin, Boston, 1929); in which a movie gunman tells of the process; Lucy L. Hazard, *The Frontier in American Literature* (Crowell, New York, 1927), is a sharp analysis.

Historical fiction has played a large part in American literary development since the eighteenth century, and within that category novels based on frontier themes are as old as American literature. Since James Fenimore Cooper made successes of his Leather-Stocking Tales the historical novel of the western frontier has been a recurring phenomenon. After desultory attempts throughout the nineteenth century, the form came into its own in the twentieth century. At the present time it is still a favorite medium, not only for belletristic writing, but for movies, radio and television. In 1957 the favorite American television show was "Maverick," tall tales of the "West." Two outstanding guides to historical fiction concerning American life are available to both teachers and students. Ernest E. Leisy, *The American Historical Novel* (University of Oklahoma Press, 1950), is divided into five parts chronologically, dealing with the various epochs of American advance through the years. Part III, "The Westward Movement," p. 114 ff., lists the novels of interest to this subject without regard to their grade placement in school. Hannah Logasa, *Historical Fiction and Other Reading References for Classes in Junior and Senior High Schools* (McKinley, Philadelphia, 1951), takes a world scope, and indicates the grade placement for reading difficulty of most of the material listed; pp. 163–176 are devoted to the expansion of the American West. Most of the novels listed below are suitable for some of the students.

Washington Irving, *A Tour on the Prairies* (1832), is a travelogue of the Jacksonian West.

James K. Paulding, *Westward Ho!* (1832), is a first novel of the Kentucky frontier.

Elizabeth Madox Roberts, *The Great Meadow* (1930), is a modern novel of the eighteenth century using the theme of movement from Virginia over the Wilderness Road into Kentucky.

Edward Everett Hale, *Philip Nolan's Friends* (1877), by the author of "The Man Without a Country," purports to be the real story of Philip Nolan, an intriguing friend of General Wilkinson in the early efforts to gain control of Texas from the Spaniards. See James R. Jacobs, *Tarnished Warrior* (1938), able, nonfictional biography of General James Wilkinson.

Samuel Hopkins Adams, *The Georgeous Hussy* (1934), is based on the activities of Peggy O'Neill Eaton, wife of the Secretary of War in Jackson's cabinet.

August Derleth, *Wind over Wisconsin* (1938); *Bright Journey* (1939); Iola Fuller, *The Loon Feather* (1940); *The Shining Trail* (1943); all deal with Indian themes based on the experiences of Tecumseh in the Ohio Valley and of the Black Hawk in the Mississippi Valley.

Walter D. Edmonds, *Rome Haul* (1929), illustrates canal life on the Erie. Herbert Quick, *Vandemark's Folly* (1922), and Samuel Hopkins Adams, *Canal Town* (1934), use the same theme.

Edward Eggleston, *Hoosier Schoolmaster* (1871); *The Circuit Rider* (1874); *The Graysons* (1887), about young Abe Lincoln; all picture life in Indiana and Illinois in the pre-Civil War period. Hamlin Garland, *Main-Travelled Roads* (1922), *Son of the Middle Border* (1917), are classics on the same sort of theme a little further west and a little later in time.

Emerson Hough, *The Mississippi Bubble* (1902); George Washington Cable, *The Grandissimes* (1880); romanticize the Louisiana Purchase and its subsequent settlement.

The Mexican War, after a hundred years, produced a crop of novels dealing with the obvious, violent side of the struggle for Texas, and also with the conflict of two different cultures; Mexican and American are shown at antipodal odds of good and evil. A few are listed here, beginning with those of highest literary merit: Robert W. Chambers, *Gitana* (1931), General Taylor's heroics and homeliness; Pendleton Hogan, *The Dark Comes Early* (1934), more patriotic and complex; J. Frank Davis, *The Road to San Jacinto* (1936), shows the irreconcilable conflict between two cultures; Anna Brand, *Thunder before Seven* (1941), intrigue; Laura Krey, *On the Long Tide* (1940), is studded with the stars of Texas—Austin, Houston, Crockett; Karl Wilson Baker, *Star of the Wilderness* (1941), romance; Herbert Gorman, *The Wine of San Lorenzo* (1945), is from a Mexican point of view.

The Far West early attracted novelists, beginning with Washington Irving, *Astoria* (1836), which became the basis for Gilbert Gabriel, *I, James Lewis* (1936), an exciting tale of adventure around the Horn to the Columbia; James Fenimore Cooper, *The Prairie* (1827), portrays the aging Natty Bumppo out on the far western frontier with the Shawnee; Francis Parkman, *Oregon Trail* (1847), is more factual history than fiction; Emerson Hough, *The Magnificent Adventure* (1916), fictionalizes the Lewis and Clark expedition; Alfred B. Guthrie, *The Big Sky* (1947), is a fine account of the hardships of the pioneers; *The Way West* (1949), carries on the theme of the former novel; Archie Binns, *The Land is Bright* (1939), and *Mighty Mountain* (1940), are set in Oregon and Washington Territory.

A special subdivision of the Far West was California before and after the American advance into the Indian and Spanish culture of the Pacific Coast; Bret Harte, *Gabriel Conroy* (1876), shows cannibalism and intrigue in the fabulous land; Mark Twain, *Roughing It* (1872), is filled with the tall tales of the West; Mary Austin, *Isidro* (1905), pre-American California; Gertrude Atherton, *The Californians* (1898), *Rezanov* (1906), show Spain, Britain and Russia struggling to hold the idyll of California; Helen Hunt Jackson, *Ramona* (1884), is still powerful sentimentalism concerning the transition from Spanish to American rule in California; Vardis Fisher, *The Mothers* (1943), depicts the tragedy of the Donner Party's mishap; Stewart Edward White, *Gold* (1913), *Gray Dawn* (1915), *Rose Dawn* (1920), present a tale of growth from lawlessness to modern economic reality in California.

Vardis Fisher, *Children of God* (1939), is the story of Utah and Brigham Young's dream.

The most prolific period of historical novel production about American expansion occurred in the twentieth century and concerned a period after the pioneering had mostly been done. The growth of population in the United States took its greatest spurt after 1890, and this seemed to produce the romantic interest in a time that was really past. With a certain realistic attention to detail the novelists wrote highly romantic tales of the last days of the mining, farming and cattle frontiers. There is also a large amount of social significance in this group of novels.

Willa Cather, *O, Pioneers!* (1913); *My Antonia* (1918), concern immigrants from Europe in the New World. They are also suitable for advanced junior and senior high school students. *A Lost Lady* (1923), is about western railroading; *Death Comes for the Archbishop* (1927), tells of a Catholic community in the Far West.

Ole Rolvaag, *Giants in the Earth* (1927); *Peder Victorious* (1929); and *Their Fathers' God* (1931); round out a gripping story of Scandinavians adjusting to the soil and customs of the New World through three generations.

Bess Streeter Aldrich, *A Lantern in Her Hand* (1928), shows the movement of farmers from Iowa to Nebraska at the end of the Civil War; Rose Wilder Lane, *Let the Hurricane Roar* (1933), and *Free Land* (1938), use the theme of corruption and neglect in the land policies of the West; Horace Kramer, *Marginal Land* (1939), is the struggle between farmer and rancher.

Joseph Hergesheimer, *The Limestone Tree* (1931), shows the American family as it passes from pioneer Kentuckian to defeat; Louis Bromfield, *The Farm* (1933), does a similar thing in Ohio; Ross Lockridge, *Raintree County* (1947), is the most recent in the "decaying family" genre, set in Indiana.

Edna Ferber, *Saratoga Trunk* (1941), moves from New York to New Orleans.

Walter Van Tilberg Clark, *Ox-bow Incident* (1940), is a special treatment of the miscarriage of vigilante justice, terrible and real.

H. L. Davis, *Honey in the Horn* (1935), is a mainly realistic book about the late coming pioneers in Oregon.

Edna Ferber, *Cimarron* (1930), glamorizes settlement of Oklahoma.

## 8. Student References

UNITED STATES HISTORY TEXTBOOKS

Junior High Level

Alice W. Spieseke, "Bibliography of Textbooks in the Social Studies, 1954–1955," *Social Education* (December, 1955), is an example of the annual listing, by Spieseke, of additions to the comprehensive listing which she prepared in *Bulletin 23*, National Council for the Social Studies (Washington, D.C., 1949. These items are merely listed, with full bibliographical information, but no annotation. Louis Vanaric is now responsible for the annual supplements.

Gertrude Hartman, *America: Land of Freedom* (Heath, New York, 1955), is a reasonably comprehensive coverage of the history of the United States, balanced well in terms of emphasis given to the various time segments. It has been adopted in The California State Textbook Series. *Making of a Democracy* (John Day, New York, 1941), by the same author, develops the background of American growth. The two books complement each other.

Mable B. Casner, *The Story of American Democracy* (Harcourt, Brace, New York, 1955), is the current revised version of the popular Casner and Gabriel text, *Exploring American History*, that has been popular for so many years. This work carries out the continuing theme of democratic growth in successive frontiers. The Turner thesis is evident here. This book is sometimes used in the eleventh grade also for slower readers.

Theodore Cavanagh and Ann Hall, *Our Country's Story* (Rand, McNally, Chicago, 1954), is a simple, straightforward text with some emphasis on the westward movement.

Edna McGuire, *Full Grown Nation* (Macmillan, New York, 1946), gives American political history from 1787 to the end of World War II. Edna McGuire and Thomas B. Portwood, *Our Free Nation* (Macmillan, New York, 1957), is a new edition of the same book brought up to date. In fact, it has a marked emphasis on presentism and broadens the base of approach to include history, geography, government and citizenship with a democratic theme. Marion Lansing, *Makers of the Americas* (Heath, New York, 1955), tells the political story illustrated with maps and pictures.

Charles H. Coleman and Edgar B. Wesley, *The Story of American Democracy* (Heath, New York, 1939), brings the American story up to its date of publication in readable fashion. It has many themes. Used in conjunction with a more recent book it is highly satisfactory. Such a book might be, Louise I. Capern, *Being a Citizen* (American, San Francisco, 1947), mainly concerned with the problem of citizenship in the atomic age.

Smith Burnham, *The Making of Our Country* (Winston, Philadelphia, 1956); Henry W. Elson, *United States, Its Past and Present* (American, New York, 1956); William B. Guitteau, *Our United States* (Silver, Burdett, New York, 1956); Ruth West, *Story of Our Country* (Allyn and Bacon, Boston, 1954); are all sound texts for junior high school use.

Special Purpose Texts

Mary Kelty, *The Growth of the American People and Nation* (Ginn, Boston, 1940), is a book oriented toward the adjustment needs of children who want to and need to learn more about themselves as individual personalities in the setting of American civilization.

Emerson M. Brooks, *The Growth of a Nation* (Dutton, New York, 1956), gives a pictorial review of United States history from colonial times to the present.

Eugene C. Barker, Walter P. Webb and William E. Dodd, *The Growth of a Nation* (Harper, New York, 1956), is a comprehensive text most suitable for senior high school students, but it could be used with very advanced junior high school people.

Earl Schenk Miers, *Rainbow Book of American History* (World, 1955), highlights the view of American history by describing certain adventurous moments in the lives of great persons. A good deal of stress is given to the westward direction of the founders of the American state, including Lief Ericson. The book is illustrated beautifully, and it is written with a highly polished literary flair.

Emlyn D. Jones, J. Warren Nystrom, Helen Harter, *Within Our Borders* (the United States); *Within the Americas* (North and South America); *Beyond Our Borders* (Canada and Latin America); *Beyond the Oceans* (Eurasia, Africa, Australia); and, at a considerably lower level, Jane McGuigan and Laura Mengert Hugley, *Many Lands* (Rand, McNally, Chicago, 1955), is a Social Studies Series prepared primarily for the elementary school, but these books are also available to junior high school students. The material covered ranges through geography and history of the United States, the Americas, Canada and topics throughout the world. These books are exploratory in nature, and have an interest level sufficient for the needs of adolescents. The language is simple enough for even a retarded seventh grader to understand. They do not have sufficient scope or detail to serve as basic texts for the eighth and ninth grade offerings in social studies, but they may be quite useful as supplementary or remedial materials.

## UNITED STATES GOVERNMENT TEXTBOOKS

Vanza N. Devereaux and Homer Ferris Aker, *Living in Our Democracy* (Harr, Wagner, San Francisco, 1955), is a new revision of an old text in civics and government; in California state series.

Edward A. Krug and I. James Quillen, *Living in Our Communities* (Scott, Foresman, New York, 1954); Nadine Clark, James B. Edmondson and Arthur Dondineau, *Civics for Americans* (Macmillan, New York, 1954); are sound texts for junior high school study of American government.

Frank A. McGruder and William A. McClenaghan, *American Government in 1955* (Allyn and Bacon, Boston, 1955), is the latest revision (since 1917) of a standard government text for high school students. It is too difficult for most eighth or ninth graders, but it might be available to the occasional accelerated student.

Howard E. Brown, *Getting Adjusted to Life* (Lippincott, New York, 1955); Judson T. Landis and Mary G. Landis, *Building Your Life* (Prentice-Hall, Englewood Cliffs, New Jersey, 1954); Harriet F. Smith with Ernest W. Tiegs and Fay Adams, *Your Life as a Citizen: Nation, World* (Ginn, Boston, 1955); Ira Wilder and Jerome Sherk, *Visualized Citizenship Economics* (Oxford Book Company, New York, 1954); are all specialized books dealing with various phases of civics and citizenship. They are useful in the degree that an eighth grade is led into the ramifications of American government and its accompanying elements of specialized citizenship. Ordinarily such subjects would not be taken up until a later time in the child's education.

In California, according to state law, children in the eighth grade are required to take and pass certain tests in American and local government, therefore a reasonable portion of the curriculum for the eighth grade must be devoted to civics. This is not the case in many other states, and we feel that the eleventh or twelfth grade is a more appropriate place in which to study the constitution in detail.

## BOOKS TO ENRICH THE STUDY OF THE WESTWARD MOVEMENT

Edith Dorian and W. N. Wilson, *Trails West and Men Who Made Them* (McGraw-Hill, New York, 1955), sketches the history of the American West by means of personal vignettes centered around the activities on the principal overland trails up to the Civil War. It is well illustrated.

Emerson, Chase and Nevins, *Pioneer Children of America* (Heath, Boston, 1955), is an interesting and entertaining way of getting at early western history.

Helen Mitchell, *Ships that made United States History* (McGraw-Hill, New York, 1950), is the story of famous voyages and ships from *Santa Maria* to the signing of peace with Japan aboard the *Missouri* at the end of World War II.

Marie Lawson, *Pocahontas and Captain John Smith: The Story of the Virginia Colony* (Random House, New York, 1950), tells of the fortunes of the first English settlers in the New World.

William C. Langdon, *Everyday Things in American Life, 1607–1776* (Scribner's, New York, 1937), shows how the early colonists lived, what they ate and how they made a living.

Van Wyck Mason, *Winter at Valley Forge* (Random House, New York, 1953), is the account of the ordeal by heroic men which marked the low point of the American Revolutionary War.

James Henry Daugherty, *Of Courage Undaunted: Across the Continent with Lewis and Clark* (Viking, New York, 1951), tells of two years of wild and terrible experience from the Mississippi to the mouth of the Columbia with all of the excitement of discovery.

Julia Davis, *No Other White Men* (Dutton, New York, 1937), dramatizes the Lewis and Clark expedition, with emphasis on the characters of the two men.

Harry Danford, *Ohio Valley Pioneers* (Rand, McNally, Chicago, 1931); Dana Hanna, *Pioneering in Ten Communities* (Scott-Foresman, Chicago, 1945); Ralph Hunkin and Regina Allen, *Trapper Days* (American, New York, 1942); Rose Nida, *Explorers and Pioneers* (Macmillan, New York, 1953); Barbara Comfort, *Flatboats and Wagon Wheels* (Beckley-Cardy, New York, 1943); Enid Meadowcroft, *By Wagon and Flatboat* (Crowell, New York, 1951); Frederick Starr, *American Indians* (Heath, Boston, 1941); all deal with various aspects of pioneering in the early nineteenth century.

The Great Plains, commencing with their "discovery" in the early nineteenth century, offer a special phase of American westward development. It was here that the typical symbolic West of the present day came into being; wagon trains, cattle herding, the gold rushes, scouts, Indians, gunmen—all had their genesis in the Great Plains. Following is a short selection of books which will prove useful in helping junior high school students to get at some of the facts and a sense of appreciation of the American West. Reading difficulty ranges from elementary to adult: Henry Cabot Lodge and Theodore Roosevelt, *Hero Tales From American History* (Century, New York); William J. McConnell and H. R. Driggs, *Frontier Law* (American, New York); Carl Rydell, *On Pacific Frontiers* (World, New York); Edwin L. Sabin, *With Carson and Fremont* (Lippincott, Philadelphia); Clarence W. Taber, *Breaking Sod on the Prairies* (World, New York). These are older books slanted at a young adult level. The better students in eighth grade can read them.

James Beals, *The Rush for Gold* (Wheeler and Company, New York, 1946); Mary Jane Carr, *Children of the Covered Wagon* (Crowell, New York, 1943); Barbara Comfort, *Prairie Schooners West* (Houghton, Mifflin, Boston, 1939); Frank Charles DeWitt, *The Story of the Mississippi* (Harper, New York, 1947); Ruth L. Holberg, *Oh, Susannah* (Doubleday, Doran, Garden City, 1940); James P. McNeer, *The Gold Rush* (Grossett and Dunlap, New York, 1938); May Yonge McNeer, *The Story of the Great Plains* (Rand, McNally, Chicago, 1938). These books represent a selection of material at average levels of difficulty to illustrate facets of the westward movement primarily centered in the central part of America in the middle of the nineteenth century.

For the purposes of incidental corrective reading in the social studies program, and for background supplementation in the subject matter, it is necessary to furnish books at a fairly low reading level of difficulty but at the same time with enough intrinsic interest and factual content so that the junior high school students will not feel that they are wasting their time in a babyish pursuit. There are many such books. It would be impossible to list them all here, but a few samples may give the idea of the type of material that is desirable. Very often, for the purpose of developing a scanty background, it is possible to use an especially good text-book from elementary school. These are usually found among the regional or specialized books, dealing in detail but simply with some small aspect of American history and life. Such a one is Lola B. Hoffman, *California Beginnings* (Sacramento,

1948), one of the California State Text Series, and designed as a text reference for the fourth grade. Its reading difficulty is at about sixth grade, but the interest level is much higher, and the quality of the factual material contained is certainly of unimpeachable accuracy. It is also illustrated very well.

Specifically for the needs in corrective reading, social studies materials organized around the westward expansion theme, there is the American Adventure Series, with its accompanying map, *Trails* (Wheeler Publishing Company, 161 E. Grand Ave., Chicago, 1957). Titles included in this series are: *Chief Black Hawk, Daniel Boone, The Rush for Gold* and *Wild Bill Hickok,* among others. The interest level of all of these is sufficiently high for the eighth grade while the reading difficulty is carefully graded from second to sixth. There are manuals to help the teacher identify the need and use of such books.

Another list of books, principally biographies, is available in the Landmark Series (Random House, New York). These have a reading difficulty ranging from sixth grade to ninth, but their interest level is universal and most appropriate for junior high school students. They are not for remedial purposes, but rather for enrichment of the faster students' appreciation of American history. The titles appropriate to a study of the West include: Armstrong Sperry, *The Voyages of Christopher Columbus;* James Daugherty, *The Landing of the Pilgrims;* Marie Lawson, *Pocahontas and Captain John Smith;* Dorothy Canfield Fisher, *Paul Revere and the Minute Men;* May McNeer, *The California Gold Rush;* Samuel Hopkins Adams, *The Pony Express;* Adele Nathan, *The Building of the First Continental Railroad;* Samuel Hopkins Adams, *The Santa Fe Trail;* Richard L. Neuberger, *The Lewis and Clark Expedition;* Quentin Reynolds, *Custer's Last Stand;* Robert Tallant, *The Louisiana Purchase;* John Jennings, *Clipper Ship Days;* James Daugherty, *Trappers and Traders of the Far West,* the story of John Jacob Astor's expeditions to the mouth of the Columbia; William Johnson, *Sam Houston, The Tallest Texan;* Stewart Holbrook, *Wild Bill Hickok Tames the West;* George R. Stewart, *To California by Covered Wagon;* Ralph Moody, *Kit Carson and the Wild Frontier;* Charlotte Jackson, *The Story of San Francisco.*

There are innumerable other biographies which fall into the same category as those listed above, such as: Fruma Gottschalk, *The Youngest General* (Knopf, New York, 1949), the life and times of the Marquis de Lafayette during the American Revolution; Marion Marsh Brown, *The Swamp Fox* (Westminster, Philadelphia, 1950), the story of General Francis Marion and his adventures in the southern frontier before and during the Revolution; Ethel Hueston, *Calamity Jane of Deadwood Gulch* (Bobbs-Merrill, New York, 1937), relates the colorful life of Jane, the last of the western wild women, who outlived her friend Wild Bill Hickok from 1875 to 1902.

Stanley Vestal, *Jim Bridger, Mountain Man* (Morrow, New York, 1946), is an exceptionally fine biography of the fabulous old scout and mountaineer who had his hand in nearly every wagon train crossing the Great Plains during the middle part of the nineteenth century. This author is exceptionally fortunate in being able to relate a biography in reasonably simple language and at the same time he can tell the salient facts about a time and place. His books are not particularly meant for children, but for persons of any age who can read they certainly can furnish a delightful intellectual experience. Other titles by the same author, covering a wide range of western themes, are: *Kit*

*Carson, Sitting Bull, Warpath, King of the Fur Traders, Bigfoot Wallace, The Old Santa Fe Trail, New Sources of Indian History, Mountain Men, Short Grass Country, Fandango: Ballads of the Old West, 'Dobe Walls, Revolt on the Border, Happy Hunting Grounds* and *The Missouri.*

## FILMS

*Educational Film Guide* (Wilson, New York), has been published in monthly increments since 1936. It contains current listings of films with annotations by teachers in the field. The following selection of films was made from the 1953 edition. They are available from the following suppliers:

ACF Academic Film Company, 516 Fifth Avenue, New York 36.
CF Coronet Films, Chicago.
EcB Encyclopaedia Britannica, 2129 NE Broadway, Portland 5, Oregon.
IGP International Geographic Pictures, 1776 Broadway, New York 19.
TFC Teaching Films Custodian, 25 West 43rd Street, New York 36.

"Story of Christopher Columbus," re-enacts the events leading up to the discovery of America, including Columbus' life from boyhood to 1492; sd 17 min, b&w EcB rental $4.00.

"Colonial Children," a colonial family's day from the morning chores to the reading of the scriptures by the fireside at night. It shows details of home, clothing and customs; sd 11 min, b&w EcB rental $2.50.

"Planter of Colonial Virginia," presents the physical and social environment of the Virginia colony immediately preceding the Revolutionary War. It considers slavery, manufacturing, transportation, medicine, penology and other social customs; sd 11 min, b&w, EcB rental $2.50.

"Our Louisiana Purchase," dramatizes the historical events in Europe and the United States in connection with the purchase from France in 1803. Napoleon, Tallyrand, Jefferson and Livingston all appear; sd 20 min, b&w, ACF rental $5.00.

"Territorial Expansion of the United States from 1783 to 1853," shows the growth of the United States from colonial times to its present size in chronological order. There are animated maps showing boundary disputes and great historical events; sd 22 min, b&w, IGP rental $4.00.

"Dixieland," is a rapid view of the South, backwater of the westward movement, emphasizing places and persons of historic interest; sd 11 min, b&w, TFC.

"Who are the People of America?" explains where Americans originally came from, how they fought together, plowed the land and built cities; sd 10 min, b&w, CF.

"English Influence in the United States," traces some of the basic influences of English culture in our own. The idea of democratic action, our body of law, freedom of speech, and other such ideas and ideals are brought into focus; sd 10 min, b&w, CF.

"French Influence in the United States," is an analysis of language, dress and architecture, showing how they were influenced by the French elements in the settlement of the New World from the explorers on down; sd 10 min, b&w, CF.

The following publications are useful guides to further film material in connection with junior high school social studies: William H. Hartley, *A Guide to Audio-Visual Materials for Elementary School Social Studies* (Rambler Press, Brooklyn, 1950); Seerley Reed and Anita Carpenter, *A Directory of 2660 16mm Film Libraries*, Bulletin 1953, No. 7, United States Office of Education (Washington, D.C., 1953); *Free and Inexpensive Learning Materials*, Division of Surveys and Field Services, George Peabody College for Teachers (Nashville, 1954).

## 9. Suggested Activities for Further Study

1. Illustrate the points of variance between two major interpretations of American political history: economic determinism and the frontier hypothesis of American democracy. In this light, contrast the approaches to history of Charles Beard and Frederick Jackson Turner.

2. In what ways does present American life reflect the continued heritage of Western democratic man's search for a rule of law?

3. What, in your opinion, would be the best approach to an eleventh-grade curricular inclusion, assuming that it must deal with American growth? For example, choose between a course in political history, one stressing some particular social theme and a course combining political history and government organization and operation. Give your psychological reasons for the choice, and develop a bibliography for student and teacher.

4. How much geography should be included in any high school course in history? Should it all be in one grade? Should it be combined with every grade's subject matter as a support for the historical core of study?

5. Draw up a plan of instruction for the eleventh grade that will accommodate both the historical and political aspects of American life as well as the humanistic growth. Make provisions for the study of American classics of literature in their true relationship to the growth of American democratic political ideals. List some books that will support your philosophy in this regard. Indicate how much time in the total curriculum your suggestions ought to take, both in hours per day and in the number of years it should cover.

6. Make a list of twenty-five political biographies of persons in United States history who have contributed substantially to our traditions. Choose books that can be read and understood by high school students with average ability.

# 10

# Teaching civic competence

Supposing that we should even be obliged to take democracy with all the disadvantages that were ever annexed to it, and that no remedy could be discovered for any of its defects, it would still be greatly preferable to the exclusive systems of other forms.

WILLIAM GODWIN, 1793

## 1. Our Democratic Heritage

In this day of nearly universal high school attendance, the upper grades in high school seem the most appropriate place for the student to examine United States political history and the dynamics of democratic government. For many, about two-thirds, it may be the last chance to study in an organized way the democratic heritage of their country. In the lower grades the ordinary student has come in contact with at least some phases of United States and world history, with some practice in applying the principles of democratic citizenship in a classroom setting. Here, in secondary school, a year or so before the young citizen will be a member of society unaided by the guiding hand of the public school, he should make a review of those responsibilities which he will legally face at age twenty-one—only two or three years after he graduates from high school.* To others, who will go on to college, it offers a preliminary chance to explore the processes of American government which can be expanded and clarified further during the baccalaureate years.

Fundamental American liberties can be analyzed as a complex arrangement of political institutions and rights, along with their growth. It is obvious that no set of rules or constitutional language can really establish a democracy, but without them and especially without knowing about them, it is impossible to have anything approaching social,

* In Georgia and Kentucky, the voting age is eighteen. In Alaska it is nineteen. In Hawaii it is twenty.

economic or political democracy. In essence, democratic procedures in government are simple. In practice, of course, it is necessary to incorporate the principles with a tradition of democratic action. Present American life is precisely that blend of republican principles and procedures and a democratic tradition that has been wrested from authoritarian beginnings and which has been protected through nearly two centuries of continual struggle—mainly through the medium of education, formal and otherwise, along with a great deal of thoughtful criticism.

In order to get at the essence of this study with high school students it is probably desirable to take up certain wide topics of interest and conflict during the various stages of growth from exploration and settlement down to this century. It is possible to organize courses covering three or four semesters which include an amalgamation of political history and government, but ordinarily the two subjects are kept separate. United States history and Problems in American Democracy are generally two distinct courses in high school although their purposes are very much the same, that is, to produce more competent citizens.

Some exemplary aspects of the historical growth of the American political heritage may be given. This listing is not meant to be exhaustive, only illustrative of the types of subjects that may lend substance to high school history and government classes.

### Sources of Authority

In the Middle Ages the divine purpose of man was to glorify God, administered on earth by absolute monarchs. This notion was first weakened by Magna Carta, then extended to a wider base by the growth of parliament in Britain and the development of a middle class. After the Protestant Reformation the divine purpose came to be identified with evidences of salvation, such as wealth which typified the newer middle classes in England and America. Religious sects such as the Dissenters, Puritans, Congregationalists and later the Quakers, moved more and more to the "left," adhering to group decisions rather than relying on autocracy. Protestant English settlers in New England identified Godliness with the Town Meeting. By the end of the seventeenth century Lockean ideas of government by compact had been combined with a growing belief in natural rights to make constitutional form into a substitute for divine purpose as the source of authority on earth. Early examples of documents bearing this message were the Mayflower Compact, Connecticut's Fundamental Constitutions, Massachusetts' rules for its General Court and Virginia's charter foundation for its House of Burgesses. In fact, each American colony had a charter which gradually turned into a written constitution, a guarantee of liberties and a source of authority.[1]

## The American Revolution

The Revolution was a social movement lasting over a century before 1776. Illustrating this is the story of Bacon's Rebellion, 1676, a conflict between back country people and the ruling oligarchy at the sea-coast.[2] The Regulator Movement just before the Revolution was further activity of the same kind. There were many. John Adams said that the "revolution was over before the war began." He meant that the social change had taken place which defined democracy as a feeling for decentralized local control of political and judicial affairs.[3] After the French and Indian War (1754–1763), British imperial control of the American colonies was resisted through a series of conflicts. For example, the Stamp Act, 1765, produced the Stamp Act Congress and almost created open revolt. It was repealed. The First Continental Congress was convened in 1774, and brought into the open a determined opposition to imperial control which finally led to American sovereignty. The Second Continental Congress proclaimed the Declaration of Independence, giving status to the war already begun. During the fighting, the Articles of Confederation became the first constitution of the United States, and clearly stated a belief in the eighteenth century idea of decentralization.[4]

## The Constitution from 1787 to 1800

Decentralization as a mode of government became intolerable after the Revolutionary War. Through the activities of the Federalists—such men as Washington, Hamilton, Madison—the Constitutional Convention met in Philadelphia in 1787 and produced a new document, the

[1] See *Problems in American History,* edited by Richard W. Leopold and Arthur S. Link (Prentice-Hall, Englewood Cliffs, New Jersey, 1957, 2nd ed.), which contains information on a number of basic elements in American political history.

[2] Thomas Jefferson Wertenbaker, *Torchbearer of the Revolution* (Princeton University Press, 1940).

[3] John Franklin Jameson, *The Revolution Considered as a Social Movement* (Princeton University Press, 1926).

[4] Merrill Jensen, *The Articles of Confederation* (University of Wisconsin Press, 1940, 1955), gives the most complete and scholarly view of the precise quality of the Articles of Confederation as a national governing instrument reflecting eighteenth century conceptions of democracy.

Constitution, ratified by nine states in 1788, thereby becoming the organic law of all of them. It was an attempt to synthesize the gains of the Revolution, safeguarding the rights of property and at the same time giving attention to the rights and the will of a majority of qualified citizens. There is still considerable controversy as to the predominant motivation of the founding fathers: whether it was the result of economic interest or a more general concern with the public welfare.[5] Whatever the reason, the new government was organized and the public debt of states and the nation was funded, establishing American credit and the national debt. Hamilton's *Report on Manufactures* suggested the future ability of the United States to sustain the debt, and was incidentally a harbinger of American future economic trends. Jefferson as Secretary of State and Hamilton as Secretary of the Treasury clashed from the outset and formed the basis for the two-party development that took place later. They represented two quite disparate points of view.[6]

### The Revolution of 1800

President Thomas Jefferson became a different figure than he was as spokesman for revolution and author of the Declaration of Independence. He accepted the responsibility of running the federal state as a centralized democracy under the Constitution. Jeffersonian liberal interpretation of the Constitution became the foil for Federalist strict construction of that document. Neither side was completely successful, but both parties made lasting impressions on the beginning phases of our state. Depending upon which group was in office the adherence to strict or loose construction passed back and forth. The Revolution of 1800 was primarily a shift in control of power from the Federalists to the Jeffersonians. John Marshall, a Federalist, served as Chief Justice of the Supreme Court throughout the Rule of the Virginia Dynasty (all

[5] Charles A. Beard, *An Economic Interpretation of the Constitution* (Macmillan, New York, 1913, 1935), is the classic statement of the direct economic influence on persons who were instrumental in getting the Constitution into effect.

Robert E. Brown, *Charles Beard and the Constitution* (Princeton University Press, 1956), purports to be a "critical analysis of '*An Economic Interpretation of the Constitution*'," and in fact is a marshalling of evidence in contravention of Beard's contentions.

Alexander Hamilton, John Jay and James Madison, *Federalist Papers* (many editions), is the contemporary argument for adoption of the Constitution. It consists of a number of separate articles prepared by those three outstanding spokesmen for the Federalist party.

[6] Claude G. Bowers, *Jefferson and Hamilton* (Houghton Mifflin, Boston, 1925), is a Jeffersonian interpretation of the growth of democracy.

of the Republican-Democratic Presidents from Jefferson to Monroe, 1800 to 1824). Jefferson tended to liberalize the state while Marshall produced one decision after another setting precedents of solidity and the rights of property.[7] The Monroe Doctrine, at the end of the era in 1823, marked the beginning of American hemispheric policy and embarkation on the sea of international relations. John Quincy Adams, Secretary of State, was its chief architect. He called himself the "last Federalist," and served in the Presidency from 1825 to 1829.

### Jacksonian Democracy

The present Democratic party was formed in 1824 through coalition of western farmers and city workers. Jackson, the first presidential candidate, received a plurality, but not a majority. In the House of Representatives Henry Clay threw his support to Adams. The next election, in 1828, saw a clean sweep for the Democrats. Jackson interjected a new note into American democracy by making it clear that there must be a sense of nationalism as well as local rights. His effect was to extend personal political participation, but also to strengthen the national state. Part of the Jacksonian surge was the opposition to it which developed and out of which came the Whig party. William Henry Harrison was inaugurated in 1841, but he died the same year. His Vice-President, John Tyler, soon reverted back to the Democrats. The Whigs did not have a positive program satisfactory to all their diverse elements. They were against westward expansion and the annexation of Texas in the North, but in the South they were expansionist. Tyler dealt them a blow when he signed the bill annexing Texas in 1845, just before he went out of office.

### Sectional Dissension

The frontier, moving west, left in its wake geographic sections of common interest which tended to produce various political points of view and aspirants to the presidency. The Northeast, mainly interested in commerce and industry, had Daniel Webster. The West, claiming the frontier and devoted to diversified farming, was represented by Henry Clay. The South, devoted to cotton culture and slavery, had as its champion John C. Calhoun. In the 1840's, as cotton culture in the South became more important, eventually becoming the single economic support of the section, and as slavery became a markedly south-

---

[7] See the cases, Marbury versus Madison, Hudson River Bridge, Dartmouth College, etc. These cases are available for review in most source books of United States history.

ern institution, the struggle for political supremacy in the whole nation assumed sectional-partisan lines: the South was predominantly Democratic and the North became the birthplace of the new Republican party in 1856. The Senate was kept in balance—half South, half North —through a series of political compromises usually involving the annexation of territory or the admission of new states. The chief ones of these episodes were the Missouri Compromise of 1820, the Compromise of 1850, and the Kansas-Nebraska Act of 1854. The contest assumed the proportions of a race to occupy the West and make it adhere to either the North or the South. "Manifest Destiny" came to be identified with sectional aspirations. The Mexican War (1846–1848) was supported by the South and Democrats while it was resisted by the Whigs of the North.

The large size of the total United States made it impossible for the South to dominate the whole country, but the North had not yet developed a representative political party. General Zachary Taylor, hero of the Mexican War, was elected President as a Whig although he had never voted in any party himself. It was little more than a majority sectional repudiation of the Southern exploitation of more cotton-growing area. Taylor died in less than a year, leaving the presidency to Millard Fillmore (1849–1853), and the pattern of Whig dissolution was repeated. Northern Democratic support gave the next election to Franklin Pierce from New Hampshire (1853–1857), but in the meanwhile the three great sectional leaders had died and the Whigs were gone forever. This left a political power vacuum which was filled soon by the new Republican party whose first candidate, John C. Frémont, in 1856, was a near success. Industrialization of the North and that section's better communication with the West gave a potential strength to the Republican-Northern political party which was ultimately bound to triumph over the South.[8]

### Civil War Politics

The Republican party dominated the scene throughout the remainder of the nineteenth century. The election of 1860 marked a turning point. Abraham Lincoln, as the candidate of the new party, represented the Northern section and the anti-slavery forces, although he was mostly interested himself in the new forces of industrial growth and strength. The Republicans were opposed by a split Democratic party offering three candidates. Stephen Douglas, Northern Democrat,

[8] Avery Craven, *The Coming of the Civil War* (University of Chicago Press, 1957, 2nd revised ed.), is the best single volume account of the development of sectional and other differences that produced the Civil War.

cared nothing for slavery, wanting to compromise and build railroads to the West. Breckenridge and Bell both represented the South, but they split over the slavery issue. In this situation Lincoln could win without a majority of the popular vote.

South Carolina immediately seceded rather than submit to Northern "tyranny," thus allowing political victory to the Republican party in the North and eliminating the South and a Democratic majority from Congress. Four years of civil war followed since the North would not allow the nation to subdivide itself. Andrew Johnson was Lincoln's vice-president and served as president after Lincoln's death (1865–1869). He had been a Democrat from Tennessee and was included with Lincoln on the Liberty ticket in 1864 when the only issue was maintenance of the Union by prosecuting the war. General McClellan was the Democratic rival. With Johnson's accession to power he attempted to rehabilitate the South politically by bringing the states back into the Union with a minimum of "reconstruction." This, however, tended to coalesce the Radical Republican forces of the North, and they refused to subscribe to his plan in Congress. The President was impeached in the House of Representatives and tried in the Senate, but was acquitted by one vote short of the necessary two-thirds for conviction. The Republican majority was secure and succeeded in keeping the Southern states out of national politics until after 1876.

### Constitutional Growth in Mid-Century

Constitutional interpretations during the rise of the Republican party offer one of the knottiest historical problems in the nineteenth century. Lincoln, during the Civil War, suspended *habeas corpus*, issued proclamations, suppressed civil rights, and, in general, assumed arbitrary executive powers never before taken by a president. It has been argued since that he gave precedents for the permanent extension of executive authority which was not envisaged in the Constitution. Congress, by eliminating the Southern representation following the war, managed to keep almost single party control of the country for about fifteen years. Gradually bipartisan political activity was restored, but congressional supremacy over the presidency gained a great impetus in the process. Acceptance of Nevada as a state during this period, even though it did not have the minimum population required for statehood, is an example of congressional high-handedness.[9]

[9] James G. Randall, *Constitutional Problems Under Lincoln* (Appleton, New York, 1926), is a good treatment of general constitutional growth. By the same author, *Civil War and Reconstruction* (Heath, Boston, 1961), is the best single volume history of the whole war and its aftermath.

## The Populist Revolt

In the heyday of Republican dominance of American politics, despite apparent success, there were serpents in Eden. The Republicans were in a majority at every level, but there was growing opposition. The Knights of Labor, organized in 1869, represented a strong dissident group of anti-Republican, low income workers. Out of this grew the great American labor movement. Agrarian unrest, due to farm depression economics, produced the Granger movement. The Populist Party tended, in the last quarter of the nineteenth century, to bring together all of the dissatisfied elements in American life. Although the Populists never managed to get much more than a million popular votes in a presidential election, they did give force to the opposition Democratic party, and the people elected Grover Cleveland, a very moderate Democrat in 1884. Cleveland (1885–1889) was not a Populist, but on the other hand, he certainly was not a Republican either. Civil service reform and a greater measure of national government control of business came out of his administration.

## Imperial Expansion, 1898

At the beginning of McKinley's term the Cleveland depression was over and business was starting to grow in the tremendous fashion that has characterized it up to the present time. Americans began to think in more than merely local terms. Admiral William Mahan's ideas on the value of sea power, coupled with the new expansiveness of American thought, led the United States to take advantage of the vulnerable position of the decadent Spanish empire in the New World. Cuba, Puerto Rico, Guam and the Philippines were seized from Spain in 1898, and the United States embarked on an international scene, really for the first time. The American people retracted from their experiment in empire building as quickly as they had gone into it, and almost as soon as the war was over the United States forswore further overseas expansion, and with few exceptions since has been attempting to get rid of its outlying possessions.

## "My Policies" and the Age of Reform

Theodore Roosevelt (1901–1909) was a Republican, but with a difference. He was not dominated by the old tradition of the party, having gained the office somewhat against the will of the chief figures of the nineteenth century, for example, Mark Hanna of Ohio. He had cut his political teeth as Police Commissioner in the city of New York, as Assemblyman at Albany and as governor of the state. As President he announced his intention of fostering reform legislation and administration in domestic affairs and an aggressive American attitude in foreign relations. He coined the diplomatic phrase, "talk softly and carry a big stick." In domestic affairs Roosevelt may have talked more than he accomplished, but there was a notable shift in American public opinion during his administration which at least paved the way for later reforms. He called himself a "trust buster," but more cases were tried under the Sherman Anti-Trust Act during the administration of his successor, William Howard Taft (1909–1913), a more orthodox and less spectacular Republican. The most important aspect of Roosevelt's administration basically had little to do with the flamboyant personality of the President, although his popularity tended to obscure everything else. A spirit of reform and reorganization was on the land —the United States was growing up, and if the President readily took credit for every social gain, still, there were other forces at work. In fact, the tireless efforts of the Populists, the unremitting zeal of the "muckrakers" such as Lincoln Steffens and Ida Tarbell, the popular interest in forest conservation, the glare of publicity thrown on the Standard Oil Company and other big business—all these things had most to do with the sweeping renovations that were started during Roosevelt's term of office. The movement was only started in this time, again accelerated during Woodrow Wilson's administration, and brought to modern fruition in the period of Franklin Roosevelt's New Deal. However, in the first ten years of the twentieth century several marked evidences of reform were visible. Direct election of senators and forest conservation were two of the items that underwent drastic change and discussion.

### Democratic Interlude

In the campaign of 1912 Roosevelt sought the Republican nomination but failed to get it. His absence from the political scene had dulled his influence too much. Taft took the Republican nomination, and Roosevelt precipitated the "Bull Moose" bolt from the convention and set up a third party. Woodrow Wilson, former president of Princeton University and governor of New Jersey, gained the Democratic nomination. He was elected without a popular majority, the Roosevelt Progressives drawing enough votes from Taft so that they both lost.

Wilson (1913–1921) directed and led a very important choice on the part of the American people. At the turn of the century the United States was increasingly faced with the necessity of choice among four possible long range philosophies of government in relation to the economic basis of our society. We could have (1) gone on indefinitely as we had since the Civil War with piecemeal legislation and a continued struggle for power in the controversy between labor and capital; (2) definitely emphasized the *laissez faire* concept of natural economic forces and the inevitable outcome of wealth in domination over politics; (3) accepted the socialistic doctrines of Karl Marx and other European political and social thinkers with a consequent rigid control of ownership of the national means of production; or (4) as a more thoughtful alternative, we could develop a long range policy of gradual reform in political and social activity accompanied by a flexible supervision of business growth and attention to social security for everyone. The last course was chosen, but there is still a large degree of doubt as to how far it should be carried. Characteristic of the choice, long range legislation tended to be based in some sort of scientific study of circumstances and background, and the national government began steadily to increase its research facilities and its encouragement of fact finding, both public and private.

Permanent reform based on national legislation was meant to safeguard American welfare for all time. Such things as pure food and drug laws were instituted, making it necessary to submit to inspection and to certify statements on labels on the parts of manufacturers. The La Follette Seaman's Act assured merchant sailors of reasonable working and living conditions aboard American ships. There were many such things that are now taken for granted as part of the national heritage, but it must not be forgotten that they came into our lives through the definite exercise of choice, ethical choice among alternatives.

## World War I

Wilson was re-elected in 1916 on the grounds of American acceptance and appreciation of the definite emphasis in the first term on domestic issues and the newly adopted philosophy of government, with, as Wilson put it, sovereignty residing in the community. The slogan, however, most useful to the Democrats was "he kept us out of war." Although the United States took a turn away from *laissez faire* in the first quarter of the twentieth century, Americans did not give up their insistence on isolationism and the belief that two oceans gave the best possible protection. Wilson was lauded for his deft aloofness from "foreign entanglements." The European war (1914–1918) was considered to be just that, a European war, not a world war. It was none of our affair. By 1917, however, two things happened to change the tenor of American thought. German submarine warfare was carried to non-belligerent nations dealing with the Allies in "contraband" goods which might be anything that could be construed to support the war effort. This was almost enough in itself to make Americans fighting mad, but when the *Lusitania*, a British ship carrying munitions and American passengers, was sunk in the Irish Sea the United States forgot its isolationist position.

Congressional elections in 1918 changed the political complexion of the national government. There was a Republican majority in both houses, and from that time on Wilson failed to get any agreement from his Congress. Americans insisted on a return to prewar "normalcy" which meant a quick disbanding of the armed forces and a retreat to isolationism. Wilson went to France and participated personally in the peace negotiations at Versailles where he lost all of his Fourteen Points but one, designed to "make the world safe for democracy." The League of Nations was Wilson's only triumph, but that was a bitter one because the United States would not join. Congress refused to ratify his treaty. President Wilson returned from his ill-advised European diplomatic venture in poor health, broken in spirit and mentality.

### Back to Normalcy

Warren G. Harding (1921–1923), a relatively unknown man from Ohio, became President. Calvin Coolidge, dour New Englander, was his Vice-President. They were both committed to old Republican principles, economy in government and the ascendancy of business. Harding's "friends," or as they were better known, the "Ohio gang," took over national politics with this election, and turned the government into the most corrupt exponent of graft that the country had ever known. The Teapot Dome scandal in which a Secretary of the Interior went to prison was the low point. Harding died while on a trip home from the Pacific Northwest. His death tended to save him from embarrassing investigation in the activities of his associates.

### "Keep Cool with Coolidge"

This became the byword in the years following his accession to the Presidency and his election in his own right in 1924. He served with impeccable honesty, completely untouched by the scandalous behavior of Harding's henchmen (1923–1929). By 1928 it was felt that in the United States prosperity and the Republican party were permanently triumphant. The stock market reached unprecedented highs. Commodity prices and amounts reached dizzy peaks. Credit and business expansion seemed to know no limits. A majority of people wondered why it had ever been thought that there was need for reform, and that the "American way" was the best in the world. There were, however, undercurrents of unrest in labor and on the farms, but these signs were disregarded.

In 1928 Herbert Hoover (1929–1933), former food administrator during World War I and an experienced civil engineer, was the Republican nominee for President. "Put an engineer in the White House" was the slogan that achieved its purpose. Coolidge had unthinkingly said "I do not choose to run," and the party took him at his word. He absorbed his disappointment and watched a triumphant Republican swing to prosperity, administrative skill and engineering dominance. In October 1929, the stock market took a spectacular plunge, wiping out millions of dollars worth of "paper profits," from which it did not really recover until after World War II. Hoover and the Republicans failed to judge the overwhelming effects that were to ensue. A world depression set in, reaching its depths in the early 1930's. Initial measures to stem the tide were neglected in favor of reminders that the American system was infallible in its reliance on the magic of "free enterprise." Hoover and his aides assured the world that prosperity was "just around the corner." The depression became worse, until by 1931, the nation had over twelve million unemployed, prices had dropped to unprecedented low levels, and it was apparent that more than confidence in the future was required.

### The New Deal

The election of 1932 was a safety valve against potential revolution in the United States. All of the ills of a depressed economy were focused in political animus against the Republicans. The hero of the day was Franklin D. Roosevelt. FDR, as he became known, was elected four times to the Presidency, dying in office (1933–1945). Roosevelt in his first inaugural address, promised a "new deal" to the "forgotten man." He said ". . . first of all let me assert my firm belief that the only thing we have to fear is fear itself—nameless, unreasoning, unjustified terror which paralyzes needed efforts to convert retreat into advance." When this Democratic President said such things they were hailed as saving utterances, whereas every time that Hoover had spoken of the need for confidence he had been rebuffed as the single person responsible for the depression. Roosevelt asked Congress and the American people to treat the economic and social condition of the time as a crisis, and on this basis he obtained wide powers for the purposes of relief and reform.[10]

Democratic measures to combat the depression divide into two time phases. The planned purposes of the measures are embraced in three parts. (1) Early New Deal, 1933–1936, was marked by whole-hearted acceptance of nearly everything which might promise to alleviate the depression. It was a time of emergency and experimental thinking. (2) Later New Deal, 1936–1941, was accented by growing political opposition and less interest in immediate relief. The dividing point between the two periods was Roosevelt's attack on the Supreme Court, which he accused of stifling his measures of initiative.

The underlying purpose of all New Deal legislation was to carry out the twentieth century choice of the United States to adhere to a middling control of economic forces through direct political action, inspired by a social ideal away from *laissez faire* but not all the way toward socialism. Government regulation of business and society rather than government ownership of the means of production was intended. The three parts of this program were directed at (1) immediate relief —Civilian Conservation Corps and Agricultural Adjustment Administration were examples; (2) economic recovery—Reconstruction Finance Corporation (set up in Hoover's administration), National Recovery Act, Public Works Administration and Works Progress Administration typified this phase; and (3) reform of a long range nature —designed to prevent recurrence of depression and to improve the citizens' social security. Securities and Exchange Commission, Social Security Act, National Labor Relations Board and Tennessee Valley Authority fall into this category.

Despite all of the best efforts of Hoover and Roosevelt alike, New Deal or otherwise, everything that could be done was not enough to drag the United States out of its depressed economic state. The apparent effects of unemployment were alleviated by artificial employment in the various agencies of government and in the "pump priming" of private industry, operating on borrowed funds or other government subsidy. Prices and wages reached a status of reasonable balance; people were employed, even though artificially; business and banks were in operation, but the economy and society had failed to recapture the inflationary, prosperous atmosphere of the 1920's. Something was

[10] See Franklin Delano Roosevelt, "First Inaugural Address," in *The Heritage of America*, edited by Henry Steele Commager and Allan Nevins (Little, Brown, Boston, 1951), pp. 1113 ff. Interesting to students.

lacking. Vice-President Henry Wallace said publicly that all that was needed was 60,000,000 full time jobs in the nation, but this seemed a fantastic impossibility, even with governmental subsidy which permeated almost all activity. Probably the real reason for the near failure of the New Deal measures was the fact that the United States was not alone in the depression. It was worldwide, affecting every industrialized nation on the globe. In Europe dictators in several nations had managed to seize power with promises to alleviate the economic problems. Chief among these were Hitler in Germany and Mussolini in Italy. By public works and rearmament they had brought an apparent prosperity to their countries. The same had been done in Japan, accompanied by a withdrawal from the League of Nations and colonial expansion into Manchuria.

As early as 1938, President Roosevelt had brought this to the attention of the American people, but it had failed to strike a chord of sympathy. The United States was still in the grip of its belief in the efficacy of isolation: two oceans were still felt to be the best possible defense against aggression, and there was very little association in the public mind between totalitarianism, the world depression and the position and welfare of the United States.

In point of fact, it remained for World War II to bring full realization to Americans that there was a possibility of "One World" (and this was also the title of a book written by Wendell Willkie a few years later after an extended political trip around the world). Gradually the aggressive nature of Nazism and Fascism dawned on Americans, and finally, after entering the war by way of economic aid to the Allies, the United States went into full production and participation in the war. As an accompanying phenomenon the United States not only recovered from the depression but embarked on a new era of prosperity which was so much greater than anything ever envisaged before that it served as a permanent shock to Americans. Even at present the United States cannot quite believe that she has become a world power in the truest sense, that no longer are two oceans enough protection, and that the welfare of one part of the world is almost immediately reflected in every other part—for better or worse.

### European Totalitarianism, American Isolationism and World War II

Political disillusion and economic depression forced the European nations into a new pattern after World War I. Kingship was fundamentally shaken, national boundaries had been altered, the Russian Revolution swept the land and altogether the way was paved for the rise of the dictators. The United States looked on until World War II became inevitable. December 7, 1941, "a day that will live in infamy," as President Roosevelt called it, the Japanese declared war on the United States by bombing Pearl Harbor. We put thirteen million men in the field in a "global war."

### United Nations, Peace and the Postwar World

Most of the nations of the world organized a successor to the League of Nations at San Francisco in 1945. The chief disability of the peace was to resolve individual national aims with those stated goals of the United Nations to abolish war forever. The veto power in the Security Council, United Nations Trust Territories and the location of the permanent home of the United Nations almost wrecked its beginning. Joint occupation of Korea by Russia and the United States finally resulted in a war there in 1950.

The United States wanted to revert to its traditional role of isolationism, but it was impossible. President Truman invoked the United Nations' police power and resisted Communist aggression in the Far East. If we could not remain isolated from the world we could at least have an armed peace.

The election of 1952 marked a reaction to the Democrats and General Dwight D. Eisenhower was elected to the White House (1953–1961). The United States embarked on a new wave of inflation and Republican optimism. This time, however, there was a difference from the days following World War I. Isolation might have its charms, but it had become a closed prospect for the United States.

## 2. Constitutional Rule of Law

Man has steadily increased his heritage since the days of the pyramid builders on the Nile, and he has pursued the quest for a principle of government that would combine the values of human dignity and the protection of worldly goods. The result of this search is the rule of law; the compact between man and man, between society and society, and as it appears in nature between environment and creature was now set down in constitutional form, by statute and legal precedent. The record of that struggle is a large component of the history of Western civilization, as it is a great part, in the words of Thomas Carlyle, of "all that mankind has done, thought, gained or been . . ." To understand the significance of the rule of law and its growth we have to read the history of man.

Specifically, in regard to our own national history, we have cleanly typified the comparatively rapid emergence of this principle in our colonial period of dependency on the British constitution and in the subsequent growth of our own constitutional body of precept from 1776 to the present.

It is trite to say that we owe anything to Magna Carta, wrested from the King of England by a group of ambitious barons for their own safety, yet it is true that we are Anglo-Saxon in cultural and intellectual descent. Present Americans are, in real truth, indebted to the whole succession of constitutional gains, including Hammurabi's Code, Greek city membership, Roman legalism, Germanic tribal custom, Norman absolutism, Angevin administrative regularity, Magna Carta, Tudor selfishness, Stuart stupidity, Oliver Cromwell's temerity, the Glorious Revolution and royal submission to law, as well as the final break from the mother country in 1776 with the blessings of William Pitt and Edmund Burke.

Present American government and politics can be studied in secondary schools as the dynamically changing result of the political heritage of the Western world. The Constitution lays down certain organizational lines from which current institutional practices have grown. The essence of any study of government is in terms of the process of change based on the historical tradition and the constitutional language that gives framework to the patterns of political choice. A high school class may be presented with contemporary problems in democratic politics to think about and from which to learn the principles and derivation of our present situation.

The first step must be the structure, but the most important aspect of both government and political history, as school studies, is the process of change and the actual working out of political behavior. The most successful teaching will be the result of combining history, political structure and dynamic process to confront students with the necessity for making reasonable and thoughtful choices. In fact, political citizenship, in constructive terms, is exactly that.

## Congress

Congress, as an item of concern in the Constitution, is of extreme importance in the administration of the American government, but of still greater importance is the congressional function as a clearing house for American controversial points of view. Members of Congress have virtual immunity from civil arrest and therefore, at least theoretically, are in the best possible position to say whatever they wish, particularly in the Senate. In effect this is curtailed somewhat by the political, economic and sectional interests of the various congressmen, but on the whole, it is undeniable that Congress has been a force in the direction of maintaining democratic political forms and therefore the democratic way of existence that is peculiar to the United States.

During the last few years more and more has been said about the need for congressional reform. Perhaps as society becomes more complicated and the demands for legislation more immediate, some more efficient means of legislative action may be instituted, but in any case, this may well be at the expense of the essential characteristic of Congress, which is free expression and widespread representation of the needs of all the people as well as their desires.

The best recent book on the Senate is William S. White, *Citadel: The Story of the U.S. Senate* (Harper, New York, 1957). The following books deal specifically with the problem of reform in congressional organization and activity: James N. Burns, *Congress on Trial: The Politics of Modern Lawmaking* (Harper, New York, 1949); Paul H. Douglas, *Economy in the National Government* (University of Chicago Press, 1952); H. H. Wilson, *Congress: Corruption and Compromise* (Rinehart, New York), American Government in Action Series, contains outstanding cases of corrupt lawmakers; George A. Graham, *Morality in American Politics* (Random House, New York, 1952); Bertram M. Gross, *The Legislative Struggle* (McGraw-Hill, New York, 1953), shows the conflict aspects of lawmaking; Stephen Kemp Bailey, *Congress Makes a Law* (Columbia University Press, New York, 1950), illustrates lawmaking by a case study of the Employment Act of 1946 in a very sensitive way.

## The Presidency

The importance of the President is undeniable.[11] As the chief of his party he speaks for a majority of the citizens; as head of the American state he exercises the sovereign power of all the citizens; as the chief executive officer of the most powerful nation on earth he is a highly respected, influential and authoritative individual. It is the highest

[11] Of special interest in regard to the Presidency are the quadrennial national elections. American party politics operate to polarize all national issues into two generalized party contenders. National nominating conventions and the subsequent campaigns have a special significance for citizens of the United States. Since 1952 television has been instrumental in bringing these events to a majority of the people, and of course, much more rapidly than has been earlier experience. National elections now have a peculiarly personal connection with the lives of all. A very useful study guide and unit outline has been prepared which might be used in connection with examination of the Presidency. *Participating in Presidential Elections, Students' Election Handbook, 1960,* Committee on Citizenship Education, Metropolitan School Study Council, an affiliate of the Institute of Administrative Research, Teachers College, Columbia University (New York, 1960).

office to which a man can be elected by his fellow citizens. As our constitutional development has taken place the office of president has become the cohesive force and symbol of the whole federal system: unitary strength without the monolithic and rigid power structure of less democratic states.

The Presidency has become a powerful and amorphous office. Its influence extends, with varying degrees of authority, over the whole political order. It encompasses, in fact, a domain far broader than appears on paper. Congress can pass a statute; the Executive must convert it into the law-in-action. Congress can decree a new agency; the Executive must endow it with the breath of life. Congress alone has the power to declare war; the President may so conduct foreign affairs that it has no alternative.*

The office of the presidency implies the most far-reaching power held by any individual in the United States. The President executes the will of Congress, but he also exercises his own will as an individual in carrying out the mandate of the people and his party. He is responsible only at election time and to the meager provisions and restrictions of his office specified by the Constitution. The President, in serving the "public welfare," has from time to time been invested with extraordinary power which has exceeded any other executive authority outside of a dictatorship, but in every case the authority has been held in stewardship, and at the end of a current emergency it has been returned to the body politic. Every time, however, an accretion of traditional authority has been left to the office, so that now it is highly responsible and powerful.

In line with the tendency to interpret the Constitution loosely and by precedent, during the past century the President has come to assume a responsibility lately called national security. This is now the chief responsibility of the office, and also the inspiration for the exercise of ever widening power. It is difficult to assess exactly what constitutes national security at any given time, and so the result has been a growing tendency to assume that there is something of a crisis most of the time, thereby widening both the responsibility and the power of the President.

Clinton Rossiter, *The American Presidency* (Mentor) is a popular paperback. Herbert Agar, *The People's Choice* (Houghton Mifflin, Boston, 1933); W. Dean Burnham, *Presidential Ballots, 1836–1892* (Johns Hopkins University Press, Baltimore, 1955); Edward H. Hobbs, *Behind the President: A Study of Executive*

* Walton Hamilton, *The New York Times Magazine*, August 29, 1943, cited in Ferguson and McHenry, *The American System of Government,* fourth edition, p. 273.

*Office Agencies* (Public Affairs Press, Washington, D.C., 1954); Sidney Hyman, *The American Presidency* (Harper, New York, 1954); H. L. McBride, *The American Electoral College* (Caxton, Caldwell, Idaho, 1953); B. D. Nash, *Staffing the Presidency*, National Planning Association, Washington, D.C., 1952); Irving G. Williams, *The American Vice-Presidency* (Doubleday, New York, 1954).

This group of books is devoted to the various powers of the presidential office, from several different positions: Wilfred E. Binkley, *President and Congress* (Knopf, New York, 1947); Joseph P. Harris, *Advice and Consent of the Senate* (University of California Press, 1953); E. Pendleton Herring, *Presidential Leadership: The Political Relationships of Congress and the Chief Executive* (Farrar, Straus, New York, 1940); W. Stull Holt, *Treaties Defeated by the Senate: A Study of the Struggle between Presidents and Senate over the Conduct of Foreign Relations* (Johns Hopkins University Press, 1933); William H. Humbert, *The Pardoning Power of the President* (American Council on Public Affairs, New York, 1941); John D. Larkin, *The President's Control over the Tariff* (Harvard University Press, 1936); United States Senate, Committee on the Judiciary, *Treaties and Executive Agreements: Hearing before a Subcommittee . . .* 83rd Congress, 1st Session (1953).

## Federal Administration

In addition to the constitutional requirements laid down by the basic organic law of the nation, as time has gradually developed more and more needs, federal government administration has come to be a veritable leviathan with millions of career employees and a myriad of responsibilities. The day to day administration of the countless details of running a great nation with an ever expanding demand on its services by a growing population has become the biggest business on earth. Naturally this is a far more complex enterprise than was ever envisaged by the founding fathers when they constructed the Constitution. Besides carrying out the numerous and varied tasks of government, the permanent personnel of the federal state must furnish a continuity that could not be consonant with periodic changes in the political complexion of policy-making officers. The electorate votes for the party of its majority choice and these people, so elected, have the responsibility of forming the basic policy, but the nearly three millions of permanent civil service employees have the continuing duty of carrying it out, of executing the administrative will.

The Constitution provides for the heads of executive departments as advisors to the President, and the first Congress in 1789 authorized three such departments. Since then the administrative structure has grown out of all recognition. There has been a continual expansion of services on the one hand, and, on the other hand, steady complaints that the whole structure costs too much.

Up until the turn of the last century most of the added functions were distributed among existing executive departments or given to new ones. Since that time there has been a tendency to create new but independent agencies of government, such as the Interstate Commerce Commission or the Civil Service Commission (two of the first ones), largely on the grounds that less partisan control will be exercised over government functions that are primarily non-political, e.g., civil service tenure is not supposed to be on a "spoils" basis, but rather a non-partisan career service. Among the independent agencies some have a single head and others are operated by a commission or board of directors. In some cases the organization has taken the form of private business enterprise and may even be called a corporation, such as the Panama Canal Company.

In addition to the large agencies and departments there are a number of minor agencies as well as a few rather important ones, such as the Central Intelligence Agency which is secretly organized and responsible to the President through the National Security Council. It may be generalized that the essential administration of the United States is passing more and more into the hands of professional civil servants employed on a career basis, and the political heads of state—those elective officers in the executive and legislative branches of government have relatively less supervisory power over public administration than was envisaged by the Constitution. The demands of a growing state oriented toward a social security goal make this inevitable. Government is now big, but it is bound to get bigger if current trends continue.

The following selected list of books illustrates tendencies in national government administration: Marshall E. Dimock, Gladys O. Dimock and Louis W. Koenig, *Public Administration* (Holt, Rinehart and Winston, New York, 1958, rev. ed.) and John M. Pfiffner and Robert V. Presthus, *Public Administration* (Ronald Press, New York, 1960, 4th ed.) are reasonably sound texts; Dwight Waldo, *The Study of Public Administration* (Random House, New York, 1955), is a concise paperback; Dwight Waldo, *Perspectives on Administration* (University of Alabama Press, 1956), is a group of lectures penetrating the subject.

### The Judiciary

As the balancing element between the executive and legislative branches of government, and sometimes as the arbitrator in the process of administrative growth, stands the American judicial system. It ranges from the Supreme Court of the United States down to the justice courts of local communities. It is essential that secondary school students learn something of the function and purpose of judicial processes. Although law and its practice is a highly technical and learned profession, some of the common legal principles can be incorporated into social studies instruction.

American courts of law form the most complex, overlapping and independent legal system in the history of the world. There are separate levels of law from the Supreme Court and Federal District Courts down through circuit courts of appeal, state supreme courts, state appellate, district, county and municipal courts. There are special courts of customs and maritime affairs, as well as the numerous and powerful administrative courts which do not try cases in the usual sense, but interpret the federal policy in matters of tariffs, insurance claims and interstate commerce disputes.

Above all, the United States Supreme Court acts as the third of the three balancing elements of our democratic system of "checks and balances": legislative, executive and judicial. In this capacity the court system has assumed the function of giving ultimate judgment as to the constitutionality of any given piece of legislation. The process is called judicial review, and is not a specified power in the Constitution, but it has grown through usage. To a certain extent the state supreme courts in the several states have taken on the same responsibility in regard to more localized legislation. This prerogative of passing on the constitutionality of congressional acts has given the court a kind of majestic power that is unsurpassed or even equalled by any other court system in the world.

Edwin S. Corwin, *Court over Constitution* (Princeton University Press, 1938, reprint by Peter Smith, New York, 1960), is a classic on judicial review; Edwin S. Corwin and Jack W. Peltason, *Understanding the Constitution* (Holt, Rinehart, and Winston, New York, 1960, rev. ed.), is an easy and clear introduction to the judiciary; Robert G. McCloskey, *The American Supreme Court* (University of Chicago Press, 1960), is the most recent treatment; *The Federal Courts and the Federal System*, edited by Henry M. Hart and Herbert Wechsler (Foundation, New York, 1953), is a case book; Arthur J. Dodge, *Origin and Development of the Office of Attorney-General*, House Document 510, 70th Congress, 2nd Session (Washington, D.C.).

## State and Local Government

Each state must have a written constitution, subject to amendment, in basic harmony with the national Constitution. This becomes the organic law of each state and it assures some degree of uniform constitutionality throughout the nation. In some states, such as California, constitutional amendment has become a favorite method of revising state law because constitutions tend to be paramount to statute law, and they are based on the principle and theory of the social contract.

All state constitutions differ in detail considerably, but all of them have in common the same characteristic which marks the federal Constitution. That is the basic Anglo-Saxon belief that a constitution is a guiding principle based in the heritage and experience of a people. In Britain this is more easily perceivable since the constitution is not a written document at all, but rather it is the traditional accumulation of precedent, custom and court decision. In the United States much the same thing is true except that at the heart of each constitutional body of growth there is a specific set of written limitations and guides to positive action. That is why the Constitution specifies that each state shall have an organic document which will transcend statute law and will not be at odds with the national document.

Since each of the state constitutions is different, and since the experience within each state has been different, it is impossible to construct a course of study around a "type" of state and local government. Rather, it is desirable to concentrate on the objective facts of one particular state government. In most states there are laws requiring a minimum competence for students in state and local history and government in order to graduate from high school.

On the other hand, since even though local circumstances vary tremendously in detail, there are common basic principles of local government. These are better illustrated in some areas than in others, for example, New England "towns," extended in area and including open countryside, and old in the direct democracy of the first Americans, make exemplary studies to determine the fundamental quality of grass roots political behavior. It is possible, then, in addition to using the local scene, to study certain general categories of action which will enhance general knowledge of state and local government while learning the particular history of the evolution of one locality.

At present the key problem involved in understanding local government lies in the growth of industrial centers with their adjacent suburban residential areas. This has been slighted in past political science studies, but it seems undeniable that the most important developments in public administration are to be made in these expanding metropolitan areas. Control of public services and mechanism for response to the public will must be perfected in the face of growing concentrations of suburban dwelling industrial workers. In other words, state and local government becomes largely a matter of public administration, growing steadily more complex.

In high school classes in government it is probably easier to study the structure of government on state, county and local levels, and certainly, to be comprehensive it would take a great deal of time and diligence to encompass only that. On the other hand, every person is the political inhabitant of a particular place, and for the most part, his direct participation in politics is at the local level. People are really most concerned with what is happening to them in everyday life. They must respond to local administration and to state laws, and their most direct political influence is exercised within a given state. Beyond general knowledge of state constitutional structure the most important field of study must then be local administration: police power, county and city organization, public utility districts, referendum, recall and initiative, public finances, social welfare, roads and public education.

There are special problems that are local in nature but which involve much larger spheres, national or international. The Great Lakes and the St. Lawrence Seaway lie across an international boundary while one of the greatest terminal shipping points in the world, Chicago, is at one end of the Seaway. Tremendous problems of organization and administration have fallen on the city of Chicago because of this. The city of Washington, D.C. does not have state or county structure between it and the national Congress. Surrounding this growing metropolis, two states, Virginia and Maryland, have become studded with suburban areas that are solely the result of Washington's needs. Thus, in one case an international waterway has created nationally important problems in one locality, Chicago; in another instance the national government expanding in services to the nation with accompanying growth of the capitol, has produced acute aggravations of local administration in two states, Virginia and Maryland. Many other cases could be adduced illustrating smiliar crisis producing effects on local government. These cases make the study material for learning about the dynamic aspects of local democratic political organization and control.

The best textbook on state and local government now available is Charles R. Adrian, *Governing Urban America: Structure, Politics and Administration* (McGraw-Hill, New York, 1961, 2nd ed.). *Book of the States* (Chicago, Council of State Government), is an annual compilation of essential information on state administration. *Capitol, Courthouse and City Hall,* edited by Robert L. Morlan (Houghton Mifflin, Philadelphia, 1960, rev. ed.), is a book of readings illustrating the various levels of subordinate government. Robert C. Wood, *Suburbia, Its People and Their Politics* (Houghton Mifflin, Philadelphia, 1959), treats the important and neglected subject of suburban growth in politics. There are many pamphlets published by the Committee for Economic Development, New York, such as *Metropolis Against Itself* (CED, March, 1959), and *Guiding Metropolitan Growth* (CED, August, 1960). All of the problems of state and local government are treated from time to time in the *Annals* of the American Academy of Political and Social Science, particularly, as an example, the issue of November, 1957. On the political structure and growth in the various states there are numerous books of varying quality. McGraw-Hill and Crowell-Collier both have series including titles on most of the states. One of the newest and best of these is Henry A. Turner and John A. Vieg, *The Government and Politics of California* (McGraw-Hill, New York, 1960).

### 3. Political Democracy

In working out political democracy under the Constitution the United States has evolved a two-party system that also has two distinct levels of operation: local and national. At the local level, seekers after political office have to associate themselves usually with one of the major parties, but their appeal to the electorate must be in terms of local issues. At the same time, however, the stand on the local issues becomes tied to national issues simply by virtue of the identity of organization in the party structure over the whole nation. This produces anomalies now and then, such as the South at the present time, which is Democratic by tradition (there being virtually no Republican party), but devoted to certain points of view such as supporting the practice of segregation of Negroes and Whites. Racial discrimination is by no means a stated principle of the national Democratic party, but the Southern Democrats will support the other Democrats against the Republicans in some matters. When the particularism of the South becomes involved, however, the Southern Democrats side with the more conservative elements in the Republican party. There is a tendency for both major parties to become more alike in their statements of purpose so as to eliminate more and more of the local differences as national issues. This makes it difficult for the voter to determine which party will best serve him, resulting in many persons' seeking to vote for individuals rather than for a party. The election of President Eisenhower in 1952 and 1956 illustrates this, because at the same time a Republican President was elected there was returned a disproportionate number of Democrats to both houses of Congress.

It may be that a reconstitution of political parties is in the making, but before that can happen there must be a sharply definable issue of universal importance that is supportable on either side. Perhaps such an issue as limitation on nuclear testing is enough of a problem. A sharp business recession resulting in an economic depression would undoubtedly catalyze a new political alignment as it did in 1929 and after. It is not so clear, however, that either existing party could be cleanly identified with one side or the other of any issue that might arise. There is a distinct possibility that a totally new arrangement of political parties might emerge. What that would be no one can predict with any assurance, although there has been a historic tendency in the United States for one party to represent a conservative position and the other to stand for a more experimental, liberal or progressive point of view.

In the beginning it may have been easier to discern than it is now what that liberal-conservative alignment was. We have all but done away with economic class lines and education is now so nearly universal that there is no longer an illiterate mass. There is no aristocracy and no group now contends for that distinction. In 1800 Jefferson and Hamilton could stand respectively for the forces of liberalism and conservatism. In the election of 1828 it was possible to identify Jackson with democratic masses and John Quincy Adams with wealthy aristocrats in the Northeast. Lincoln was the outspoken adherent of the liberal tradition of the industrial revolution against the aspiring aristocracy of the South which was trying to hang on to the old values of an outmoded age. Theodore Roosevelt appeared in 1901 as a crusader for liberal thought against the "bossism" in all parties. When Wilson attempted to carry on the tradition of reform he was seen as a liberal opposed to the conservatism of Senator Henry Cabot Lodge. Harding, Coolidge and Hoover represented conservative points of view—*laissez faire* and honest virtue, while Franklin Roosevelt was hailed as the great liberal who could reorganize human political forces in the interest of bettering mankind and especially those fortunate enough to be American citizens.

Although liberal-conservative struggles can be recognized almost up to the present moment, it has become increasingly difficult to discern the difference as represented by the two parties. Perhaps the secret lies in the blurring of class distinctions and the rising standard of living for everyone. Now most Americans can honestly claim a middle class mentality, but this has ceased to have its old meaning, since there is no upper or lower class. Everyone cannot be in a "middle class" if by definition where there is a middle there must be two ends. The only explanation would be that "middle class" does not mean a social relationship to other social classes, but a point of view, and therefore it becomes more and more nearly impossible to be liberal or conservative. Everyone tends to be seeking the same political ends, and in turn, these ends seem to be more and more identifiable with complete social security.

The great issues of the future are likely to be those things which will concern the whole world and necessarily the role of the United States in that world. World peace, international control of nuclear power, economic and educational equality, the resolution of nationalistic claims and interest in the betterment of mankind—these are the types of political issue that must become the concern of the citizen of the United States in order for him to survive. It is the sort of thing which will dominate future American thought both domestically and in terms of international relations which must tend to become more nearly the same. The day of local or national partisanship without regard to the whole world is of necessity on the wane. Even though just now, despite any idealism to the contrary, nationalism is the only identifiable vehicle of world relations, this situation will ineluctably alter, and the only direction of change short of destruction must be toward tolerance and understanding among all men. Political choice even at the lowest level comes to mean the involvement of every man in the affairs of all.

Out of all the centuries of growth, struggle and animadversion, in all parts of the world, one current truth is unavoidable: the constitutional rule of law has persisted and grown to proportions that cannot be overlooked or even minimized. One development yet remains to materialize—perhaps the most difficult step of all—and that is to realize that constitutional minutiae may differ and yet not subvert the whole idea of representative self government. In other words, there is not a black and white difference between any two constitutions in the world; there are only variants in customary procedure outside the basic acceptance of the validity of a rule of law. It is the spirit of acceptance of man's equality of opportunity and before the law that counts, not the particular concept of rightness of wrongness of the specific law, or for that matter, of the prevalent political philosophy. Man's unimpeachable right to dignity and a minority position if he wishes it so long as he refrains from "hurting to the extent that he must be hurt" are to be included among the privileges that give the breath of life and liberty to a rule of law. American and world political institutions must bear this out.

It becomes the responsibility or the duty of every citizen in the process of passing through our schools, public or private, to learn the present machination and the past growth of our version, at least, of the way a rule of law has been perpetuated in the United States. The high school furnishes the curricular means for coming upon the subject matter involved, and it remains the student's share to gain as much as he can at the eleventh grade.

In regard to best techniques for accomplishing this objective there is considerable controversy. It may be that some sort of participating activity in the actual process of government would be the best method; however, at the age of fifteen or sixteen, school citizens do not have the legal qualification to vote in public elections. They may participate in a school government of some kind, or there may be an artificial political situation created, as a mock court, or a model legislature or a United Nations facsimile. All of these lack reality since in the government of a student body, administrative authority must always be apparent in the background, and in the case of synthetic legislative arrangement, the atmosphere, by definition, is unrealistic. Field trips to various governmental agencies are possibly desirable, but unless the location of the school is favorably placed in relation to an important governing installation this procedure is not feasible.[12]

It remains true, as in most other secondary school social studies, that young people must read, study and write about the factual matter concerned with the subject at hand, in this case American political history. It is extremely difficult for anyone to experience something which has gone by and still understand it except in his own contemporary terms.

As far as political participation is concerned, the realistic involvement in current political issues need not be dependent upon the knowledge of how to push voting levers in an election booth. This is a trivial procedure which may be mastered by any citizen when he first goes to the polls as an adult to exercise his constitutional right upon attaining the proper age. On the other hand, however, understanding and appreciating the importance of the rule of law and representative self government can be learned effectively by high school students in an intellectual atmosphere through operation of the adumbrative process. The one absolute requisite is knowledge— knowledge of the current process and past development. Other experiences may be useful adjuncts to learning, but one must know the facts and relationships of political history and principles.

It must follow "as the night the day" that the teacher of such students will be required to know the subject rather well, somewhat

---

[12] See Edwin T. Ingles, "The Community—A Social Studies Laboratory," in *Educating Citizens for Democracy: Curriculum and Instruction in Secondary Social Studies*, edited by Richard E. Gross and Leslie D. Zeleny (Oxford University Press, New York, 1958), for some interesting suggestions in this regard resulting from the author's experience with the Columbia Citizenship Education Project.

better than the average citizen, and certainly better than the students. It is simply another example of the need for social studies teachers to possess more than the general education requirements of our society.

## 4. Humane Knowledge and General Citizenship

It may be seen that political citizenship in the United States consists of several different levels; local and county, state, and federal representation is enjoyed by every American citizen. He must, if he it to be considered competent, know the basic issues at all these layers of public administration. This in itself is a continuing and exacting assignment, and often, unfortunately, is not taken as the serious obligation that it really is.

In addition, there are two other major aspects of citizenship. First, along with political democracy, social and economic democracy have always been considered to be important. Merely being able to vote is not the sum of democratic citizenship. Modern Americans find themselves involved in all sorts of semi-political or non-political considerations requiring judgment and knowledge in order to achieve a reasonable democratic outcome. For example, important economic considerations are at stake in any assessment of the position of labor unions. Usually labor unions figure extensively in political campaigns. The relationship is obvious.

Next, in the expanded view of citizenship, world affairs figure largely, and for the future the best guess is in the direction of more interdependence among nations and quicker and more adequate communication throughout the world. The American citizen is obligated to know about the rest of the world. Immediately there arises necessity to evaluate and choose among alternative attitudes toward other nations, toward race, cultural differences, foreign traditions and ideologies. The total answer to these questions is most implicit in adequate United States political participation. In fact, such participation is now not even adequate unless it embraces awareness of the whole family of nations in a global concept.

Secondary school courses in citizenship or civics should also include some consideration of the general nature of citizenship and its international overtones.

### Current Events

What are current events? What use do they have to social studies in schools? What are the objectives of the study of current events? Where may they be found for school use?

First of all, current events are those happenings in the world which have significance to many people. They are not in the histories yet because they have just happened, but they will be. Most current happenings are trivial and they will never be recorded for posterity except as passing occurrences which are used to pad out newspapers. The reader must discriminate in order to tell what may be of value for study and remark. It is not possible to set up an easy criterion for selection, such as politics or international diplomacy, since current events of significance may fall into any of the major categories of learning. The simple news that an Indian won the Nobel prize in literature might be of tremendous importance to posterity; it would depend on the subject of his effort, the social milieu in which he and his readers live, the historical derivation of his material, training, interest and motivation, the *future* of the world.

The importance of carefully chosen current events as subjects for study is in their furtherance of a prime aim of education: critical thought. Criticism and discrimination provide man with much of his differentiating quality. Simple choice and selection in the use of current events in a social studies classroom can provide exercise in critical thought. First, the material should fit the curricular pattern if it is to be any more than simply news of the moment. Second, the problem should have some worldwide meaning in terms of American values, inculcation of which is a responsibility of social studies teachers. Preservation of political democracy in the world is one of those values. Third, current developments in regard to any of the thought provoking problems of man should extend and exercise the faculties of criticism and creative thinking. Mere acquisition of news in order to keep up with current modes and styles so as not to be "left out" has no justification as a school learning process. Ability to think critically and creatively *about* something and with substantive content is a high goal of achievement in social studies. Current events, as they add to past events, contribute to the solution of man's problems and to the augmentation of his heritage.

Here are the criteria for selecting current events, listed under nine headings:

1. Determining the Importance of the Issue.
2. Defining the Issue to Make it Specific.
3. Putting Issues in Perspective.
4. Persisting Nature of the Issue.
5. Relating the Current Issue to the Curriculum.
6. Readiness of Students to Handle Current Issues.

7. Background and Knowledge of the Teacher.

8. Adapting Methods of Instruction to the Use of Current Issues.

9. Materials Available for Adequate Study of the Issue.[13]

As an extension of the examination of the history and geography of Europe, speculation on the probability and advisability of there developing a United States of Europe can be a fruitful way in which to apply the knowledge of places, people, resources and their story.

One high school teacher, seeking to broaden and deepen the knowledge of her students, discovered that the American constitution offered a theme for current events. "Most of us," she wrote, "when we explain the meaning of the Constitution, are plagued with the question of how we can present the full meaning with 'true-life' experiences in order that the student will understand the topic." She explained that while ". . . studying each section of the Constitution, each student was required to read the daily newspaper and cut out all items that referred to Congress, the President, or the Supreme Court . . . . the superior student was challenged not only to read the papers but to consult old magazines that were in his home and bring in the clippings. Others went to the library to check the *Congressional Quarterly* for certain laws and to see how they applied." [14]

This can be a delightful and rewarding way to stretch young minds, and at the same time to meet the objectives of studying current events. No child who learned about the timeless and flexible living constitution of his own country could ever possibly be bored with it.

The United Nations, from its inception in 1945 to the present, offers another theme around which current events study might be focused. Hardly a news organ in the world encounters a week without major coverage of the events in the United Nations. As a supplement to any historical sequence, news of the clearing house of nations furnishes deeper and more consequential knowledge of man. In fact, as an additional project for any class in social studies, it might be desirable to keep a United Nations corner on the bulletin board, with a special committee in charge. The United Nations Secretariat in New York maintains a public relations section which will be happy to furnish on

[13] William H. Connor, "When Teaching Current Affairs: Nine Suggestions" (*Social Education*, November, 1955, pp. 306–308). Cf. Edgar Bruce Wesley, *Teaching Social Studies in High Schools* (Heath, Boston, 1950), 3rd ed., p. 388 ff., gives a somewhat different view of the purposes of current events study.

[14] Doris R. Brosnan, "The Constitution in Action," *Social Education* (December, 1954), p. 352. Every social studies teacher should read this half page of wisdom and experience.

request summaries of the periodic actions and deliberations of the General Assembly, the Security Council and the various subordinate agencies.

There can be no doubt that the political and economic fragmentation of Europe has been both a cause of war and an obstruction in the way of progress. For hundreds of years mistress of the world, Europe has looked on helplessly in recent decades as other powers wrested the mantle of leadership from her. She has watched uneasily as a new economic and political system absorbed more than 800,000,000 of the world's peoples, and she has seen a former colony, profiting in part from her decline, become a colossus of democratic strength. While she dissipated her energies on the battlefield in a useless struggle pitting sovereignty against sovereignty, new giants arose on the world scene: the U.S.S.R. and the United States of America came of age.

And it is generally agreed by thinking people on the Continent that only a United States of Europe, based on the American plan of federation, will save Europe from being absorbed, economically or militarily, by one or the other of these powers.[15]

This offers an appropriate theme for a study of "current events." It is not the only one, of course, but it meets the criteria for selection of contemporary material for social studies use. In the same article cited above, three outstanding European political figures give their views on the problem. Robert Schumann, Paul-Henri Spaak and Jean Monnet present their views in interview form with the author concerning the prospect of United States of Europe in the foreseeable future. No precise prediction was extracted from those statesmen, but that they were willing to talk about and to show concern over the international propagation of the idea is promising from a democratic standpoint, and certainly it gives cogency to a type of problem which should interest all citizens, those of our country as well as of Europe. It is feasible to conduct a continuing program of current events built around such a topic. Boys and girls of junior high school age might not be able to solve world problems, but they can learn about them as the events develop.

Education aims at the preservation, extension and use of knowledge for man's good, therefore any assistance is welcome. The Constitution of the United States and the Charter of the United Nations, in order to serve the needs of a dynamic national and international community, must live and expand along with that society and community. For this to happen, citizens must learn about all that is going on now, and moreover, they must think about those things in the light of what man

[15] Anthony Scarangello, "In Quest of European Unity," *Social Education* (December, 1954), p. 340.

already knows, and they must speculate critically about the future of knowledge. Movement in the present world, especially technological and political, is so rapid that it is impossible to expect the most recent developments to be found anywhere recorded except in the daily, weekly, monthly and quarterly journals of man's activities. Although a few days, weeks or months of delay in learning of a truly important event will not alter the event itself, it is certainly true that any delay in subjecting new events to sharp critical analysis may radically alter the future course of effects which the event might have. The humane ideals of Christ were not altered by his crucifixion, but the dissemination of those ideals and their permanent preservation as living doctrine were deeply affected by the Roman execution of law which swept up the Christian Savior to martyrdom on Golgotha.

At present in the United States, every city has some sort of daily newspaper and access to radio broadcasts of current news. These outlets are mainly dependent upon a few international news services operating in all the nations of the world. In short, all parts of the world receive almost simultaneously, and with very little lag after the event, news of what is happening around the world. The standards of journalism demand a fair degree of accuracy in substantive reporting, but the principles of human behavior and nature make it impossible for any man to be absolutely objective. There is bias in the news. Unfortunately the speedy technical triumphs of communication which news agencies use tend to spread uniformly and rapidly whatever bias happens to get into the first reporting of a news event. This fact makes doubly important the necessity for critical scrutiny of the news of any current event. Notwithstanding this much caution, the daily metropolitan newspaper is probably the best source of current events for school use.

Next, there are several rather comprehensive weekly news magazines. They are similar to the best dailies except that much of the winnowing of time is done for the reader. After the lapse of a week the volume of what might otherwise appear to be enduring news is reduced to the compass of a single magazine. Most important among these in the United States are *Life, Time, Newsweek* and *U.S. News and World Report*. There are many others of less comprehensive character or more specialized in some way, such as *The Reporter*. All of these have value as raw sources of selected news. Perhaps *Life*, since it is essentially a news picture magazine, has the widest and most easily applicable use in junior high school.

Still more selective, but with correspondingly greater lag, are the monthly and quarterly journals. These are usually less concerned with the news items themselves and more with criticism and interpretation of events as they become part of our civilized heritage. The *New Yorker* or the *Economist* (London), although weeklies, contain much of this type of news treatment. *Foreign Affairs,* a quarterly, is devoted to analysis of recent developments in diplomacy and it represents a quasi-official American point of view in the world. *Harper's Magazine* and the *Atlantic Monthly* represent a more sophisticated level of current event criticism in every field from poetry to politics. These would hardly be suitable for ninth grade students, but they might be of interest to the ninth graders' teachers.

A series of specially graded news magazines exists for the current events uses of schools in *My Weekly Reader* (with vocabularies adjusted for grades three through six), *Junior Scholastic* and *Current Events* (for upper grades and junior high school). These carefully graded journals are particularly useful for the reluctant readers which are found in every grade. The stories are likely to be of significance, but unnecessary verbiage is eliminated and the exposition is as simple as the subject will allow. Very often in junior high school these materials form the standard basis for a regular period of current events study.

A last most important source of current events information is the almost unlimited stream of United States government publications. The range of coverage in this category is very wide, and the presentation is usually authoritative. For such things as recent developments in the Pacific Trust Territories there is no better place to seek information. Each issue of *Social Education* in the department, "Pamphlets and Government Publications," under the direction of Manson Van B. Jennings, gives a short survey of the current offerings from this prolific source.

As to the techniques to be employed in utilizing these materials, there are as many possibilities as there are teachers. Each person will, in time, determine his own particular bent in the matter. To begin with, it is probably advisable to establish a regular time each week for the discussion of current events. A desirable length of time is about twenty minutes a week. This is generally sufficient to cover the major happenings, and it is still short enough so that interest will be kept at a maximum. Naturally, the time and duration of any such discussion should be flexible, since some things require more consideration than others. The death of a king or president does not demand the same order of analysis as the launching of an earth satellite. Oral presentation of the item is usually more spontaneous than reading or writing it might be. Although a one or two minute report is sufficient to introduce an item of significant news, the source of information should be placed on the bulletin board in the form of a clipping from journal or newspaper for more mature perusal and consideration.

As suggested before, if the news items are integrated into a theme of enduring importance it will be easy to organize them on a bulletin board, perhaps under such general headings as might appear in a news magazine's regular features: religion, education, medicine, science, personalities, books, television and radio, inventions, etc. As a topic of broad interest is developed over a long period of time, such as current illustration of the growth of United Nations work on boundary arbitration, the students could be expected to build scrap books or special sections in their notebooks. Perhaps this is a good place to use special committees of students, each group being charged with a particular department of news as it applies to the whole class project of attempting to understand a major movement in the nation or in the world. There are limitless possibilities.

### The Legacy of War

A. During and after World War II a wrenching change came to the world, not only in political geographic rearrangement in Europe, Africa and Asia, but in psychology, technology, business, and in a drastic new realignment of the world power structure. Germany and Japan and Italy emerged from the struggle dismembered, weak, broken and disillusioned. Britain and France found themselves stripped of empire, treasuries drained, and faced with political crises. Great Britain came under the control of Labor, long in the majority and only held from power by the exigency of war. India, Burma and Ceylon clamored for their long-promised independence. South Africa, almost untouched by the war, fell into a pattern of white supremacy power dominance and since 1945 has become more and more out of sympathy with the mother country. France doggedly faced one cabinet crisis after another while waging unsuccessful combat in Indo-China and North Africa. Russia came out of the war realizing a centuries-long ambition to take her place in the sun. She was, for the first time, a first class nation rivaled only by the United States in wealth, prosperity, strength and technological progress. China made another step in her revolution which started with the Tai P'ing in 1850. The Nationalist regime of Chiang Kai-shek fell to Mao-tse Tung, and a new Communist China arose from the ashes to threaten Asia and to attempt to fulfill the old Japanese war aims: "Greater East Asia Co-Prosperity," now changed to "Asia for the Asians." Even the United States had to remake the map of overseas possessions; the Philippine Republic sprang into being, no longer a colonial dependency.

1. New developments in war itself.
   a. Refinement of aviation techniques and equipment.
      1. American money and engineering.
      2. German ideas in rocket propulsion.
   b. Specialized technological developments such as radar, sonar, nuclear weapons.
2. Psychological adaptations to war.
   a. Application of science and technology to psychological warfare.
   b. "Fifth column" and Quisling techniques of internal subversion. Guerilla warfare.
   c. Attack of civilian targets in massive attempts to degrade the total morale of combatants.
3. Essentially non-military developments which came directly out of the war.
   a. The "wonder drugs," such as penicillin and other antibiotics which portend great alterations in the death and birth ratio of the world's underdeveloped countries.
   b. Jet and rocket propulsion of aircraft and vehicles as applicable to peacetime business.
   c. Nuclear and thermodynamic power sources which can be applied to capitalistic enterprise, such as generation of electric power.
   d. Specific techniques of travel, diet, survival and rescue which grew out of necessity in the widely diverse arenas of battle, but which have since been applied to everyday living.
   e. Impetus to basic scientific research which has resulted in space investigation, expansion of astronomical and meteorological knowledge, discoveries and speculations in and concerning the arctic and antarctic regions.
B. Problem of international cooperation
   1. Joint occupation of Germany by England, France, Russia and the United States.
      a. War crimes trials.
         (1) German jurisdiction divided between Russia and the West. United States dominated.

(2) Japanese jurisdiction strictly American.

(3) Russia established a unilateral system of reprisals in both Germany and in East Asia.

b. Ideological split between Communism and Democracy.

2. At San Francisco in 1945 a majority of the nations of the world met and adopted the charter and organization of the United Nations with the avowed intention of eliminating future wars through the process of community arbitration of disputes before they became out of hand.

3. The old functions of the League of Nations were taken on by the new United Nations.

a. Small nations were given a voice in the collective deliberations of the General Assembly.

b. The great nations became the final arbiters in the Security Council.

c. The old colonial mandates were given in trust to the United Nations.

(1) Colonial problems in Africa and Asia were debated and gave way to the rising nationalism in those areas. Many new nations were born.

(2) The Pacific islands were awarded in trusteeship to the national interests most involved, such as Great Britain, Australia and the United States.

4. National interests in the family of nations seemed to outweigh most international considerations, and the chief product of the United Nations was a radical realignment of the world power structure. It was obvious that the ancient balance of power in Europe was not to be the determining factor in the new global relationship of peoples. Europe is still important, but for different reasons than in the past. The whole world faced the future together after World War II—either for peace on new terms or for destruction on new terms.

a. Germany was partitioned between the West and Russia, part of it being added to the Iron Curtain of eastern Europe which shields Russia from the old power combination of western Europe.

b. Communist China perforce became the easternmost flank of Russia, which was now one of the two major power centers of the world.

c. The other power factor, the United States, being deeply involved in the affairs of prostrate Japan, came to blows indirectly with Russia and directly with China in the Korean conflict. Russia and China hid behind North Korea as a sovereign state while the United States prosecuted the Truman Doctrine of containment of Communism under the banner of the United Nations, of which South Korea was a member. The result was stalemate.

    d. The United States led the West and Russia led the Communist bloc in what we now know as "cold war," without much bloodshed.

C. The United Nations is not a failure, but it has failed to settle many problems of the modern world. It functions in a limited sphere with major success in those regions of activity and thought where interests are international, such as suppression of the slave trade and reduction of narcotics transportation and sale; in maritime matters such as international rules of the road at sea, detection and arrest of pirates, and international dissemination of welfare information. The United Nations keeps open an avenue of communication among the nations of the world. It is a clearing house of ideas concerning the political, economic and social well being of men everywhere. On the other hand, however, the United Nations has not furnished a substitute for nationalism, for indivisible, national sovereignty. Where the national interest prevails then the United Nations cannot function. It can restrain and admonish, suggest and veto, but it cannot rule. Until some new dimension in political thought is discovered, such will probably continue to be the case. The United Nations, in being in existence, is one of man's noblest and farthest reaching group endeavors. It must be preserved, but it is not omnipotent.

Outside the structure and function of the United Nations, there remains a bilateral system of political alliances: Russia and the Communist nations on the one hand, and the United States with her allied democracies on the other. In addition, there is a group of relatively neutral states, such as India and Indonesia. These are completely unpredictable. The vehicles of alignment are treaties of accord and mutual assistance pacts: the Japanese Peace Treaty, the North Atlantic Treaty Organization and the Southeast Asia Treaty Organization, as examples in the West; or the Tito-Stalin Accord and the Polish Peace Treaty, in the East.

There is a tremendous power struggle in the world between the two great colossi of East and West. It is in old terms of national sovereignty and interest but with newly phrased disguises: German unity, disarmament, satellite races, displaced persons, economic cooperation and others. The real struggle is between national interests and the problems are not always identified by the participants.

It is difficult, for example, to appreciate the price of 150,000 American casualties suffered under the banner of the United Nations by American men in a conflict between North and South Korea. What was gained in return? The United Nations survived. The Truman Doctrine was vindicated because Communism was contained beyond certain specified borders and lines. Still, the problem was nationalistic in character, and whatever success may be identified was strictly limited and unsatisfactory, but better than submission. Was the price too high?

The world is full of strange, new, and unresolved problems, public and private, left over from World War II. The United States is now the "fairy godmother" to all answer-seeking suppliants. The above discussion offered some ideals and some tragic conundrums that are the result of the nation's position.

### 5. Specific Application of Method

Topics listed under the American growth of political activity in pursuit of a constitutional rule of law could be used in a high school classroom in many different ways. Two examples will be sketched in the following pages, both based primarily on the use of study guides, homework and a socialized recitation methodology. As usual, the social studies teacher must keep in mind several principles, one of which is to pay attention constantly to individual differences and ability. This is perhaps the most difficult problem that faces teachers in a time when enrollments are increasing and time for individual attention to students is continually contracting. Another problem, related to the first one, is the selection of appropriate reading and teaching material for various groups of different ability. The method must be adjusted as well as it can be to the upper and lower limits of any particular class.

Study guides and carefully graded textbooks possibly offer some of the best means of meeting the situation mentioned above. Students of greater ability can be entrusted with more and complex homework than can those of lower capacity. In any case, the homework policy of the local school district must be consulted and current practices should be followed. For average eleventh and twelfth grade students, two or three hours a week outside class ought to be a reasonable expectation in connection with a single course in history or government. Of course, this will vary with the situation.

First of all, it is desirable for the teacher to outline for himself rather carefully and in some detail, the actual material to be covered by the students. This should form the basic guide for the teacher in preparing and assigning lessons to his class. Such an outline should be keyed to whatever text material that is furnished.

For an average class, for further specific guidance in outside study, a list of study questions could be developed. These might be drawn from a class discussion or they might be given directly by the teacher. They should be reproduced on sheets of paper with spaces left blank under each question in which the students could write out their answers. For more dependable students, the whole list could be issued at the beginning of the week to be completed for the following week's discussion. For less mature or less capable people, perhaps it would be better procedure to make the assignments more frequently and in smaller bulk. The following suggested questions were extracted from a standard high school text and actually used over the period of one week by a student teacher in Ventura, California.

Upon completion of the several phases of homework attending a chapter outline and study questions, the questions ought to be discussed in class meetings. It might be desirable to use a small group or committee technique if the size of the class and the facilities warrant that. Sometimes it is quite satisfactory simply to conduct a structured question and answer session, framing a more detailed inquiry around the study questions that have already been posed. One thing occurs here that the teacher must watch carefully. Sometimes the students are inclined to simply copy answers out of their textbook and then read them to the class instead of discussing the possibilities and ramifications of thought that are available. One device that can be used to forestall this is to require the student to stand up and deliver his comments without notes.

As a supplementary exercise, either in class or as homework, a blank outline map with a set of specific questions may be given to each student. This does two things: (1) it offers reinforcement in fixing certain concepts, and (2) it emphasizes the natural setting and geographic factors that often have such an important determining relationship to human activity. Here is a sample of the type of map exercise which might be given in connection with the subject just now under discussion:

Study Questions
United States History
Grade 11
Text: Everett Augspurger and Richard Aubrey McLemore, Our Nation's Story
      (Laidlaw, New York, 1956), Chapter 23, Part I, pp. 490-503.

1.  How had reform movements shown their effects by 1900?

2.  What was the Australian ballot?

3.  What was the purpose of introducing the direct primary?

4.  What is meant by:

    a. Initiative--

    b. Referendum--

    c. Recall--

5.  How did the 17th Amendment, providing for direct election of
    senators, become law?

6.  What were the beliefs of Theodore Roosevelt about:

    a. Big business--

    b. Labor unions--

7.  What did the "muckrakers" attack? Were they effective?

8.  What was the Northern Securities Case?

9.  What were the results of the Northern Securities Case?

10.  How did legislation aid the government in dealing with monopolies?

11.  What was Roosevelt's view on conservation?

12.  What was the Newlands Reclamation Act of 1902?

Outline Map of the United States
Reference: Augspurger and McLemore, *Our Nation's Story*, pp. 494, 501, 510, 512

On the map mark the states and the dates for those which had granted woman suffrage before the adoption of the 19th Amendment.

Indicate the national parks in the United States.

Put a heavy line around the twelve Federal Reserve Districts and number them.

Shade in the states which were considered dry at the time prohibition was enacted.[16]

Another facet of the same general period in American political growth might be treated with the same methodology, but directed toward the needs of a more highly selected and superior group of students. One might take the topic, "Heyday of Republican Dominance of Politics," from the Civil War to World War I. In the first instance, the teacher's initial responsibility would be to outline the material. Next, he would want to prepare study guides for the various parts of the topic. This time the period of coverage is greater and there will probably be more time devoted in class for its discussion. Also there can be more emphasis on homework, possibly even to include the assignment of a term paper on special subjects, such as biographies or political campaigns. In the class discussions, a major part of the time can be devoted to exploring the niceties of definition and semantic contingencies arising from description of the political phenomena. Current usages of words and concepts as well as recent modifications of principles can be related to the historical context.

The following study guide might be used as a basis for class discussion or writing, or it could be assigned as homework. Again, it is only one sample. It might have infinite variations.

Based on Henry W. Bragdon and Samuel P. McCutcheon, *History of a Free People* (Macmillan, New York, 1958), chapter 23, pp. 462–474, it will be found that prior to the Civil War politics flourished as a primary means for an individual to become prominent in national affairs. After the war, business assumed this role as politics sank into a corrupt state of confusion.

I. Political corruption.
   A. Meaning of corruption and the reasons for its growth.
   B. Corruption on the local or municipal level.
      1. Tweed Ring in New York. What was it?
      2. Why did good men tend to stay out of politics?

---

[16] These study guides were prepared by Wayne Haight, Santa Barbara, California, 1960. See also Ellen Semple and C. F. Jones, *American History and Its Geographic Conditions* (Houghton Mifflin, Boston, 1938).

    C. State level. What were examples?

    D. National level.

       1. Why was corruption less at the national level?

       2. What was the Credit Mobilier?

       3. Grant's administration. Why did the worst corruption occur then?

II. Major political parties.

    A. Why was it so difficult to tell just how the major parties stood on the various issues? What did sectionalism have to do with this?

       1. The silver issue.

       2. High and low tariff.

    B. Republican party.

       1. In power from 1861 to 1912 with one exception. Why was this so? Who were the main party backers? What problems did this present?

    C. Democratic party.

       1. Main strength in the South.

       2. What effect did the Civil War have on the party and its strategy?

    D. Pressure groups.

       1. What is a pressure group?

       2. Were they successful in this period? The Populist movement.

       3. Name and describe some pressure groups active in the era. Labor, various churches, suffragettes, etc.

Define the following terms:

    tariff, trust, cartel, holding company, monopoly, Grangers, Mugwumps, soft money, hard money, cornering the market, Muckrakers.

Identify the following persons:

    Mark Hanna, Boss Tweed, Jay Cooke, Jim Fiske, John Sherman, William Jennings Bryan, James G. Blaine.[17]

Either preceding or after discussion of the material in the foregoing outline, students should learn the factual content of the party structure, then and now. The names of personalities, the political campaigns and general chronology may be put into some kind of graphic or chart form. The students may be made wholly responsible for this if they have the capability, or in the case of slower students it might be a joint class effort, perhaps even a permanent blackboard or bulletin board display. In any case, the lowest common denominator of learning in political history must be the basic chronology. Beyond this, any possible degree of enrichment and examination of cause and effect relationship should be furnished as the students can absorb it.

Only one methodology has been indicated here because of the lack of space. United States history or any other social studies subject is amenable to, and should have, a variety of methods applied to its study. The study guide and socialized discussion have been suggested here as a way to start. Any of the other methods may also be used.

[17] Study guide prepared by Frank Whittington, Santa Barbara, California, 1960.

In addition, there should be a program of continual testing. Preferably at the end of each unit or chapter, a comprehensive test should be administered. Nearly every day some sort of progress mark can be recorded, and at the end of a quarter or semester it is usually desirable to give a review test over a major section of the course. This helps to reinforce learning and to encourage a systematic review of work covered. The teacher has the obligation to remind students of this, and to conduct review lessons periodically over each unit of work finished. Both in daily discussion and in the review sessions it is very important to make sure that a maximum number of the students in the class be given opportunity to express themselves. It is often the easier road to allow one or two highly verbal persons do all of the talking, but too often such procedure will leave a majority of the class in a completely passive situation, neither developing their learning nor correcting their mistakes.

Supplementary reading should also, in most cases, accompany the study of history, but this as a particular technique of teaching will be discussed later.

### 6. Bibliographies of Content and Method

#### GOVERNMENT AND POLITICAL PHILOSOPHY

James M. Burns and Jack W. Peltason, *Government by the People* (Prentice-Hall, Englewood Cliffs, N.J., 1960), 4th ed., including seven chapters on state and local government, is the most popular college text. Almost every publishing company has some such book, each of which has merit. Many of them can be used with the better high school students.

In regard to local government there is no possibility of getting such generalized yet valid statements as can be made for national government. Further, there is little distinction between the types of material useful for the teacher and for the students. Among things to be found in this field, The Maxwell Graduate School of Citizenship and Public Affairs, Syracuse University, has published *The Structure of Local Government* (1945), and *Parties and Politics in the Local Community* (1951). Specific state texts are mentioned elsewhere.

*Roots of Political Behavior, Introduction to Government and Politics,* edited by Richard Carlton Snyder and H. Hubert Wilson (American Book Company, New York, 1949), is a collection of essays by various authorities on different phases of the subject. It has long been used as a text for an introductory course in politics at Princeton University.

John Locke, *The Second Treatise of Government,* edited by J. W. Gough (Macmillan, New York, 1957), 2nd ed., is a reprint of the famous seventeenth century Englishman's views on the civil state from which we have derived most of the essential philosophy of our government. This is the place where classic expression was given to the doctrine of "life, liberty and property," pejorative element in our constitutional nexus.

James Bryce, *The American Commonwealth* (Macmillan, New York, 1893, 1914, 1919), 2 vols., in very friendly fashion, pointed out to Americans long ago that the time now here "may be the time of trial for democratic institutions."

Alexis de Tocqueville, *Democracy in America,* edited by Phillips Bradley (Vintage Books, New York, 1957), 2 vols., is a paper bound edition of the famous French commentary on the American political scene in the first part of the nineteenth century. Its comments are still valid and refreshing.

Robert M. MacIver, *The Web of Government* (Macmillan, New York, 1947), makes clear the complex interdependent ramifications of government, national and international.

## MISCELLANEOUS

*Social Studies Notebook,* is a quarterly service bulletin for teachers of social studies published and distributed by Scott, Foresman, Chicago. It is not specialized in the field of government, but often it is very useful in that field. For example, the spring, 1960, issue contains a chart of generalized government function which is also available as a wall chart.

## TEXTBOOKS ON GOVERNMENT

Junior High

Jack Allen and Clarence Stegmeir, *Civics* (American, New York, 1959), is a lively, sound text for the study of government; good bibliographies.

Judson T. Landis and Mary G. Landis, *Building Your Life* (Prentice-Hall, Englewood Cliffs, New Jersey, 1959), incorporates personal and social adjustment into the greater role of citizenship.

Senior High

Jack Allen and Fremont P. Wirth, *This Government of Ours* (American, New York, 1955), revised edition, is a comprehensive yet simple enough presentation of the elements of American government.

Bruce Findlay, *Your Rugged Constitution* (Stanford University Press, 1950), is a unique analysis of the constitution. On facing pages throughout a passage from the document is quoted and analyzed, with illustrations.

Frank A. Magruder and William A. McClenaghan, *American Government* (Allyn and Bacon, New York, 1959), is the latest yearly revision of this standard work since 1917. It is sound.

Laurence G. Paquin and Marian D. Irish, *The People Govern* (Scribner's, New York, 1958), reviews the American democratic heritage including the meaning of democracy.

*We Hold These Truths,* edited by Stuart Gerry Brown (Harper, New York, 1948), second edition, is described as "documents of American democracy" in the subtitle. It contains annotated copies of all the major political documents which we consider as landmarks in the growth of our present governmental form and philosophy.

In addition, there should be a wider selection of texts which range in point of view and difficulty, even including some multi-volume general histories used at the college level and a number of source books and selections of philosophic value in regard to both government and history. Since students, aged sixteen or seventeen, are about as adult mentally as most of them will ever be, there is absolutely no reason why they should not be given recognition in this regard and also the responsibility of bearing out the promise of adult mentality. They can and should read mature books.

Two rather simple yet sufficiently sophisticated volumes exist covering both political and historical facets of American development. In politics, Edward S. Corwin and Jack Peltason, *Understanding the Constitution* (Dryden Press, New York, 1958), rev. ed., is a simple and effective review of the main points in the document itself and its application. Richard Hofstadter, *The American Political Tradition and the Men Who Made It* (Vintage, New York, 1958), rev. ed., discusses the characters of many chief figures in American political history and their relative positions as to conservatism and liberalism. These inexpensive paperbacks are a real asset in teaching a high school course in United States history and government.

Clara Atwood, *The United States in the Western World* (Ginn, New York, 1950), is an attempt to present American life in its expanded setting of Western civilization.

Joseph Peck, *The World in Our Day* (Oxford Book Company, New York, 1954), is a good guide to general subjects for current study as events develop in the world. It relates the United States to the rest of the world.

## GENERAL MATERIALS ON CITIZENSHIP AND CIVIL RIGHTS FOR STUDENT AND TEACHER

Citizenship Education Project, *When Men Are Free* (Houghton Mifflin, Boston, 1955), is a new text for students on America's heritage of freedom.

Joseph Cottler, *Champions of Democracy* (Little, New York, 1936), contains brief biographies.

Stanley E. Dimond, *Citizenship for Boys and Girls* (Science Research Associates, Chicago, 1953), is a pamphlet in the Junior Life Adjustment Series, defining the good citizen.

*Good Citizen. The Rights and Duties of an American* (American Heritage Foundation, New York, 1948), is basic citizenship material for senior high.

Harold Hansen and others, *Fighting for Freedom* (Winston, New York, 1947), contains historical documents with interpretive comments.

Robert E. Merriam and John W. Bethea, *Understanding Politics* (Science Research Associates, Chicago, 1952), Junior Life Adjustment Series Booklet on American democracy and political parties.

Robert E. Merriam, *Politics for Boys and Girls* (Science Research Associates, Chicago), Junior Life Adjustment Booklet on politics for the junior high level.

Alison Reppy, *Civil Rights in the United States* (Central, New York, 1951), is a review of civil rights court cases, 1948–1950.

Films and recordings

Charles Boyer, *Liberté, Egalité, Fraternité* (78 rpm), 5-12″ records. Decca.

*Democracy*, 1 reel, Association Films.

*Declaration of Independence*, Teaching Film Custodians.

Poetry

William Rose Benét and Norman Cousins, *The Poetry of Freedom* (Random House, New York, 1945), contains many selections suitable for reading to a class.

## CONSTITUTION AND BILL OF RIGHTS

President's Committee on Civil Rights, *To Secure These Rights* (Simon and Schuster, New York, 1947), is part of the report which summarized the national record in civil rights enforcement and recommended steps to improve that performance.

Public Affairs Committee, *New Threats to American Freedom* (pamphlet) and *These Rights Are Ours to Keep* (pamphlet) (22 E. 38th Street, New York, n.d.).

United States Immigration and Naturalization Service, *Federal Textbook on Citizenship, Our Constitution and Government* (U.S. Government Printing Office, Washington, D.C., 1954), rev. ed.

Paul Witty and Julilly Kohler, *You and the Constitution of the U.S.* (Children's Press, New York, 1948), is for upper grades and junior high.

Films and recordings

*Bill of Rights.* Association Films.

Civil Rights Film Association, *The Challenge.* 16 mm., 30 min. March of Time Forum Films, 369 Lexington Avenue, New York, dramatizes the conclusion of the President's Committee on Civil Rights.

*Growth of Democracy.* 78 rpm, 10-12" records. Instructional Films. These sounds illustrate democracy from Magna Carta to the Constitution.

Robert E. Sherwood and Ernest Kinoy, *The Battle for the Bill of Rights.* 33⅓ rpm. Cinemart, Inc., 565 Fifth Avenue, New York. Civil rights are the same for all; the principle is indivisible.

Documents

National Archives, *Charters of Freedom and Formation of the Union* (Superintendent of Documents, Washington, D.C.), are facsimiles of basic documents in the growth of the American state.

## FREEDOM OF SPEECH AND PRESS

Robert E. Cushman, *Keep Our Press Free* (Public Affairs Committee, New York, pamphlet), illustrates a modern threat to freedom of the press.

Edgar Dale, *How to Read a Newspaper* (Scott, New York, 1941), demonstrates a method for evaluating the contents of newspapers.

*Democracy in Our Everyday Lives* (Building America, New York, pamphlet), discusses privately-owned opinion polling agencies.

*Documents of American History,* edited by Henry Steele Commager (Appleton-Century-Crofts, New York, 1949), in particular the "Northwest Ordinance," I, 128–132, which guarantees freedom of worship.

Jeanette Eaton, *Lone Journey—the Life of Roger Williams* (Harcourt, Brace, New York, 1944), illustrates the separation of church and state as a prerequisite to freedom.

Morris L. Ernst, *The First Freedom* (Macmillan, New York, 1946), deals with freedom of communication.

Jerome Frank, "Fight for Freedom," articles in *Life,* reprints available from Department E., 9 Rockefeller Plaza, New York, 20 (1951), shows how freedom of the press was established in colonial America.

Jerome H. Spingarn, *Radio Is Yours* (Public Affairs Committee, New York, 1946), holds that the public can control the radio.

## FREEDOM OF INQUIRY AND CRITICISM

*Heritage of America,* edited by Henry Steele Commager and Allan Nevins (Heath, Boston, 1949), "Dr. Morton Discovers Anesthesia," pp. 394–399, shows how men must be free in order to advance science and thought.

David E. Lilienthal, *This I Do Believe* (Harper, New York, 1949), is an illustration of the same thing.

## PUBLIC EDUCATION

*Education—An Investment in People* (Committee on Education, United States Chamber of Commerce, Washington, D.C., 1954), indicates the direct relationship between economic status and educational level.

## RIGHTS TO LIFE AND LIBERTY

Carl Carmer, *For the Rights of Men* (Hinds, New York, 1947), includes "William Lloyd Garrison," an example of the uncompromising attitude necessary to aid the cause of human freedom.

*American Issues,* edited by W. Thorp, Merle Curti and C. Baker (Lippincott, Philadelphia, 1944), has the famous speech of Patrick Henry ". . . give me liberty or give me death," March 23, 1775, I, 90–92.

## RIGHT TO A FAIR TRIAL

Stephen Vincent Benét, *The Devil and Daniel Webster* (Rinehart, New York, 1937), is a short story which has been made into a stage and television play, showing how Webster won the soul of Jabez Stone from the devil in a court trial.

Carl Carmer, *For the Rights of Men,* pp. 59–64, "John Peter Altgeld," illustrates the fulfillment of justice despite odds and initial mistaken justice.

Chester S. Williams, *Fair Trial* (Row, Peterson, Evanston, Illinois, 1941), contains stories dramatized to present the essence of democratic personal liberty.

## INDIVIDUAL RIGHTS AND NATIONAL SECURITY

Dumas Malone, "Jefferson Still Survives," *New York Times Magazine,* July 2, 1950, shows modern application of Jefferson's philosophy. Reprints available from Citizenship Education Project, Columbia University.

*National Security and Our Individual Freedom* (Committee for Economic Development, 444 Madison Avenue, New York, 1949), is a pamphlet recalling the necessity of insuring individual rights in the face of pressure for national defense.

## WORTH OF HUMAN BEINGS

*Civil Liberties; Civic Responsibilities* (Building America, 2 West 45th Street, New York), are pamphlets outlining the two sides of citizenship.

Harry Lee Shaw and Ruth Davis, *Americans One and All* (Harper, New York, 1947), is a collection of twenty-three stories showing the common humanity of all Americans.

Films and recordings

*Americans All.* 16 min. March of Time Forum Films. Stresses intergroup relations.

*Boundary Lines.* 10 min. Film Foundation, 1600 Broadway, New York.

Earl Robinson, *Ballad for Americans* (78 rpm), RCA, is adaptable to choral speaking at the junior high level.

Gilbert Seldes, *Americans All—Immigrants All* (28 rpm, 24 recordings), shows how the whole American population derives from immigrant sources.

## SELF-GOVERNMENT

Stuart Chase, *Democracy Under Pressure* (Twentieth Century Fund, New York, 1945), describes how various pressure groups work in a democracy.

Edna McGuire, *With Liberty and Justice for All* (Federal Security Agency, United States Government Printing Office, Washington, D.C., 1950), is a documentary history of the growth of self government in the United States.

National League of Women Voters, *Is Politics Your Job?* (Washington, D.C., n.d.), is a pamphlet stressing the universal responsibility of citizens.

Chester S. Williams, *Right of Free Speech* (Row, Evanston, Illinois, 1940).

Film

Preston Sturges, *Every Vote Counts*, excerpted from Paramount's *The Great McGinty*, 7 min. Teaching Film Custodians.

## CITIZENSHIP MATERIAL FOR THE TEACHER

Grace M. Anderson, "Practical Experiments in Student Government," *Social Education* (December, 1938), pp. 627–629, gives some pointers.

Ben A. Arneson, "Trends in the Teaching of Government," *Social Education* (December, 1945), pp. 35–54, emphasizes the growth of government.

Louis J. Capen, *Being a Citizen* (American Book Co., New York, 1953), points out citizenship qualifications at all age levels.

Albert Coates, "Educating Citizens for Their Responsibilities as Local Government Officials," in *The Citizen's Participation in Public Affairs* (New York University School of Law, 1948), pp. 146–158.

Stanley E. Dimond, "The Detroit Citizenship Study," *Social Education* (December, 1948), pp. 356–358, illustrates a relationship between schools and life.

Kermit Eby, "Can We Teach Citizenship?" *Phi Delta Kappan* (November, 1949), pp. 130–137, is a comment in the affirmative, but there is always the question of how to do it. Perhaps the only way is to teach substantive material and hope for a good behavioral outcome.

William H. Eells, "Preparing for Politics," *Social Education* (October, 1956), pp. 262–263. In a sense we must all be politicians.

*Education for Democratic Citizenship,* edited by Ryland W. Crary, Twenty-second
Yearbook, National Council for the Social Studies (Washington, D.C., 1951),
in particular "Characteristics of the Good Democratic Citizen," and "Evaluation of Citizenship Education."

*Evaluation of Citizenship Education in the High School: A Report of the Kansas
Study of Education for Citizenship* (Kansas State College Press, Manhattan,
Kansas, 1950), is a practical curricular guide.

*Goals for Political Science,* report of the committee for the advancement of teaching, American Political Science Association (William Sloan, New York, 1951),
is a straightforward appraisal, by specialists in political science, of what ought
to be taught in secondary schools and why it should be so.

Lamar B. Johnson, "General Education for Citizenship," *Junior College Journal*
(October, 1952), pp. 91–97, shows what society should expect of everyone
who achieves the first two years of college.

Leonard S. Kenworthy, "The World View in Civic Education," *Social Education*
(December, 1953), pp. 379–382, stresses the idea that although Americans
are citizens of the United States they are also members of a world community.

Raymond Nelson, "Citizenship Laboratory," *School Review* (March, 1948), pp.
156–162. Every community and every school offers opportunities to practice
the arts of citizenship merely by putting out the effort.

I. James Quillen, "The World Minded Citizen," in *Education for Democratic
Citizenship,* Twenty-second Yearbook, National Council for the Social Studies
(Washington, D.C., 1951).

William S. Vincent, "Principles and Practices of the Citizenship Education Project," *Teachers College Record* (March, 1954), pp. 261–268, tells about a
very useful enterprise. C.E.P., aside from many hints on procedure, contains
the most comprehensive bibliography in usable form that is available to
teachers of secondary school citizenship and government.

Stanley P. Wronski, *How to Locate Useful Government Publications,* How to Do
It Series, No. 11, National Council for the Social Studies (Washington, D.C.,
1952).

## CURRENT AFFAIRS TEACHING METHODS AND MATERIALS

Howard A. Anderson, "Magazines and Education," *School Review* (December,
1954), pp. 511–512.

*Current Affairs and Modern Education,* Delbert Clark, ed. (*New York Times,*
1950).

Howard H. Cummings and Harry Bard, *How to Use Daily Newspapers,* How to
Do It Series, National Council for the Social Studies (Washington, D.C.,
1949).

Leonard W. Doob, "The School's Potential as a Determinant of Public Opinion,"
in *The Teaching of Contemporary Affairs,* Twenty-first Yearbook, National
Council for the Social Studies (Washington, D.C., 1950).

*Current Affairs and Social Studies,* Junior Town Meeting League (Middletown,
Connecticut, 1955).

Jewell Phelps, "Geography Behind the News: An Experiment in Educational
Television," *Journal of Geography* (April, 1955), pp. 187–192.

*Report of the Teaching of Current Affairs,* National Council for the Social Studies (Washington, D.C., May, 1948).

*The Teaching of Current Affairs, A Teacher's Manual,* Commission on American Citizenship, Catholic University of America (George A. Pflaum, Washington, D.C., 1949).

See in particular two yearbooks of the National Council for the Social Studies on several phases of citizenship: *The Teaching of Contemporary Affairs,* Twenty-first Yearbook (1950), and *Citizenship and a Free Society: Education for the Future* (Washington, D.C., 1960).

## GENERAL BACKGROUND AND AMERICAN HISTORY

*American History Atlas* (Hammond, New York, n.d.), is a paper covered simple atlas containing very valuable information concerning the political development of the United States.

Elizabeth Chesley Baity, *Americans before Columbus* (Viking Press, New York, 1951), is a text and picture account of the native inhabitants of the two Americas. Useful for students also.

John Bartlet Brebner, *The Explorers of North America* (Doubleday Anchor, Garden City, 1955), is a paperback reprint of what has become a classic in the field of American exploration. Each chapter is furnished with a list of original narratives and descriptions.

*Guide to Historical Literature,* American Historical Association (Macmillan, New York, 1961), is the most recent compilation of historical materials. It contains 20,000 items. Very valuable.

Among the many one or two volume surveys of American political history, only two will be listed here. There are many, and most of them have some particular merit. In addition, there are a good many textbook histories of the United States which take in much more than the political narrative. Of these, perhaps the most widely used college text is John Hicks, *The Federal Union* and *The American Nation* (Houghton Mifflin, 1955, 1957), 3rd ed. Samuel Eliot Morison and Henry Steele Commager, *Growth of the American Republic* (Oxford University Press, New York, 1960), 6th ed., is a classic that continues in popularity and effectiveness year after year. It is the most comprehensive college text, and also one of the most gracefully written books, therefore a few copies should appear in high school libraries.

*Documents of American History,* edited by Henry Steele Commager (Croft, New York, 1960), 6th ed., has become a standard acquisition of historians and libraries, and serves as a basic political guide in United States history. Most of the important American political documents appear here.

*Readings in American History,* edited by Oscar Handlin (Knopf, New York, 1957), represents another type of source book, of which there are many, giving various selections by contemporaries of past events.

*Narrative and Critical History of America,* edited by Justin Winsor (Boston, 1884–1889), 8 vols., was, up to the time of its publication, a remarkably well documented statement of what was known about American history.

*The American Nation: A History from Original Sources by Associated Scholars,* edited by Albert Bushnell Hart (Harper, New York, 1904–1918), 28 vols., was, until recently, the most comprehensive and definitive collection of historical writings in one series. Lately the *New American Nation Series* was begun under the editorship of Richard Morris, but so far it is incomplete.

*Encyclopedia of American History*, edited by Richard Morris (Harper, New York, 1953), is a collection of abbreviated materials concerning American history with some illustrations and maps.

## DIPLOMATIC HISTORY

Howard K. Beale, *Theodore Roosevelt and the Rise of America to World Power* (Johns Hopkins University Press, 1956), treats foreign policy and domestic politics in the Progressive era at the beginning of the twentieth century.

Foster Rhea Dulles, *China and America* (Princeton University Press, 1940), by one of the outstanding authorities on Far Eastern affairs, this book handles the matter of the Boxer Rebellion and the Open Door Policy. By the same author, *America's Rise to World Power, 1898–1954* (Harper, New York, 1954), New American Nation Series, is a concise and interesting account of half a century of American politics and diplomacy.

Thomas A. Bailey, *A Diplomatic History of the American People* (Appleton-Century, New York, 1958), 6th ed., is the most widely used college text.

Julius W. Pratt, *Expansionists of 1812* (Macmillan, New York, 1925; reprinted by Peter Smith, New York, 1949), links the War of 1812 with western political aspirations. See also Alexander DeConde, *New Interpretations in American Foreign Policy* (Service Center for Teachers of History, American Historical Association, Washington, D.C., 1957), for different approaches.

Julius W. Pratt, *Expansionists of 1898* (Peter Smith, New York, 1952), makes another attempt to link politics with sectional expansionism and a revival of Manifest Destiny at the turn of the century.

## PROFESSIONAL AIDS TO TEACHERS

The American Historical Association has set up a Service Center for Teachers of History which has the function of publishing pamphlets bringing to the profession various items of information—new literature, interpretations, bibliographies—focused on the problem of teaching history in secondary schools. The list of titles now in print includes Edmund S. Morgan, *The American Revolution;* Charles Grier Sellers, Jr., *Jacksonian Democracy;* Hal Bridges, *Civil War and Reconstruction;* George E. Mowry, *The Progressive Movement, 1900–1920;* Alexander DeConde, *New Interpretations in American Foreign Policy;* Eric E. Lampard, *Industrial Revolution;* Otis A. Singletary, *The South in American History;* Ray Allen Billington, *The American Frontier;* Charles Gibson, *The Colonial Period in Latin American History;* Margareta Faissler, *Key to the Past* (bibliography for high school students). More titles will be forthcoming.

## COLONIAL PERIOD AND BACKGROUND

Wilbur Cortez Abbott, *The Expansion of Europe* (Holt, New York, 1918), shows how America happened historically.

Samuel Eliot Morison, *Admiral of the Ocean Sea* (Little, Brown, Boston, 1942), is a magnificent biography of a significant figure, Christopher Columbus.

Francis Parkman, *The Old Regime in Canada* (many editions), by one of the greatest American historians, is a typically American book. It shows very well why monarchical France lost out to "middle class" England in the New World.

S. H. Brochunier, *The Irrepressible Democrat, Roger Williams* (Ronald, New York, 1940), is a sensitive biography of the founder of Rhode Island; *Bradford's History of Plymouth Plantation* in *Original Narratives of Early American History* (Scribner's, New York, 1908), gives a view of early resistance to the idea of theocratic control, and is useful for students.

Charles M. Andrews, *Colonial Self-Government, 1652–1689* (Harper, New York, 1904) and Leonard W. Laboree, *Royal Government in America* (Yale University Press, 1930), illustrate the beginnings of sovereignty in the British colonies which finally led to revolution. Charles M. Andrews, *Our Earliest Colonial Settlements* (Cornell University Press, Great Seal Books), is a current paperback reprint which carries a simple version of the author's ideas.

## INDEPENDENCE AND A NEW NATION

Clinton Rossiter, *Seedtime of the Republic* (Harcourt, Brace, New York, 1953); John C. Miller, *Sam Adams: Pioneer in Propaganda* (Little, Brown, Boston, 1936); Catherine Drinker Bowen, *John Adams and the American Revolution* (Little, Brown, Boston, 1950), popular treatment; Carl Becker, *The Declaration of Independence* (Harcourt, Brace, New York, 1933); Willard M. Wallace, *Appeal to Arms* (Harper, New York, 1951), on the war itself; Nathaniel W. Stephenson and W. H. Dunn, *George Washington* (Oxford University Press, New York, 1940); Merrill Jensen, *The New Nation* (1950); Max Farrand, *Framing of the Constitution* (Yale University Press, 1913), cf. Beard, *An Economic Interpretation* . . . ; Nathan Schachner, *Alexander Hamilton* (Thomas Yoseloff, New York, 1957, reprint), cover the growth of the United States up to about 1800.

Nathan Schachner, *Thomas Jefferson, A Biography* (Yoseloff, New York, 1957, reprint), 2 vols., is the best current study of Jefferson.

## JACKSONIAN DEMOCRACY

Samuel Flagg Bemis, *John Quincy Adams and the Union* (Knopf, New York, 1955); Arthur M. Schlesinger, Jr., *The Age of Jackson* (Little, Brown, Boston, 1946); Marquis James, *Andrew Jackson: The Border Captain* (Bobbs-Merrill, Indianapolis, 1933), and *Andrew Jackson: Portrait of a President* (1937).

## SECTIONALISM

Roy Nichols, *Advance Agents of American Destiny* (University of Pennsylvania Press, 1956); Clement Eaton, *A History of the Old South* (Macmillan, New York, 1949); Oliver P. Chitwood, *John Tyler: Champion of the Old South* (Appleton, New York, 1939); Glyndon Van Deusen, *The Life of Henry Clay* (Little, Brown, Boston, 1937); C. M. Wiltse, *John C. Calhoun, Nationalist, 1782–1828* (Bobbs-Merrill, Indianapolis, 1944); C. M. Fuess, *Daniel Webster* (Little, Brown, Boston, 1930), 2 vols.; Bernard De Voto, *Year of Decision, 1846* (Little, Brown, Boston, 1943); R. S. Henry, *The Story of the Mexican War* (Bobbs-Merrill, Indianapolis, 1950); Allan Nevins, *Ordeal of the Union*

(Scribner's, New York, 1947), 2 vols., on the decade after the Mexican War; George Fort Milton, *The Eve of Conflict: Stephen A. Douglas and the Needless War* (Houghton Mifflin, Boston, 1934), on the Compromise of 1850; Robert Forrest Wilson, *Crusader in Crinoline: The Life of Harriet Beecher Stowe* (Lippincott, Philadelphia, 1941), all show the relationships among sectionalism, politics and two wars.

## CIVIL WAR AND RECONSTRUCTION

No other topic in American history has had such a huge bulk of literature, both source and secondary; to attempt to annotate even a small part of it is like washing an elephant with a toothbrush, therefore, here will be given only those easily obtainable items which should give a fair comprehension of the basic political and constitutional problems involved in the great struggle between the states. To begin with, the standard college text for upper division courses in the subject is J. G. Randall, *The Civil War and Reconstruction* (Heath, Boston, 1953). The most recent note on possible revisions of Randall's view may be seen in Hal Bridges, *Civil War and Reconstruction* (American Historical Association, Washington, D.C., 1957), and Otis A. Singletary, *The South in American History* (American Historical Association, Washington, D.C., 1957), pamphlets issued by the Service Center for Teachers of History.

In order to put the Civil War issues in a reasonable perspective it is necessary to pose several problems immediately, such as, slavery as a cause, sectional politics, southern nationalism, the economic base of politics, or Lincoln's constitutional position. This may be done satisfactorily by reference to *Problems in American Civilization*, edited by George R. Taylor and others (Heath, Boston), a series of separate paper bound titles consisting of various views, contemporary and secondary, on the central problem posed, i.e., *Slavery as a Cause of the Civil War*, edited by Edwin C. Rozwenc (1949); *The Compromise of 1850*, edited by Edwin C. Rozwenc (1957); and *The Transcendentalist Revolt Against Materialism*, edited by George F. Whicher (1949), all apply somewhat to the Civil War (there are a good many other titles in the series dealing with other problems).

Good general and special works on the war include Kenneth Stammp, *Causes of the Civil War* (Spectrum); Arthur C. Cole, *The Irrepressible Conflict, 1850–1865* (Macmillan, 1934), Vol. 7 in *A History of American Life;* Nathaniel W. Stephenson, *Abraham Lincoln and the Union: A Chronicle of the Embattled North* (Yale University Press, 1921), Vol. 29 in *Chronicles of America;* William E. Dodd, *Statesmen of the Old South, or from Radicalism to Conservative Revolt* (Macmillan, New York, 1911); Sir Frederick Maurice, *Statesmen and Soldiers of the Civil War, A Study of the Conduct of War* (Little, Brown, Boston, 1926); Arthur C. Cole, "Lincoln's Election an Immediate Menace to Slavery in the States?" *American Historical Review* (1931), XXXVI, 740–767; Edward S. Corwin, "The Dred Scott Decision in the Light of Contemporary Legal Documents," *American Historical Review* (1911), XVII, 52–69; Harold M. Dudley, "The Election of 1864," *Mississippi Valley Historical Review* (1932), XVIII, 500–518.

A few selected biographies may be very useful: Henry Adams, *The Education of Henry Adams* (1918), (many editions); Hamilton Basso, *Beauregard: The Great Creole* (Scribner's, New York, 1933), concerns the man who thought that he could have been the savior of the South; Oswald Garrison Villard, *John Brown, 1800–1859* (Houghton Mifflin, Boston, 1910); Hans Louis Trefousse, *Ben Butler* (Twayne Publishers, New York, 1958), depicts the colorful commander-politician of New Orleans after the North defeated that city. Benjamin Franklin Butler represents the Northern political general.

Varina Howell Davis, *Jefferson Davis, Ex-President of the Confederate States of America: A Memoir by His Wife* (1890), 2 vols., is a rather sharp analysis of the headstrong leader of secession by the one person who should have known him best.

Gamaliel Bradford, *Lee the American* (Houghton Mifflin, Boston, 1912); Douglas Southall Freeman, *R. E. Lee: A Biography* (Scribner's, New York, 1934–1935), 4 vols., give different views of the great Southerner.

Albert J. Beveridge, *Abraham Lincoln, 1809–1858* (Houghton Mifflin, Boston, 1916–1919), 4 vols.; Carl Sandburg, *Abraham Lincoln: The War Years* (Harcourt, Brace, New York, 1939), give a slim sample of the hundreds of books on Lincoln; Nathaniel W. Stephenson, *Lincoln . . . An Account of His Personal Life* (Bobbs-Merrill, Indianapolis, 1924), is a fair single volume attempt; George Fort Milton, *The Age of Hate: Andrew Johnson and the Radicals* (Coward-McCann, New York, 1930), shows what happened to the political policies of Lincoln in the hands of his successor, after Lincoln's death. Bruce Catton, *Mr. Lincoln's Army* (Dolphin Books), is a popular paperback.

For a quick view of Reconstruction see: C. Vann Woodward, *Reunion and Reaction* (Anchor Books), a recent paperback; Howard K. Beale, *The Critical Year: A Study of Andrew Johnson and Reconstruction* (Harcourt, Brace, New York, 1930); Claude G. Bowers, *The Tragic Era: The Revolution after Lincoln* (Houghton Mifflin, Boston, 1929); Allan Nevins, *The Emergence of Modern America, 1865–1878* (Macmillan, New York, 1927), Vol. 8 in *A History of American Life.*

## LATE NINETEENTH CENTURY

R. M. Robertson, *History of the American Economy* (Harcourt, Brace, New York, 1955), shows the economic development that has evinced itself in American political change. Wilfred Ellsworth Binkley, *American Political Parties, Their Natural History* (Knopf, New York, 1945), could serve as a basic text in high school.

Richard Hofstadter, *The Age of Reform: From Bryan to F. D. R.* (Knopf, New York, 1955), treats the two great reform parties of American history, the Populists and the Progressives.

Walter Prescott Webb, *The Great Plains* (Grossett, 1957), is a paperback reprint of a classic explaining much of American behavior in terms of the frontier.

Allan Nevins, *Grover Cleveland: A Study in Courage* (Dodd, Mead, New York, 1932), describes the career of the only Democratic president from before the Civil War until Woodrow Wilson.

Catherine Drinker Bowen, *Yankee from Olympus: Justice Holmes and His Family* (Little, Brown, Boston, 1944), covers a period from the eighteenth century almost to the present, but it is focused on the problems of reform which marked the middle period of American history.

## THE TWENTIETH CENTURY

Oscar Theodore Barck and Nelson Manfred Blake, *Since 1900* (Macmillan, New York, 1952), revised edition, is a comprehensive survey of the United States from the beginning of the century. Arthur S. Link, *American Epoch: A History of the United States Since the 1890's* (Knopf, New York, 1955), is a competent political history of the period indicated.

George E. Mowry, *Theodore Roosevelt and the Progressive Movement* (University of Wisconsin Press, 1946); Arthur Link, *Wilson: Road to the White House* (Princeton University Press, 1947), and *Wilson: The New Freedom* (Princeton University Press, 1956), give adequate introduction to the progressive and reform movement of the early twentieth century. See also Edwin O. Rozwenc, *Roosevelt, Wilson and the Trusts* (Heath, Boston, 1950) one of the series, Problems in American Civilization.

Mark Sullivan, *Our Times* (Harper, New York, 1928–1935), 6 vols., is a social commentary on the first quarter of the twentieth century. It is invaluable in understanding common American life. Henry Bamford Parkes, *Recent America* (Crowell, New York, 1942), brings the social record a little further into the present.

Material concerning the New Deal and World War II is so profuse that no one really has sifted out the chaff yet. From the standpoint of political history it is just as well to start with Franklin Roosevelt, *Looking Forward* (John Day, New York, 1933), and *On Our Way* (1934), giving the late President's own first impression of his job and his first progress report.

Various estimates of Roosevelt's character and stature are available, and they vary almost as much as their authors. Here are some completely diverse pictures of FDR: Gerald W. Johnson, *Roosevelt: Dictator or Democrat?* (Harper, New York, 1941); John T. Flynn, *Country Squire in the White House* (Doubleday, New York, 1940), written as Republican campaign ammunition in the third term controversy; Edgar Eugene Robinson, *The Roosevelt Leadership* (Lippincott, Philadelphia, 1955), more recent and scholarly, but no less vindictive; Dexter Perkins, *The New Age of Franklin Roosevelt, 1932–1945* (University of Chicago Press, 1957) and Dennis Brogan, *The Era of Franklin D. Roosevelt: A Chronicle of the New Deal and Global War* (Yale University Press, 1950), are both scholarly books and rather sympathetic to the President. Edward Stettinius, *Lend Lease: Weapon for Victory* (Macmillan, New York, 1944), helps understand the New Deal position in relation to the war, written by a former Secretary of State.

Peter Drucker, *America's Next Twenty Years* (Harper, New York, 1957), points up the need of the United States to expand its outlook in politics and philosophy to embrace the rest of the world. The same problem is developed in technical political science terms in Karl W. Deutsch, *Political Community at the International Level* (Doubleday, Garden City, 1954).

## NON–PROFESSIONAL HISTORY

Stephen Vincent Benét, *America* (Rinehart, New York, 1944); William Carlos Williams, *In the American Grain* (New Directions, Norfolk, Connecticut, 1925), are prose comments by poets on the story of American development. Sometimes it is possible to get a penetrating insight into the body of history by studying a poet's subjective truth which is denied to a professional historian's writing by the nature of his creed. At least, it offers an interesting perspective. See also John Berryman, *Homage to Mistress Bradstreet* (Farrar-Straus-Cudahy, New York, 1956), which is a rather long poem devoted to seventeenth century life and literature, only incidentally using Anne Bradstreet as the vehicle.

In regard to historical fiction, a similar sort of observation can be made: the historian who does not read many novels is likely to be pedantic and narrow. Rather than list historical novels, reference should be made to those in Chapter 9 and also to Ernest Leisy, *The American Historical Novel* (University of Oklahoma Press, 1950), which discusses most of the significant novels concerning American history.

### 7. Student References

UNITED STATES HISTORY TEXTBOOKS—Senior High Level

The selection of a particular book depends upon the technique of instruction favored by the teacher. Because of the diversity of ability to be found in any unselected high school group it is probably desirable to use a variety of methods and therefore a variety of text materials. As in the other grade levels one may assume a minimum competence in reading ability on the part of everyone (although there are exceptions, with some students being almost non-readers), and to require mastery of a basic text in United States history. It follows that a class should have common access to one book selected by the teacher assigned to each student.

In addition, there should be a wider selection of texts which range in point of view and difficulty, even including some multi-volume general histories used at the college level and a number of source books and selections of philosophic value in regard to both government and history. Since students, aged sixteen or seventeen, are about as adult mentally as most of them will ever be, there is absolutely no reason why they should not be given recognition in this regard and also the responsibility of bearing out the promise of adult mentality. They can and should read mature books.

Students of history at any level need to be instructed in the methodology of history writing, in the elements of historiography, and they need to be constantly reminded of the existence of source materials. If it is not guarded against rigorously, students will come to think of history as being what can be read in the textbook at hand. Critical analysis of the bases from which a historical narrative is drawn must always be encouraged. The best way to do this is certainly by example; students should have access to the materials of history at first hand whenever it is at all possible. Usually this is a difficult matter, and it always entails knowledge and appreciation on the part of the teacher. The instructor must know, first of all, the basic difference between source and secondary material. To do this he must be thoughtful and he must have been instructed himself in the fundamental methods employed by historians in locating and using sources. At present there are not nearly enough printed collections of historical documents available to the capabilities of young students. There are, however, a few items of genuine usefulness in this regard. *The Spirit of 'Seventy-Six,* edited by Henry Steele Commager and Richard B. Morris (2 vols., Bobbs-Merrill, Indianapolis, 1958), is a fine addition to the category under discussion, dealing with the American Revolution. *American Heritage Book of the American Revolution* (American Heritage, New York, 1958), carries an interpretive text, but its main value is the contemporary documentation in pictures. *Times of Trial: Great Crises in the American Past,* edited by Allan Nevins (Knopf, New York, 1958), documents some of the outstanding episodes in United States history.

The following is a list of high school textbooks in United States history:

David S. Muzzey, *Our Country's History* (Ginn, Boston, 1955), is the latest edition of a classic in the teaching of many generations of American students. Fremont P. Wirth, *United States History* (American, New York, 1955), is another equally useful test, a little longer, and of less venerable reputation. Both books are attractively illustrated and are accompanied by teachers' manuals and other teaching aids.

The following group of textbooks has the characteristic of having been prepared specifically for modern high school students, with special attention to the general level of interest and ability. They all tend to be a little over simplified and generally lack the mature intellectual interest of more adult books. They have the advantage of being geared to standard teaching methods and have adequate guides and testing material: Everett Augspurger and Richard A. McLemore, *Our Nation's Story* (Laidlaw, New York, 1954); Henry W. Bragdon and Samuel P. McCutcheon, *History of a Free People* (Macmillan, New York, 1954); Leon H. Canfield and Howard B. Wilder, *The American Story* (Heath, Boston, 1954); William A. Hamm, *From Colony to World Power* (Heath, Boston, 1953); Samuel Steinberg, *The United States: Story of a Free People* (Allyn and Bacon, New York, 1954).

In view of the varied composition of current high school classes in United States history there are bound to be some students who simply do not have the capacity for the more mature titles so far listed, and therefore one remedial book will be included. Eugene C. Barker, Henry S. Commager and Walter P. Webb, *The Standard Building of Our Nation* (Row, Peterson, New York, 1953), is written by three highly reputable historians; it is not slipshod nor "written down," but simply does not treat as many topics or give as much detail as do some of the larger books.

For the occasional adult student who has neglected learning the basic facts concerning our government and history, or who has forgotten them and needs a concise reminder, there are four books that taken together should form the foundation of American general education in regard to political citizenship. They are: Allan Nevins and Henry Steele Commager, *A Short History of the United States* (Modern Library, New York, 1942); Ernest S. Griffith, *The American System of Government* (Praeger, New York, 1954); Clinton Rossiter, *The American Presidency* (Signet, New York, 1956); and Stuart Brown, *We Hold These Truths* (cited above).

## SPECIAL REFERENCES

Alfred H. Kelly and Winifred A. Harbison, *The American Constitution: Its Origins and Development* (Norton, New York, 1955) revised edition, is a solid constitutional history.

Samuel Eliot Morison, *The Maritime History of Massachusetts, 1783–1860* (Houghton Mifflin, Boston, 1941), is important not only for its application in economic history, but because of the significance of the Northeastern section in particular, and because of the relationship existing in American politics between economics and politics and sectionalism and politics.

Foster Rhea Dulles, *Labor in America: A History* (Crowell, New York, 1955), emphasizes the significance of labor in American political growth.

Pre-revolutionary

Samuel Eliot Morison, *Christopher Columbus, Mariner* (New American Library, New York, 1955), grew out of the author's longer and earlier work on Columbus, *Admiral of the Ocean Sea.*

Harold Lamb, *New Found World: How North America Was Discovered and Explored* (Doubleday, New York, 1955), is by a master storyteller and should intrigue any young person.

*Parkman Reader: From the Works of Francis Parkman,* edited by Samuel Eliot Morison (Little, Brown, Boston, 1955), is a selection from the works of one of America's truly great historians who dealt so forcefully with the history of the great struggle between France and Britain for possession of North America in the colonial period.

Verner W. Crane, *Benjamin Franklin and a Rising People* (Little, Brown, Boston, 1954), gives an adequate sketch of the fascinating personality of Franklin, the first American.

Revolution

Esther Forbes, *Paul Revere and the World He Lived In* (Houghton Mifflin, Boston, 1942), is a best seller and it can produce a thrilling experience for any American.

Nathaniel W. Stephenson and Waldo H. Dunn, *George Washington* (Oxford University Press, New York, 1940), 2 vols., is the best short biography of Washington. Marcus Cunliffe, *George Washington: Man and Monument* (New American Library), is a good paperback.

Louis Gottschalk, *Lafayette Joins the American Army* (University of Chicago Press, 1937), presents the romantic and materialistic facts concerning the young French aristocrat in a most charming manner.

Claude Bowers, *The Young Jefferson* (Houghton Mifflin, Boston, 1945), by an expert on Jefferson, history and foreign affairs, this is a sympathetic estimate of the character forming period of the father of the Declaration of Independence.

Early Nineteenth Century

Saul K. Padover, *Jefferson* (Harcourt, Brace, New York, 1942), is about the mature Jefferson and political involvements.

Francis F. Beirne, *The War of 1812* (Dutton, New York, 1949), is a journalistic account of the military and naval aspects of the war.

Marquis James, *The Raven* (Grossett, New York, 1956), reprint of an earlier edition, this life of Sam Houston is a gripping adventure story built out of the authentic fragments of history.

Civil War

Clement Eaton, *A History of the Southern Confederacy* (Macmillan, New York, 1954), shows the position of the South as it was caught up in a fratricidal conflict.

Margaret Leech, *Reveille in Washington* (Harper, New York, 1941), shows life as it went on in the nation's capital during the Civil War.

*The Lincoln Reader,* edited by Paul M. Angle (Pocketbooks, 1947), was compiled from Lincoln's own papers, and it contains wisdom and anecdotes sufficient to recompense the many hours of effort spent on it.

Bruce Catton, *A Stillness at Appomattox* (Doubleday, New York, 1953), possesses the fascinating power of a great novel, it shows hour by hour the travail and triumph of heroic men during the last year of the Civil War.

Since the Civil War

James MacGregor Burns, *Roosevelt, The Lion and The Fox* (Harcourt, Brace, New York, 1956), is a recent and readable biography of Franklin Roosevelt, four term President, and his political maneuvering in order to stay in power.

Eric F. Goldman, *The Crucial Decade: America 1945–1955* (Knopf, New York, 1956), stresses the people, individuals and societies, in the current time—or within the memory of even very young people.

In addition to the above lists which might reasonably be expected to appear either as texts in a classroom or in a school library, there are several series of books covering the history of the United States in its various aspects. Perhaps larger high school departments might have some of them in a special departmental library where they would be available to both teacher and student.

Typical of this group is *The Chronicles of America,* edited by Allen Johnson and Allan Nevins (Yale University Press, 1918–1921 and 1950–1951), 56 vols. Some of the more applicable titles include Edward S. Corwin, *John Marshall and the Constitution: A Chronicle of the Supreme Court,* Vol. XVI; Charles M. Andrews, *The Fathers of New England: A Chronicle of the Puritan Commonwealth,* Vol. VI; Allen Johnson, *Jefferson and His Colleagues: A Chronicle of the Virginia Dynasty,* Vol. XV; and Denis W. Brogan, *The Era of Franklin D. Roosevelt: A Chronicle of the New Deal and Global War,* Vol. LII.

*Teach Yourself History Library,* edited by A. L. Rowse (Macmillan, London, 1947), consists of small biographies written by Englishmen concerning those figures of most interest to English people, but many of them are very useful to American students, such as: Max Beloff, *Thomas Jefferson and the American Democracy* (1948); Kenneth B. McFarlane, *John Wycliffe and the Beginnings of English Nonconformity* (1952); Sir Charles Grant Robinson, *Chatham and the British Empire* (1948); and James A. Williamson, *Cook and the Opening of the Pacific* (1948).

Supplementary Reading: Non-fiction

Charles A. Beard, *Presidents in American History* (Messner, New York, 1946), revised edition, goes through the time of Franklin Roosevelt.

Vladimir O. Key, *Politics, Parties and Pressure Groups* (Crowell, New York, 1958), 4th ed., is useful for both students and teacher.

F. A. Ogg and P. O. Ray, *Introduction to American Government*, rev. by W. H. Young (Appleton-Century-Crofts, New York, 1960), 11th edition, is a standard old text for political science in secondary schools.

A. M. Schlesinger, *The American as a Reformer* (Harvard University Press, 1950), is a mature book for thoughtful students.

In regard to a special topic that should be of interest to every boy in high school, military service, there are few books that have much value. There are, however, some, such as: Sidney Forman, *West Point* (Columbia University Press, 1950), a history of the military academy; and a very recent publication, Cleon E. Hammond, *The Marine Corps . . . From Civilian to Leatherneck* (Viking Press, New York, 1958), which carries out the promise of its title.

Under the classification of pictorial history of the United States there are several publications that might be useful, but only two will be listed here: *Pageant of America*, edited by Ralph H. Gabriel and others (Yale University Press), is a pictorial supplement to literary material on the history and life of the American people; *American Heritage*, edited by Bruce Catton, is a unique periodical in United States history, appearing every two months in hard cover format and lavishly illustrated in color. It is an experiment in the presentation of history in terms that the layman can understand yet with scholarly accuracy as a criterion (551 Fifth Avenue, New York 17).

Sometimes statistics, in connection with history and government, are very necessary, and surprisingly, they may be very interesting also. There is a periodic publication that should be available to secondary students at all times: *United States Statistical Abstract* (United States Government Printing Office, Washington, D.C., annual), a selection of current statistics taken from the official reports of the various executive departments and independent agencies.

## SUPPLEMENTARY MATERIALS

### Periodicals

For illustration of past American experience, nothing surpasses *American Heritage* (mentioned above) for high school students. For keeping up with current developments that affect the United States and its citizens there are two periodicals published by the Civic Education Service, 1733 K Street, NW, Washington 6, D.C.: *American Observer*, for upper grade high school students, and *Weekly News Review*, at a sightly lower ability level. These journals appear in thirty-four issues during the year, and they may be accompanied by *Civic Leader*, a companion manual for the teacher.

### Films, Filmstrips and Recordings

Educational films are available in prolific quantities and variety from a number of sources, and are especially illustrative of later developments in American history; but it must be remembered that such supplementary devices should only be used when they can do the teaching job at hand better than any other medium. There can, therefore, be no attempt here to make any sort of exhaustive listing of the items that may be employed. The following list is only a recommendation supplementing the material in one topic for American history: civil rights. For more detailed exploration of the subject, see the section on audio-visual materials in

Chapter VII, and the file boxes of the Citizenship Education Project (Teachers College, Columbia University, New York 27).

*Bill of Rights,* Association Films.

*Americans All,* 16 min., March of Time Forum Films, 369 Lexington Avenue, New York.

*Boundary Lines,* 10 min., International Film Foundation, 1600 Broadway, New York 19.

*Every Vote Counts,* Preston Sturgis, excerpted from Paramount feature, *The Great McGinty,* 7 min., Teaching Film Custodians.

*Growth of Democracy,* Magna Carta to Constitution, 78 RPM recording on 10-12″ records, Instructional Films.

*Americans All—Immigrants All,* Gilbert Seldes, 78 RPM recording of 24 programs concerning the contributions of foreign immigrants to the United States, U.S. Office of Education, Washington, D.C.

*Ballad for Americans,* Earl Robinson, 78 RPM recording, RCA.

## 8. Suggested Activities for Further Study

1. Where, in the United States, does the bulk of the police power lie? Give an analysis of legal and constitutional provision for police power. How can this information best be taught in secondary school?

2. Compare the "due process" clauses of constitutional Amendments V and XIV. Decide how this distinction could be presented to high school students.

3. Determine what some of the overlapping responsibilities of local and national authority are, and decide how they might be eliminated. What should high school students learn about governmental jurisdictions?

4. Design a chart showing the main functions and agencies in the federal government. Make clear, simply and graphically, the division and balance of power, legislative procedure, administrative function and judicial processes. Show the sources of authority—agencies, documents and electorate.

5. Make a similar chart for your own county, city or borough. Include the names of incumbent officers. How could this project be used in high school?

6. How could the procedure and philosophy of judicial review best be presented to high school students?

7. Define the position and function of the electorate in our politics. Why do we have a two party system instead of the multi-party fractioning that has taken place in France? How do we, on the other hand, safeguard ourselves from a one party organization such as appears in the Soviet Union?

8. Illustrate the points of variance between two major interpretations of American political history: economic determinism and the frontier hypothesis of American democracy. Contrast the approaches to history, in this light, of Charles Beard and Frederick Jackson Turner.

9. In what ways does present American life reflect the continued heritage of Western democratic man's search for a rule of law?

10. What, in your opinion, would be the best approach to an eleventh grade curricular inclusion, assuming that it must deal with American growth? For example, choose between a course in political history, one stressing some particular social theme and a course combining political history and government organization and principles. Give your psychological reasons for the choice, and develop a bibliography for student and teacher.

11. Make a list of twenty-five political biographies of persons in United States history who have contributed substantially to the tradition. Choose books appropriate for high school students.

# 11
# Teaching geography

Again and again we see the wisdom, even the vital necessity, of Man's entering into alliance with Nature instead of regarding himself as freed by his inventions from natural laws.

*Land for Tomorrow*
L. Dudley Stamp, 1950

## 1. Introduction

There is little doubt that geographic knowledge is important. Most educators realize and agree that geography should be taught as part of the social studies. There is, however, considerable disagreement as to when and how this should be done. For a variety of reasons very little attention has been paid in the last twenty years or so to formal instruction in geography at any grade level. Unlike United States history which usually finds its way into the curriculum three or four times in the course of twelve years, geography may receive cursory treatment only once or perhaps not at all. Ordinarily some teaching in this subject is found in the later elementary grades, but it is rarely emphasized in junior or senior high school.

One answer might be to incorporate geography into every social study. Man's setting in the world must be taken into account in any study of his behavior or history. The various unified social studies programs purport to do this, and sometimes with a degree of success. Unfortunately, in many states geography as a college subject is not required of prospective teachers, and as a result they are often unequipped to carry out such a unified program. There is no substitute for knowledge of geography on the part of the teacher. If he does not learn in school, then his clear duty is to teach himself after he becomes a teacher. In California, for instance, geography as a part of elementary teacher training, is a clear requirement by law.

The student as he enters secondary school is psychologically adapted to learning about his place in the expanded world community, and of his cultural heritage; he is also ready and curious to know about different places in the world. He can absorb with understanding some of the principles which cause world geography to be what it is. He can and should know about landforms, weather, erosion, land masses and oceans. He can understand the movement of his earth and its sister planets around the sun; of the tilt on its axis which makes the world subject to seasonal change and the variations in that change from pole to equator; of latitude and longitude as a system for locating places on the earth; of time zones and their practical use; of the international date line and night and day on opposite sides of the earth at the same time. These things are all part of common human knowledge, but they will not be acquired by any individual without effort and some guidance.

However the task is done, whether by itself as geography, or as part of a unified approach to the understanding of a culture or region, the facts are still the same. The job is still the same. The material must be presented in some form and learned by the students in some manner. It would appear to be more interesting and perhaps less painful to incorporate geographic information about a place with the other aspects of knowledge needed for understanding.

Whether or not geography is taught as a separate subject or as part of a fused social studies effort, the import and function are the same. Geography must serve as a vehicle for the coordinating elements in the study of human relations. Basically, man exists in an environment, a set of natural and man made circumstances. Bodies of land and water, continents, islands, oceans and seas, mountains, hills, valleys and plains with rivers and streams coursing downward to the seas and lakes, are the basic habitat of man. Lands covered by forest, scrub and grass, an envelope of gas containing oxygen, nitrogen, carbon dioxide, rare gases, micro-organisms and water vapor, a subterranean structure of iron core, rock mantle, various deposits of mineral and underground water lying below a surface dusting of soil—these three major components make life possible on our planet and form the landscape in which man first found himself.

As human civilization set in, differentiating man from the other creatures of the world, he began to alter the landscape. He tilled the soil and scoured the forests and grasslands for game and other food; he built cities, bridges, roads, canals, docks, dams, and rail lines. Man invented politics, wars and economic systems; he constructed a maze of communication facilities and set up national boundaries around his complicated activities. Human culture became the record of human achievement. History was recorded and the social scientists began to study man in the different aspects of his organization and growth.

After the study of history, or the record of mankind, geography is one of the oldest of social studies. Really half physical science and half social science, geography is the coordinating study, the bridge from natural science to the humanities. It is the general study, without a discrete body of source material, of man's habitat both natural and cultural.

For secondary school purposes, such study can be classified into a few major categories dealing with most of the important aspects of men's lives. This can also be said of history, but the approach is different. Geography is concerned mainly with space, its organization and relationships as they affect people. History is concerned with the story of man as he occupies space in time. Both studies aim at the same thing by different means—an understanding of man.[1]

The two principal divisions of geographic study are physical and cultural, or human. Each area or region, inhabited by man, can be viewed and studied in terms of the items under these two headings. A convenient checklist of the headings to be considered is included here, taken from a standard introductory text in college geography.

All of the items on the checklist are applicable to every part of the habitable world, but with varying emphases. The nature of geography requires a comparative type of study of the parts of a whole. The total study of geography embraces examination of the variable character of the Earth's surface, but this makes no sense to the student unless there are points of contrast and comparison. To facilitate such comparison, the earth can be divided into eight or nine major regions, each of which has enough characteristics in common to lend some kind of descriptive unity to it. There are eight well defined cultural areas each centering on a major civilization which in turn is placed in a relatively common setting. Maps and other teaching materials are available that recognize these major regional divisions. It is also agreed that the most important single concept in teaching elementary geography is regionalism, regardless of what the regions are or how they are derived.

[1] John Wesley Coulter, "Human Geography and History," *Social Education* (November, 1954), pp. 307–308.

## GENERALIZED CHECKLIST OF ELEMENTS
## OF THE HUMAN HABITAT [2]

**Physical or Natural Elements**

A. Atmosphere (Air)
   1. Weather
   2. Climate
B. Lithosphere (Earth)
   1. Earth materials
     a. Bedrock
     b. Regolith, especially soils
     c. Minerals
   2. Surface configuration
     a. Continents and islands
     b. Major landforms
     c. Minor landforms
C. Hydrosphere (Water)
   1. Oceans and seas
   2. Waters of the land
     a. Surface water
     b. Ground water
   3. Glaciers and icecaps
D. Biosphere (Life)
   1. Native plants
   2. Native animals

**Cultural or Human Elements**

A. Man
   1. Population
     a. Numbers
     b. Distribution over the earth
     c. Density
   2. Cultural groups
     a. Major groups
     b. Other groups
   3. Cultural institutions
     a. Languages
     b. Religions
     c. Political units
B. Works of Man
   1. Settlements
     a. Rural
     b. Urban
   2. Forms resulting from econo-
     mies or ways of life
     a. Hunting, fishing, and gath-
       ering
     b. Pastoralism
     c. Agriculture
     d. Exploitation of earth re-
       sources, i.e., lumbering,
       mining, etc.
     e. Manufacture
   3. Routes of transportation and
     communication.

---

[2] Kendall, Glendinning, MacFadden, *Introduction to Geography* (Harcourt, Brace, New York, 1958), Second Edition, p. 5. Quoted by permission of the publisher.

Esthetic experiences and developments are also part of the current cultural environment, and they could be listed and studied. Although geographers seldom do this, possibly they should; at least high school teachers of geography ought to include some of that material, such as art, music and philosophy. It is difficult to draw a line between the humanities and the social sciences.

Regionalization of the world added to the checklist of physical and cultural characteristics will make a firm point of departure for the study of geography in any secondary social studies course. The emphasis on organization or the priority given to one discipline or the other will only be incidental to the basic concepts and facts to be learned. In this way, for example, the national state can be placed in its proper perspective in relation to general culture. In studying Western Europe, it is necessary to consider the common characteristics of Germany or of France, but at the same time it is useful to regard the Saar Basin as an entity; or in learning about Anglo-America, it is best to study the Canadian Shield as a single unit even though it laps over from Canada into the United States.

The world can be divided into eight major regions, and by the same token each region be separated into subregions, each with more minute common characteristics. In France there is the Rhône Valley, the Paris Basin, the Atlantic coast and hill region and the Mediterranean Riviera. By further subregionalization the Paris Basin contains rural and urban areas. In each case examination of the region rests on data of the cultural development, but in a particular physical setting giving rise in turn to generalized physical principles. The order of sequence of study, then, is first, physical principles; next, local variations in physical structure and process, and third, cultural differentiation among major regions and in a more strictly local sense.

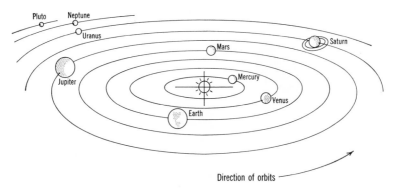

FIGURE 10. Diagram of the planets and their orbits, showing the sun and its immediate family of planets. The sun is necessarily drawn may times smaller than it really is in relation to the other bodies. The planets are roughly proportional to each other. The distance from the earth to the sun is approximately 93,000,000 miles.

## 2. Physical Principles of Geography

### Gross Features

At some point in the social studies curriculum, in junior or senior high school, there should be a specified treatment of the principles of physical geography. These basic concepts are usually part of all social studies instruction, with some introduction as early as the first grade; but it is essential to review and reinforce a minimum knowledge of basic physical attributes of the earth in the secondary school. Some high schools now have required courses in physical geography. Regardless of the name or scope of any social studies course, however, there is a deep necessity to organize formally physical geography into a unit of instruction and present it. As an example of this philosophy the Chicago City schools now require either a course in world history or one in world geography of every high school student. In these courses the physical principles of geography are taught.

Minimum inclusion in such a course or unit should contain a general view of the universe and our own solar system with emphasis on size, distance, movement and relationship among the units of the visible universe. The names of the nine planets in our system and their relative distances from the Sun, the planes of their axes, the speed of their rotations and revolutions, make up a dramatic bit of information that students should know. The philosophic and semantic connotation of such a word as isostasy is fascinating to young people, especially now at the dawn of space travel and rocketry.

### Axial Tilt and the Seasons

Every person should know the fundamental principles that make possible different seasons and different climatic zones on the earth. The fact that the earth's axis is tilted $23\frac{1}{2}$ degrees from that of the sun produces the phenomenon of the "midnight sun" in the north and south polar regions. This is useful and interesting knowledge to the secondary student. As the yearlong trip of the earth around the sun makes a different angle of incidence between its surface and the sun's rays, each place on the earth, depending upon its latitude, receives a different amount of heat from the sun.

The teacher should develop visual means of reinforcing the students' perception of these physical phenomena. Blackboard diagrams and still or moving pictures of the various processes should be used to the fullest. The individual teacher may prepare his own projection material either in transparency, slide or film strip form or he may procure adequate sequences from commercial sources.[3] The students themselves can manipulate various materials to help them visualize the importance of the axial tilt of the earth. For example, one student can represent the earth, carrying a globe, and actually revolve around another student representing the sun. In this way the rest of the class can be shown exactly how the earth's inclination remains constant yet changes in relation to the sun because of its movement in orbit. At the same time the dark and light hemispheres of the earth can be demonstrated by rotating the globe on its axis. A light directed against the globe from one side in a darkened room will further emphasize "day" and "night."

At this stage of instruction it is important that each student learn and appreciate thoroughly the seemingly simple yet very important small facts that go to make up the principles of geography. Simply reading a text is not enough. Explanation by the teacher, actual handling of real objects and reflective thought are all necessary. Coverage of a great body of material is definitely subordinate to learning well a few fundamental principles. Words and their definitions are critical at this level. *Rotation,* the twenty-four hour movement of the earth on its own axis toward the east, as contrasted to *revolution,* the 365 day movement of the earth in an elliptical orbit around the sun toward the east embodies several principles. The facts themselves are simple, but they must be learned and put together in a total appreciation of the basic principle of *isostasy,* or balance of the whole system. Seasons—spring, summer, autumn and winter—are the direct result of the earth's revolution; day and night and the length of the cycle—twenty-four hours—are directly due to the earth's rotation at a fixed rate. Both phenomena are tempered in their effects by the constant angle of inclination.

A number of simple problems in arithmetic can be devised to illustrate further the variable results of these repetitive and constant patterns. The angle of the earth's inclination is always $23\frac{1}{2}$ degrees, but as the earth and the sun are in a different relationship each day during any year, the date and the position of any point on the earth in regard to the equator will make it possible to calculate the angle of incidence between the earth's surface and the direct rays of the sun. Because the earth's surface is curved upward and away from the equator (or downward in the southern hemisphere), the sun's direct

---

[3] The Herbert E. Budek Company, Inc., 324 Union Street, Hackensack, New Jersey, supplies a varied line of slides and filmstrips in both physical and cultural geography.

(90 degree) rays can only strike one series of points all the way around the earth on a given day. On March 21 and September 21 at noon (when the sun is directly overhead) this series of points, or line, will be the equator. Either three months earlier or later the inclination of the earth will be maximally toward or away from the sun, therefore the sun's direct rays will strike a line (at noon) 23½ degrees away from the equator north or south. Either above or below these lines the sun's direct rays never reach. Various problems can help illustrate this phenomenon.

In midsummer (June 21) on the northern border of the United States (49 degrees North Latitude), what is the angle of incidence of the sun's rays with the surface of the earth at noon? At this time the earth is tilted toward the sun a maximum amount, therefore the rays are vertical (or directed in a 90 degree angle) to the north sun line (Tropic of Cancer), 23½ degrees above the equator. We are concerned with a point 49 degrees above the equator. Subtracting 23½ from 49 will give us 25½ degrees. We must then add 25½ degrees to the vertical or 90 degree angle of incidence at the Tropic of Cancer. Adding 25½ to 90, we get 115½ degrees. The angle of incidence formed by the

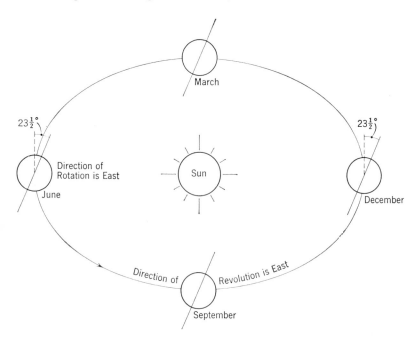

FIGURE 11. Diagram of the earth's 23½ degree tilt and the different orbital positions.

sun's rays and the earth's surface is 115½ degrees at the time and place specified. This makes the sun appear to be 25½ degrees away to the south from directly overhead along the Canadian border in mid-summer. This problem also explains why it is often sunny on the south sides of houses and fences and never so on the north sides of structures during summer in the northern hemisphere, above the sun line, in such places as the United States.

Another type of problem that is useful for instruction of high school students in finding the latitude is to go outside on a sunny day, set up a vertical pole at noon and measure the relative lengths of the pole and the shadow that it casts. A right triangle may be plotted on paper using the length of the pole for one leg, the distance from the pole to the end of the shadow on the ground for the other leg, and the distance from the top of the pole to the end of the shadow for the hypotenuse. The angle at the bottom of the hypotenuse subtracted from 180 degrees will give the angle of incidence of the sun's rays with the earth at that point and time. This can be arrived at either by geometric calculation or by simple measurement with a protractor. Suppose the result turns out to be 124 degrees and the date is March 21. Since on this date the direct rays of the sun are pointed at the equator, then it must be discovered by subtracting 90 from 124 that the latitude position of observation is 34 degrees (the vicinity of Los Angeles). By interpolation, any other date will give the same latitude in the

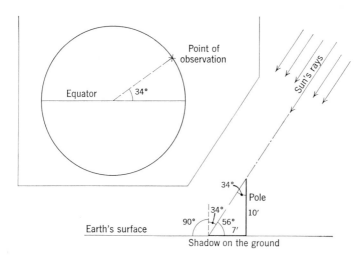

FIGURE 12. Diagram of the sun's rays angle of incidence. The Northern Hemisphere on March 21 (Spring Equinox): sun's rays are vertical to the equator on this date. Source of sun's rays: overhead, but to the south of the meridian.

same place. Similarly, if the latitude was known to be 34 degrees, we could find the angle of incidence for this latitude on March 21 by adding 34 degrees to 90 degrees (or the angle of incidence at the equator); this would give us our answer: 124 degrees. The angle of 34 degrees (the latitude) is the angle from the center of the earth formed by lines directed at the equator and at the point of observation.

A great variety of problems may be constructed by changing the requirements of position and date or by altering the known and unknown elements. Students can perform some of these problems on the blackboard and they can do others as part of their homework. They may be required to develop some problems of their own to be solved by other members of the class.

### Weather and Climate

One of the most important results of fundamental physical processes in man's world is climatic conditions. To a very large extent the character of human occupance is determined or modified by the weather and climate conditions in which man finds himself. These conditions can be observed and analyzed; their causes can often be determined, and as a consequence, some type of prediction of weather can be made. Climatology and meteorology thus become important subdisciplines of geography. As a part of physical geography in secondary school, then, weather and climate are essential considerations.

First of all it is necessary to arrive at some satisfactory definitions with the students. Climate is the overall, recurrent, long term pattern of atmospheric conditions typical of any given place in the world. Weather is the day by day, sometimes unpredictable, short term phenomena of atmospheric disturbance in a locality. Atmosphere can be defined as the relatively thin gaseous envelope that rotates and revolves around the earth, clinging to it in all of its movements. The atmosphere is composed of 80 per cent nitrogen, about 19 per cent oxygen, and various other gases and material to make up the means of existence for all living things on the earth. The other components of the atmosphere are carbon dioxide, the result of animal respiration and the source of one basic element in the photosynthesis process of plants, rare gases such as argon, xenon, krypton, neon and helium, water vapor, dust particles and micro-organisms. There are traces of hydrogen, ozone and other poisonous or explosive gases, but they are usually at high altitudes and associated with certain noxious elements of solar radiation such as gamma rays.

The most ordinary ways in which the atmosphere can be affected or disturbed to produce the familiar weather patterns on earth can be classified into precipitation, temperature changes, air movement (wind), cloud formation and atmospheric pressure. These are the features by which weather is described. We say that the temperature is 70 degrees Fahrenheit, no precipitation, light breeze (5 miles per hour), 25 per cent cloud cover (cirrus-cumulo) and atmospheric pressure normal (30 inches of mercury will stand in an open tube at sea level). The day just described in weather data terms is a typical June day in Southern California near the beach. The weather on a stormy day in mid-winter in Chicago might appear in a weather report as: temperature 34 degrees, precipitation 5 inches (snow), atmospheric pressure 68.7 (falling) and overhead visibility zero or complete cloud cover. Since Chicago is in a mid-latitude position and it occupies an internal continental position, one should expect this kind of weather in December when the earth is tilted 23½ degrees away from the direct rays of the sun. This makes for the generalization that the climate in the vicinity of Chicago is of a typical character, in fact it is called mid-latitude continental or continental humid. The same type of generalization can be made about Los Angeles except that because of its different location and proximity to an ocean the general classification is different. It is a subtropical variation of the marine west coast climate, sometimes called Mediterranean with a little less accuracy. Interpolating these generalizations to other parts of the world one might expect, then, to find similar climates in similarly situated places elsewhere in the world. For example, the climate of Chicago is almost duplicated in Berlin, and Barcelona's climate approximates that of Los Angeles. Since the climates in these pairs of places are similar, so also are the weather conditions on the same day likely to be similar, for instance, in both Barcelona and Los Angeles, and can be predicted with some degree of accuracy.

New and dynamic developments in recent research have produced knowledge about such things as the jet stream and cosmic storms. The jet stream may be the way in which polar high pressure areas are continually fed by very high altitude winds.

## The World as Regions

In relationship to the historic derivation of the characteristics of any nation or the interaction of all the nations in the world, it is necessary to classify the whole world and its parts into some grouping of states or regions. This may be done on various grounds: geographic, cultural, economic, sociological. Perhaps any classification into regions must be primarily geographic since there is a determinant factor in geography that cannot be long denied as one considers any individual nation and its development. For example, there is a tendency for areas with the same climatic conditions to produce similar economic bases; or, geographic regions with similar terrain, such as mountainous, tend to produce the same cultural characteristics if the other factors are relatively fixed.

For adequate understanding of the American position in our present world it is absolutely essential to have a general knowledge of basic similarities of geographic structure and character throughout the world. It is necessary to know where one may expect sub-zero temperatures, a short growing season, year-round seaports, or continual humid heat; nations in the trade belts or surrounding a major ocean will develop in far different ways than those states completely surrounded by towering mountains and whose population is continually subjected to very high altitudes, such as the Indian principalities along the rim of the Central Asian plateau.

### Climatic Regions

One fruitful yet simple method of classification is by standard climate characteristics. There are four such major divisions, with several subclassifications. (See Figure 13.)

The physical principles that tend to make climates constant are the tilt of the earth, the annual revolution of the earth around the sun and the earth's diurnal rotation on its axis. There are, of course, other factors such as landforms and moisture—mountains, plains, rivers, lakes and oceans. Very important among the reasons for certain climatic phenomena is the fact that large bodies of land cool and heat quicker than do large bodies of water. The difference in temperature of the earth along an ocean shore is much less from summer to winter than it is in an inland situation away from any large sea or ocean. This explains why, for example, the winters in central Russia are so much colder than along the Norwegian coast although both places are at the same latitude and therefore have the same angle of incidence with the sun's rays. It is simply that the North Atlantic Drift tends to keep the Norwegian coast at a higher stable temperature throughout the year. By the same token summers in Norway are cooler than they are in Moscow.

Such principles as these are both important and useful to secondary students. They can learn about weather and climate and about the distribution of world patterns of wind, rainfall and temperature with profit. A good learning exercise is to consider the world as a group of climatic regions as has already been suggested. Weather maps may be prepared by the students, both on a world and regional basis and for one's own locality.

## Weather Observation

A good device for instructing in basic weather observation technique is to have a group of students set up an amateur weather station in the school. The various devices needed for weather data collection are simple and can be constructed by the students themselves. Precipitation is very simple to measure merely by collecting, in the open, a sample of all precipitation in a straight sided can open at the top. Merely measure in inches the amount of moisture that has fallen into the container. A barometer, for measuring atmospheric pressure, may be purchased from which the reading in inches of mercury can be read from a dial, but a fairly accurate barometer may be made from a glass tube filled with mercury and up-ended in a dish of mercury. At sea level the column will normally remain at 30 inches, but normal readings for any given place will vary with altitude. Records should be kept in inches or fractions of inches of variation from the normal. A thermometer can be made by the students but thermometers are cheap and easily obtainable. Ordinarily American temperatures are recorded in degrees Fahrenheit with the reading being taken at the same time each day in a shaded place protected from wind. Wind velocity is measured in miles per hour. The device for this is a shaft, exposed to the wind in the open with four cups attached to one end to catch the wind; as the shaft revolves, its speed can be determined by a counting mechanism at the bottom where it is attached to a bearing which allows it to turn freely. The number of revolutions per minute can be converted into miles per hour. Wind direction is easily determined by a wind sock, a light cloth bag, open at both ends, and attached to a swivel at the top of a pole.

With this simple basic equipment any high school student can observe and record the fundamental aspects of weather data. The most strict requirement is to keep a rigidly punctual schedule of observation and recording. This may be done once or more each day, always at the same hour, and after a length of time it will be very rewarding to have an accurate and complete record of weather phenomena stated in the same terms used by professional climatologists and weather experts. After a whole year's cycle it will be found that prediction of recurrent patterns will become more and more familiar. Aside from

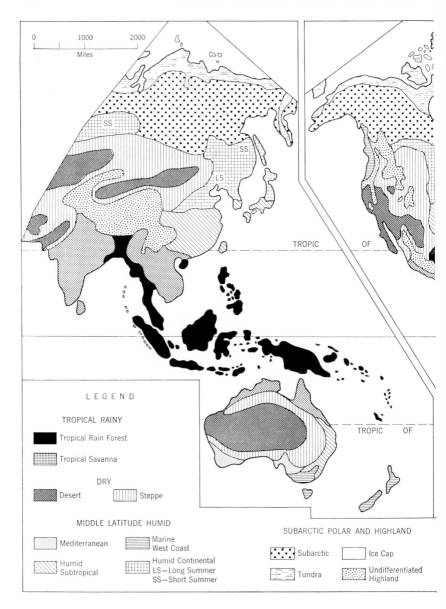

LEGEND

TROPICAL RAINY

Tropical Rain Forest

Tropical Savanna

DRY

Desert          Steppe

MIDDLE LATITUDE HUMID

Mediterranean          Marine
                       West Coast

Humid                  Humid Continental
Subtropical            LS—Long Summer
                       SS—Short Summer

SUBARCTIC POLAR AND HIGHLAND

Subarctic          Ice Cap

Tundra             Undifferentiated
                   Highland

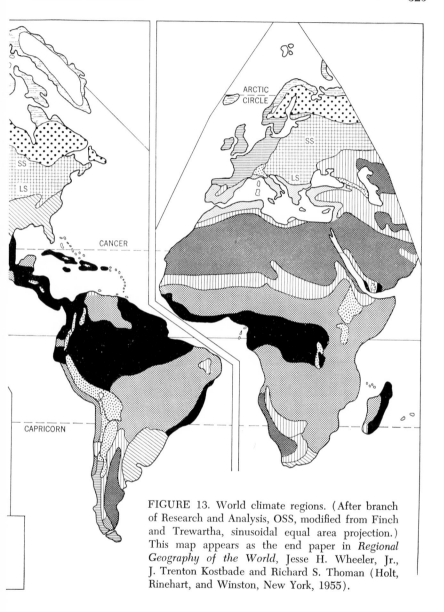

FIGURE 13. World climate regions. (After branch of Research and Analysis, OSS, modified from Finch and Trewartha, sinusoidal equal area projection.) This map appears as the end paper in *Regional Geography of the World*, Jesse H. Wheeler, Jr., J. Trenton Kostbade and Richard S. Thoman (Holt, Rinehart, and Winston, New York, 1955).

its utility as a learning device it will be found also that such a weather bureau activity will undoubtedly add measurably to the amount of interest that students will show in the pursuit of study of physical geography.

One of the most interesting outcomes of such an activity can be achieved by comparing the periodic results of the students' work with the official reports and forecasts of weather that are issued by the Department of Interior Weather Bureau or by the Civil Aeronautics Authority. It will be found immediately that the students will begin to read the weather reports and predictions which usually appear on the front page of nearly every newspaper.

### Physiography

Shape, size and position of land masses are the most fundamental aspects of physical geography that can be used in description. The surface configurations of the land masses are further refined and differentiated by landforms in relief, that is, the size and shape of areas measured in vertical terms. The study, in physical geography, of these phenomena and the processes by which they came about is called physiography. Secondary school students can begin to appreciate some of the subtle determining influences of the landscape, the total shape and appearance of the land, and they should be given opportunity to examine the ". . . function of process, stage and structure. The relative importance of these is indicated by their order." [4] Best methods for teaching this kind of appreciation are description by the teacher with as many illustrations as possible—pictures, maps and relief models—and actual participation by students in the process of building relief maps.

During the past forty or fifty years there has not been a marked interest among professional geographers in the study of physical geography. More emphasis has been placed on cultural or human geography: on demography, conservation and regional study; but now several very careful scholars have begun to examine again the physical structure of the landscape and how it became what it is. Many new hypotheses have been advanced and new vital generalizations have begun to emerge. These should get into the minds of high school and elementary students as soon as they are available. This means, obviously, that social studies teachers must become more mindful of geography, especially physical geography.

[4] L. C. King, "Canons of Landscape Evolution," *Bulletin of the Geological Society of America* (1953), pp. 721–752.

For example, it has been assumed for years that the normal and general effect of erosion was the reduction of slope gradient, and that high hills gradually became low hills, then valleys; that the ordinary tendency of physiographic change has been in terms of hills and mountains, alluvial plains and valleys. Such has been the empirical basis for description of landscapes.[5] Now, in view of more modern and thoughtful interpretation of data, a newer view of geomorphology is available which generalizes that "the standard or 'normal' type of landscape, both now and in the geologic past, is the semiarid type with broad pediments and parallel scarp retreat."[6] This leaves a characteristic landform pattern over most of the world consisting of a broadly sloping plain or pediment, of which only a few remnants of the original material appear as upstanding escarpments with steep sides—island-mountains in the pediplain or universal flatland.

The implication of this particular generalization as well as for many others in physiography is clear to the social studies teacher. "There are many classrooms in America through whose windows these features can be seen, or which are at least located close to places where landscapes can be observed out-of-doors."[7] It is important to note that there are exceptions to this and all other vital generalizations, as in the case of landscapes formed by glaciation, but this is simply the subject for another phase of study. Field trips, then, are in order for the purpose of first hand experience with the evidence going to make up grounds for a new and dynamic generalization affecting the whole of geographic description. Field trips are time and effort consuming, and it is easier to remain in the classroom. Think, however, of the reinforcing value of direct observation of the kind of data that geographers must use in order to arrive at a valid generalization. After a detailed study, description and illustration of a particular landform, a trip to view it in reality, on the ground, may be the deciding factor in students' remembering the vital generalization that every teacher hopes will be the result of study.

Personal photography and the many fine color reproductions in magazines may be used by the teacher to advantage in this connection.

[5] Preston E. James, *A Geography of Man* (Ginn, Boston, 1959), pp. 100–102, is a good example of empirical description without much regard to the process, the geomorphology.

[6] Thompson, *loc. cit.*, discussed in Clyde P. Patton, "Professional Contributions to Physical Geography," in *New Viewpoints in Geography*, Twenty-ninth Yearbook of the National Council for the Social Studies (Washington, D.C., 1959), p. 22.

[7] *Ibid.*, pp. 23–24.

*National Geographic Magazine, Natural History, Holiday* and *Life*,
to name a few, abound in pictures that may be used for attractive and
informative bulletin displays. Such topics as bathyscaph descents and
mapping of the ocean floors are often illustrated by striking pictures
in news releases and stories.

"Study and description of the earth's surface is an integral part of
the long history of man's effort to understand the world around him.
The winning of wider knowledge and keener insight in this discipline
is fully as important a part of man's history as the social and economic
revolutions of the past, not to mention battles and dynastic turmoil.
In the context of the history of knowledge, physical geography takes
its natural place, and the older generalizations and beliefs can be
presented as they should be. Presently held views can then be shown
as inevitable changes resulting from new information or new tools of
attack, and the tentative nature of many of the current hypotheses will
serve as a reminder and a challenge to the student. If this challenge
is properly presented the field of physical geography will experience a
renaissance directly attributable to the transmission of new ideas from
scholar to student by the teachers of this century." [8]

### Maps and Map Making

The basic tool for any study of geography is the map. It is the simplest convention for complicated description of areas and landforms.
Whether the subject be physical or cultural, maps are necessary for a
proper and universally understandable description. Secondary school
students should learn about the principal types of maps and the general ways in which they are made. Again, as in other phases of geography, actual participation in an activity is useful. Students can
construct maps themselves from data that they themselves gather.
Such projects need not be elaborate and deal with huge areas. A good
map project for a high school class might be a detailed plan of the
school campus and its installations. The ground can be measured,
directions determined, sizes and shapes of installations and landforms
assessed, and the whole transformed into a map.

The first and indispensable principle in mapping is the need to appreciate accuracy and that all maps must be drawn to a scale, that is,
a very accurate reduction of the actual size of objects on the ground
so that a large area may be depicted on a small piece of paper. Scale
should be studied and students made to give evidence of their understanding of the principle. A map is not a fanciful representation of

[8] *Ibid.*, p. 33.

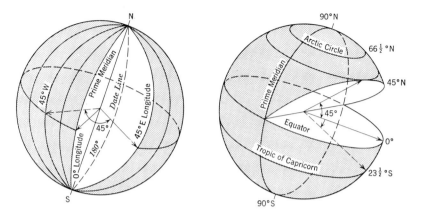

FIGURE 14. Longitude and latitude as measures of angular distance on the surface of the earth, starting from the earth's center.

reality nor an interpretation of geographic phenomena. It is a detailed and dependable description, by means of a convention, of a piece of terrain drawn smaller than the original and usually only in two dimensions. It is, above all, accurately drawn to scale.

On most maps there is a grid, or cross hatch of vertical and horizontal lines which divide up the map into smaller squares so that identification of specific points is possible by reference to the intersections of the vertical and horizontal grid lines. Such a coordinate system makes it possible to state the position of a point on a map in numbers or letters, or as in the case of the world polar coordinates, in degrees of latitude and longitude.

Lines of longitude on the globe or world map are north-south lines from pole to pole such as would result from bisecting the earth with a plane passed through both poles. The base point for measurement of longitude is the one that passes through Greenwich (London, England) and is called the Prime Meridian or 0 degrees. One hundred and eighty degrees both eastward and westward from this line would reach the exactly opposite side of the earth. This meridian is numbered 180 and substantially coincides with the International Date Line, running from pole to pole down through the Pacific Ocean. Each meridian line, in both directions, from 0 to 180 is numbered by degrees east or west (e.g., 72 W) of Greenwich. Thus each theoretical line on the earth from pole to pole represents a degree of angular measurement from the exact center of the earth, starting at an arbi-

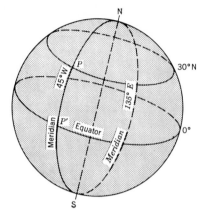

FIGURE 15. Polar coordinates: typical latitude and longitude designation of a point. Point P on the earth's surface is identified at the intersection of the parallel of latitude at 30 degrees north and the meridian of longitude 45 degrees west of Greenwich. The designation, then, of 30 N 45 W can mean only this particular point on the surface of the earth. Similarly, point P' is 0 (equator) 45 W. Any other point can be plotted in the same way. This system is known as plotting by polar coordinates.

trarily selected point on the surface (Greenwich). Subdivisions between degrees are expressed in minutes ('), or sixtieths of a minute, seconds (").

Lines of latitude are formed on the earth as parallel rings, or the result of passing parallel planes through the earth at a right angle to the pole. Start with the equator and mark angular distance as measured from the center of the earth upward and downward toward the polar extremities, 90 degrees north or south. The north pole is at 90 N latitude. The south pole is at 90 S latitude. Similar to the longitude measurement, latitudinal subdivisions of degrees are expressed in minutes and seconds.

As lines of latitude and longitude are placed on the surface of the globe a criss-cross network is produced which can be made to designate every point on the earth's surface. Each place can be enumerated exactly by means of two coordinate numbers associated with directions north or south of the equator and east or west of the prime meridian. Accurate compass directions are then possible between any two points so named.

To facilitate usefulness of the globe as a map, land surface shapes have been projected from it onto flat surfaces, thus giving what is defined as a map. In order to read the projection a system of polar coordinates has to be superimposed on the map. These lines are generally north-south and east-west, sometimes straight and sometimes curved, depending on the type of projection. They still mean, however, the same thing: angular distance from the center of the earth measured in two planes, vertical and horizontal.

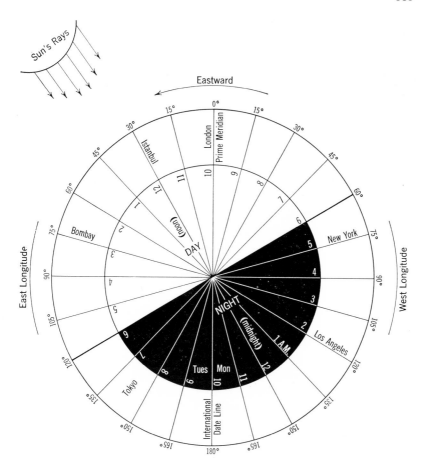

FIGURE 16. Standard time zones. Every fifteen degrees of longitude equals one hour in time difference: 1 hr = 15° = 1,000 mi; so that when it is 2 A.M. in Los Angeles, it is 10 A.M. in London.

## Time Zones

Longitude lines serve another useful function in the use of maps and general geographic study. Every fifteen degrees of longitude passes a given point each hour in relation to the sun as the earth rotates. In twenty-four hours any spot on earth will pass through all the stages of day and night. As man keeps track of time by his relative position in regard to the sun, apparent times in different places are simultaneously different. The sun's direct rays produce the phenomenon of "noon" at only one longitude at a time, and at the same moment it is 12:00 A.M. in Los Angeles and midnight over central Asia. Longitude and a simple convention make it possible to assess quickly relative "times" all over the world.

The circumference of the earth is 360 degrees and the length of time for each rotation is 24 hours. Each hour, then, equals 15 degrees of longitude. This is approximately 1,000 miles along the equator.

Students can make a simple device to illustrate time zones and relative time around the world. Cut two circles of cardboard, one smaller than the other, and with a means of fastening them both on common center so that the smaller may be revolved on the larger. Mark the outer circle with longitude divisions every 15 degrees and the inner circle in twenty-four equal divisions, numbered opposite to the clock. As the diagram shows, when it is 2:00 A.M. in Los Angeles, it is 10:00 A.M. in London, 120 degrees or eight hours further past the sun.

Easiest to use and probably most frequently encountered is the type of map with polar coordinate grid based on Mercator's cylindrical projection. This map has straight lines representing both latitude and longitude and the areas of the world are exaggerated at the lower and upper extremities and in the oceans. Students can easily see the method of locating places by polar coordinates, but it is very difficult to understand the principle by means of that map only. It is important and interesting for students to understand the principle of angular measurement from the center of the earth. It not only tends to make them remember the material better, it also gives opportunity to establish a relationship between mathematics and geography.

Incidentally, the cylindrical projection is the type used for navigation since directions shown are in straight lines. For example, a great circle course over the Pacific Ocean will appear as a straight line accurately giving the proper direction. Any area far to the north or to the south, such as Greenland, will appear to be far too large. By a comparison with other kinds of world maps, Greenland will appear to be as large as South America.

Students should be urged to compare the shapes and sizes of land masses on different type maps of the same scale. They should always then refer to a globe to keep in mind the necessary distortion on flat maps of size, shape or surface curvature. No matter what the map used, the student must, through practice, become accustomed to visualizing the globe—the only truly accurate map.

An exercise which will dramatize the difficulty of showing "roundness" on a flat map is to take a hollow ball, such as a tennis ball, and

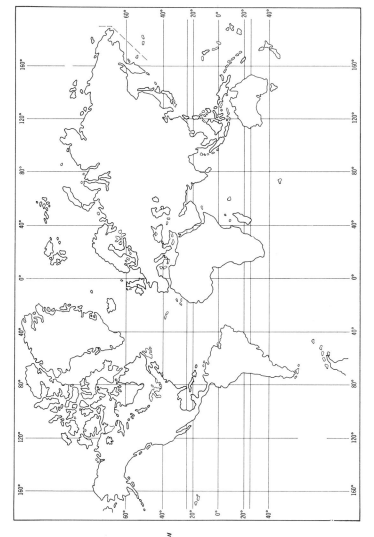

FIGURE 17. The World: Mercator's projection.

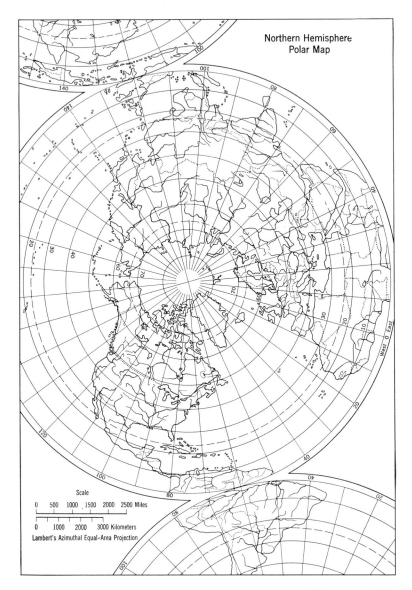

FIGURE 18. Northern Hemisphere—polar map. From Goode's series of base maps. Copyright, 1938, The University of Chicago.

slit it down the sides. It will be seen immediately that it cannot be pressed into a contiguous flat sheet.

The polar grid may be applied to another type of map which is most accurate as to both direction and distance from the center of the map, the azimuthal or polar map. This map is used for aviation navigation. The drawback is that distance and direction between points on the map are not accurate, only from the center to any point. It is necessary to have a different azimuthal map for every point of reference.

This is the type of the air age map that has become popular in this day of common air transportation. British Overseas Aircraft Corporation has one centered on London. Other companies use maps with centers in their various headquarters cities. A student might make a collection of the many different azimuthal air age maps which abound.

Still using the polar grid, but with lines of varying curvature, other types of orthographic projection can be used to produce maps of the world. One of the most generally accurate world maps is Goode's interrupted sinusoidal projection which simply leaves out the areas between the continents that in the Mercator would be incorporated into the ocean portions. On this map Greenland is properly shown as to size in relation to the rest of the world. The lines of latitude and longitude are neither straight lines nor smooth curves, but they still serve the same function of showing position by coordinates.

THREE TYPES OF MAP GRID. Various combinations of straight and curved latitude and longitude lines may be used as grids for certain

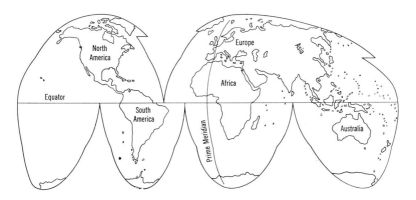

FIGURE 19. The World: Goode's interrupted projection. This map is perhaps the most accurate as to all of the features, size, shape and distances between points. It is a little harder to use because of the interruptions, and because the longitude lines are not smooth curves.

maps, depending upon what degree of distortion can be tolerated. For an area such as South America that crosses the equator vertical distortion is more tolerable than lateral because of the length of the area. It is therefore desirable to adjust the apparent width of the extremities by the use of curved grid lines running longitudinally.

For a smaller region with the emphasis on lateral accuracy, curved latitude lines are useful. The Mediterranean area illustrates this combination.

To obtain accuracy of equal area representation in an area the size and shape of Europe both latitude and longitude lines are best curved.

The following three outline maps illustrate different combinations of curved and straight latitude and longitude lines making up the polar coordinate grids used for locating places on the maps. Incidentally, such outline maps of the various regions should be regularly given to students in geography and history upon which to perform various exercises. Place location, practice in identifying coordinates, construction of surface features and configurations, economic, political and other cultural activities—all these can be shown on specialized maps, as well as many of the historical events in different regions. Each student should have frequent assignments of problems to be worked out on outline maps.

### Three–Dimensional Maps

The basic disability of all maps is that the world is a huge sphere and through no means can it all be shown accurately at once on any sheet of paper. By reason of the earth's curvature at the surface it is also impossible to depict *exactly* on a flat surface what is actually on the ground. It is therefore necessary to use a variety of maps depending upon what aspect of the earth's surface is to be studied. Finally, especially with young people, it is necessary to have access to a globe. Although all sides of the globe are not visible at once, at least it actually possesses a three-dimensional reality and it is possible to depict more nearly the precisely accurate landforms and shapes that appear in nature. In other words, although not technically a true map, the globe is the only truly accurate map.

Especially for small areas, the relief map or terrain model has many of the advantages of the globe. Three dimensions can be shown. Relief, or vertical distance above a datum plane, can be shown as *realia*. The student can touch it and through another kind of sense perception he can achieve greater appreciation of the surface configuration of the land. Such maps may be based on any one of many schemes of projection, but in small scale maps of large areas they are not likely to be highly accurate nor do they usually have a very good grid system exactly because the surface is not smooth. Relief maps must have two separate scales, one for horizontal distances and one for vertical distances. Relief scales have to be much more exaggerated than scales for horizontal distance even to be felt or appreciated. For example, a relief map of the United States with both scales at one to ten thousand would show the Rocky Mountains about an inch high and the whole country would take up a map about six thousand feet long! The vertical scale must be increased, then, and the horizontal scale decreased. Vertical scale of 1/5000 and horizontal scale of 1/1,000,000 would be more appropriate.

### 3. Cultural and Regional Geography

The other side of geography, the human or cultural aspects of man's relationship to the land, is extremely complex and yet it is most interesting and most important. Obviously generalizations about all men in all places are hard to make and seldom would they really hold true. It is necessary to think of these facets of geography concerning restricted areas, one at a time. "It is difficult," as Jean Brunhes wrote, "to make out at first glance what is really and strictly geographical in the manifestations of human life in vast and dissimilar settings, each corresponding, for example, to a 'whole' as complex as France or the United States. Only by the careful study of a small unit can one learn to discern and evaluate the strictly geographical relations between physical and human destinies." [9] The key to study of geography in secondary school, then, is to take advantage of the large cultural regions into which the world falls, and to organize their study along topical and sometimes national lines.

Each region and subregion can be examined with the aid of the checklist of physical and cultural characteristics that has already been given. Certain major topics of overriding importance should, of course, be given more consideration than others. Aside from purely physical determinants of human occupance there are such things as water and land use, food, clothing and housing habits, communication, circulation and population, to name only a few. Each of these is somewhat dependent upon physical factors, but beyond those there are almost purely cultural developments that must be studied.

[9] Jean Brunhes, *Human Geography,* translated by I. C. LeCompte, edited by Isaiah Bowman (Rand, McNally, Chicago, 1920), p. 52.

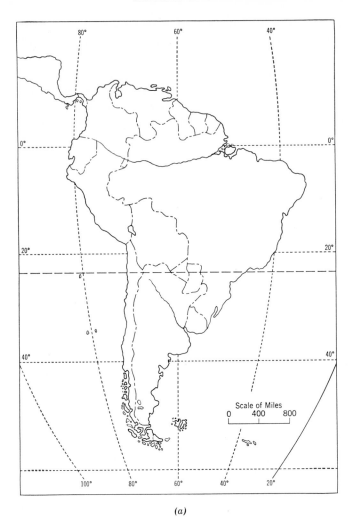

(a)

FIGURE 20. Three maps with different arrangements of coordinates: (a) South America (straight latitude and curved longitude lines).

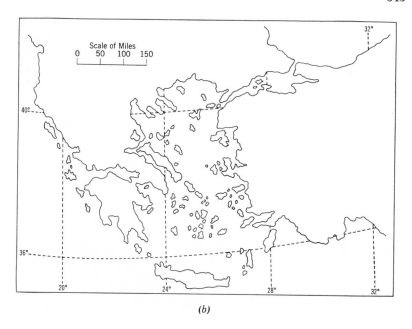

(b)

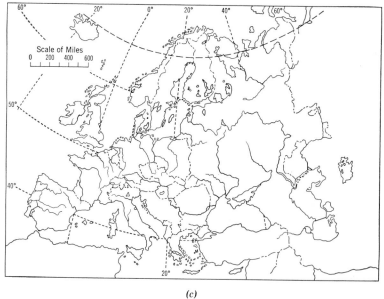

(c)

(b) The Grecian World (curved latitude and straight longitude lines).

(c) Europe (curved latitude and longitude lines).

FIGURE 21. Air age map of the World.

## Major World Cultural Regions

Eight divisions make up the habitable portions of the earth. Cultural and other characteristics add to the geographic considerations to give order to such a classification.

### REGIONAL DISTRIBUTION, 1960
#### (Area in Millions of Square Miles)

|                  | Area | Population        |
|------------------|------|-------------------|
| Europe           | 1.9  | 430 millions      |
| Soviet Union     | 8.6  | 230               |
| Middle East      | 7.0  | 200               |
| Orient           | 8.0  | 1500              |
| Pacific World    | 3.3  | 14                |
| Africa           | 11.7 | 240               |
| Latin America    | 7.9  | 180               |
| Anglo-America    | 8.4  | 200               |
| Total Population  |      | 2,994,000,000 *   |

* Figure obtained by extrapolation of regional growth rate estimates made by the United Nations.

POPULATION. As of mid-year 1959, the world total was estimated by the United Nations at 2.9 billion, distributed over the 197 million square miles of the earth (57.4 million square miles exclusive of oceans) at the average density of about 55 persons per square mile of land. United States density at that time was 50 persons per square mile. Density in the Netherlands amounted to 812 per square mile while Australia, the size of the United States, has only 3 persons per square mile.

## Topics of Significance

WATER AND HOUSES. "Among the natural facts and forces to which man is geographically bound almost as closely as he is to the air, water deserves a place in the first rank. Water is pre-eminently the economic wealth: it is, for men, more truly wealth than either coal or gold." [10] It is a commonplace to note that all of the great civilizations have grown up around or adjacent to oceans, streams or lakes. Economic life has usually been tied to communication and transportation. The first availability was the natural waterways, and they are still important despite the recent emphasis on other means of communication.

As a supplementary project in social studies classes it is sometimes fruitful to assign students to detailed studies of local harbor or transportation facilities. A particular student or committee of students may find great profit in a series of field trips to a particular local installation, such as a habor, for the purpose of finding out at first hand what is going on there. Many of the geographic skills can incidentally be utilized in such a project. Mapping, tabulation of statistics, interviewing and analysis of the results—all of these skills might be cultivated in the pursuit of intimate knowledge of one example of man's earliest geographic support: water.

Professor Brunhes, father of human geography, stressed the manner in which houses have always taken their basic pattern from the availability of water. "Not a house or human shelter has been built without some attention being given to the availability of a water supply; the humblest chalet in the high mountains is situated first of all near a spring or a stream; every village must have its spring or its well. In some countries where the climate brings a prolonged period of dryness, the roofs and terraces are arranged so as to catch all the rainwater in cisterns." [11] First of all, the location of houses (and therefore

[10] Brunhes, op. cit., p. 52.
[11] Ibid., p. 52.

towns and cities) is often determined by the proximity of water; then the actual design and structural materials are quite naturally sought in the vicinity so chosen for habitation.

As houses and other cultural factors gain respectability with age and usage, the particular society tends to perpetuate its pattern of existence without much alteration. After the first stages of bare existence have given way to a more settled culture, with security for the many and affluence for at least a few, housing tends to take on two aspects. The rich live in one type of house and the poor in another. History abounds in illustrations of this geographic generalization. For example, the mud huts (with flat roofs) of the Egyptian *fellahin* have been about the same for several thousand years; in contrast, the stone palaces (with flat roofs) of the pharoahs indicate a rise to great affluence of one segment of the ancient Egyptian population. The master could use stone, not native to his habitat, but the servant had to use the local materials because he could not afford anything else. It is noteworthy that both stayed with the flat roof on which to catch water, because even great wealth cannot free man from dependence on water.

The form of the house is nearer to nature in the less developed regions, and as men become less bound to the rigors of bare subsistence and as they approach higher degrees of civilization, houses take on more aspects of amenity. Since the industrial revolution has helped raise standards of living, in many parts of the world it is common for people to have glass windows, carpets, sanitation facilities and central heating systems in their houses. The house, in industrialized societies has tended to escape more and more from the strictures of natural determinants as to its location and form, but culture has decreed that houses of certain cultures will retain identifying features, although as world communication becomes easier even this is less marked than formerly.

ROADS. Much the same thing can be said concerning roads. First they followed the clumps of houses, from one village to the next. In modern America, for example, main roads are between cities, although recently there is a tendency to bypass all save the most important cities. This again illustrates the conflicting forces of geographic determination, the persistent force of cultural tradition and the physically liberating influence of technology.

A most attractive project for the secondary school study of geography is to trace the growth of a group of nearby villages and their linkage by a road net. Los Angeles offers a typical opportunity in this respect, since it has grown into a great metropolitan agglomeration which has tended to swallow up all of the originally independent settlements. Here and there, however, it is possible to identify the older village enclaves even though they have been overgrown by encroaching suburbs. Sometimes major alignment of arterial highways has been determined by the chance location of several old villages.

Roadways and cities have a most interesting relationship. Many great roads stem from ancient animal trails. A central Appalachian crossing from Cumberland, Maryland to Pittsburgh is based on an Indian path which followed an animal trail. Braddock crossed that way. It became the National Road, and finally U.S. Highway 60. Nearly the same route is followed by all the airlines from Chicago to Washington, D.C. Natural factors seem to have largely determined both the location of settlements and the alignment of the road between them; the cities are at favorable sites on rivers and a natural path over the mountains between joins them.

Sometimes the roads themselves are the determinants of settlement as in the case of some imperial Roman arteries. Watling Street, running northward from London, still persists as a main road. It was built from Roman London to Hadrian's Wall on the Scottish border as a military and administrative line of communication, and thereby dominated subsequent village and town establishment along its route.

In any case, it is hard to separate roads and towns in geography. This is, incidentally, a commentary on the importance of communication in man's life. Roads gave access to the first rapid communication, examples of which may be found among the ancient Inca as well as the ancient Romans.

GEOGRAPHY OF CIRCULATION. It is a vital generalization that people have tended to stay in permanent abodes and thus to alter their environment while perpetuating their culture. Man is at the same time conservative and imitative, but he is also adventuresome and imaginative. He tends to stay in one place, but under the inexorable forces of technology and expanding population new societies have been formed; new places settled and different ideas blended into the old. It is not too much to say, in this light, that man is part of his own environment to which he reacts in establishing and nurturing his culture.

"One of the best ways to study human geography is to examine man on the move; his population fluctuation settlement patterns, modes of movement and communication are all keys to human geography. Demographic studies have shown, for example, that business enterprises have often gravitated to regions of amenities—good climates, pleasant surroundings. This becomes more and more possible and likely as technology increases." [12]

High school students can be introduced to demographic study by means of actual problems in their own community. Population and its movement, land use and possible reasons for these phenomena are practically inexhaustible possibilities for the imaginative teacher.

NEW DEVELOPMENTS. Perhaps the most important consideration in teaching geography is to remain sensitive to new developments. In both physical and cultural geography there are constant changes in the discovery of new facts and methods of observation and also in fresh ways of interpretation. For example, recent high altitude aircraft pilots discovered the jet stream, very swift, high wind currents which have forced a completely new evaluation of world wind patterns. Cloud seeding, humidity control and solar heating open new vistas of enterprise in another phase of climatology. Transmission over great distances not only of hydraulic electrical power, but of the water itself, is now a potential reality. Nuclear power has opened a whole new concept of energy application hitherto unavailable. Movement of water from mountains to desert, with an accompanying change in weather and demography must expand and alter geographic study. Technology, the application of pure research freeing man from the hampering elements of environment, should also help him to make the ultimately necessary compromises and adjustments to nature which are essential to survival.

Anthropology, sociology, economics, geography, psychology and history all contribute to the knowledge necessary for secondary students' understanding of man's adjustment to his environment. At the seventh grade level these elements are relatively indistinguishable, but to the teacher they must be clearly recognized bodies of disciplined information upon which he can draw. For most successful presentation to a class, especially in junior high school, the subject should be divided into units or problems to be worked out with text and illustrative material. Textbooks vary considerably in their approaches to man's adjustment to geography and society, but perhaps since the underlying theme of technology is everpresent and the scene is American, problems should be chosen which are of present concern in time and place. In any case, historic and geographic illustration should be provided.

One way of approaching the problem is to choose a text which in-

[12] Edward Ullmann, "Amenities and Regional Growth," *Proceedings XVIIth International Geographical Congress* (Washington, D.C., 1952).

corporates both the basic geography and history of the Americas or Europe. Starting somewhere near the present, half of the course might be devoted to a historical resumé or highlighting of the place, and the other half could then be concerned with geographic information. As an alternative both basic aspects might be integrated into one continuous process.

In addition to the basic text the teacher could set up a succession of topical units designed to meet the specific objectives, and study these with the aid of varied reading and visual activities.

Experience in the Americas offers an excellent body of subject matter. The United States lies in the choice middle part of a continent, the northern half of the second largest major land mass of the world, the Americas. From earliest times it was relatively unexploited and relatively new geologically speaking. The inhabitants numbered not more than three million persons at the time of their "discovery" by Europeans. The Indians had arrived in North America, possibly from Asia, sometime between ten and twenty thousand years before the present. They had developed in small independent groups scattered all over North and South America without much appreciation of each other except as local enemies. They all competed for wide expanses and the meager usable natural produce of the land. They adapted to their environment in a way entirely different from the obvious facts of modern existence.

Columbus, as the twelfth or thirteenth "discoverer" of these people, commenced a train of migration to and exploitation of the New World at the end of the fifteenth century. More and more Europeans came to the Americas until, in the nineteenth and twentieth centuries the prevalent culture had lost most of its originally "American" flavor. At the present time the typically American society of the New World is found best expressed in the United States because of the almost universal acceptance of the effects of the industrial revolution. On the other hand, in a comparative way South and Central America and Mexico represent more of the old American culture in various stages of emergence into technologically modern life. For example, the relatively primitive Mosquito Indians of Nicaragua live in proximity to the Panama Canal, one of man's modern mechanical achievements in engineering.

A similar illustration of cultural development may be seen in the Middle East and in Europe. The *fellahin* grubbing in the Nile Delta is only a short distance from the immaculate metropolis of Tel Aviv. Oil from Saudi Arabia, extracted by the most advanced technical means by recently illiterate nomads from the desert, is used to operate the highly complicated machines of production in Western Europe which in their turn may be located in old cities of medieval origin. The Saar Basin is within sightseeing distance of Mont St. Michel and Chartres.

Behind the development of modern Europeans and that of the natives of Peru in Pizarro's time there are the same basic human characteristics, but different physical and cultural factors. Civilizations grew in both places and then made impacts upon each other. As a present day citizen in a highly cohesive world community, the seventh grader is in a psychological position to learn about these things.

Man in the New World, having come from the Old World, was faced first of all by a frontier of wilderness. He took lessons from the native inhabitants and conquered the frontier of space. This was done in various ways in different parts of the New World and in terms of the varied backgrounds of experience brought to the task. English, Spanish, French explorers, settlers, missionaries, traders and thinkers all brought their own special gifts to the frontiers of America.

After the frontiers of space were subdued to the civilizing process of Western man's occupance, new ideas of equality and democratic self-government began to percolate. Out of the American experiment in revolution and rule by law came an ideal for re-export to the rest of the world. The South American popular revolutions of the early nineteenth century immortalized such persons as Simon Bolivar and exemplified the universal application of our own revolutionary principles which had been forged out of the thinking of ancient and modern Europeans. In this way, some of the republican dreams of Plato came into real being among the descendants of Montezuma and the Inca rulers in the New World, as well as among the English speaking Europeans of North America.

Along with the growth of democratic self-governing political forms, the industrial revolution began to make a decided impression on the people of the world, Old and New. During the nineteenth century perhaps the most important thing that happened to man was his adaptation of scientific principles to the production of goods. Western man invented and built out of all reasonably expected proportions to his previous accomplishment. In the past fifty years man has come a greater distance mechanically than he had in the previous four thousand years. At present we are in possession of both a potential for utter destruction and for the most leisurely and easy life imaginable. Man is now truly *stupor mundi*—O wonder of the world! We must stop wondering and begin to understand. The way to understanding is through knowledge of the present and the past.

Two specific and coordinated ideas are suggested to achieve the general objectives of social studies: nature and nurture. Assuming the use of a basic text, a minimum objective is established for learning the geography, history and cultural aspects of a given area.

Along with the text and its unifying sequence of particular information the teacher should adopt an interesting, cogent theme which is highly important to the modern age and at the same time having historical roots in our cultural heritage. This is an air age, so study of the world or its parts in our time must be based on an understanding of that world in an air age context. Outstanding purposes in this regard are:

1. To help the young citizen understand his physical and social environment.

2. To encourage the young citizen to accept individual responsibility for solving his own and social problems.

3. To assist the young citizen to develop a pattern of behavior based on understanding of other people and appreciation of the proximity of all peoples in an air age.

As one unit of instruction it would be well to introduce the concept of life in the air age. If the students have funds available, a short air trip to a nearby city is a most instructive activity. Oftentimes the parents will be interested in accompanying such an excursion. This makes a fine culminating activity to a unit on the air age. An obvious substitute for a class trip is individual reporting on some air trip already completed by a member of the class.

Photographs taken informally from the cabin windows of commercial aircraft can often be very enlightening and interesting illustrations of geography. They are not of the precise quality of professional aerial photographic maps, but if taken by students, they would have the advantages always inherent in direct participation in a vital activity.

### Regional History and Geography for Gifted Students

As a method of enriching the learning of superior or more energetic students, areal or regional studies may be undertaken independently or as class projects. Generally, the average competence will be taxed by covering the material represented in the foregoing comments, but occasionally some student may want to go more deeply into one special geographic-historical case. As a matter of fact, some of the more esoteric doctoral degrees are now being offered in area studies. The candidate, after preparing himself in a discipline such as history, will specialize in the Middle East or Europe, and then, equipped with the languages necessary to further and more intensive study of the area, he will spend a year or more in that place and emerge with a dissertation based on an internship spent on the spot amid the influences and varied stimuli which can only be extensively appreciated at first hand. This type of study is not common. Only a few persons have either the diligence or the intelligence for it. The rare person who does possess the quality of mind needed, certainly also has it at younger ages than at the level of doctoral study. It is that sort of student to whom this section is addressed.

At any level, if the time and ability allow, there is more that can be done concerning the increase of individual knowledge about the great ideas and sources of inspiration of modern man. Any of the regions of the world or any of the enduring questions of civilized man can furnish the vehicle for additional study at this level.

The questions of nationalism, the precise nature of nations, their dependence upon climate, position, size, shape and population, the proximity of one nation to another, natural resources and their common use, and the geographic relationship to modern economics, all offer fruitful fields of inquiry. Specific areas of the world, such as Europe, Africa or Asia, may be studied in detail by means of the data available through all of the social and physical sciences. For example, certain questions for the future might be posed, as, how would a United States of Europe function?

### Conclusion

Geography is a vital and dynamic study. It is the coordinating discipline between natural science and the humanities, bringing into social study the necessary formulations and generalizations to make: for instance, the study of history from both human and scientific vantage points. Geography has no discrete body of source materials from which it must draw exclusively, no set pattern of methodology. All human knowledge is its reservoir. The method is comparative and descriptive for the most part, but theoretical formulations also abound.

In social studies application, geography may be taught as a separate subject at any level, or it may be incorporated into any one of the several subjects that contribute to social studies. In either method of teaching, the components are the same: physical principles of the universe and the earth, human adaptation to those principles and the cultural result of man's interaction with nature. Since areal description and differentiation are the basic purview of geography, most geographic studies should probably be in terms of a regional concept. It is most fruitful for students to begin with a unit, the earth, break it up into major cultural regions, and then into subregions of ever decreasing size and expanding detail.

Human nature is fundamentally the same in all time and in every place, but the varying conditions of environment from place to place and the different types and stages of culture from time to time make life very different in different places. We speak of underdeveloped or highly industrialized societies, of types of social organization, of disparate landscapes; the way to understand these differences is through geographic and historical study of them. It is a fair generalization to say that fear and distrust diminish in direct proportion to the increase of general knowledge. The average American and the average Thai, living in very different landscapes, probably seldom give each other much thought. Both are foreign, one to the other, but basically each is the same as the other, a human being struggling for adaptation and survival. Only a glance at two sets of typical scenes, one from each place, may serve to strengthen this impression.

During the period of agricultural dominance in the United States (and still, in some rural areas), it has been common to see great herds of horses domesticated to the usual farm tasks. In Thailand, which is still predominantly agricultural and rural, the most common draft animal is the water buffalo or *kwai*. Thousands of the great beasts roam the countryside most of the year. They are used for the annual plowing, principally because this operation is carried on while the land is flooded and the buffalo can withstand the hazards of the job. In any event, to the average American, there is a sharp contrast in the appearance of horses and water buffalo as they are respectively the chief draft animal of two separate and different agricultural economies.

Commerce and industry, as they emerge in conjunction with a basically agricultural mode of livelihood, always must be accompanied by increased means of transportation. Again presenting a marked contrast, in present day Thailand most of the transport is accomplished by means of cows and two wheeled carts. Now, in the United States, diesel trains and highway transport trucks perform the essential function, but only a few years ago it was most ordinary to see steam railways. Thailand has not yet advanced technologically to that stage while the United States has gone far beyond it.

FIGURE 22. Contrasts in technology and transportation: Thailand and the United States.

The two sets of pictures (Figure 22) illustrate how geography may be affected either by cultural influences or by the degree of technology employed, as in contrast between rapid transit machines and two wheeled carts.

As a final admonition to teachers of social studies, geographic knowledge and concepts are continually subject to new discoveries both substantive and by way of interpretation. Who can say what the future changes may be in climate control, agricultural production, transportation and communication, to say nothing of the fathomless possibilities in creation, storage and use of energy from the sun, from nuclear fission and fusion, or for that matter, from yet undiscovered advances in science and technology. It will be the task of historians and geographers to assess each change as it appears and recedes into the record of human culture.

### 4. Bibliographies of Content and Method

METHODS IN TEACHING GEOGRAPHY

*Journal of Geography,* published ten times a year by the National Council for Geographic Education, is the single best magazine for geography teachers. It carries both substantive and methodological articles of current interest to the teacher. Next in importance for geography instruction is *Social Education,* which, of course, is not devoted exclusively to geography but to the whole social studies field.

*New Viewpoints in Geography,* edited by Preston E. James, Twenty-ninth Yearbook of the National Council for the Social Studies (Washington, D.C., 1959), is a most interesting symposium of points of view and ideas expressed by both experts in geography and people with great experience in teaching.

Zoe Thralls, *The Teaching of Geography* (Appleton-Century-Crofts, New York, 1958), is a well organized, simple guide to instruction in geography. A reliable handbook.

Forest E. Long and Helen Halter, *Social Studies Skills* (Inor, New York, 1942), is specific in techniques for teaching the use of maps, globes and atlases.

*Free and Inexpensive Materials,* George Peabody College for Teachers, Field Services (Nashville, n.d.); Bruce Miller, *Sources of Free and Inexpensive Pictures for the Classroom,* Box 222, Ontario, California.

METHODS IN STUDYING GEOGRAPHY

*American Geography: Inventory and Prospect,* edited by Preston James and Clarence F. Jones (Syracuse University Press, 1954), contributed by many scholars, is the most comprehensive survey, now existing, of what geography is.

Isaiah Bowman, *Geography in Relation to the Social Studies* (Scribner's, New York, 1934), although somewhat old, gives useful emphasis to the present school need for attention to geography.

Richard Hartshorne, *Perspective on the Nature of Geography* (Rand, McNally, Chicago, 1959), is a timely reappraisal of the author's former work in defining the scope and methods of geographic study.

Earl B. Shaw, "Forces Contributing to Changes in Geographic Education," *Professional Paper No. 16* (National Council for Geographic Education, March, 1958), presents compelling arguments for teaching geography.

## 5. Substantive Works for Teachers of Geography

### WORLD GEOGRAPHY

George F. Deasy, Phyllis R. Griess, E. Willard Miller and Earl C. Case, *The World's Nations: An Economic and Regional Geography* (Lippincott, Philadelphia, 1958), is a comprehensive and somewhat detailed survey of all of the world regions with an emphasis on their economic development.

Specialized information concerning particular aspects of regional economic activities is available in many forms through the agencies of production or promotion in many countries. Examples of this sort of material are *The Story of Tea*, produced by the Tea Bureau, Inc. (American Education Press, Columbus, Ohio, 1948); *Coffee, the Story of a Good Neighbor Product*, Pan-American Coffee Bureau, 120 Wall Street, New York 5, New York (1954); *Rubber*, Wesleyan University and the Firestone Tire and Rubber Company (Columbus, Ohio, 1954). The technical information contained in such pamphets is not easily available in any book, nor is it generally applicable to the purposes of all students, but in special cases there is no better substitute. Such material is useful to both student and teacher when the need arises.

Jesse H. Wheeler, Jr., J. Trenton Kostbade and Richard S. Thoman, *Regional Geography of the World* (Holt, New York, 1955), is a simple yet comprehensive description of the world in regional sections. The book contains enough of physical geography to make comprehensible any of the particular or general statements about the world and its occupance.

*The University Atlas*, edited by Harold Fullard and H. C. Darby (George Philip, London, 1958), 8th ed., is a rather fully detailed world atlas. *Hammond's Word Atlas and Gazeteer* (Hammond, New York, 1955), is a convenient paper covered collection of essential and pertinent information concerning the places of the world. It is a valuable supplement to the larger, more expensive atlases available in all libraries.

### HUMAN GEOGRAPHY

Jean Brunhes, *Human Geography* (Rand, McNally, 1920), is an old work by a French scholar of the nineteenth century, but it has the great merit of thoughtful synthesis of a broad knowledge of man and the world.

Preston E. James, *A Geography of Man* (Ginn, Boston, 1958), 3rd ed., is a standard modern treatment of man in his physical setting.

L. Dudley Stamp, *Land for Tomorrow* (Indiana University Press, Bloomington, 1952), is the revised form of a group of lectures illustrating the necessity of man to live with his environment, to adapt to nature while at the same time getting the most out of it.

## ECONOMIC GEOGRAPHY

Nels A. Bengston and William Van Royen, *Fundamentals of Economic Geography* (Prentice-Hall, Englewood Cliffs, N.J., 1956), is sound and comprehensive.

Isaiah Bowman, *Geography in Relation to the Social Sciences* (Scribner's, New York, 1934), deals with economics as well as the other social sciences.

Theodore L. Hills, *The St. Lawrence Seaway* (Praeger, New York, 1959), treats the new international cooperative effort to use the natural facilities of this inland waterway.

O. O. Maxfield, "Principles: An Approach to Economic Geography," *Journal of Geography*, Vol. 52 (1953), pp. 25–32, gives a fresh view of the subject.

## PHYSICAL GEOGRAPHY

Carl O. Sauer, "Early Relations of Man to Plants," *Geographical Review*, Vol. 37 (1937), pp. 1–25, is basic.

Arthur N. Strahler, *Physical Geography* (John Wiley, New York, 1960), 2nd ed., is one of the most comprehensive texts in the general subject available. It has a fine bibliography arranged by topics.

Edward Ullman, "The Railroad Pattern of the United States," *Geographical Review*, Vol. 39 (1949), pp. 242–256, is typical of a certain kind of treatment of many aspects of the geography of circulation. All sorts of factors are involved in the establishment of means of transportation, movement and communication. These are both physical and human—topography, weather, amenities, chance.

S. W. Woolridge, *The Physical Basis of Geography* (Longmans, Green, New York, 1937), is by one of the world authorities on geomorphology. See also H. D. Thompson, "Canons of Landscape Evolution—A Discussion," *Bulletin of the Geological Society of America*, Vol. 66 (1955), pp. 1205–1206, for a newer view of pediplanation as compared with peneplanation.

## WEATHER AND CLIMATE

Lincoln Barnett, *The World We Live In* (Live Publishing Company, New York, 1955), is about the simplest introduction and general view.

C. F. Brooks, *Why the Weather?* (Harcourt, Brace, New York, 1935), is sound and simple.

Howard Critchfield, *General Climatology* (Prentice-Hall, Englewood Cliffs, N.J., 1960), is a concise review of the principles and application of weather and climate phenomena.

W. Koppen and R. Geiger, *Handbuch der Klimatologie* (*Handbook of Climatology*), (Berlin, 1936), 5 vols., is an accepted basis of classification for world climates.

Special Topics

L. M. Gould, "Antarctic Prospect," *Geographical Review*, Vol. 47 (1957), pp. 1–28.

Pierre Gourou, *The Tropical World* (Longmans, New York, 1953), is an especially penetrating treatment of all of the world's tropical regions, treated generally and as individual places.

Gilbert F. White, editor, *The Future of the Arid Lands* (American Geographical Society, New York, 1957), is a symposium of prospects for many formerly uninhabitable places.

## POPULATION

*The Determinants and Consequences of Population Trends,* United Nations Population Studies No. 17 (New York, 1953), is a comprehensive analysis of world population growth and projections.

"The Malthusian Mischief," *Fortune,* Vol. 45 (May, 1952), pp. 96, 210, 213, shows how "overpopulation" is a direct function of underproduction.

F. W. Notestein, "Population—The Long View," in *Food and the World,* edited by T. W. Schultz (University of Chicago Press, 1945), comments on technological support for an expanding population.

## CARTOGRAPHY

C. H. Deetz, *Cartography* (United States Government Printing Office, Washington, D.C., 1943), is a concise description of principles and processes.

A. K. Lobeck and W. J. Tellington, *Military Maps and Air Photographs* (McGraw-Hill, New York, 1944), discusses aerial photography in map making, although many new developments have taken place in the last fifteen years.

Arthur H. Robinson, *Elements of Cartography* (Wiley, New York, 1960), is the latest manual in this field.

Earl B. Shaw, *Anglo-America: A Regional Geography* (Wiley, New York, 1959), includes a good deal of information on cartography.

## STUDENT REFERENCES

Basic texts at various levels of maturity include Loyal Durand, *World Geography* (Holt, New York, 1958), for high school; Preston E. James and Nelda Davis, *The Wide World: A Geography* (Macmillan, New York, 1959), for junior high; Oliver H. Heintzelman and Richard M. Highsmith, Jr., *World Regional Geography* (Prentice-Hall, Englewood Cliffs, New Jersey, 1956), suitable for high school or junior college; and Leonard O. Packard, Bruce Overton and Ben D. Wood, *Geography of the World* (Macmillan, New York, 1953), adapted to the use of beginners 12 to 18 years of age. There are several others.

For less advanced or less able students other materials must be sought, such as:

Elsa Jane Werner, *The Golden Geography* (Simon and Schuster, New York, 1952), presents the most simplified version of world geography with many illustrations. It might be useful for retarded readers in the seventh grade.

*Compton's Pictured Encyclopedia* (F. E. Compton, Chicago, revised annually), is a multi-volume general reference with illustrations, suitable for use in junior high school. Its coverage is broader than any other encyclopedia available to public school use.

*The World We Live In,* editors of *Life* (Life-Time, New York, 1956), contains anthropological, historical and geographic material with wonderful illustrations.

ATLASES

George T. Raisz, *Atlas of Global Geography* (Harper, New York, 1944), is a reference atlas prepared by one of the world's outstanding authorities on cartography.

BOOKS ON WORLD GEOGRAPHY FOR JUNIOR HIGH SCHOOL

Senior high students will probably have to resort to the many adult books on specialized or regional subjects.

Merlin Ames and others, *America, Heir of Yesterday; My Country's Heritage* (Webster, Chicago).

Wallace Atwood and Helen Thomas, *Nations Overseas* (Ginn, Boston).

Harlan Barrows and others, *Old World Lands* (Silver, Burdett and Company, New York).

Frances Carpenter, *The Pacific: Its Land and Its People* (American, New York).

Ralph W. Cordier, *History of World Peoples* (Rand, McNally, Chicago).

Grace S. Dawson, *Your World and Mine* (Ginn, New York).

Mabel Grimm, *The Old World* (Row, Peterson, New York).

Gertrude Hartman and Lucy S. Saunders, *Builders of the Old World* (Little, Brown, Boston).

George and Violet Hoffman, *Life in Europe—Switzerland* (Fideler, Grand Rapids).

R. O. Hughes and C. H. W. Pullen, *Eastern Lands* (Allyn and Bacon, New York).

Edward Kolevzon and others, *Our World and Its People* (Allyn and Bacon, New York).

Vincent and Ruth Malmstrom, *Lie in Europe—Norway* (Fideler, Grand Rapids).

Edna McGuire, *Backgrounds of American Freedom* (Macmillan, New York).

J. G. Meyer and others, *The Old World and Its Gifts* (Follet, Chicago).

Clyde Moore and others, *Building Our World* (Scribner's, New York).

Gerhart Seger, *Life in Europe—Germany* (Fideler, Grand Rapids).

Clarence Sorenson, *A World View* (Silver, Burdett and Company, New York).

Lewis P. Todd and Kenneth Cooper, *World Ways* (Silver, Burdett and Company, New York).

W. de Groot Van Embden, *Life in Europe—The Netherlands* (Fideler, Grand Rapids).

Gertrude Whipple and Preston E. James, *Neighbors on Our Earth; Our Earth and Men; Living on Our Earth; At Home on Our Earth* (Macmillan, New York).

H. E. Wilson and others, *Out of the Past* (American, New York).

AIR AGE BOOKS

Richard E. Byrd, *Alone* (Putnam, New York, 1938), is an early story of aerial discovery and exploration in the Arctic.

Thomas Collison, *This Winged World* (Macmillan, New York, 1943).

E. E. Harrison, *Look at the World* (Knopf, New York, 1944), is global in concept.

A. T. Hellring, *Jobs in the Aircraft Industry* (Science Research Associates, Chicago, 1943), analyzes and presents the positions available in aviation and related industries.

Chester H. Lawrence, *New World Horizons* (Duell, Sloan and Pierce, New York, 1942), is a little out of date now, but it still is useful in giving a world view of places and people.

Charles A. Lindbergh, *We* (Grossett and Dunlap, New York, 1927), is the incomparable story of the romance and scientific conquest of the Atlantic by air. It is the story of an all time "first."

Burr W. Leyson, *Aeronautical Occupations* (Dutton, New York, 1938), is of historic interest.

De Forest Stull and Ray W. Hatch, *Journeys Through Many Lands* (Allyn and Bacon, Chicago, 1943), sees the world from the air.

AUDIO–VISUAL

"The Twentieth Century," Columbia Broadcasting Company television program, highlighting man's achievement in the air age.

List of 16 mm. sound films on aviation subjects, produced by industry for the use of classroom teachers, Parks College of Aeronautical Technology, St. Louis University, East St. Louis, Illinois. Gratis.

Maps, charts, globes, pictures and other visual materials are available from:
National Geographic Society, 16th and M Streets, Washington 6, D.C.
Rand, McNally & Company, 536 South Clark Street, Chicago 5, Illinois.
Informative Classroom Pictures, 40 Ionis N.W., Grand Rapids, Michigan.
Boeing Aircraft Corporation, Boeing Airport, Seattle 8, Washington.

## 6. Suggested Activities for Further Study

1. Prepare a list of basic terms used in geography that students ought to know in order to be able to read about the subject intelligently. Remember that many words ordinarily used have special meanings in geography, such as landscape.

2. Draw up a supplementary reading list of biographies, novels and travel books that illustrate geographic generalizations and that might add to interest and utility in a high school course in world geography.

3. Work out a unit for physical geography by which common mathematics can be integrated with the social studies. Include some appropriate problems.

4. How can the study of geography help in high school history classes? List some specific activities that a teacher of world history could use to enrich his presentation.

5. What should high school social studies include concerning world population? Make a compilation of necessary facts and figures with reasons for their inclusion, for each major world region.

6. What recent political events have caused a reappraisal of African geography? How does Afro-Asian demography affect the U.N.?

7. Write an essay justifying one or the other of two approaches to geography teaching: as a separate subject or as a unified effort with history.

# 12

# Teaching
# economic competence

When the division of labour has been once thoroughly established, it is but a very small part of a man's wants which the produce of his own labour can supply.

*The Wealth of Nations*
ADAM SMITH, 1776

## 1. Introduction to Economics

How did man come to be involved in the intricate economic organization in which he now finds himself? It is difficult to understand, and certainly every economic development cannot be predicted. Therefore much is still unknown about how men and nations maintain their economic integrity. As Adam Smith wrote over and over again, "Every man is rich or poor according to the degree in which he can afford to enjoy the necessaries, conveniences, and amusements of human life. The far greater part of them he must derive from the labour of other people, and he must be rich or poor according to the quantity of that labour which he can afford to purchase." [1] Thomas Hobbes had enunciated, even earlier, that power consists of wealth, and that the relationship is very close between private affluence and public policy.

From a purely selfish point of view, then, it is desirable to gain understanding of the following overwhelmingly important problems of modern economics: the causes of depression, unemployment, and inflationary booms; and the causes of prosperity, full employment, and rising standards of living. But no less important is the fact—clearly to be read from the history of the twentieth century—that the political health of a democracy is tied up in a

[1] Adam Smith, *An Inquiry into the Nature and Causes of the Wealth of Nations,* Modern Library Edition (Random House, New York, 1937), p. 30.

362

crucial way with the successful maintenance of stable high employment and living opportunities.[2]

In order to achieve competence in general citizenship and to acquire the stance of an educated person, the student must learn some of the fundamental concepts and facts of economics. It seems inconceivable that any socal study can be comprehensive without some consideration of the way in which man organizes himself to satisfy basic economic needs and amenities. In fact, economics as a subject of investigation and as a pervasive force in people's lives could be presented as the coordinating study among all of the social sciences. In this book, geography has been assigned that coordinating role because of its affinity to the natural sciences as well; but for the social studies teachers, economics can very well fill the same role.

There are, in general, three ways to present the necessary information: (1) through a systematic examination of principles and theory accompanied by both historical and contemporary illustrations, (2) by an historical approach to the growth of economic institutions, and (3) through examination of current organization and recent developments. A high school introduction to the subject should contain elements of all three methods. Perhaps most important, but also most difficult, is an emphasis on principles and theory. Appropriate illustrations would seem to be the key to success no matter which approach is used.

### Historical Approach

At the end of the eighteenth century a classical economics had developed which, in accord with Newtonian physics and the beliefs of the Age of Reason, was based on immutable laws. The Law of Supply and Demand, the Law of Diminishing Return, the principles of economic rent, Gresham's Law (that poor money drives out good) and others less well known, were thought to exist; it was the province and task of economists to discover them. If man, knowing natural laws, adhered to their clear dicta he would prosper economically. In truth, these economic rules were not really laws (which are immutable), but rather principles that operate optimally during periods of full employment and expansion. During most of the time in the past full employment has been more of a hope than a reality. Only now is it a real possibility, although Alfred Marshall considered this problem as early as 1890.

[2] Paul A. Samuelson, *Economics: An Introductory Analysis* (McGraw-Hill, New York, 1958), 4th ed., p. 3. Quoted by permission of the publisher.

Before the end of the nineteenth century, but most markedly at the time of the great depression which began in 1929, economists began to think more seriously about the actual problems that confronted the whole world. Although starting much earlier, this emphasis is now popularly attributed to Lord Keynes. Mass unemployment, declining production and low level of investment became acute, in some cases threatening the stability of governments. Economics turned more and more to a study of current affairs and immediate trends. Capitalism and the whole profit system underwent a profound re-examination, and the result was a much clearer understanding that the so-called economic laws operated best when a society approached its maximum of employment and enjoyed expansion of consumption and therefore of production. This can be conveniently called either Keynesian or neo-classical economics, but it is actually a long historic growth stemming from the beginning of the industrial revolution and studded with the formulations of economic theorists all along the way.[3]

Posing a classical theory of economics, based on natural laws, accepted at the beginning of the nineteenth century, on the one hand, and a rather different theory of economics prevalent after the first quarter of the twentieth century, on the other, the result of thinking during the nineteenth century amounted to a neo-classical synthesis. Various components of this theory include the natural laws, such things as the principle of marginal utility, developed in the last half of the nineteenth century, and emphasis on the need for increased production which stemmed from the industrial revolution.

The law of supply and demand operates, but it may require governmental intervention in the natural processes of production and trade in order to forestall overproduction of a particular item and a consequent depression. Rather than a free enterprise capitalism, then, there developed a "mixed" free enterprise system in which planning on a national scale is necessary and in which government and corporation both participate to better resultant ends of full employment and maximum purchasing power of the labor force.

### Current Organization and Development

"Economics is . . . the study of how society produces and distributes the goods and services it wants."[4] Man in societies depends for

---

[3] See O. H. Taylor, *A History of Economic Thought* (McGraw-Hill, New York, 1960), which elaborates the history of economic theory.

[4] *An Introduction to Economic Reasoning*, edited by Marshall A. Robinson, Brookings Institution (Washington, D.C., 1959, rev. ed.).

existence (aside from his political institutions which are historically secondary) on adequate and continued procurement of (1) food, (2) clothing, (3) shelter, (4) communication facilities and (5) amenities. These are the goals of economic activity. The manner in which man gets these things constitutes his economic structure. Depending upon the stage of development in which a group finds itself, the system and philosophy of economic organization varies; but in all societies at all times there are certain fundamental patterns of need and action common to everyone.

At first, in human groups at a very low level of sophistication, when subsistence was directly related to hunting and gathering and when the specialization of labor was not marked, there was a great difference in the economic mode, for example, as compared to the twentieth century in nearly all of the world. Each man had to be fairly self-sufficient. Presently, however, all peoples have accepted the necessity for a definite division of labor and increasing specialization. This obviously makes each individual more dependent on others, but it also provides for a wider variety of commodities and a rising standard of consumption.

Given the essential specialization of productive labor there are four main regions of study in the realm of economics: (1) natural resources must be available, as well as (2) capital and entrepreneurial direction, (3) labor and (4) a market for the finished goods. According to some thinkers, Adam Smith notable among them, labor is the most important of these, since, in view of a labor theory of value, goods are valued precisely in accord with the amount and kind of effort required to produce them. It has been recognized from the middle of the nineteenth century increasingly to the present that value depends not solely on the cost of production, but on both *utility* and *cost*. In more and more cases sheer demand becomes the dominating factor in establishing value, as in the case of clothing style.

In our society in this century, labor value has become uniquely important in another sense, in that the preponderance of the consuming market is synonymous with labor, and consumption as the key to economic health must depend upon a laboring group with considerable purchasing power. The bulk of consumption is effected by the very persons who make up the labor force. Even in the intrepreneurial field the same effect has been felt. Although not in direct managerial control, each stockholder does have some influence on production policies, and certainly the vast accumulation of capital now in use could not have been achieved without the tremendously widespread participation in stock purchasing by millions of members of the labor force. This was possibly the most important factor overlooked by Karl Marx in his analysis of economics. He put so much emphasis on the rigid existence of economic and social classes that he failed to anticipate the wide participation by labor in the actual support of capitalistic effort.

The outstanding responsibility and chief efforts of economists now ought to be, and sometimes is, to describe means to achieve and keep full employment and a rising standard of living, to accommodate the needs and desires of a constantly increasing population and to explain and assist in the monumental task of equitably distributing the world's goods to that population. Some economists would deny this, not wanting that much responsibility. The domain of decision in formulating public policy belongs, of course, to the statesmen, but more and more economists' views and predictions are weighed as major determinants.

Every economic activity entails a choice among alternatives. Often they are not easy choices, therefore political organization is always closely tied to economic life. This does not mean that politics is determined by economics, nor does it mean that economists are responsible for policy decisions. It is not that simple. For example, the exigencies of national defense, depending directly on the procurement of highly specialized technical devices and other products of the economic machine, may demand the reduction of national consumption of some common item such as steel. The area of choice might entail a stepped-up program to reach the moon or expansion of the national highway system. The country could produce more than enough steel to build all of the highways proposed, or it could produce all of the guns, rockets and devices needed to project man into space in a limited time, but it cannot produce all of *both* that everyone wants or could use. A choice has to be made. This becomes the province of the national state, and through established political procedures a balanced choice is made. In a democracy such as ours it is even more difficult than in a totalitarian state where the direction is given by fiat and the provisions carried out by force.

Steel is a good current illustration among economic alternatives now, but in the future it might be another commodity, such as aluminum, or another economic consideration, such as the proportion between public and private investment in production. In any case, the economist must advise, and describe results of different courses of political action.

## They're All His Hats

FIGURE 23. Cartoon from the *Santa Barbara News-Press*, September 5, 1960. The implication of this cartoon may be deceptive and construed to mean that there are no economic class differentiations. It would be extremely unsophisticated to assume that there are no dominant working-class pressures against investors, or that controlling blocks of corporate stock were held by laboring people. The "average" holding of the 10,000,000 American investors in corporate enterprise is 19 shares, and this is largely confined to families with incomes in the top half of the economic brackets. Despite these facts, the idea conveyed in the cartoon is extremely important in American economics.

*Economics in Secondary School*

Regardless of the philosophy or approach, and no matter what the particular topics of study might be, there are major considerations that can be served by a secondary school study of economics. They may include (1) general liberal learning, (2) embellishment of the historical display of our human heritage, (3) consumer information, and (4) economic opportunities: students will become job seekers, businessmen and investors.

One way to meet the requirements of the objectives suggested above is to select topics for study and discussion pertaining to the following list of major items in economics. Depending upon the time available and the skill of the students, each topic could be expanded or not as circumstances warranted.

SUGGESTED OUTLINE

1. Central problems of every economic society
   a. Economic organization
   b. Technological choices open
   c. Population basis of any economy
2. Functioning of the profit system
   a. How a free enterprise system solves the basic economic problems
   b. Capital, division of labor, money
   c. Markets, prices and costs
3. Individual and family income
   a. Budgeting and security
   b. Individual relationship to the society
4. Business organization and income
   a. Forms of business organization
   b. The modern corporation
5. Economic role of government
   a. Federal taxation
   b. Federal government as biggest consumer and employer
   c. Local financing
   d. Federal and local ownership of capital
6. Labor and industrial relations
7. Social security; federal government as an economic regulator in the welfare state
8. National income and gross product
9. Saving, consumption and investment
10. Prices and money

11. Banking
12. The public dept and modern fiscal policy
13. Current international economic problems
14. Economics of the nuclear age

If the task is to present an introduction to economics in a class of seniors who have elected the subject and have a semester to devote to the study, then the teacher might by means of lectures, a textbook, discussions and outside reading and reports cover some aspects of most of the topics listed.

### Labor and Industrial Relations

As an example, the topic of labor in the modern economic organization may be taken. Every child is, or should be, aware of some of the immediate problems that his family faces in making a living. A job is essential to most members of our society. Among boys and girls of high school age probably a majority have been employed themselves, at least during summers. The subject has intrinsic interest. On the other hand, do high school students know how many people are in the national labor force, what proportion of that force is employed, what types of work are chiefly represented?

Almost any newspaper, on its financial pages, carries periodic charts of employment-unemployment. One of these might be selected for a bulletin board display to introduce the role of labor in the national economy. First, the question should be raised as to how many persons must be gainfully employed in the United States in order for the economy to maintain its upward tendency. This sort of question, of course, has no ready answer, but it is necessary to do thinking along these lines to appreciate the importance of labor economics. In 1940 the figure was suggested at 60,000,000. The truth is that it varies according to total population, living standards, degree of technological development and the general world outlook. Full employment, of course, also depends upon what is defined as the labor force—how many old and young are employed, how many wives and mothers are working for wages.

At the start of such a unit a questionnaire could be circulated among the class asking for information on the employment of the parents (type of job, length of tenure, salaries and so on). The answers should be anonymous to avoia any embarrassment. The data received could be analyzed in comparison with the composition of the national labor force as determined by the census. An important consideration is

FIGURE 24. An example of an employment-unemployment graph showing growth pattern. With the economy asked to supply new jobs for one million more workers each year, economists consider the slight percentage increase in unemployment at mid-year as normal. (From the *Los Angeles Times,* August 20, 1960.) See the *Survey of Current Business* to correct and update any newspaper selection made for classroom use.

the effect on production and consumption wrought by sudden surges in population, as after World War II. A convenient reference for such data is *Statistical Abstract,* published periodically from material furnished by various government agencies.

As study progresses a committee can be appointed to collect and coordinate information in each of the major categories of employment, e.g., agriculture, basic extraction, manufacturing, entertainment, protection, personal service, etc. Some of the groups might extend their questionnaire to the whole student body. In the end there could be enough data to compare the community labor force to the national pattern. Incidentally, help in this enterprise is often available from chambers of commerce, business firms and various consulting specialists. Visiting lecturers and field trips might be in order at several points.

Labor force, employable persons, including seasonally adjusted groups must be identified. As new technical terms arise they should be explained and defined at once, and written on the blackboard. A permanent listing on the board and notebooks should be started. Individuals or groups might be assigned to find out the specialized meanings from the textbook or from other references. As in other aspects of economics here is an opportunity to prepare permanent large scale charts to be displayed in the room.

### Controversial Topics

Soon after the introduction of any consideration of labor, controversial attitudes concerning labor unions and management will arise. Many points in economics have strong adherents to different positions. The natural outcome of such study and discussion could be a panel or debate. Each side should learn all they possibly can about the history of organized labor and about the recent legislation and events which have been aired in magazine and newspaper.

For example, one may find the statement that labor "has an inadequate share of the national income on the one hand, and unequal bargaining powers in industrial relations on the other. Both conditions could be remedied by compelling the legal recognition of trade unions and by legislation fixing minimum wages and maximum hours of work." [5]

This may easily be set over against a more recent avowal that the "economic and political power of unions will be curbed considerably if two controversial labor issues are decided against the unions. One issue is before the United States Supreme Court. The court will answer the question: May unions force workers to join and then use part of their dues money to seek economic and political objectives which some workers may oppose?" [6] This position implies that workers do have adequate voice in their own affairs if they are allowed to make individual agreements as to their conditions of employment, that in a natural state of competition in free enterprise the best will emerge. The question arises as to the degree of competition that actually exists.

Adherents of these variant points of view have become quite heated in their clashes, and possibly no real accommodation of emotions is possible, but certainly, in a classroom, even though there may be a good deal of emotional commitment, objective analysis of a problem

[5] Louis M. Hacker, "The Third American Revolution," *The New Deal: Revolution or Evolution*, Amherst Problems in American Civilization (Heath, Boston, 1949), p. 3.

[6] "Workers Attack Union Politics," *Nation's Business* (June, 1960), p. 14.

should be possible. For one thing, a short review of the history of labor unions ought to be fruitful. It should become readily apparent, also, that during the time since the founding of the Knights of Labor after the Civil War a great many changes have taken place in economic structure. There should also be some evidence of the truth of Hobbes' dictum avowing the identity of power and money. The problem, of course, remains as to who or what group will control the wealth, therefore the power. Without advocating the interests of any particular group the teacher of economics in high school can help students learn the persistent truth of certain principles and their altered significance in the modern world.

### Population and the Labor Force

Every economy must solve in some way three fundamental problems: (1) Types and quantities of all possible goods and services to be produced; (2) use of economic resources in the production of these goods; (3) distribution of income among the various groups and individuals in the society so that consumption of goods produced can be facilitated. Very important to these problems, on the national scale, is the size and composition of the population. In a society such as ours that is highly industrialized, with great technological achievement and a high standard of living, a certain trend has developed in relation to full employment. This tends to make the labor force appear to be proportionately smaller than would be the case in less technically advanced areas such as West Africa. Here, in the United States, the per capita production is very high and consequently more older and younger members of the total population must be dependent on a smaller labor force. Whereas, in West Africa, an agricultural area, the labor force accounts for a higher percentage of the population. Several non-economic factors affect this also, such as increased longevity and reduced infant mortality in the industrialized areas. These are the direct result of sanitation, medical discoveries and the generally increased standard of healthful living, and so, indirectly, they are economic. In any event, the composition of population by age and occupation bears directly on the way in which full employment, and therefore solution of fundamental economic problems, comes about.

Can it be concluded that population growth is a good thing? Is it inevitable in a condition of full employment? Should population growth be regulated or can economic activity keep up with it under certain circumstances? Is there any limit to how many people the world can support? What relationship does population increase bear

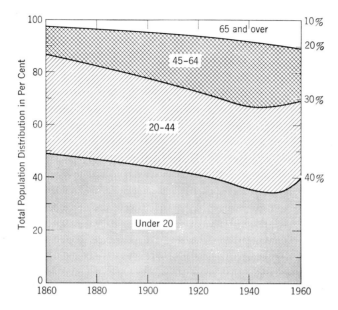

FIGURE 25. Age composition of the population of the United States, 1860–1960. (For example, in 1960 40% of the population was under 20 years of age, 30% was 20–44, 20% was 45–64, and 10% was 65 and over.)

to technology? Economics alone cannot answer these questions, but in the interest of adducing all the evidence available in the attempt at solution, economics can offer a great deal of enlightenment.

## Charts and Graphs

A class can make its own large scale charts showing the composition of population by occupation and income, thus illustrating how one of the fundamental economic problems is met. The same can be done for consumption of the national product. In fact, there is hardly a limit to the kinds of picture graphs that can be devised to illustrate various phases of economic life. *U.S. News and World Report,* among weekly newsmagazines, is especially good for this sort of illustration.

Large charts make very attractive and useful displays, calling attention forcefully to their subject matter and constantly reminding students of the application of economic principles that they are learning.

Analysis of statistics and the construction of graphs make possible the use of several related skills in many different disciplines. This aspect of economics gives the social studies teacher opportunity to cooperate with the mathematics teacher as well as to bring in findings from geography, sociology and psychology which he should do whenever possible.

### Automation and Labor

Automation is a new and frightening word. It means only a facilitated electronic control of machines which have been doing repetitive and menial jobs in manufacturing for a long time. In fact, technological displacement of laborers has been going on ever since the first organizations of industrial output. Every factory operator, every society, has wanted to achieve the most efficient and most rapid means of production. Characteristically, with every wave of improvement in technology that has resulted in a machine doing what several persons previously did, there has been pained protest on the parts of workers. The very word sabotage comes from the phenomenon of peasants throwing their wooden shoes, or *sabots*, into the new machines so they could have their jobs back. The cotton gin was expected to destroy the need for a labor force in the South. Automatic control of the processes of production in automobile factories is now feared as a means of eliminating the need for automobile workers.

In all of these considerations it is often forgotten that another result also follows technological displacement of workers: production goes up, more goods are available and more and new jobs are created, not only for the number of persons displaced but for the new entrants into the labor market.

Automation need not be a fearful threat to individual workers' security. If the proper fiscal and economic policies are adopted as they become necessary and in sufficient magnitude, our society can look forward to the continued and increased benefits of increased production along with full employment that constitute prosperity. We must understand the elements of the situation and it is well to heed the advice of "Satch" Paige, the great baseball player, "Never look back; someone may be gaining on you." Automation may complicate the problems of economic organization, but it does not alter the basic principles, and the solution of basic and constantly recurring problems does not lie in the past. For example, full employment might have been achieved at a certain point, and immediately automation might halve the number of workers needed to produce the *same* amount of goods. Something like this has actually happened in agriculture in the United States. Naturally there will be a displacement of the labor force, but not necessarily to a status of unemployment. As people work less and produce more and different goods, the capacity for consumption increases. The problem is not to find ways of curtailing production, but of facilitating consumption. From this point of view automation is the greatest boon of mid-century.

## 2. Economics as an Adjunct of History

Most high school students do not study economics formally, but all people get two or three years of history in the secondary schools. On two grounds, then, economics assumes importance: as a very useful and interesting aspect of history, and as an irreplaceable part of general knowledge for the liberally educated person. It is quite necessary for the informed and competent citizen to know something about the principles, theory and application of economics. Economic structure is perhaps basic in any social organization. It may not, on occasion, be as evident as the political structure, but it is just as important, although much more often neglected in the educational process.

In high schools, even if economics is taught as a separate course, required or elective, it is one of the most fascinating adjuncts of the study of man's heritage, his history. The way in which man makes a living is equally significant with his setting, his social and political organization and his biological derivation in learning the total story of human development which is the scope of history. Analysis of the growth of economic institutions and the establishment of economic theory can be a substantial part of almost any secondary school history course.

In world history courses common in many high schools, some time is usually devoted to pre-literary beginnings, using anthropological materials. One of the most important aspects of study is examination of the two great upheavals in human organization that took place five to twenty thousand years ago: the tool-using revolution and the agricultural revolution. These made possible and necessary the specialization of effort and the division of labor. Such a development was definitive in the subsequent civilizations that grew up, and in the modern world if one economic fact of greatest consequence can be stated it is the practice of division of labor. Modern industrialization could not exist at all without specialization, and the present standards of living would not be possible without industrialization. This is only one example of how economic institutions have been historically significant.

The history of Florence is usually centered about the great Renaissance age of art production. The mighty Medici family is pictured as patrons of artists and the arts, and Michelangelo is not usually thought of as an economic unit. In truth, Florence is more fundamentally tied historically to the growth of an economic institution: banking. The first Medicis were money lenders and usurers, as they were often called. They made their vast wealth from the professional care of other people's money. Patronage of the arts was a secondary result of amassing wealth. In a world history class the story of how goldsmiths turned into bankers should not be overlooked.

During the Middle Ages, when towns began to develop and urban life required the services of goldsmiths, about the only place for safekeeping valuables was the goldsmith's vault. It became the practice for people to entrust their money and jewels, for safety's sake, to the goldsmith. He began to charge a fee for this service and in return guaranteed against possible loss. This is the essential foundation of two economic institutions: banking and insurance. Very soon the goldsmith discovered that it was possible to conduct transactions with the money he was safeguarding without physically moving the money at all. For example, A deposits $1,000, for which the goldsmith charges a fee. A owes B $1,000. A, instead of withdrawing the money, simply arranges with the goldsmith to transfer its ownership to B, who leaves it on deposit and pays his fee. More simply, A can write a check on the goldsmith for $1,000 and give it to B who, in his turn, can do the same to pay some debt of his own. The transaction may be multiplied many times and still the original sum will never leave the vault. The goldsmith is by now pretty much a banker. He must make one more refinement in his procedure, however. Assume that the goldsmith–banker now has ten depositors, each having claim to $1,000. Viewed from the banker's standpoint this represents a total capital of $10,000 which could be loaned or otherwise invested. The owners of the capital can write checks back and forth to each other without ever removing the money itself, so why could not the banker lend the money in the same way—by writing checks himself on the deposited capital? The only requirement would be that the investors would not claim their money in cash without notice. Depositors were attracted by the promise of interest on their money if they would leave it in the bank for a protracted period. With the original $10,000 on deposit for a year it was found that easily five times that amount could be loaned (for repayment within the year) and because of checks written instead of risking the hazard of transporting actual gold in the open, the sum in the vault remained substantially unchanged. The benefit to the depositors and borrowers was convenience and safety from robbery. The gain to the banker was the difference in the interest he charged to many borrowers and the amount that he paid to the investors. Banking was thus begun.

There is just such a fascinating story in connection with all of the essential institutions of modern capitalism. Joint stock investment for procuring large capitals, insurance for sharing single risks with a number of similar investors, the bourse or stock exchange—all are historical growths from the end of the Middle Ages into the period of modern history. Each presents a bit of history in itself and each is highly illuminating of the rest of man's story. They all add up to the development of what has been called capitalism, the profit system, by which men venture capital in the hope of economic gain and enhancement of living standards.

### The Industrial Revolution

From the dawn of civilization down to the middle of the eighteenth century trade was the principal economic enterprise, first barter and then a gradual shifting to a cash nexus with the growth of banking and insurance. It is often overlooked that the Greeks in the last centuries before the Christian era were equally successful in trade and philosophy. Through the Middle Ages, commerce was a continual occupation of some of the population. Most emphasis in modern history teaching is perhaps placed on political and social practices in medieval history, but economic life was not restricted to manorial subsistence. Trade did flourish and towns grew. In fact, such words as burgher and bourgeoisie came from the fact that a class had grown through the Middle Ages into a city dwelling middle class living on the fruits of commerce.

In the seventeenth century dawned an Age of Reason, a scientific and questioning age, out of which practical mechanics developed a system of factory production of goods. During the eighteenth century and on up into the present a revolutionary economic change took place. All sorts of devices were invented for the manufacture of more and more diverse goods. The industrial revolution put the bulk of population into cities and employed them in factories. The whole of human life altered so markedly that now we are almost totally interdependent on each other because the division of labor has become so specialized that practically the whole purchasing public is employed in some phase of the productive machine that keeps on growing in size and technical complexity.

Coming down to recent history, the industrial revolution has now spread over the whole world, but there are still countries much less developed in this sense than others. Africa and the Far East are still comparatively non-industrial although their recent strides have been tremendous. Russia, since her revolution in 1918, has emerged from a totally unindustrialized rural nation of peasants and lords to become a contender for position among the leaders of the world. The Soviets profess to have done this as the result of their adoption of Marxist socialism or communism, but in reality their economic structure is fundamentally the same as any other except that it is controlled by a monolithic state and individual freedom of enterprise is almost completely curtailed. Basically, industrialization is the key to whatever gains in living levels the Russions have achieved. Despite their great gains they are still far behind the United States in achieving standards of production and consumption but their *rate* of increase is very significant. The total comparative amounts of coal and steel produced each year, if allocated in the same way as are those of the United States would yield a much higher level of consumer goods than is the case at present. Russian allocation of basic hard goods to defensive or other state projects effectively keeps them out of the consumer market. Therefore Russian people have fewer refrigerators and automobiles than Americans, but the Russian missile systems are just as good as or better than American counterparts.

**Comparative Levels of Living in Russia and the United States, 1958**

| Per Capita Annual Consumption | Russia | United States | Times Greater in United States |
|---|---|---|---|
| Automobiles | 0.0003 | 0.047 | 156.7 |
| Refrigerators | 0.0007 | 0.022 | 31.4 |
| Vacuum cleaners | 0.0006 | 0.021 | 35.0 |
| Washing machines | 0.0004 | 0.026 | 65.0 |
| Selected food items | | | |
| Butter (pounds) | 4.9 | 8.8 | 1.8 |
| Milk (pounds) | 332.2 | 940.5 | 2.8 |
| Sugar (pounds) | 38.1 | 96.3 | 2.5 |
| Meat (pounds) | 44.5 | 160.7 | 3.5 |
| Clothing and shelter | | | |
| Shoes (pairs) | 1.4 | 3.9 | 2.8 |
| Housing (square feet) | 51.7 | 344.5 | 6.7 |

Industrialized nations such as the United States or Russia must make choices in the allocation of their production, either to private consumption or to state enterprises. In Russia the allocations to state projects is greater, for a variety of reasons; national strength is of higher value to them than individual affluence, and the total amount of basic production is smaller. Therefore apparent levels of living, personal consumption indices such as the use of automobiles or washing machines, are much lower. It will be noticed that although consumption of food, shelter and clothing is also lower than in the United States, it is not significantly so. The items constituting differences in standards of living are in the amenity classification.

A different view is achieved when basic production of hard goods is compared with the same items in American industry. Coal and steel production in the Soviet is quite high, and still more impressive, capacity for such production is more nearly reached each year than it is in the United States. If the rate of increase of Russian production persists for a few more years, the Soviets can divert more of their total production to amenities if they so choose.

### Comparative Coal and Steel Production in Russia and the United States, 1959

| Per Capita Annual Consumption | Russia | United States |
|---|---|---|
| Steel | .317 tons | .517 tons |
| Coal | 2.7 tons | 2.4 tons |
| Total Production 1959 | | |
| Steel | 66,009,800 tons | 93,000,000 tons |
| Coal and lignite | 558,052,800 tons | 432,000,000 tons |

Other significant factors in the analysis of these figures are that United States steel production represents only about half of current capacity, while Russian production is equal to Russian capacity. Further, total Russian industrial production is increasing at about 11 per cent per year, causing a faster Russian growth in gross national product than can be claimed by the United States.

As has been said, Soviet production in practically all items is less in gross amount and in per capita amount than American industrial output. However, the rate of gain is greater in Russia, and the power of the monolithic state to make national allocations of materials can be applied directly and rapidly in most matters. The chief deterrent to Soviet superiority in industrial production is the undeniable fact that agricultural output necessary for maintenance of minimum standards still requires about one-half of the Russian labor force. For the same purposes in the United States only 8 per cent of the labor force is required.[7]

### Economic Development

World history of the current moment is most keenly concerned with economic development. Every nation is classified according to its degree of development in industrial production. "Underdeveloped" nations receive the focus of international attention in the struggle between the polarized forces of East and West. In Asia and Africa the important theme is economic development—how "to escape from the misery and poverty which are the common settings of all the new locales of history."[8] There is a great deal to be known about the actual process of growth from agrarian dependence to industrial economic strength.

Most of the underdeveloped areas of the world are tied securely to an agricultural system of production. The great emphasis and the major part of productive energy has to be devoted to furnishing enough food so that the population can subsist. Little labor and practically no capital are left over for expansion of industry. There seem to be at least two prerequisites to the initiation of economic development: capital and specialization of labor. Economic theory, from the time of Adam Smith, has furnished classical patterns for the utilization of both these things. However, it is also necessary to establish a general predisposition, a social precondition to industrialization, also. Sociologists find that role and status sometimes govern the degree of labor specialization that is considered desirable. In addition, a standard of living model and capacity must be established in an underdeveloped area. In other words, there must be a local awareness of the desirability for economic development utilizing economic theory and modern economic activity.

China is one of the best examples of what may happen in the first stages of industrialization. China has been traditionally an agricultural economy for thousands of years. Just in the last ten years, by

[7] For further statistics see *Economic Almanac* (The Conference Board, New York), annual, and for analysis of the problem see Robert W. Campbell, *Soviet Economic Power* (Houghton Mifflin, Boston, 1960).

[8] See Robert L. Heilbroner, "The Literature of Development," *Harper's* (May, 1961), p. 88. He says that the best introduction to the problem is Eugene R. Black, *The Diplomacy of Economic Development* (Harvard University Press, 1961), by the head of the World Bank.

political fiat and with unilateral control of people and resources, the Chinese government has undertaken widespread industrialization of the productive output of the country. The impetus was first given in the form of a promise of more equitable distribution of *land,* but this was not really the important thing. It lulled the laborers and gave a political unity to the Chinese effort to outstrip some parts of the West. *Some* land for every peasant, in contrast to no land for the masses, constituted a rise in living standard for many millions. In order to pay for the process, expropriation of existing land and other wealth went some of the way, and there was a little period of fancied affluence that allowed the Communists to shift at least some of the labor force to industrial production. What industrialization that has already taken place in China has not raised the standard of living very much, but specialization of labor has begun, and the role of workers is being transformed into the necessary pattern for industrial production. Capital is harder to acquire than it was to shift the role of workers. Here it has been necessary to use makeshifts, such as very small, hand operated manufacturing units, the backyard smelting furnace and manpower transport for interchange of items in the productive machine. The shortage of capital in all underdeveloped areas is acute, and international political considerations always color the needs and availability of investment funds from outside the countries in question. For example, how could United States investment funds find their way into Red China? Would it be desirable if possible?

The whole problem of economic development is extremely complicated and fraught with political and social difficulties. The Aswan Dam in Egypt, very necessary to the development of the Nile Valley, not only for the benefit of Egyptians but also for the security of the rest of the world, required the expenditure of capital far in excess of anything that could be obtained in Egypt. The United States and the West in general found itself engaged in an international political struggle with Russia for the right to help finance the dam. The United States is said to have lost in the contest, but Egypt is going to have the dam. At what expense to the security of the world was this investment made?

In essence, the same problem exists in every underdeveloped nation in Africa, Asia and South America. It is generally agreed that economic development needs to take place. It is generally known that capital is required and that industrialization ought to be the goal, along with the necessary specialization of labor. What would be the best political means of achieving the desired result has not been agreed upon, and of necessity, therefore, the ideological forces of East and West are pitted in direct opposition in every area of the world which is agricultural but which aspires to a higher standard of living.

Avowedly, economic development is a difficult subject for anyone, but at least an introduction to the problem may be accomplished in high school. The first economic information requisite to understanding is some idea of comparative standards of living in the industrial and underdeveloped portions of the world. Fundamental comparisons may be made between per capita income and purchasing power, for instance, in Ghana and in the United States. Gross national products can be compared for all of the nations in question. This kind of information will not insure understanding of the need for economic development, but it can serve as a starting point.

### Economic Theory

Just as the industrial revolution was getting under way, and by the same token, just as commerce was giving way to manufacturing as the dominant economic mode in the Western world, Adam Smith produced his monumental *Wealth of Nations*. Published in 1776, this book purported to be the classic statement of economic theory and principles under the system of mercantilism. Smith really, however, illustrated the concept of *fin de siècle*, in which the finest flowering of an age comes just as the plant withers. His main emphasis was on the economic matters involved in world trade and the relationship of national strength to economic power. He did, however, give a foundation for the development of a classical economics which maintained its vogue into the twentieth century. Based on Adam Smith's careful study of economic factors, David Ricardo, James Mill (John Stuart Mill's father) and Jeremy Bentham established the first school of classical economists at the start of the nineteenth century. Ricardo enunciated the various economic laws that are still mentioned: supply and demand, diminishing return and economic rent. These ideas were put into their final classical form by John Stuart Mill in the middle of the century.

Classical economics, mainly concerned with the belief that natural laws govern economic life, combined with the Malthusian theory that the world would become overpopulated unless checked and the neo-Darwinian ideas that social behavior followed the patterns of biological survival, dominated thinking on both sides of the Atlantic until well into the twentieth century. In United States history of the nineteenth century, the figure of the captain of industry is famous indeed. John

D. Rockefeller, Andrew Carnegie and J. Pierpont Morgan are the most enduring representatives of the group of believers in rugged individualism and the survival of the fittest in the economic struggle.[9]

Alfred Marshall in England and Richard T. Ely in the United States gave economic texts to high school and college at the opening of the twentieth century embodying the essence of the classical economics. The study of economics became a respectable school and college offering, but the economic theory thus presented failed to answer the questions posed by recurring depressions and by the persistent growth of labor unions. Legislation failed equally to settle these foreboding dangers to social equilibrium. Classical economic theory had been devised for a society at a certain stage in the industrial revolution and in terms of a static population and economy. Those were not the conditions at the end of the first quarter of the present century. Depression followed boom in dismal recurrence until the Great Depression of 1929. After several years of continued depression something besides reliance on natural laws that did not operate had to be the recourse of at least the Western nations.

Some of them turned to political nostrums, as in Germany and Italy, and handed over total control to dictators. In Britain and the United States other measures proved at least equal to the task of survival and the Roosevelt New Deal along with England's Labour Party produced data for the expression of a new economics. In 1936 John Maynard Keynes, Lord Keynes, theorized that to make the classical economic principles operate, governments must exert a great deal of forceful interference in the natural economic workings. Providence could not be relied on to supply full employment and a rising standard of living which was hopefully expected for at least some segments of society at the beginning of the nineteenth century. Keynes propounded that direct government investment must supplement inadequate private capital to produce desirable economic and social results. As in the New Deal measures taken in the 1930's, if full employment could not be achieved by private industry, then the government must furnish it. Since that time Keynesian policies have been adopted by most governments. Social security, old age insurance, socialized services to workers, paid vacations, trade and securities control—in short, "cradle to grave" security for everyone—underwritten by the state and paid for out of taxes, came about largely as the result of increasing

[9] See *Democracy and the Gospel of Wealth* and *John D. Rockefeller: Robber Baron or Industrial Statesman,* Amherst Problems in American Civilization (Heath, Boston, 1949). These can be used in advanced high school courses.

government responsibility for the economy. Public investment accompanied by guaranteed security appeared to be the only way in which an expanding economy could be assured with full employment and a rising standard of living for everyone.

These ideas have by no means been accepted by everyone, not all economists agree, but it is clear that the public segment of the economy has produced results so deeply imbedded in our political and social life that they will not easily be eradicated even if we decide they ought to be. Old age security, for example, is not only a guarantee to the elderly that they will not starve, but it also keeps them out of the labor market which must be left open to the proportionately shrinking age group between 20 and 65. A long period of preparation and training and retirement from work at an early age and secure enjoyment of a long old age are now part of the expectation of American youth. It is always interesting to ask a class of high school seniors what they expect to do when they retire, and if they expect their children to support them after they quit working.

It is a long and tortuous cycle from the position of the early classical economists to the present. Their theory was always a projection into an ideal future, never really applying to the actual conditions prevailing at the genesis of the industrial revolution. Now, it can be speculated that, for the first time, full employment as a precondition for classical analysis has a possibility of becoming a reality. Human struggle is the essence of history and one of the most fruitful struggles of modern times has been to find a way to make everyone economically secure if not affluent.

One way to get at an understanding of the struggle and of the evolution of economic theory and practice, not the easiest but perhaps the most stimulating, is by means of biographical study of the figures involved from Adam Smith through John Stuart Mill to Lord Keynes and the modern organization man. There are suitable high school biographies of at least some of the figures and there are certainly materials that can be read to classes by the teacher which could be employed very usefully as adjuncts to any course in modern history.

### 3. Consumer Education

A majority of students in high school do not elect economics. Because of this, modern high schools have instituted courses in problems of various kinds, and usually there is one part of such courses devoted to problems of economic life of the individual—consumer education.

Regardless of the extent of anyone's knowledge, he must become a member of the vast army of economic consumers. Most of his income will be spent nearly as fast as he acquires it, and it would seem reasonable that all high school graduates should know the best ways in which to spend their money in order to further private happiness and public policy.

Consumer economics ought to occupy some place in the secondary curriculum, whether it be in an economics course or as a sequence of units in a problems course, or in still some other way. In order to achieve competent citizenship all persons should know the principles of budgeting income, providing security for their families and for their old age, how to judge and choose various products of industry that they consume, and the means of investment including the stock market, real estate, insurance and cash saving. These things can be taught in social studies courses incidentally to the main subject of investigation. In economics this becomes merely the application of theoretic knowledge to the everyday problems of family living.

There is currently a certain generalized standard of living enjoyed by the "average" or ordinary urban family. It is somewhat higher than the equivalent at any time in the past, partly due to increased values and prices, including wages, and partly to the increased and improved products from the great industrial machine of modern capitalism. In any case, this average is the usual base for budgeting income, whatever it happens to be from year to year. At present, for a city family of four, according to the Labor Department Bureau of Labor Statistics, about $6,000 annually is required to pay for a modest but adequate version of the normal standard of consumption. Incidentally, such "average" families usually have incomes ranging from $7,000 to $7,500 a year. These figures represent a forty per cent increase between 1951 and 1960, and well over half of the increase in expense is due to an enhanced standard of living.[10]

Facts of this kind are understandable to high school students and have great significance and interest when related to total national income, the gross national product and the national debt. There is also a relationship here with the problem facing every young person in choosing a career.

Since the beginning of the twentieth century social science has become so actively incorporated into daily living and the activities of government that all sorts of data are available concerning living expenses, stock market fluctuation, national and private debt and

[10] Associated Press, Washington, D.C., August 25, 1960.

credit, commodity costs and buying habits. People now can learn very quickly about what others do in these respects and the results of such knowledge are sometimes far-reaching and definitive in future developments in consumer economics. Societies tend to set patterns of spending (as well as other activities) and they tend to continue them only so long as they remain generally satisfying. With quick communication and much social scientific information, buying and consuming patterns shift rather rapidly. Thus it is important for high school students to learn as much applied economics as they can to get the most out of their future earnings.

In illustration of the above phenomenon, although personal incomes are steadily rising (faster than basic subsistence costs) more money is going into savings and less into large items of consumption such as automobiles and major appliances for the household. For example, the immediate success of foreign and American compact cars is directly attributable to their lower prices and more economical operation. People have been willing to forego luxury and ostentation in favor of greater saving. The same thing is generally true of a number of other items such as clothing and houses, although Americans are always attracted by the new and/or improved versions of the old. We have been accused of living in a "gadget civilization." We are willing to pay more and more for better packaged and more completely prepared foods than was ever the case before.[11]

In view of these things consumer education in high school should consist basically of two things: budgeting and personal security. Related to budgeting, as another social problem, is the matter of choosing a career and estimating lifetime income.

I. Budgeting
   A. Expenditures                                         Income
      1. Food
      2. Clothing
      3. Housing (rent)
      4. Medical service
      5. Entertainment and travel
      6. Saving for security and contingencies
         a. Emergencies
         b. Education
         c. Security
         d. Taxes

[11] Sam Dawson, business news analyst, Associated Press, New York, August 27, 1960.

B. Long and Short Term Spending      Increases in Income
1. Daily, weekly and monthly
2. Annual expenses (taxes, insurance, etc.)
3. Recurring capital outlay (house, car, clothing)
4. Non-recurring expenses (births, funerals, investments)

The last three items entail a program of saving on a regular basis and must be incorporated into the budget. Saving is the hardest item to budget and the hardest item to control in actual application of the budget. In fact, it might be guessed that a majority of failing marriages founder on some facet of that problem. It is often very difficult to forego an immediate expenditure in favor of saving for the proverbial "rainy day." Precisely because of the difficulties inherent in saving to pay taxes the federal government has devised the system of salary withholding from each worker's pay check a proportionate amount of his annual estimated income tax. For the many other items that a family has to save for, the budget provides the plan for doing the same thing.

II. Personal Security      Anticipated Income
  A. Short Term Security      and
1. Cash reserve      Career Planning
2. Health insurance
3. Immediate risk insurance
4. Installment buying
  B. Long Term Security
1. Life insurance
2. Retirement and social security
3. Real estate purchase and property improvement
4. Education

Budgeting is the process of balancing income with anticipated expenditure, taking into consideration all of the elements of earning and maintaining a standard of living commensurate with national norms. In a high school class an interesting exercise might be to assign as a term project to each student the preparation of a budget for the "average" family of four. Each student could expand on the skeletal outline provided above to include all of the small specific items that might fit into each of the categories. At the same time class exercises could be conducted investigating the intricacies of product analysis and choice, the principles and extent of insurance and investment possibilities.

For example, a class might go through the method used by product

analysis foundations such as Consumers Research in deciding what
is the best automobile for the money in a given year. A particular
problem might be posed in the following terms: Prepare two different
budgets for a family of four based on a salary of $6,000 with one wage
earner and an income of $9,000 with both the mother and father
working at steady jobs. What car or cars should be purchased? Obviously, a good many things would have to be taken into account, such
as the types of jobs, location of the family home, taste and many
others.

In the complex modern economy in which we live insurance has
become the most important single factor in individual security and
therefore of great significance in budgeting. In a time past when
people lived on farms or in a subsistence situation there was little
risk and slight dislocation in the event of death. Little money was
used in the normal course of events and a relatively simple reallocation
of duties was the chief necessity even in the case of a young father's
accidental death. Now it is very different. Much larger incomes are
the rule, the standard of living is greatly increased and most of the
things used in modern living are produced by someone other than
the consumer and therefore require purchase in cash or short term
credit. The loss of a major wage earner in the modern family is severely
dislocating unless sufficient insurance is available. Recently this
has even extended into health insurance against loss of income through
relatively short periods of unemployment.

Since 1933 a kind of super insurance has come into being, social
security, which tends to become very far-reaching and more important than private insurance, but it is really, in effect, an extension of
the system of private insurance in this industrialized age. In any case,
students in high school should learn what they can about insurance
of all types, of sharing the risk of modern living. The cost of insurance
thus becomes an important part of budgeting income, and the benefits
of insurance are part of the increased standard of living enjoyed by
modern society.

#### 4. Bibliographies of Content and Method

CLASSICS IN ECONOMICS

John R. Commons, *A Documentary History of American Industrial Society,* 11 vols.
(Arthur H. Clark, Cleveland, 1910–1911), reprinted (Russell and Russell,
New York, 1958), is the only comprehensive American book on the subject.
It is based on classical economics, but it is primarily an exhaustive study of
what actually took place. Commons, *History of Labor in the United States*

(1918) and Richard T. Ely, *Outlines of Economics* (1923) were for nearly half a century the chief texts used in American schools.

Henry George, *Progress and Poverty* (1886), numerous later editions, presents an American version of the physiocratic conception that all wealth stems from the land. George advocated a single tax on land.

Thomas Hobbes, *Leviathan* (1651), reprinted in many editions, such as Everyman's Library (1937) and Oxford (1946), along with John Locke's ideas concerning natural rights presents the basis for mercantilistic economics at the beginning of the classical tradition.

*Marx on Economics*, edited by Robert Freedman (Harvest Books, Harcourt, Brace, New York, 1961), is a paperback selection of Marx's economic ideas. It is much easier to read than the repetitive *Capital*.

John Stuart Mill, *Principles of Political Economy* (1848), new impression (Longmans, Green, New York, 1920), is the definitive form of classical economics as it evolved by the middle of the nineteenth century. Mill influenced everyone subsequent, down to the time of Lord Keynes.

Adam Smith, *The Wealth of Nations* (1776), reprinted in Modern Library edition (Random House, New York, 1937), is perhaps the most important single book in the development of economic theory in the modern world.

Richard Henry Tawney, *Religion and the Rise of Capitalism* (1926), available in paperback (Mentor, New York, 1953), traces the growth of the profit system and the relationship to religious morality. Tawney is as much a sociologist as he is an economist.

Thorstein Veblen, *The Theory of the Leisure Class* (1899). Because "every brash, upcoming generation should discover Veblen, and most complacent adults need to rediscover him," this book appears in a cheap edition (Mentor, New York, 1953).

## ECONOMIC THEORY AND APPLICATION

William H. Beveridge, *Full Employment in a Free Society* (Norton, New York, 1945), although applying to Great Britain, deals with modern problems of economics in terms of the neo-classical synthesis.

Peter F. Drucker, *Concept of the Corporation* (Day, New York, 1946), describes the theory of big business organization as it applies to American economy.

Paul T. Ellsworth, *The International Economy: Its Structure and Operation* (Macmillan, New York, 1950), is mainly descriptive.

Gunnar Myrdahl, *The International Economy* (Harper, New York, 1959), makes an appeal for a truly world economy.

John Maynard Keynes, *The General Theory of Employment, Interest and Money* (Harcourt, Brace, New York, 1936), is the most revolutionary book on economics since the nineteenth century. Keynes' ideas form the basis of nearly all modern economic thinking.

Alfred Marshall, *Elements of Economics* (1892) and *Principles of Economics* (Macmillan, London, 1935), 8th ed. reprinted (1949), were written by the last great economist before Keynes. He is still considered by some to be superior in his theoretic formulations, but the currents of inflation and the struggle for full employment have obscured the classical tradition.

Wilbert E. Moore, *Economy and Society* (Doubleday, New York, 1955), is a very simple yet penetrating treatment of the essentials of social economics.

Paul A. Samuelson, *Economics: An Introductory Analysis* (McGraw-Hill, New York, 1961), 5th ed., is the most extensively used textbook in college classes. It stresses a national income approach.

Joseph A. Schumpeter, *Capitalism, Socialism and Democracy* (Harper, New York, 1942), attempts a synthesis of the holdings of socialism and democracy in regard to economics.

## HISTORY OF ECONOMICS

Robert Heilbroner, *The Worldly Philosophers* (Simon and Schuster), is a short paperback giving the nub of content of the great philosophical thinkers in the field of economics and placing them in their historical perspective.

J. Bronowski and Bruce Mazlish, *The Western Intellectual Tradition* (Harper, New York, 1960), is actually in the field of intellectual history, but it does a very fine job of weaving the economic strands into the general pattern of evolving philosophy and organization in the Western World.

*Gateway to the Social Sciences,* edited by Arthur W. Thompson, rev. ed. (Holt, Rinehart and Winston, New York, 1959), especially those sections dealing with "The Economic Institutions," is helpful in getting various points of view on the historical evolution of economic theory.

## ECONOMIC HISTORY

G. D. H. Cole, *Introduction to Economic History* (Macmillan, London, 1952), deals with Europe.

Harold Underwood Faulkner, *Economic History of the United States* (Macmillan, New York), current paperback, is an adequate survey of the field which can also be used in high school. It is based on his *American Economic History* (Harper, New York, 1960), rev. ed., a textbook.

## CONSUMER EDUCATION

Orin E. Burley, *The Consumer's Cooperative as a Distributive Agency* (McGraw-Hill, New York, 1939), is a readable and factual investigation of cooperatives. Students can use it.

Paul D. Converse and Harvey W. Huegy, *The Elements of Marketing* (Prentice-Hall, New York, 1958), 6th ed., is a text in marketing, a branch of economics, but it can be used to illustrate consumer education in high school. A good reference.

Leland J. Gordon, *Economics for Consumers* (American, New York, 1958), 3rd ed., takes the consumers' position and treats abuses as well as positive practices in production that purchasers must know. The section on insurance is quite adequate. Useful as a text for high school.

## TEACHING METHODS AND CURRICULUM SUGGESTIONS IN CONSUMER EDUCATION

Gladys Bahr, "Consumer Education: Do Students Need It?" *Educational Leadership* (March, 1950), pp. 411–415.

*Journal of Educational Sociology,* issue on "Economic Education," edited by G. Derwood Baker (March, 1950).

Sherman E. Gunderson, "Weakness of Current Economic Education," *Social Education* (January, 1956), pp. 15–18.

Henry Harap and Ray G. Price, "Preparation of Teachers of Consumer Education," *Educational Record* (October, 1949), pp. 458–464.

*Improving Economic Understanding in Public Schools* (Committee for Economic Development, New York, 1950).

*Social Education,* issue on "Economic Education" (November, 1953).

GENERAL METHODS IN TEACHING ECONOMICS

G. Derwood Baker, "Educating Citizens for Economic Effectiveness, 1960–1980," in *Citizenship and a Free Society: Education for the Future,* Thirtieth Yearbook of the National Council for the Social Studies (Washington, D.C., 1960), pp. 117–139, contains much material and many suggestions for procedures.

*Economic Education,* edited by Harold F. Clark, Eleventh Yearbook of the National Council for the Social Studies (Washington, D.C., 1940).

M. L. Frankel, *How to Cooperate with Community Agencies,* National Council for the Social Studies How to Do It Series, No. 17 (Washington, D.C., 1954), is helpful in discovering how to go about getting help from outside the school, in economics as well as other fields.

Kenneth A. Fuller, "Using Graphs," *Social Education* (October, 1953), pp. 268–270.

John D. Garwood, "Uneconomic Teaching in Economics," *Social Studies* (April, 1955), pp. 128–130.

Thomas J. Hailstones, "The Right-to-Work Laws: A Changing Attitude Toward Labor," *Social Studies* (November, 1956), pp. 260–261.

Charles W. Marrifield, "Economic Competence: New Frontier in Civic Education," *Social Education* (February, 1959), pp. 71–74.

Frank Meyer, "The Tax Court of the United States," *Social Studies* (December, 1954), pp. 283–286, is an illustration of the kind of topic in economics that can be used to extend the scope of history instruction.

Mack Ryan, "The Stock Market in the Classroom," *Social Education* (December, 1955), p. 365.

Max Seham, "Medical Economics in the United States," *Social Education* (December, 1954), pp. 348–352.

Lawrence F. Pisani, "Overpopulation and Poverty," *Social Studies* (November, 1956), pp. 247–249.

Daniel E. Stines, "The Role of Private Investment in Latin America," *Social Education* (November, 1958), pp. 342–344.

Paul P. Vouras, "The Soviet Iron and Steel Industry," *Social Studies* (November, 1955), pp. 260–263, is an example of material that can be used to help implant a world view of economics.

Mary Margaret Scobey, "Industrial Field Trips," *Social Education* (April, 1955), pp. 161–162.

*The Teaching of Elementary Economics,* edited by Kenyon A. Knopf and James

H. Stauss (Holt, Rinehart and Winston, New York, 1960), is the report on the Conference on the Teaching of Elementary Economics, Merrill Center, 1958. It contains bibliographical material and pointers particularly helpful in teaching gifted children.

## HIGH SCHOOL TEXTS

Sol Holt, *Economics and You* (Scribner's, New York, 1962), is concerned with applied economics.

Jacob Klein and Woolf Colvin, *Economic Problems of Today* (Lyons and Carnahan, New York, 1959), is a recent popular text.

Richard W. Lindholm and Paul Driscoll, *Our American Economy* (Harcourt, Brace, New York, 1959), is a Keynesian view written at appropriate high school level.

Augustus H. Smith, *Economics for Our Times* (McGraw-Hill, New York, 1959), has the best section on consumer economics.

## SUPPLEMENTARY MATERIALS

Committee for Economic Development, New York, publishes many timely items such as *Soviet Progress vs. American Enterprise* (1958).

The Conference Board, 247 Park Avenue, New York 17, furnishes a series of charts, Road Maps of Industry, which are useful.

The Education Department, National Association of Manufacturers, 2 East Forty-eighth Street, New York 17, furnishes free to teachers a great deal of teaching material including units of instruction, special papers stating the views of management and numerous very valuable charts and graphs that can be used in the classroom. This is naturally not the best place to get information concerning labor, but for data on the condition of American business it is unsurpassed.

Nearly every major industry has an educational service, supplying information and teaching suggestions concerning their products. Some of them are very sound, such as *Rubber* (American Education Publications, Columbus, Ohio, n.d.), or *The Story of Tea* (American Education Press, Columbus, Ohio, 1948).

Joint Council on Economic Education, 2 West Forty-sixth Street, New York 36, has available for the asking curriculum materials and resource units for secondary school economics study.

Public Affairs Pamphlet published by the Public Affairs Committee, New York, embrace all sorts of topics and are priced at twenty-five cents each. Typical titles that might have some application in economics are Richard Neuberger, *Our National Resources and Their Conservation* and Jack Barbash, *The Labor Movement in the United States*.

## 5. Suggested Activities for Further Study

1. Prepare a list of basic terms in economics that a high school class should know.

2. Draw up a list of biographies that might supplement a course in economics.

3. Assume that high school students will have no formal instruction in eco-

nomics, but that they will all have a course in United States history. What topics of economic significance should be incorporated into the history instruction, and as a result, what history must be left out?

4. In the United States, at any given time, how is it determined what full employment means? How many people must this be, for example, in 1960, with a total population of 180,000,000? Must it always be the same for that population?

5. Which is best for high school social studies: to teach economics separately or as part of the other courses such as history or geography?

# 13
# Teaching social justice: problems

A hundred years are but a moment of sleep.
Translation from the Chinese, 822 A.D.

## 1. World Problems

Of all the secondary social studies, world history or the history of civilization is the most difficult to present. It is considered to be essential to any understanding of the modern world and its problems, but it also has proved too large a bite for a single year, and it always lacks contemporaneity if it includes enough coverage. History of civilization shows up regularly twice from grades nine through fourteen, and each time it receives similar reactions: the students cannot cover the necessary material, chronologically they rarely get anywhere near the present, and prerequisite geographic knowledge is often sketchy or lacking altogether.[1]

Knowledge of world history is absolutely essential to the education of modern man, but it is probably best covered in a more leisurely fashion than that represented by the traditional attempt. The objective is to make students aware of their heritage as it impinges upon the present, and to make possible for them as citizens to contribute appropriately to that heritage for the future. The tenth grade world history outline is usually a selection of outstanding institutional developments in Western civilization intended to anticipate amplification of the whole subject of civilization after graduation whether the student goes to college or not.

[1] Alex Weingrod, "Anthropology and the Social Studies," *Social Education* (January, 1956); J. Russell Smith, "Geography and World History," *Social Education* (May, 1957); Joe Park, "Trends in Social Studies: Grade 13 and 14." *Social Education* (April, 1955).

In the last few years, since the method of teaching world history has been unsatisfactory and inadequate when it is presented only in the ninth or tenth grade, many states have adopted another course designed to expand the subject and correct some of the defects mentioned above. Contemporary world history, geography and problems —the course name of one such adoption—implies knowledge of the cultural descent, areal significance, and recognition of debatable hypotheses in regard to global situations.[2] Such a concept is meant to give to students an opportunity to work toward a method of problem solution utilizing the general and specialized knowledge of the social sciences. Perforce, it must be based upon some familiarity with the historical derivation of those problems while it supplements and prepares for future learning in the progress of civilization.

Although this section is devoted to world problems, the problems approach may be applied to any of the social studies: world history, United States history, problems of American democracy, contemporary social problems, and many other variants. Any subject matter dealing with human relationships in a certain environment can be organized into problems to be analyzed; it is merely a matter of choice of objectives and techniques.

There is no prescribed, specific method for achievement of the general aim. Choice of immediate objectives will determine the type of problem to be studied. The overall objectives of any course in world problems are twofold: improvement of general understanding of the world and its civilization, and increased ability in critical thinking. The first one is prerequisite to the second, and therefore more important; although critical thought is more far-reaching as an educational aim it is impossible to achieve if there is nothing to think about. The one is knowledge and the other is technique. Sheer technique is pragmatically worthless without content, but content alone is only vacuum-packed facts which are possibly interesting but not useful until applied in the framework of an identifiable process. Critical comparison, or scientific methodology in deriving objective values (as techniques) are worthless without content (facts). The assumption must be made that there is a relationship between knowledge and the desired outcome of learning a process of thought; therefore the immediate objectives of study of a problem will be, first, to learn as much as possible about the subject, and second, to apply this content in a systematic and scientific way to the end of critical thought. Assuming the problem approach, there are two categories of topics

[2] Washington, Iowa and Michigan presently have such requirements.

available. One might be called problems that have confronted man since he first emerged as a civilized being, such as land, people, technology, institutional changes, and international relations. Such broad subjects would have to be redefined in more specific, disciplined form, and would probably require a high degree of specialization in several fields on the part of the teacher as well as a student body selected for high intellectual aptitude. The advantage in this type of selection is its flexibility and adaptability to the needs of accelerated students.

From the standpoints of geography, sociology, anthropology, history, political science and economics the following arrangement of problems and subtopics might be derived:

## GENERAL PROBLEMS

   I. Can contemporary man organize one political world?
      A. Political boundaries in international relations
      B. To what extent does political unity depend upon economic unity?
      C. Cultural unity?
      D. Who owns the oceans?
      E. Ancient Rome's shadow as a stimulant and deterrent
      F. Linguistic barriers
  II. Bases of National Power
      A. Natural resources and national strength
      B. Cultural bases of national strength
      C. Location as a factor of national strength
      D. Population and national power
      E. Technology as a factor in national power
      F. Nationalism as a singular product of the modern world
 III. Can man continue to feed himself?
      A. What is population pressure?
      B. How can food production be increased?
      C. Does poor land have to breed poor people?
      D. Malthus and Neo-Malthusianism
 IV. Socialism versus individual enterprise
      A. What does history show?
      B. How is economic fact or fancy involved?
      C. USA versus USSR
      D. Western economic theory under the impact of modern technology

V. The Doctrine of Progress
  A. What is the nature of man, culture, civilization?
  B. How does physical evolution affect world problems?

## References for Teachers and Young Adults in Regard to General World Problems

As a humble substitute for the learning of the ages which would be the optimum reference for the solution of any problem in the modern world, here is a very small list of practical and applicable suggestions.

First of all, it is essential to be cognizant of the current happenings in a rapidly changing world. There is a plethora of daily newspapers in English. Among those foremost in circulation and news coverage are the *London Times,* the *New York Times,* the *Washington Post,* and the *Christian Science Monitor.* These are supplemented by daily radio broadcasts on all the major networks and summarized in weekly newsmagazines such as *Time, Newsweek,* and *U.S. News and World Report,* or, more facetiously in *The New Yorker* or *Punch.* For a more immature or graphically oriented audience *Life* magazine furnishes much the same coverage while *National Geographic Magazine* selectively illustrates certain points of interest in world problems.

Geographic knowledge is essential to any attempt to unravel the problems of the world. Atlases too numerous to mention exist. Specifically, as a shortcut, there are three paper bound items: *Hammond's Modern World Atlas* (C. S. Hammond, New York, 1955), *American Historical Atlas* (C. S. Hammond, New York, n.d.), (both retail at 59¢ each), and Breasted, Huth, Harding, *European History Atlas* (Nenoyer-Geppert, Chicago, 1947).

Modern technology and development of the capitalist system have produced a unique phenomenon: the paper backed book. A great deal of the world's knowledge is now available in that form. The following ten books are suggested as a guide to the mastery of basic knowledge needed in identifying and illustrating world problems:

Fred Hoyle, *The Nature of the Universe* (Signet).
Ruth Benedict, *Patterns of Culture* (Mentor).
Gordon V. Childe, *What Happened in History* (Penguin).
Bronislav Malinowski, *Magic, Science and Religion* (Doubleday).
Richard Henry Tawney, *Religion and the Rise of Capitalism* (Pocketbooks).
Ortega y Gasset, *Revolt of the Masses* (Pocketbooks).
Ritchie Calder, *Science in Our Lives* (Signet).
Alfred North Whitehead, *Science and the Modern World* (Mentor).

George Soule, *Introduction to Economic Science* (Pocketbooks).

J. B. Bury, *The Idea of Progress* (Dover).

In addition, ranging from whimsy to chronology, one may read these important recent books:

Walter Blumenthall, *Rendezvous with Chance* (Exposition Press, New York, 1954); whimsy.

A. A. Berle, Jr., *The Twentieth Century Capitalist Revolution* (Harcourt, Brace, New York, 1954).

Louis L. Snyder, *The World in the Twentieth Century* (Van Nostrand, New York, 1955).

William Ebenstein, *Today's Isms* (Prentice-Hall, New York, 1958), 2nd ed.

*An Encyclopedia of World History*, edited by William L. Langer (Houghton Mifflin, Boston, 1948); chronology.

The other type of problem selection, better adapted to the needs of average students and more closely oriented to the smaller specialization of most teachers, consists of topics conceived spatially, historically, or for reasons of cogency at the present time. Here one might find subjects such as nationalism, capitalism, and world organization; or, areal studies of underdeveloped lands, the Mohammedan world, colonialism in Africa, Asia for the Asians, comparative world sea power, Latin-American democracy, modern communication in a shrinking world, or nuclear weapons in military preparedness. The list of topics is almost inexhaustible, depending upon the imagination, ability and training of students and teacher.

## 2. Specific Problems

A unit might be evolved around the problem of imperialism in an underdeveloped area, Southeast Asia, as an example. First of all it would be desirable to dwell on certain concepts and definitions necessary to an understanding of such a topic.

Nationalism is perhaps the strongest international force in the world at present, and it is basic to all world problems. How did it come about? Two definitions, germane to such study, are first needed: (1) nation—an area with a recognized boundary often the same as natural and physical barriers to invasion, and with a people having a common purpose and organization, usually with a common language; (2) sovereignty—permanent unquestioned authority, stemming from tribal assignment of temporary power in time of war or emergency. The next step in development can usually be seen in the personal relationship of the monarch or emperor to a settled agricultural group, such as that of the Angevin Empire under Henry II.

Sovereignty in the modern world can be traced historically from very early times. Greek city states had their tyrants. The Roman empire had its unlimited *imperium*. Possibly the first modern European nationalistic sovereignty is identifiable with the attempt of France in 1499, to incorporate French-speaking people in northern Italy into the French state. The wave of nationalism in modern Europe definitely rose after 1485, in England with Henry VII and Henry VIII, in France with Francis I, in Spain with Emperor Charles V of the Holy Roman Empire. Anachronistic and rigid sovereignties, in contrast to those listed, still persisted in the Hapsburg Austrian Empire and the Ottoman Empire. Both of these retained almost their original entity down to World War I.

The national self-consciousness thus begun (later called nationalism) was joined with three other forces. (1) An economic revolution came about which has produced an approximate one per cent per year price index inflation since 1500. (2) The Protestant Reformation and the Catholic Counter Reformation marked the beginning of the sixteenth century, and, among other things, encouraged development of the modern business ethic. (3) A spirit of adventure, the feeling of the Renaissance, swept over the West, and led to the voyages of discovery and the opening of the New World. The natural outgrowth of these forces was accretion of colonial dependencies around the established national states of Europe, thus forming the imperialism of the 17th century, and growing into the "old colonial system" of the 18th. This broke down and flourished again in the 19th century, to dwindle in the 20th. Portugal and Spain entered the field first, followed by England and France. With the Treaty of Paris, 1783, the United States won its own sovereignty and gradually became a contender for imperial stakes. Along with Manifest Destiny in North America, the Latin dependencies in South America sought and achieved sovereignty. General identification of nationalism, colonialism and imperialism in the modern sense began to take shape.

Modern imperialism began about 1800 with Great Britain in India, Singapore and Hong Kong; with France in North Africa and Indochina; with Germany, Italy, Japan and the United States toward the end of the century. After the United States seized the Philippines in 1898, out of the wreckage of the Spanish empire, the doctrine of the "white man's burden" grew, and responsibility to the "little brown brothers" became a slogan of imperialism. A real sense of responsibility to underdeveloped areas and peoples finally began to emerge in the 20th century.

Growing democratic institutions in England, France and the United States permeated the colonial areas. Territorial status came to Hawaii and Puerto Rico. The Philippines were promised independence. Libertarian ideas even penetrated such as absolutist state as Siam, never subjected to colonial rule, and in 1933 she became a constitutional monarchy.

With the decline of colonialism at the time of World War II, many new national states grew up out of the ashes of the older empires. In Asia there were India, Pakistan, Burma, Indonesia, North and South Vietnam, Cambodia, Laos, the Philippine Republic and others. The "White Man's Burden" has now been supplanted by "Asia for the Asians." There has been a great deal of recrimination and confusion between democracy and imperialism. The United States, Great Britain and France (democracies), Russia and China (Communist dictatorships) all stress anti-imperialism, at the same time accusing each other of colonial imperialism and exploitation of peoples. In truth, the new Asian nations tend to follow the patterns of nationalistic jealousy of their sovereignty that were developed in modern Europe after 1500.

In view of international Communism as a world movement, there are particular problems in Asia. For example, there are two Chinas, one on the mainland, and one on Formosa. Indigenous Communist activity in the smaller nations has been acute, as the Huks in the Philippine Republic, North Vietnam, Malaya, and Indonesia.

Southeast Asia Treaty Organization was formed in 1953 as a bulwark against Communist encroachment. The Columbo Conference and the Bandung Conference produced a number of unilateral treaties of mutual aid among certain Western nations and the emergent nationalities of Asia. These treaties have tended to point up certain Asian national interests which are basically the same as older nationalist ideals and counter to new Western concepts of nationalism which have altered to include service and global consciousness as well as a repudiation of colonial imperialism. Here is an unresolved problem.

What is the future of Asian nationalism? Questions are outstanding in regard to Communism in China, India and Southeast Asia, in regard to world organization and sustained peace. Asian nationalism is being affected by cultural factors such as religion and language, social organization, communications, technology and diplomacy.

Geography or economics as coordinating bodies of knowledge in the social studies may be used to supplement, in conjunction with, or as the core of learning in such a study. This depends upon the organization of the curriculum and the specialization of the teacher as well as the interests and needs of the students. The same may be said for anthropology or sociology. In any case, no matter how the material is organized the teacher has an obligation to know the principal facts concerning an area under consideration.

If the above suggestion were used as a beginning, specific problem study of Southeast Asia could proceed with the following outline, each heading of which might be expanded as the need arose:

## SOUTHEAST ASIA

I. Southeast Asian Land and People (geography and anthropolopy)
   A. Geographic factors making for a natural region
      1. Topography
      2. Demographic movement
      3. Political boundaries
         a. Ancient national states (Siam)
         b. Old empires (Kmer, French Indochina)
         c. Enforced nationalism (Geneva settlement of 1954)
      4. Drainage systems
      5. Salt water communication
      6. Natural history (flora and fauna)
   B. Ethnic derivation
      1. Racial variations
      2. Cultural variations
      3. Basic similarities in culture and social organization
         a. Religions
         b. Languages
         c. Family patterns
         d. Ethnocentrism
         e. Wars
         f. Population
      4. Intrusions of Western civilization (Thailand, Burma, Philippines, Anzac; coca-cola, clothing, Christianity)
II. Basic system of subsistence (economics)
   A. Village agriculture
   B. Extractive industries (tin, rubber)
      1. For domestic uses
      2. For export

    a. Manufactures

    b. Raw products such as timber

C. Imports

    1. Impact of Western culture and capitalism

    2. Regional interchange of products

    3. Political effects

D. Fiscal support of new national states

    1. Internal taxation and exploitation

    2. Western assistance

    3. Colonial exploitation by European states

### *Future of a Region in Relationship to the Rest of the World*

"In all countries of Southeast Asia structural reforms in economic life are necessary . . . The economic and welfare problems of Southeast Asia cannot be solved unless the majority of citizens develop a sense of civic interest and responsibility." [3] Each nation must, in order to survive in the modern world, develop its own feeling of worth—of belonging to the family of nations. Possibly this will be in terms of modern democratic socialism; at least, nationalism will play a leading role. It is possible that the Communist ideology will be temporarily the guiding force in the growth of national self-consciousness of Asian countries, but only for a short time. Because of the interrelated nature of the modern world in economics, in communication, and in the field of international relations, there must be a recognizable basis for agreement and dispute among the nations. This is nationalism. Each nation must meet nationalistic qualifications before all nations together can begin to think of another form of sovereign organization.

Such a goal for the underdeveloped regions of the world where colonialism has played such an important part must be accepted by the peoples of those countries first. Responsibility for achievement of stable nationality in those countries is jointly held between themselves and the older, stronger and well established democracies of our time.

### 3. Propaganda Analysis

Knowledge and understanding of a wide range of ideas are the essential components of social justice. Nationalism is only one element in the organization of all of the peoples of the world into an integrated

---

[3] Justus M. van der Kroef, "East and Southeast Asia," in *Approaches to an Understanding of World Affairs*, edited by Howard R. Anderson (National Council for the Social Studies, Washington, D.C., 1954), p. 219 ff.

whole. Beyond that, even though there is no other substitute for operational sovereignty at the present time, it must be recognized that people everywhere in all time have basically the same rights and aspirations. Some are merely more fortunate or more highly developed than others. Social justice is not confined to one area nor only to be administered by one nation inside one set of boundaries. The nation is certainly responsible for safeguarding its own traditions, rights and privileges, but at the same time all of the people in all of the nations have a more diffuse but perhaps even deeper responsibility to each other to keep open and improve lines of communication leading to a more universal social justice. The study of world problems offers such an opportunity.

Along with the subject matter of world problems, as an objective in the mastery of knowledgeable technique, one may study propaganda analysis. In fact, it would be difficult to avoid it and also avoid the pitfall of ethnocentric indoctrination. Information of any kind, and especially information concerning controversial and contemporary problems, is sometimes almost indistinguishable from propaganda, from interested attempts by all kinds of agencies to influence men's minds and therefore their actions and beliefs. To arrive at sound opinions, based on true understanding, requires a great deal of discrimination. Such discrimination is not a natural consequence of intelligence or experience; it must be learned as a technique of thought.

If high school students are trained and encouraged in scientific methods of study and thought continually in all of their intellectual enterprises there is a much better chance that they will arrive at the ability to discriminate in the matter of separating propaganda from useful information in the study of world problems. Nonetheless, it is a good idea to set up the conscious objective of critical analysis of data as part of the work in any problems course.

One of the first things that a teacher can do at the outset of study is to develop with his class a set of criteria for the selection of data. If the problem is put directly to the students they can often produce the necessary points of view to be codified and followed in analyzing their study material. After such a set of working principles is derived, constant care must be exercised by the teacher that the students pay attention to it, because the imprint of early habituation is strong, and the prejudices that students bring to school from their personal backgrounds are often as persistent as recurring hunger. For example, it is easy to get a class of students to agree that labor unions, representing a great many persons, have basic and definable rights guaranteed by law; but the child in that class, offspring of a business man employing several workmen in his plant, will experience real difficulty in acting out his moral determination that the laborer's rights are equal to his own. The reverse might be equally true in the opposite case.

It is easier in a larger problem, in the international field and more remote from the individual, to get agreement and adherence to a code of discriminating choice in sifting propaganda. Students can be brought to see that informational documents produced and disseminated by national governments will probably be most interested in putting the best face on the history and present posture of their own states. It would be ridiculous to expect that a travel bureau in Austria would extoll the virtues of South Africa. Unless, however, the students' attention is directed to the matter such flagrant discrepancies might escape notice. More subtle are nationalistic or ethnic messages carried in philosophical discourses which sometimes accompany the types of material that students will use for the study of world problems. For example, it is possible to find in a Polish magazine very glowing descriptions and pictures of Soviet agriculture, all positively presented and without any apparent attempt to glorify the idea of the collective farm. In this case, it is quite reasonable to appreciate the fine photography and pay attention to the description and statistics concerning the precise region under discussion, but in order to detect the propaganda quality of such a piece it is also absolutely necessary to gain access to wider information, data concerning the whole of Soviet agriculture, average yields per acre and per capita worker over the entire country. Needless to say, such information may be hard to get.

Reducing the analogy to more familiar and simpler things, domestic advertising often can give the model for rules of propaganda analysis. Certain products are presented quite often as the choice of "thinking people," with the obvious hope (with a little thought) that the prospective purchaser will not think at all, but simply buy the product. As a preliminary exercise in the development of a code of judgment for the class, it might be a good idea to have each student bring in an advertisement from a national magazine which actually tells a minimum about the product under discussion and which at the same time has some sort of appeal to cultural, racial, national or class prejudice which it is hoped will sell the product regardless of its merits or defects. This kind of exercise might have considerable carry-over to the analysis of news and other data concerning problems of international importance.

Certain generalized guides to the critical evaluation of information might include:

Source of information
(reliable, not reliable, unknown)
What country does it come from?
Is it private or public?
Does it represent a widely known point of view or ideology?
Reason for its existence
Was it produced for a particular audience? Why?
Is it truly a contribution to universal knowledge regardless of its origin?
Is the information actually an objective document or is it an interpretation?
Content
Is it complete?
Is it recent or old?
Can it be corroborated? (true, false, indeterminate)

Each group can work out its own criteria and, of course, each bit of information will have to be handled in the context of its own significance. It must always be remembered that propaganda effect is never a complete turn about. Rather, a slight bending of opinion in a general direction already established is usually the maximum effect of successful propaganda. Also it must be remembered that people are inclined to believe what they want to believe; they like to reinforce their prejudices if possible. During the Korean conflict, as an example, there were persistent reports, emanating from several different places, that the Chinese had developed a Marine Corps and that they were consistently and continually expanding it. Naturally, this was disconcerting to the United Nations forces, and considerable analysis of the problem had to be made in order to ascertain the truth or falsehood of the rumored intelligence. First of all it was discovered that the source of the reports, although coming from different places, was always the same. Nationalist China, on Formosa, had diligently planted duplicate reports in several different Far Eastern cities. Next, it was discerned that the reports corroborated each other—but then, naturally they would, since they all came from the same place. Each report of a new increment of the Chinese Communist Marine Corps gave it as a precisely organized division, each of a uniform size and equipment, and numbered in a completely obvious and logical manner. The last doubtful element of information was that the divisions were being organized and put into the field too fast, faster than troops could be trained. Finally, it was determined by means of linguistic comparison that the Chinese characters which had been translated into "Marine Corps" were the same as those which had been used in World War II by the Japanese to indicate their Special Naval Landing Forces which, in turn, had been translated into "Marine Corps" by certain American newsmen. The fact was that the Japanese, in World War II, had never had a marine corps—and during the Korean conflict, the Communist Chinese never had one either.

Basically, the Nationalist Chinese wanted to insure the continued support and protection of the United States, and they had taken this as a vehicle of propaganda to try to influence the United States to augment its naval forces in the Pacific. Secondly, Americans were quite willing to believe any evil of the Communist Chinese while at the same time inclined to go along with points of view expressed by the Nationalist Chinese. Without exercising the critical discrimination implicit in propaganda analysis the United States might have been stampeded into spending a great deal more energy in a war that was already more costly than most Americans were willing to underwrite.

A useful technique in teaching world problems is to follow two steps in each assignment. First, have two or more students evaluate independently the sources of information, and second, assign the same topic to more than one individual. Small groups, or committees of students, each taking a problem, can fruitfully study, combine their efforts and share their findings with the whole group. Perhaps thus the objectives of widening knowledge of fact and of propaganda analysis technique may both be furthered.

### 4. Teacher References

It is impossible to list a number of books that will answer the teacher's every question. If it were possible, no one person could read them all in any available, reasonable time. The teacher of world problems must first define his objectives and limitations, then strive to stay within reasonable bounds. In general, there are two types of source material for teacher preparation in this field. A number of publications attempt to give philosophies or methodologies for teaching world problems. Another group of books, comprising most of human knowledge is available for the specific information needed to illustrate the study of any specific or general problem. In the former category we can list with some assurance those titles that have been helpful to some teachers. In the latter group only a few sample items can sensibly be presented. It is up to the individual to determine his own particular needs and proceed to acquire the needed materials.

## CATEGORY I

*Approaches to an Understanding of World Affairs,* edited by Howard R. Anderson, Twenty-fifth Yearbook of the National Council for the Social Studies (Washington, D.C., 1954), is a thoughtful collection of diverse points of view on the general subject. This book is a good starting point.

Stuart Chase, *Roads to Agreement* (Harper, New York, 1951), presents a laudable but futile appeal to the "better senses" of men to quit bickering on an international level.

*Education for International Understanding in American Schools* (National Education Association, Washington, D.C., 1948), is most concerned with spreading democratic attitudes concerning the solution of international problems. This book is oriented to the present time and most interested in crisis types of problems.

J. Montgomery Gambrill, "Experimental Curriculum-Making in the Social Studies," reprinted from *The Historical Outlook* (December, 1923 and January, 1924), is an older view of the problem which stresses world history as essential.

David Krech and Richard S. Crutchfield, *Theory and Problems of Social Psychology* (McGraw-Hill, New York, 1948), is a rather thorough analysis of the factors which go into social organization. It would be a good handbook for the international propagandist.

Lester B. Pearson, *Democracy in World Politics* (Princeton University Press, 1955), is a refreshing analysis of nationalism in today's world. ✓

Lord Percy of Newcastle, *The Heresy of Democracy* (Regnery, Chicago, 1955), is an appeal to a new interpretation of democracy which would eliminate all socialistic elements in establishing satisfactory world agreements.

*Readings in Social Psychology,* edited by Guy E. Swanson, Theodore M. Newcomb, and Eugene L. Hartley (Holt, Rinehart and Winston, New York, 1952), is a tremendous collection of learned articles dealing with identifiable social issues.

*Suggested Scope for Programs in Contemporary World History, Geography and Problems* (Washington State Department of Education, Olympia, Washington, 1955), mimeo., gives the composite recommendations of one hundred high school teachers and administrators. Their opinions seem to favor a contemporary emphasis with a good deal of attention to the history of Western civilization.

*Teaching World Affairs in American Schools,* edited by Samuel Everett and Christian O. Arndt (Harper, New York, 1956), emphasizes activity means of learning about world affairs and problems.

## CATEGORY II

These are books which are merely representative samples illustrating the types of information available on a few of the countless problems in the world.

Donald G. Bishop, Wallace E. Lamb, Emily B. Smith and Edith E. Starratt, *Community Planning in a Democracy,* National Council for the Social Studies, Bulletin Number 21 (Washington, D.C., 1948), shows how democratic planning takes place at a local level.

Donald G. Bishop and Edith E. Starratt, *The Structure of Local Government*, National Council for the Social Studies, Bulletin Number 19 (Washington, D.C., 1945), along with the two former pamphlets may be used with students also.

Delmer M. Brown, *Nationalism in Japan* (University of California Press, 1955), gives an honest and scholarly view of past and present trends in nationalistic growth in Japan.

*Consumption of Food in the United States,* United States Department of Agriculture, Miscellaneous Publication Number 691 (United States Government Printing Office, Washington, D.C., 1949), presents and analyzes the facts concerning the topic. This sort of information is essential in any consideration of comparative standards of living.

*Elections in Israel* (Israel Office of Information, New York, 1955), sheds light on Jewish nationalism in the Middle East.

Marguerite J. Fisher and Edith E. Starratt, *Parties and Politics in the Local Community*, National Council for the Social Studies, Bulletin Number 20 (Washington, D.C., 1951), localizes one problem, local politics, which may be used as a pattern in nearly every country.

A. L. Goodhart, *The British Constitution* (British Information Services, New York, 1945), gives an English point of view, but the factual content is unimpeachable.

Harry N. Howard, *United States Policy in the Near East, South Asia, and Africa* (Department of State Bulletin, February, 1955), reprinted as a State Department Circular, 1955), presents the official American record of achievement in the areas listed.

Preston E. James, "On the Treatment of Controversial Topics in Geography," (Banquet address at the annual meeting of the National Council of Geography Teachers, November 26, 1948), illustrates various geographic factors, such as the crucial quality of water supply in Israel, as controversial items in world interaction.

*Landmarks in Democracy* (British Information Services, New York, 1945), is, again, a British propaganda arrangement of important documents in the growth of democratic nationalism.

*NATO: Its Development and Significance,* Department of State Publication Number 4630 (United States Government Printing Office, n.d.), is the official explanation of the North Atlantic Treaty.

John B. Rae and Thomas H. D. Mahoney, *The United States in World History* (McGraw-Hill, New York, 1955), could be used as a guide to world problems if the center of interest were always the United States. It is a fairly usable history of American life, especially in the last half century.

Burton Sapin, Richard C. Snyder, and H. W. Bruck, *An Appropriate Role for the Military in American Foreign Policy-making: A Research Note* (Organizational Behavior Section, Princeton University, 1954), is filled with facts concerning the problem stated.

L. Dudley Stamp, *Land for Tomorrow* (Indiana University Press, 1952), is a geographic guide to the world's problem regions.

*The Teaching of Contemporary Affairs,* edited by John C. Payne, Twenty-first Yearbook of the National Council for the Social Studies (Washington, D.C., 1950), gives a guide to the necessary information in presenting current affairs.

Teaching World Understanding, edited by Ralph C. Preston (Prentice-Hall, New York, 1955), is the joint effort of a number of Quakers to point the way to world knowledge through tolerance.

*The U.S. Stake in the U.N.* (The American Assembly, Columbia University, 1954), gives the views and findings of several authorities on international organization.

*Topics of Current Interest in International Economic Relations* (National Association of Manufacturers, New York, 1953), is a particular point of view on international agreements affecting American business.

Harold M. Vinacke, *International Organization* (Crofts, New York, 1934), gives the form and history of attempts at international organization up to the disintegration of the League of Nations.

Charles Wagley, *A Conference on the Study of World Areas,* Social Science Research Council Pamphlet 6, Area Research and Training (New York, 1948), analyzes the requirements for an integrated social science approach to the examination of problem areas.

*Water in Industry* (National Association of Manufacturers, New York, 1950), presents facts needed in estimating the importance of water as a factor in developing backward areas.

*Western Germany: An Economic Appraisal* (National Association of Manufacturers, New York, 1952), illustrates how Germany has effected a major economic recovery in a short time by means of capitalistic methods.

Howard E. Wilson, *Universities and World Affairs* (Carnegie Endowment for International Peace, New York, 1951), presents a problem in getting acquainted among the national groups in the world by way of education.

Bibliography

Jenning B. Sanders, *Methods Used by College Social Science Departments to Improve Students' Understanding of Post-World-War II International Tensions,* Federal Security Agency Circular Number 362, mimeo. (Washington, D.C., 1952), is an annotated listing of sources of information.

## 5. Student Materials

No textbook could satisfy even a small part of the requirements of the course objectives or scope of knowledge. The very need for such a course precludes any stereotyped organization of its content. The needs and interests of the students could not conceivably be incorporated into one book—existent or nonexistent. Diverse books and other materials will be required for the students just as they are for the teacher. In fact, since students taking this course will probably be in grades twelve to fourteen, they will be seventeen to twenty years of age and will have attained an optimum of skill in reading and using adult material. Therefore such students can use much the same kind of informational sources as their teachers.

As a basic guide the course should always take on a historical aspect in order for the students to understand the background of whatever problem is under consideration. This does not mean that it will be a repetition of world history, but rather, each problem must be developed in its own setting, and more individualized and specialized aspects of history will be required. By definition, history is a humanistic, integrative record of social experience. It is sometimes classified as a social science, but it impinges on all fields while at the same time using techniques and information from every discipline. Above all, history, in order to find an audience and therefore become usable, must achieve success in communication. The story, if it incorporates a high degree of literary art, can emphasize historicity, human interest, timeliness and broad integration and still provide a sequential background for each problem under consideration.

Within one general problem, such as nationalism, each student could start with the common record of European nationalism and then proceed to individual consideration of different nations, with final emphasis on the particular nation in a contemporary setting. In this way a whole class, collectively, could get some acquaintance with a great diversity of material through a classroom exchange of information in the form of reports or forums.

In providing lists of books for such an enterprise no selection could be ultimately adequate because of the wide range of topics and because of the rapid change in the status of affairs. The following list is one selection arranged in one fashion. There could be almost infinite variations in the selection and many different organizations.

A.  Economic Realities of Subsistence

Jesus de Castro, *The Geography of Hunger* (Little, Brown, Boston, 1952). Deals with the problem of productive scarcity and underdeveloped social growth.

*Focus*, published monthly by the American Geographical Society, New York. A geographical interpretation of current events.

Charles E. Kellogg, *Food, Soil, and People* (UNESCO New York, n.d.). One of the UNESCO series about "Food and People."

W. Van Royen and O. Bowles, *The Mineral Resources of the World* (Prentice-Hall, New York, 1952). Very valuable maps and graphs.

W. S. Woytinski and E. S. Woytinski, *World Population and Production* (Twentieth Century Fund, New York, 1953). A comprehensive economic view of the world as a whole.

B.  Nations Cooperate

Daniel S. Cheever and H. Field Haviland, Jr., *Organizing for Peace: International Organization in World Affairs* (Houghton Mifflin, Boston, 1954). Very comprehensive treatment of European and American attempts at international understanding.

Linden A. Mander, Foundations of Modern World Society (Stanford University Press, 1947). A book for the advanced student in theory and practice of international organization.

Amry Vandenbosch and Willard N. Hogan, *The United Nations: Background,*

*Organization, Function, Activities* (McGraw-Hill, New York, 1952). A most recent textbook on the United Nations.

United Nations Bulletin, published semi-monthly by the Department of Public Relations of the United Nations, Columbia University Press, New York.

Filmstrips

Eighteen 35mm. filmstrips are available through McGraw-Hill, Text-Film Department, New York, produced by the United Nations to illustrate its functions.

C. The United States and World Affairs

Charles A. Beard, *Idea of National Interest* (Macmillan, New York, 1934). An economic interpretation of nationalism.

M. W. Graham, *American Diplomacy in the World Community* (Johns Hopkins Press, Baltimore, 1948). Diplomatic history used to promote internationalism.

George F. Kennan, *American Diplomacy, 1900–1950* (University of Chicago Press, 1951). An analysis of diplomacy made by a professional diplomatist.

Robert E. Osgood, *Ideals and Self-Interest in America's Foreign Relations* (University of Chicago Press, 1953). An appeal for a more realistic foreign policy in terms of American needs.

*New American Nation Series,* edited by Henry Steele Commager and Richard B. Morris (Harper, New York). Not yet complete, it will contain forty volumes and it will give a thorough coverage of American history topics. Very useful for students and teachers.

D. Latin America

Ciro Alegria, *Broad and Alien Is the World,* translated by Harriet de Onís (Rinehart, New York, 1941). A penetrating novel depicting the position of the Indian in Peru.

Robert S. Platt, *Latin America, Countrysides and United Regions* (McGraw-Hill, New York, 1942). Detailed views of individual farms and communities with summaries by regions.

Luis Quintanilla, *A Latin American Speaks* (Macmillan, New York, 1943). The political tug of war in Latin America as seen by a Mexican scholar.

T. Lyn Smith, *Brazil: People and Institutions* (Louisiana State University Press, Baton Rouge, 1946). A sociological examination of one South American nation.

Charles Wagley, *Amazon Town, A Study of Man in the Tropics* (Macmillan, New York, 1953). An anthropological study of an Amazon village.

George Wythe, *Industry in Latin America* (Columbia University Press, 1945). Shows the progress of manufacturing since World War II.

*Hispanic America Reports,* monthly, edited by Ronald Hilton, Stanford University Press, Stanford, California.

E. Western Europe

*Rise of Modern Europe,* edited by William L. Langer, 20 vols. (Harper, New

York, 1934–). Extensive history of Europe done by American scholars. Fine reference.

Wilbur Cortez Abbott, *The Expansion of Europe: A Social and Political History of the Modern World, 1415–1815* (Crofts, New York, 1938). Four centuries of well illustrated development of European culture and its movement abroad.

*The United Nations Series,* edited by Robert J. Kerner (University of California Press, 1945–). Provides modern and historical data on most of the European nations with, in most cases, a volume devoted to a single country.

*The American Foreign Policy Library,* edited by Sumner Welles and Donald G. McKay (Harvard University Press, 1946–). Planned for twenty-five volumes, this series is now about half finished. It stresses the information needed by Americans for an understanding of the problems of the nations in the world in relationship to the United States.

United Nations, *Demographic Yearbook* (Department of Social Affairs of the United Nations, New York, 1947–). An annual compilation of statistics pertaining to every problem which might arise in the United Nations.

*Pageant of Europe: Sources and Selections from the Renaissance to the Present Day,* edited by Raymond P. Stearns (Harcourt, Brace, New York, 1947). Fine one-volume compilation of selected source materials in European history.

William Robert Shepherd, *Historical Atlas* (Holt, New York, 1929). Unfortunately out of print, this atlas is a very handy one-volume reference of invaluable use to high school and college students.

F.  Central and Eastern Europe

*Readings on Contemporary Eastern Europe and Challenge in Eastern Europe,* edited by C. E. Black (New York, 1953 and 1954). Two volumes of sources and comments on the situation in Eastern Europe.

Hans Kohn, *Pan Slavism* (Notre Dame University Press, 1953). Good exposition of the pan-Slavic ideology.

There are three recent Russian films available which have value for students interested in Russian history:

*Alexander Nevsky*

*Ivan the Terrible*

*Peter the First*

G.  China

H. F. Bain, *Ores and Industries of the Far East* (Council on Foreign Relations, New York, 1933).

J. L. Buck, *Land Utilization in China* (University of Chicago Press, 1937).

George B. Cressey, *China's Geographic Foundations* (McGraw-Hill, New York, 1934).

George B. Cressey, *Land of the 500 Million* (McGraw-Hill, New York, 1954).

T. H. Shen, *Agricultural Resources of China* (Cornell University Press, 1951).

Joseph E. Spencer, *Asia, East by South* (Wiley, New York, 1954).

Warren S. Thompson, *Population and Peace in the Pacific* (Chicago, 1946).

The above books deal with economics, geography and demography of China and the rest of the Far East. Like nearly all works on the subject they are reluctant to acknowledge a Chinese population in excess of five hundred million. Some recent estimates have placed the figure at six hundred fifty millions.

Kenneth Scott Latourette, *The Chinese, Their History and Culture*, 2 vols. (Macmillan, New York, 1947). The best available comprehensive history of China written in English.

Kenneth Scott Latourette, *The American Record in the Far East, 1945–1951* (Macmillan, New York, 1952). Brings the former work up to date.

There are several good general reference books on China which do not classify as either history or geography:

Lin Yu-tang, *My Country and My People* (Halcyon House, New York, 1938). Written in English for Americans.

*China*, edited by Harley F. MacNair (University of California Press, 1946). All kinds of information on China.

G. F. Winfield, *China: The Land and the People* (Sloane, New York, 1948). A sociological view.

Two earlier travel accounts offer much firsthand information of China before the present revolutionary period.

Harry A. Franck, *Wandering in Northern China* (Century, New York, 1923), and *Roving Through Southern China* (Century, New York, 1925).

H. East and Southeast Asia

J. C. Caldwell, *The Korea Story* (Regnery, Chicago, 1952). A useful and popular account of the Korean war including descriptions of personalities and society.

J. L. Christian, *Modern Burma* (University of California Press, 1942). Burmese politics and government covering the pre-war period.

J. S. Furnivall, *Netherlands India* (Macmillan, New York, 1944). Dutch colonialism in the East Indies is shown in relation to social and economic conditions.

Ellen J. Hammer, *The Struggle for Indo-China* (Stanford University Press, 1954). Most recent treatment of the events between World War II and the present which led to Indo-Chinese independence.

*Asian Nationalism and the West*, edited by W. L. Holland (Macmillan, New York, 1953). A symposium dealing especially with public administration and government policy.

Shirley Jenkins, *American Economic Policy Toward the Philippines* (Stanford University Press, 1954). Treats of the obstacles to Philippine economic development.

Kenneth Scott Latourette, *The History of Japan* (Macmillan, New York, 1947). A good short history of Japanese cultural growth and traditions.

*The New World of Southeast Asia*, edited by L. A. Mills (University of Minnesota Press, Minneapolis, 1949). A symposium on all the nations in various aspects which make up Southeast Asia.

E. O. Reischauer, *The United States and Japan* (Harvard University Press,

1950). An analysis of American policy in the Japanese occupation, including a brief historical background.

*Southeast Asia in the Coming World,* edited by Philip Thayer (Johns Hopkins University Press, 1953). A symposium dealing with various aspects of the area. Good section on the economy.

The Institute of Pacific Relations publishes two periodicals: *Pacific Affairs* (quarterly), and *Far Eastern Survey* (monthly) which regularly publish articles on Southeast Asia as well as the rest of the Far East.

I. India and Pakistan

Chester Bowles, *Ambassador's Report* (Harper, New York 1954). A fine description of the social and economic problems of modern India.

Jawaharlal Nehru, *The Discovery of India* (Day, New York, 1946). Impassioned and non-objective account of new India.

Eleanor Roosevelt, *India and the Awakening East* (Harper, New York, 1953). A travel book by a sympathetic and keen observer.

Sir Percival Spear, *India, Pakistan and the West* (Oxford University Press, London, 1949). A thoughtful examination of the impact of Western culture on India.

Richard Symonds, *The Making of Pakistan* (Faber, London, 1949). A brief account of the formation of the new state of Pakistan.

T. Walter Wallbank, *India in the New Era* (Scott, Foresman, Chicago, 1951). This histroy shows the importance of the problem of Moslem-Hindu relations.

J. Islam Around the World

Matta Akrawi, *The Arab World: Nationalism and Education,* The Yearbook of Education (Evans Brothers, London, 1949). An examination of Moslem customs and social organization which are often unknown in establishing relations between Christian and Moslem rations.

W. B. Fisher, *The Middle East: A Physical, Social and Regional Geography* (Dutton, New York, 1950). Besides the physical geography this book deals with the social structure and with economics.

J. C. Hurewitz, *Middle East Dilemmas: The Background of the United States' Policy* (Harper, New York, 1953). Historical and political circumstances leading up to the present.

S. A. Morrison, "Arab Nationalism and Islam," *Middle East Journal* (April, 1948). An important treatment of a pressing problem. This journal carries contemporary scholarship in the field.

K. Africa: A Changing World

On resources and change in Africa there are only a few items of interest. Much study has yet to be done in order to understand this least developed continent. With about two hundred million people, according to the best guess, the world's second largest continent offers unlimited opportunity for study. In view of its recent growth in export of essential materials it may become quite important in the affairs of the world.

James S. Coleman, "Nationalism in Tropical Africa," *American Political Science Review* (June, 1954).

Walter Fitzgerald, *Africa, A Social, Economic and Political Geography of Its Major Regions* (Dutton, New York, 1943).

Sally Herbert Frankel, *Capital Investment in Africa* (Oxford University Press, London, 1938).

William Miller MacMillan, *Africa Emergent: Survey of Social, Political and Economic Trends in British Africa* (Faber, London, 1949; Penguin Books, New York, 1949).

Dudley Stamp, *A Study in Tropical Development* (Wiley, New York, 1953).

*Review of Economic Conditions in Africa,* United Nations, Department of Economic Affairs (New York, 1951).

In present day Africa the pattern for the future is not at all clear. There is no unity and no single direction which the diverse African people will take. It can best be studied from current journalism until such time as more scholarly work is available.

L. The British Commonwealth and Great Britain

Charles F. Mullett, *The British Empire* (Holt, New York, 1938). Presents a good summary of the backbone of organization in this democratic empire.

Goldwin Smith, *A History of England* (Scribner's, New York, 1949). Gives the postwar development in Britain and treats the problems of housing, economics and the loss of empire.

W. P. Hall and R. G. Albion, *A History of England and the British Empire* (Ginn, Boston, 1946). Good survey of the whole history of the nation and Commonwealth.

Geoffrey Bruun, *The World in the Twentieth Century* (Heath, Boston, 1948), Alfred E. Kahn, *Great Britain in the World Economy* (Columbia University Press, New York, 1946). These two books give elaborate and detailed explanations of the present place of Great Britain in regard to the Commonwealth and to the world.

Foster Hailey, *Half of One World* (Macmillan, New York, 1950). If one world, or international organization on a total scale, is impossible at the present time, at least that part of the world under the influence of the British Empire can maintain a democratic unity.

*The World Today* (monthly), published by the Royal Institute of International Affairs, New York.

*British Civilization and Institutions* (Books and Periodicals Committee, British Council, American Library Association, Chicago, 1946). A selective and comprehensive list of books on the subject.

*International Conciliation* (periodical), published by the Carnegie Endowment for International Peace (New York). The British Information Service maintains a free film and filmstrip service available through its many offices in the United States, or from the headquarters, 30 Rockefeller Plaza, New York 20.

The above lists and outlines are merely suggestions of ways in which world problems as a course in school can be approached. There are almost innumerable organizations possible. The wealth of material available could not possibly be listed in any one place. The imagination, skill and knowledge of students and teacher offer the only limitations.

Students should be encouraged to pose their own problems and seek out their own illustrative materials. Each country in the world maintains an information service of some kind in the United States. These organizations produce a plethora of both good and bad information, and they are quite anxious to have it circulated in the American schools. A simple request to any of the foreign agencies through their embassies or consulates will usually produce something useful. It is only necessary that a reasonable amount of precaution and discrimination in its use be undertaken. In addition to the study of any particular problem this also offers a concomitant opportunity to encourage discrimination, selectivity and propaganda analysis which are all very important adjuncts to an understanding of world problems.

## 6. Suggested Activities for Further Study

1. Prepare a list of the addresses of foreign embassies or consulates in the United States and request them to send you educational materials.
2. Make a detailed outline for the study of any single problem cogent to the present world situation.
   a. Prepare a bibliography for retarded readers which would illustrate that problem.
   b. Gather pictures which might supplement the literary sources of information.
   c. Make a list of novels and other belletristic writings which might supplement the same problem for more advanced students.
3. Prepare a statistical table and world map showing the relative disposition of the world's population by major regions or linguistic groups.
4. Select a problem which is important now, such as dictatorship, and compare it with the same problem in the past.
5. Analyze and define "population pressure." Prepare a list of books and articles on the subject.
6. List the major efforts toward or suggestions for international organization.
7. How could music have any bearing on world problems?
8. Does such a matter as the American problem of racial integration have any important bearing on world problems? If so, in what way?
9. Prepare and describe a classroom activity which would best dramatize an extended study of current world tensions.

part **V**
# JUDGING THE EFFECTIVNESS OF SOCIAL STUDIES PROGRAMS

# 14

# Evaluation in social studies: theory and practice

Man is his own measure.

St. Augustine

## 1. A Theory of Evaluation

Evaluation includes many facets. It is both objective and subjective. It comes both from within and without. Success in evaluation rests on the ability of teacher and student to withhold judgment; this might seem to be the denial of evaluation, but if a scientific value is placed on tentative conclusions, then final judgment on any grounds is impossible.

The most apparent aspect of evaluation has to do with measuring and reporting the progress and achievement of students, but this is only part of the whole process. It also includes an understanding of and choice of evaluating instruments and the construction of tests. By the same token no curricular pattern can become sacredly impervious to change, and every teacher's program is constantly subject to re-evaluation, both by himself and by society as a whole through its various influences and institutions. Self-evaluation on the part of the teacher, thus, becomes a part of student evaluation, choice and construction of tests and total assessment of the school program.

That man is his own measure is true. Man in society sets his values and therefore no truer judge can exist. Each man as a mirror of his time must select his goals and evaluate his attainment of them. No effective evaluation is ever really outside the individual, as no real discipline is ever completely administered from authority alone. In fact, self-discipline entails self-evaluation. These must be basic principles of education. A successful scheme of evaluation for social studies must center in the student. Naturally there will be varying degrees of student achievement, and there will be authority, usually represented by the teacher. As self-discipline is achieved slowly, so is a sense of self-evaluation.

Above all, in establishing evaluative techniques, the aims of social studies must be held firmly in mind. The objectives of social studies are complicated and serious, and they are tied to evaluation and skill mastery. Their complexity invites measurement of subject achievement in order to produce apparent simplicity. Testing subject matter is the simplest form of evaluation. This alone, however, is not sufficient for school purposes.

After objectives have become clear to teachers and students (among these should be the aim of self-evaluation) specific means must be established. In general, these divide into two main categories: long range and immediate. The first group has mainly to do with such things as developing self-evaluation and attitudinal or behavioral outcomes. These are equally the concern of students and teachers, and, of course, society also has an acute interest in the behavior and beliefs of its citizens. Another aspect of long range evaluation is curricular planning in which the students do not play an active part. Teachers and administrators must continually assess their programs of instruction and seek the advice of lay advisory groups in order to meet the needs of changing situations and altered student bodies. The chief purpose of schools and teachers is to help students in all of the various ways possible. Every teacher enters his first classroom with this in mind, and therefore commences immediately the never ending process of observation and evaluation by which he can improve the type of help he gives to the students.

Such long range evaluation is quite subjective, although certain scales and checklists do exist which may be used to supplement individual and group observation. Long range behavioral changes are hard to observe because the changes are slow and subtle, and the continuity of observation is difficult. It is also, at present, quite difficult to isolate the specific items of behavior and attitude that can be measured.[1] There is some question as to how much of a measureable attitude carries over into behavior. This is especially true in regard

---

[1] Franklyn S. Haiman, *Group Leadership and Democratic Action* (University of Chicago Press, 1951), p. 237 ff., gives the *Barnlund-Haiman Leader Rating Scale*. See also I. James Quillen and Lavone A. Hanna, *Education for Social Competence* (Scott, Foresman, Chicago, 1961 rev. ed.), section on evaluation.

to such things as race prejudice or democratic political practice.[2]

Certain scales exist for measurement of behavior such as the *Barn-lund-Haiman Leader Rating Scale*. The same result may be approximated with the use of a scale locally developed; or attitudinal change may be completely the subjective judgment of the teacher. Many checklists and personality rating scales are available, or they may be constructed to suit individual needs in a given situation. On a still more subjective level, the anecdotal record may be used to keep an accurate running documentation of characteristic individual behavior. The teacher writes down in some sort of journal periodic examples of statements or acts of each student (without any judgment stated). At the end of any given period, if enough entries have been made, one has a series of data which may be used to analyze progress in attitudes and behavior. This may very often serve as the basis for a parent-teacher conference concerning the achievement of a young person in the non-academic aspects of his social studies work. Some school systems have a policy of maintaining a cumulative file of such material on each student from his entry into school until he graduates. When that is the case, and when the entries are made in a spirit of "withheld judgment," a cumulative personnel file can be of great value to both teachers and students.

In any case, the methods of evaluation should always bear direct relationship to the stated objectives, and the students should know at every stage what they are expected to achieve and how this is to be measured. The Educational Policies Commission has stated objectives for education as (a) self-realization, (b) civic responsibility, (c) economic efficiency, and (d) satisfactory human relationships. Much of this is supposed to be taught in social studies, but only the knowledge and skills upon which these objectives are based and from which they are derived is susceptible of immediate test and measurement.[3]

Therefore evaluation must be of a dual nature: long range assessment of progress toward behavioral goals and short range testing of subject matter achievement. In short range testing the assumption must be made that a positive relationship exists between mastery of

[2] Dean G. Epley, "A Survey of Human Relations Programs," *The Journal of Educational Sociology* (May, 1956), pp. 378–385.

[3] *The Purposes of Education in American Democracy*, Educational Policies Commission (Washington, D.C., 1938), cited in *Social Studies for Young Adolescents*, edited by Julian C. Aldrich (Washington, D.C., 1951), p. 5.

social studies subject matter and attainment of the long range objectives stated.

Fundamentally evaluation is a kind of practical tool important to anyone who is going anywhere in any operation. It is the tool that says, "Are you moving? Are you moving in the direction you intend to move? Should you change the direction or should you change the rate?" In view of this sensible interpretation, . . . most of us will admit that if we are to be evaluated, we would rather be evaluated on real facts than on somebody's casual observation of us. . . . First of all, evaluation is a process. There is a scientific approach which requires the statement of objectives, some statements of what these mean in behavior, then some effort to make an evaluating instrument. . . .[4]

Such an instrument should include all the elements mentioned above and should emphasize both teacher-made and more highly standardized tests of both subject and behavior. The report of evaluation is best done with a combination of subject matter grade and written statement of growth, preferably accompanied by a conference of student, teacher and parent.

In summary of the theory of evaluation, man is educable and this is primarily a matter of the intellect. Objectives of learning are hoped to produce behavior patterns acceptable to society and expressive of worthy values. Progress can be measured in terms of mastery of the knowledge and thought content of the curriculum, but only if the objectives are clear and the evaluating instruments are conceived in direct relationship to those objectives.

## 2. Evaluating Students

Evaluation is always a comparative matter; by definition it means placing persons in relationship to each other and to a standard of some kind. Two completely opposed philosophies exist in this regard: either students are compared individually to a set standard of achievement, or they are placed in a relative standing in regard to the group in which they happen to be.

In the first case, if only a previously fixed standard of achievement is used, then all of the students may fall short of it or all of them may gain near perfection in that light. It depends entirely upon what the standard may be and what the abilities of the students are.

[4] Maurice Freehill, "Some Possible Approaches to Evaluation," *Proceedings of the Annual Summer Conference and Institute*, Western Washington College of Education Bulletin (Bellingham, Washington, 1955), pp. 22–24.

On the other hand, by comparing only within a particular group, standard patterns of probability will determine that about sixty per cent can be placed in the middle with a bell-shaped curve of distribution to either side of the central tendency. Thus every class will have a top, middle and bottom. Obviously, if no extraneous standard is introduced, each group will set its own criteria, and regardless of the level of ability or achievement most persons will emerge as apparently "average."

Neither system is satisfactory in all cases. A blend of the two points of view is needed in properly evaluating students in public schools. First of all, there should be a standard of achievement which could be met by a majority of the students involved. It must be understood and accepted by the students, and the teacher must instruct in accordance with it. In some instances, of course, it can be quite inflexible. For example, if all of the world's political capitals are to be learned in a unit on geography, then only perfect knowledge of them can be sufficient. In contrast, if the subject of study is the American family and its role in modern politics, then the standard must, of necessity, be flexible. The ability and experience of the students must be considered. The resources for study and the length of time must be sufficient. The means of testing competence in achievement cannot be merely a series of short answer questions such as would suffice for testing mastery of place name knowledge. In all likelihood written essays and oral reports would be principal testing devices, and such examinations not only depend on skill in writing and speaking but are not subject to easy comparative marking by the teacher.

Evaluation of the individual student must be in terms known to the students and clearly identified as to its character, that is, in knowledge acquired, attitudes exhibited or stated, or a matter of total growth from one known point to another. In every case the student must know how he is being judged, and the basis for his comparison to others and to a standard.

The grade report card is the most common expression of teachers' evaluation of students. Sometimes this is supplemented or even replaced by a conference between teacher and parent. Sometimes two sets of grades are issued for each subject. One has to do with subject matter comprehension and the other rates the student as to behavioral development. Thus a student may get a grade of A in United States history accompanied by a mark of 1 in citizenship characteristics or personal traits. Often there is confusion as to exactly what the two grades may mean, and there is a marked tendency to equate the two sets of marks, that is, C goes along with 3, and F is usually accompanied by a personality marking of 5.

It is desirable to have two sets of marks, but it is also essential that the basis for grading in the two categories be definitely separated and understood by the students and teachers. One method is to restrict the subject achievement grade to the results of tests in subject matter, and to make the trait evaluation in a prose comment based on the results of an anecdotal record kept over a considerable period of time. This might tend to define the separation between short range and long range objectives also.

Grades are an important part of the evaluation procedure. Nearly every secondary school is obligated to inform its patrons of the standings of its students. This should be both in relation to the group in school and to standards of achievement which are set on a nationwide scale and thought of most commonly in terms of subject matter skill. Grades establish acceptance or rejection of a high school graduate for entry into college.

Evaluation is a continuous process by teachers, students and society of the curriculum, procedures of instruction and students' performance. It indicates an interrelationship among society, the schools as an institution of society, the body of knowledge, instruction and social behavior; evaluation is a continuous and mutual enterprise of all concerned.

## 3. Evaluating Instruments: Tests and Test Making

### Achievement Tests

If subject achievement is to be the basis for grades, as it usually is, then it is absolutely necessary to administer a testing program based on the objectives and procedures of the specific course that is to be tested and graded. This is best done in most cases by the application of two general types of test: the standardized or commercial test and that made by the teacher of the particular class. The Educational Testing Service, Princeton, New Jersey and Los Angeles, California, publishes a wide variety of social studies tests covering all of the commonly taught subjects in American secondary schools. They also distribute several brochures and pamphlets describing test construction and administration such as *Selecting an Achievement Test: Principles and Procedures* (1958). Their advice to teachers seeking a test is to make "careful inquiry into the following topics: I, the nature of the pupil population; II, the content and objectives of the curriculum; III, the purposes in testing; IV, the ways in which test scores may be used to accomplish those purposes; V, the readiness, willingness, and ability of the school staff to administer tests and interpret scores; VI, the amount of time and money available for testing (p. 3)." There are, of course, many other publishers of tests.

If sufficient care is exercised in the selection of a test with a wide base of standardization, obviously the results will give a much broader comparative judgment of the achievement accomplished in any particular group. This is relatively easy in a widely taught subject such as United States history in grades eight and eleven. Certain other social studies courses, such as local history and government, or the various types of problem offerings that are found in grade twelve, are less amenable to standardized testing because of the disparity of subject matter inherent in the local nature of the courses. Where a standardized test is available, if it meets the needs of the testing problem, it should be used in order to make a wide comparison with other students.

In every case, regardless of whether or not a standardized test is available, students should be accustomed to taking frequent tests made by the teacher and specifically adjusted to the material that is being taught. This serves a triple purpose of allowing the teacher to check on his own competence and coverage of material, to determine periodic achievement progress of the students, and to assist in instruction and learning (tests should always be thought of as teaching devices as well as evaluation instruments).

Such tests usually fall into two categories: the short answer variety depending on a choice among alternatives, direct recall of a fact or matching of related items; or the essay type in which the student is given a statement or question (perhaps in some detail) upon which he is expected to comment in paragraphed prose. The criticism most often leveled at the latter kind of test is that it tests more than merely the subject content of the course being measured. This is true, but since we live in a world in which semantic relationships expressed in formal language constitute the vehicle by which culture is transmitted there should be no fundamental objection to a little added practice in writing English. It should be remembered, however, that the chief reason for giving a test in history is to determine achievement in history. The teacher giving an essay test should, in scoring it, always use a factual checklist prepared in advance to make sure that the answer includes the proper material to answer the question adequately. Credit should not be given merely for fluent expression regardless of the content.

### Standardized Tests

Typical illustration of short answer test items and essay items may be given in two examples, both of which are from published materials, but either of which might be approximated in a teacher-constructed test. The difference in the multiple choice item and one made by a particular teacher in a specific situation lies in the standardizing element that would be very difficult for a single teacher in one class to achieve. For the essay item there can be little chance of standardization, therefore the teacher-made item would be preferable because it could assumedly be made to fit the current, local need.

From the *General Achievement Test, Social Studies* (Educational Testing Service, Princeton and Los Angeles, 1947), Form XX, by Jeanne M. Bradford, is the following item designed to test knowledge of a specific point:

The New Deal was primarily a reaction against
(A) isolationism
(B) fascism in Europe
(C) communism in Russia
(D) economic depression
(E) federalism

The correct answer is (D) which is a distinct choice among several alternatives, and the assumption is made that the student must know considerably more than the mere statement involved in the test item in order to be sure that he is making a correct answer. This assumption becomes reinforced in direct proportion to the number of times the item has been shown to produce consistent results in different situations.

From the *Instructor's Manual* to accompany *The American Nation*, John D. Hicks (3rd ed., Houghton Mifflin, Boston, 1956), is an essay question designed to test similar knowledge:

What principal objectives were sought by the establishment of the TVA (Tennessee Valley Authority)?

The center of any answer to this question would be the attempt to alleviate economic depression, just as that was the best choice in the other item, but for this kind of question there is no specific, single "right" answer. The response of the student would be in terms of his knowledge, ability to reason, skill in syntax and eloquence. The answer might be of great value in allowing the teacher to evaluate the student, but there is very little chance of ever producing a coefficient of reliability or validity for such a test item.

## Short Answer Tests Made by the Teacher

Short answer tests are often wrongly identified as "objective" in a generic way, as though the mere format of their exposition insured a degree of validity and reliability not achievable in the essay test. Short answer or any other kind of tests are only as objective as the method used in making and scoring them. Short answer examinations can be objective, but then, so can essay tests. The chief difference lies in the point of objectivity or its absence. The essay is vulnerable in the process of scoring while the short answer test may absorb much of the subjective quality of its author. In other words, the short answer test is only as objective as the person who constructs it.

There are generally four types of short answer tests, but there may be a great many variations or combination of these types. In descending order of desirability for social studies testing, they are: direct recall, matching, multiple choice and true-false. The true-false is least useful for several reasons; it is subject to easy guessing and it may reinforce a wrong answer as readily as a right one. Multiple choice may be criticized on somewhat the same grounds, but it is less culpable, at least having more ways of being wrongly answered.

Direct recall items are usually in the form of sentences or statements with a key word left out which the student is required to fill in. Sometimes a list of blanks is presented to the student with directions to fill in a series of names, events, dates, etc. In any case, the element of objectivity may be introduced by following a sampling procedure tempered by recognition of major ideas to be covered. It is simple if only a series of names or events is to be memorized, but in the case of such an idea as that tested in the foregoing items on the New Deal a more careful test item is required. For example, in assessing a student's knowledge of the Tennessee Valley Authority in relation to the New Deal, the question might be phrased thus:

Give the name of the largest public power project in the United States at the time of the New Deal   (TVA)   .

Along with the rest of New Deal policies, it was meant primarily to combat   (economic depression)   .

This kind of question is more difficult to answer than the multiple choice, but it is probably more challenging and requires more exactness in thought. Again, it must be warned that trivial points are to be avoided, and in judging the answers a certain amount of latitude must be allowed in the choice of words employed.

Matching questions offer a great range of various approaches.

They may be used in conjunction with maps as well as with all sorts of social studies information. This is an especially good kind of test item to examine place name knowledge in connection with items of produce or characteristic activity in those places. As an example:

Place the appropriate letter from the right-hand column in the left margin beside the number it best describes.

| | | | |
|---|---|---|---|
| (a) | 1. Roman Britain | a. | Imperialism |
| (e) | 2. Union of South Africa | b. | Socialism |
| (b) | 3. Modern England | c. | Sugar |
| (h) | 4. Mexican plateau | d. | Recent emergence from monarchy |
| (j) | 5. Florida | e. | Racism |
| (g) | 6. Algeria | f. | Dense population |
| (i) | 7. United States | g. | Tangerines |
| (c) | 8. Cuba | h. | Aztecs |
| (d) | 9. Thailand | i. | Industrialization |
| (f) | 10. China | j. | Real estate speculation |

## Other Ways of Testing Knowledge in the Evaluation of Students

One of the most important aspects of evaluation is the teacher's diligence in accumulating a great mass of testing data upon which to form an evaluative judgment. Almost every teaching activity offers some means of making a mark of some kind to add to the cumulative record of achievement for each student. The teacher should devise some system of recording marks in a continuous fashion for all of the many and varied activities that go into everyday class work. The anecdotal record has been suggested as a means of developing cumulative evaluation material for evidence of attitudinal and behavioral growth. A similar thing can be done for academic growth.

Things that can contribute to overall appraisal of a student's progress include oral discussions, debates and round table presentations, oral reports, projects such as term papers and construction jobs as well as outside reading. There is no definite prescription as to the method that should be used. Each teacher will probably figure out his own system of observation and recording. It is important to remember that many marks are desirable, taking into account many different aspects of performance. Credit should be given for pertinent contribution and partial credit should be recorded for answers and contributions that are partly right.

Testing should always take into consideration the ability of the group being measured. Accelerated students need a different kind of examination than do the less capable. There are many ways of accommodating this need. The chief means is simply to adjust the difficulty of the material to suit the class. One specific way to challenge advanced students is to administer examinations in which the students are allowed to consult their textbooks or other references. The open book test is disarmingly deceptive in that a time limit is always imposed and if the student has not studied his lessons in advance there will not be time for him to do it during the test. On the other hand, if he is allowed to look up a specific point, such as a date or a place, this may enhance the organization and style of his answer but it will not consume much of his time.

For slow students an interesting variation of the true-false test may be used to meet the needs both of examination of outside reading or research. The true-false test, especially as prepared by the classroom teacher, is often quite unsatisfactory and subject to much bad guessing and wrong learning. If, however, the items are marked as either true or false and then checked by means of library references, the assignment tends to serve two functions: it is a test of knowledge and at the same time a learning device. Guessing can be practically eliminated by requiring a terse statement justifying the answer. The following is an example of such a device which was used successfully with a slightly below average class in American history as a homework assignment and for the purpose of recording achievement marks.

## RESEARCH ASSIGNMENT

The American Indian

Directions:  Find proof or disproof of each of these assumptions about the American Indian in our history. On a separate sheet of paper copy the statement proving your answer.

Give the name of the book, author and page number for each reference.

Try to use as many different sources as possible.

1. The American Indian is rapidly becoming a vanishing race.
2. The United States government is doing very little to educate the American Indian.
3. American Indians are not citizens of the United States.
4. The ancestors of the American Indian came from Asia.
5. The first contacts between the white man and the Indian were made by Spanish explorers.
6. Indian culture has had no influence on the white man's way of living.
7. Many different languages were spoken by the American Indians.
8. Many white men were killed in the Battle of Wounded Knee.
9. American Indians dressed in white sheets during the "Messiah Craze."
10. By 1870 the number of Indians north of Mexico had decreased to one–third of what it had been in 1492.
11. American Indians are lazy and dull and incapable of being taught to do anything useful.
12. American Indian population is now approximately the same as it was in 1492.
13. Some of the Indians were cannibals.

Many cities and states take their names from Indian tribes. This is true or false for:

Seattle, Washington                    (Explain each answer.)
Pueblo, Colorado
Iowa
Oswego, New York
Pottowattamie, Kansas
Chicago, Illinois
Choptank, Maryland
Picqua, Ohio
Cheyenne, Wyoming

## Teacher-Made Essay Tests

A subsumption of the philosophy expressed in this book is that educated persons will behave in a socially constructive way, and that education can be achieved in some degree by almost everyone. Further, education is not merely the accumulation of facts and skills, but their integration into useful and interesting means of adapting to society and improving it. First, then, a substantial amount of factual knowledge will accrue to the educated person, and secondly, he will be in command of a group of skills commensurate with his intelligence and needs. Among these skills, as the result of social studies learning, there should be the ability to conceptualize, to generalize and to adapt principles to actual situations. Another skill of importance, not necessarily learned in social studies, but certainly to be practiced there, is writing—expressing social concepts and facts in acceptable English diction. If these points have any validity, it is rather obvious that social studies students all along the course of their education must be made to write out their thoughts and learning achievements in the form of essay tests.

The tyranny of short answer tests, especially true-false or multiple choice, is such that intelligent and otherwise well educated students may proceed through high school without ever learning how to digest, organize and write about a statement or question regarding the materials which they have studied for years. The objection is often raised that in the essay test a student is only tested in English, and not in the subject of his study, that is, United States history or world economics. This objection is not only false, it is vicious, in that knowledge is worthless unless it is subjected to an adumbrative process. Speech is only verbalized thought, and written speech is the only true way of testing the processes of thought.[4a]

The principal difficulty to be encountered by secondary teachers is that their students will, in all likelihood, have been subjected to numerous short answer tests but to very few exercises in writing. It simply is easier to follow the accustomed pattern of more short answer tests. On the other hand, even though students of high school age may not be adept at writing out their ideas, there is no substitute for experience in this regard. Secondary social studies teachers should use essay tests, even though at first the results may not be inspiring. For the high school

[4a] See Banesh Hoffmann, "The Tyranny of Multiple-choice Tests," *Harper's* (March, 1961), pp. 37–45. He says "Testing in this country is too crucial an activity to be accepted on trust" (p. 45).

graduate who goes on to college this may be very important, because a vast majority of college course examinations are of the essay type.

Although there are difficulties surrounding the administration and scoring of essay tests, they should be used. One reasonable guide to the selection of items can be the criterion of critical thought and reflection. The primary skill to be tested is penetrating expression of ideas, always couched in language conveying knowledge of the subject matter involved.

Several essay items drawn from a particular chapter in a specified textbook, with some alternative choices, may be offered as an example of a teacher-made test that was actually administered in a classroom. It must be remembered that the subject had been read and discussed for several days in class, and that the students were aware of the objectives of their study. This combines group comparison with an outside standard of achievement.

## UNIT QUIZ

Chapter 36, "United States Influence in the Far East"

*Making of Modern America,* Leon Canfield and Howard B. Wilder (Houghton Mifflin, Boston, 1958).

Choose two questions from those below and answer them in as much detail as possible, keeping the subject of the question well in mind. Write on only one question if you choose number 5.

WARNING: Organize your thoughts *before* writing.

1. Describe the Open Door policy. Why was the United States interested in maintaining this policy in the Far East?
2. How did Japan try to close the Open Door? Why did she dislike the American policy?
3. What is Japanese imperialism and how did it threaten the policy of the Open Door?
4. Describe the relations between Japan and America with the development of Japan as a world power (for example, friendly, hostile, neutral? give specific events to illustrate).
5. Discuss America's Far Eastern policy during the twentieth century, including relations with both Japan and China. Note understandings or misunderstandings on either side, treaties signed, agreements reached and the subjects of controversy.

In scoring such a test the teacher should prepare a numerical scale, giving a value to each possible point of information that could be gleaned from the chapter covered. In addition, point value should be assigned to organization and skill in presentation—logicality, grammar, vocabulary, etc. Each paper should then be given a number mark so that all of them can be arranged in ascending order from poorest to best. One way to accomplish this is to arbitrarily establish 100 as the top, then allow a variation of ten points for skill in presentation. Divide up the remaining 90 points equally among whatever number of specific items of information that might be reasonably presented in the essay. Care should be exercised not to equate very minor factual points with major ideas and concepts. In fact, two sets of point values can be established: a smaller value for each of many small points, and greater numerical value for a small number of major ideas. If the scoring is carefully handled the essay test can be just as objective as the short answer test, and it will have the added advantage of giving practice in writing and organizing. This is especially important for college preparatory students because a great majority of college courses are tested by means of the essay examination.

All types of tests should be used frequently, drawn from both commercially standardized versions and from the ingenuity of the teacher. For further expansion of this theme consult the following bibliography:

Doris Baron and Harold W. Bernard, *Evaluation Techniques for Classroom Teachers* (McGraw-Hill, New York, 1958), is a late manual on the use of tests, giving emphasis to standardized tests but encouraging the use of teacher–made devices, principally for their motivational value.

*Educational Measurement*, edited by E. F. Lindquist (American Council on Education, Washington, D.C., 1951), is the most comprehensive book on the problem of constructing short answer or objective tests. It is the cooperative effort of many specialists in the field of measurement.

H. A. Greene, A. N. Jorgenson and J. R. Gerberich, *Measurement and Evaluation in the Secondary School*, 2nd ed. (Longmans, Green, New York, 1954), discusses especially the role and use of teacher–made tests.

Joseph E. King, "Using Tests in the Modern Secondary School," *Bulletin of the National Association of Secondary School Principals*, 32:158 (1948), pp. 3–92, is mainly devoted to a discussion of specific standardized tests.

## 4. Evaluating Teachers and Courses of Instruction

Evaluation of beginning teachers and assessment of appropriate personality for teacher trainees has been discussed already in the section on teacher preparation. The basic personality characteristics of the good teacher will be expected to improve with experience, and their continual appraisal by rating officers will be a teacher's expectation throughout his career. It is each teacher's continuing responsibility to try to develop along useful and satisfactory lines.

Beyond this is the realization that must come to every teacher that as he progresses in his profession new ideas and new techniques must be incorporated into his professional personality. In the last analysis it is the personal task of each teacher to scrutinize his own practices and to improve them constantly. It becomes a matter of professional pride to become not only a specialist in social studies but a more and more highly skilled and proficient teacher.

Among the administrative duties of school system officials, often shared with teachers, is evaluation of school programs. This is closely allied to curriculum revision and the personal assessment of staff members who are striving to meet the objectives of the curriculum. It is mainly a matter of careful, close and continuous scrutiny of the offerings, goals of education and the particular procedures employed to reach them. Nearly every school, school system, county, state or national educational body is engaged in the study of how to improve the curriculum and its administration. At the level of the school, teachers are usually involved along with the administrators in this enterprise. There are curriculum revision committees at all levels employing the evaluative cooperation of teachers.

In the social studies there are some particular problems of evaluation that are possibly more acute than in some of the other fields. The nature of the subject matter is of necessity changing constantly and current problems are always involved. Since one of the major purposes of social studies is to produce competent citizenship the current needs of citizenship must be considered, and when they change curricular content must also change.

Under the auspices of the National Council for the Social Studies, Ole Sand, in 1955, prepared a list of procedures to follow in the assessment and revision of social studies curricula. He gave the following ten points:

1. Study children and youth.
2. Study contemporary society, including problems which endanger international relations and those which endanger interpersonal relations.
3. Study what others have done.
4. Formulate and use a philosophy.
5. Develop a defensible theory of learning.
6. Formulate clear objectives which indicate both behavior and content.
7. Develop creative learning experiences.

8. Select instructional materials.
9. Organize learning experiences to provide for continuity, sequence, and integration.
10. Evaluate the extent to which each individual attains the objectives, with particular emphasis on behavioral change.

The order in which these steps are followed need not be the same as the order of presentation. . . . The initial point of attack depends upon the concerns of the faculty and students, the problems already identified, available data, and the like. The social studies curriculum may be improved by beginning at any point, providing all 10 aspects are eventually studied and revised. Each task requires the united efforts of individual teachers and groups of children, individual schools, school systems, universities, state agencies, and study councils. The National Council for the Social Studies has a unique function in coordinating the efforts of these groups.[5]

The total aim of education is to produce generally educated citizens in a process which in itself is an experience in citizenship, with an interesting and beneficial atmosphere. Social studies encompasses a very broad slice of this experience, and its success is measurable in the attainments of the students. Evaluation of students in a sensible and efficient way points to the needed evaluative procedures to be followed in assessing and improving the programs of instruction. The evaluation of social studies varies from teacher to teacher and from school to school. The important thing is that it be done continuously.

### Summary

Evaluation must be based on some kind of theory, preferably a broadly based one. Measurement must be accomplished, and those being measured ought to know what the standards consist of. Subject matter alone is not enough to test; attitudes and behavior can be assessed also. Social studies, being almost as broad as the whole curriculum, cannot be measured merely in terms of chronological facts. Expression in writing and the mastery of basic processes of thought have to be tested along with the learning of separate facts. Above all, the process of evaluation must be continuous.

### 5. Suggested Activities for Further Study

1. Make up a test of fifty short answer items based directly on a standard textbook in American history for senior high school. Analyze each question carefully, attempting to include only one bit of information in each,

---

[5] Ole Sand, "Tasks to be Done in Improving the Social Studies Curriculum," *Improving the Social Studies Curriculum,* edited by Ruth Ellsworth and Ole Sand, Twenty-sixth Yearbook of the National Council for the Social Studies (Washington, D.C., 1955), p. 237.

rigorously excluding items with alternative answers and "hidden" irrelevancies.

2. Select a passage from some common source document in United States history, such as Bryan's Cross of Gold speech, and attempt to phrase an essay examination question that will elicit the type of understanding statement you consider to be appropriate learning from having studied that document. Try to get the chance to administer the examination to some of your own contemporaries.

3. In a teaching procedures class it is an interesting exercise to get each prospective teacher to contribute one short essay question, from which the instructor can prepare a test to be administered to the whole group. The next step is, obviously, to have each student mark someone else's test.

4. Write out your philosophy of evaluation in regard to students, teachers and programs of instruction in social studies.

## 6. Suggested Further Reading

TESTS AND TESTING

Howard R. Anderson and E. F. Lindquist, *Selected Test Items in American Government*, Bulletin 11, National Council for the Social Studies, rev. ed. (Washington, D.C., 1950).

Susan Bentel, "A High School Senior Looks at the Social Studies," *Social Education* (January, 1951), pp. 29–30.

Howard H. Cummins, "Evaluation of Citizenship Education," *Education for Democratic Citizenship*, Twenty-second Yearbook, National Council for the Social Studies (Washington, D.C., 1951).

J. R. Cunningham, "A Self-Rating System," *Social Education* (December, 1952), pp. 373–374.

Helen E. Deans, "Student Self-Evaluation in a Core Program," *Social Studies* (March, 1954), pp. 83–91.

William Dunwoodie, "How to Give Oral Examinations," *Social Education* (March, 1953), pp. 123–124.

L. B. Ezell, "A Device for Scoring Chronology Tests," *Social Education* (November, 1949), pp. 329–331.

H. H. Negley, "Using Checklists," *Social Education* (February, 1958), p. 74.

Neville Scarfe, "Testing Geography Objectively," *Journal of Geography* (October, 1953), pp. 275–278.

THEORY OF EVALUATION AND CURRICULAR IMPLICATIONS

Donald G. Bishop, W. E. Lamb, Emily B. Smith and Edith E. Starratt, *Community Planning in a Democracy*, Bulletin 21, National Council for the Social Studies (Washington, D.C., 1948).

Ryland W. Crary and John T. Robinson, *America's Stake in Human Rights*, Bulletin 25, National Council for the Social Studies (Washington, D.C., 1949).

*Improving the Social Studies Curriculum*, edited by Ruth Ellsworth and Ole Sand, Twenty-sixth Yearbook, National Council for the Social Studies (Washington, D.C., 1955).

*Skills in Social Studies,* edited by Helen McCracken Carpenter, Twenty-fourth Yearbook, National Council for the Social Studies (Washington, D.C., 1953), especially Chapter XIII, "Developing a Program for the Effective Learning of Skills."

Leonard Haas, "Evaluation in the Social Studies," *Social Education* (November, 1948), pp. 314–316.

Robert I. Ebel, "The Problem of Evaluation in the Social Studies," *Social Education* (January, 1960), pp. 6–10.

Earl A. Johnson, "How Did You Teach? Testing and Evaluation," *Theory and Practice of the Social Studies* (Macmillan, New York, 1956), Chapter 17.

Joseph Sher and others, "The Regents Evaluation Committee in Social Studies," *High Points* (May, 1954), pp. 5–12.

A. Somit and others, "Evaluating the Effects of Social Science Instruction," *Journal of Higher Education* (June, 1955), pp. 319–322.

Hugh B. Wood, "The Measurement of Social Values," *Social Education* (February, 1953), pp. 76–77.

OTHER

Hubert M. Blalock, Jr., *Social Statistics* (McGraw-Hill, New York, 1960), is an advanced textbook in statistical procedures which might possibly be of interest to the sophisticated student of evaluation.

# part VI
# GETTING STARTED
# IN THE PROFESSION

# 15

# Student teaching
# or internship

Beginners should work strictly according to models; more advanced pupils should work without models in front of them; accomplished students should work independently.

*Analytical Didactic*
COMENIUS, 1649

## 1. First Application of Methods

After the credential candidate has completed his major and minor and has mastered the theoretic work in professional education he is ready to attempt application, as a student teacher, of the methodology he has learned. Directed teaching under a qualified teacher in a regular junior or senior high school class is the most common way in which this experience is acquired. Such student teaching is usually for one term or semester, and will comprise two or three one–period classes a day. College credit is given for the work and it is normally part of the professional equipment required for certification. There are many variations in the precise way in which candidates are introduced to teaching, including internship which will be discussed a little later. In any event, the first application of teaching methods, the first real opportunity for instructing students, is the most critical and thrilling part of teacher preparation.

It is here, for the first time, that the aspiring teacher has a chance to test the theories he has so laboriously learned; he can find out at first hand how a philosophy of education can be put to use. The student teacher can discover his strengths and weaknesses, decide what more he needs to learn, and find, really for the first time, how effective he is likely to be in the profession he has chosen. "Student teaching is a period for exploration and continuous self-evaluation." [1]

For all candidates, regardless of their fields of specialization, certain specific objectives stand to be evaluated and modified in the process of student teaching. From a great deal of collective experience they have been found to be:

1. To determine whether teaching is really a good choice for a lifetime profession.
2. To gain actual teaching experience based upon democratic concepts of education, and to test the methods and theories which have been previously learned.
3. To gain a better understanding of children through teacher-pupil relationships.
4. To relate the curricular content with the collective needs of learners.
5. To become familiar with effective use of instructional resources.
6. To learn to evaluate student growth as well as individual teaching ability.
7. To develop essential enthusiasm for the learning process.
8. To develop an understanding of the functions and operation of a well planned school system.
9. To gain insight into school-community relations through participation.
10. To assess the teacher's position in regard to personal, civic and academic freedom. [2]

In meeting these goals three persons are involved: student teacher, classroom cooperating teacher and supervisor. Ordinarily, the supervisor is on a college staff and very often is the person who also instructs in teaching methodology, therefore, particularly in social studies, it is desirable that this person be a specialist in one or more of the social sciences as well as adept in the teaching process itself. The supervisor is often responsible for selecting the cooperating teacher and for working out, in conjunction with the student teacher and the cooperating teacher, appropriate activities whereby the student teacher may achieve the greatest value from his experience and at the same time promote the welfare and learning of the students. One of the most frequent criticisms of student teaching is that the children, the real center of the public schools, are sometimes slighted. It is the greatest responsibility of the college supervisor to see that such a criticism is not warranted. Student teachers must be well prepared. If they are, they become a positive asset to the school and they are able to offer the children something extra that they would otherwise not get, in the

---

[1] Lawrence O. Haaby, *How to Plan for Student Teaching*, Number 18, How to Do It Series, National Council for the Social Studies (Washington, D.C., 1954), p. 1.

[2] *Ibid.*, p. 1, based on the *Oak Ridge Student Teaching Project Report* (College of Education, University of Tennessee, Knoxville, 1951), pp. 1–2.

form of special projects, closer personal attention and a fresh viewpoint.

The first thing a student teacher must do is to get acquainted with the school, the school system and the surrounding community. It is not enough merely to know the one class to which he is assigned and the one resident teacher to whom he is responsible. The whole community participates in the matter of education, and for the social studies teacher who is above all a student of social relationships, it is extremely important to assess and learn about the total situation in which public education takes place. Specifically, the person in charge of a particular school is the principal. He is responsible for all of the activities that take place in and around the school. The principal of a school will usually have some sort of orientation program for the new student teachers. If he does not, the student teacher will do well to seek him out at the earliest opportunity. During this time student teachers can become acquainted with the teachers and other staff members of the school.

Student teachers, or for that matter any beginners, can avoid much embarrassment by refraining from quick judgments and unthinking criticism of procedures and customs. It is far better to learn what the established procedures are and then to operate within the familiar pattern that has grown up in a particular school. If in doubt about anything, large or small, a question is always in order. The student teacher should ask his room teacher or college supervisor. The student teacher who enters a school with the attitude that he is going to correct the abuses and stamp out all of the bad practices he thinks he sees is doomed to failure. The period of student teaching is a time of learning and adjusting to a future profession. It is a peculiarly vital and critical experience in which the student teacher holds an important position without complete authority. He is not a fully qualified teacher, and yet he is in direct control of the classroom much of the time. He is subject to the supervision, even though it may on occasion seem arbitrary, of the classroom teacher and the supervisor. The student teacher is more than a helper but he is less than the one in charge.

### The Three Way Conference

In order to meet the needs of the student teacher and at the same time to preserve the function of the public school and of the teacher training process, one of the most useful devices is a series of regular conferences during the period of student teaching among the student teacher, the classroom teacher and the supervisor. At such meetings the all-important matter of planning can be discussed and specific ways of proceeding worked out that are satisfactory to all parties. At these meetings all of the three separate yet interacting objectives of the three personalities can be integrated into a cohesive program for the student teacher. They also serve as a medium for expressing the three-way evaluation that is always going on. If each party will speak freely and honestly there will be no inadvertent misunderstanding that may lead to embarrassment.

## Planning

At the outset of student teaching, there is usually a period of a week or two in which the student will have the opportunity to be in the classroom and observe the teaching of an experienced person. In this preliminary period the student teacher may be asked to do some of the necessary chores of teaching, such as grading papers, preparing materials and perhaps handling a small group discussion with a portion of the class. His main purpose at first, however, is twofold: (1) to learn about the class, its character and composition, and (2) to get acquainted with the procedures of the cooperating teacher and to prepare himself to take over the responsibility of the class. It has been found to be good advice to beginning student teachers to have them start their own teaching in a manner quite similar to that of the regular teacher. This serves two purposes: (1) the high school students are less upset by the transition and (2) the teacher is gratified at being able to serve as a model.

To plan properly it is necessary for the student teacher to find out all he can about the individual students. He can get from the counseling staff cumulative records on each child showing aptitude, achievement marks, personality characteristics, home background, health records, any special data that a student might have produced and comments about many of them from previous teachers. Every student teacher should, before he takes a class, know the names of all students in it and outstanding or special facts about any of them who are exceptional in any way. The value of being forewarned is obvious in the cases of the very brilliant student, the one who is most likely to create disturbances, or the chronic epileptic who may have a seizure any time. Knowing something about each child makes it possible to take into account the inevitable individual differences that confront every teacher. It also helps the student teacher establish the essential rapport and trust which will ease his job.

While the student teacher is learning about and observing the children he must also accomplish another task. He must learn the established patterns of school housekeeping, the location of supplies and equipment and the manner of procuring them. For example, he has to know how the library operates, how and when to check out books, when he can take or send students there for research and how many can go at once. One of the first things to do is to get acquainted with the librarian. It is necessary to learn the routine connected with the use of typewriters and reproduction equipment. Find out where the workroom is located and, above all, the hours of its availability. Few things are more irritating to veteran teachers than to be subjected to interference from beginners in their regular practices in using the mimeograph machine. The same thing applies to the use of audio-visual equipment and materials. If the student teacher uses a projector or tape recorder he should request it properly and return it promptly. If he needs an operator he must plan in advance and follow prescribed procedures.

In every school there are emergency procedures for disaster, fire, earthquake or cyclone, for referring children to the medical or psychological service, for handling serious disciplinary problems. The student teacher must learn them and follow them in case they are invoked. It would be disconcerting to hear the bell for a fire drill and not know what it meant or what to do. It might be more than just a drill, and the student teacher would be suddenly placed in a position of extreme responsibility. He must know what to do.

Important also to initial planning is observation of the technique used by the teacher in charge. The student teacher should pay special attention to the way in which the experienced instructor handles individual differences in students, how he allows for the speed of comprehension of slow learners, and how he stimulates the quicker ones. There is no prescription for the best way to teach; every teacher works out his own methodology, and it is certainly not advisable to follow slavishly the precept of anyone in this regard. It is evident, however, that almost any beginner can profit from watching one who is adept and smooth in his approach. After the student teacher has learned and tested some of the procedures of his cooperating teacher, then he should experiment with his own ideas, but for the generality of novices it is a good idea to become familiar first with his immediate model.

As soon as the student teacher has become somewhat familiar with the school, the particular class and with the procedures of a master teacher, he should begin to outline the material he hopes to cover in the units he is to teach. This outline should be derived in cooperation with the teacher and the supervisor, and of course, it must be in consonance with the curriculum and philosophy of the school. This is not a lesson plan, but merely an overall guide and an agreement among the teacher, the supervisor and the student teacher as to what he ought to do. This step implies, just as all of the others in teacher preparation, the candidate's subject knowledge blended with his willingness to adapt that knowledge to the best procedures in presenting it that can be devised.

### Lesson Planning

Planning is implicit in the establishment of an objective. To propose learning about United States history, or to examine the American family, to set out to explore three or four thousand years of Western civilization, may be the objective. Whatever the course, a wise teacher will prepare an outline covering the whole thing with some sort of tentative time schedule and a list of the intended activities. This is the first stage in planning the teaching of a given course of instruction. In many cases the textbook will furnish the basic outline, but it almost always must be modified to suit the local conditions and the maturity of the students.

The next factor to consider is the weekly allocation of time, divided into daily or other periods, which is to be devoted to the particular subject in hand. Again, the wise teacher will plan in advance about where he will be at the end of any week in the year. There is no need to adhere rigidly to a timetable, but if one does not exist the teacher's greatest pitfall will loom continually—unexpected and unfruitful digression. This is not to say that digression is bad, but it should always contribute to the objective of advancing the students' learning in the field under consideration. School systems have established sequences of courses (some have programs that extend over fifteen years, or through the junior college level) and it is the individual teacher's responsibility to contribute his own share to the sequential learning of the students.

The final step logically becomes the daily lesson plan which should be prepared in groups of two to five, depending upon the number or times the class meets each week, and about one week in advance of their use. As well as keeping the teacher from wandering and assuring consistent advance toward the objective, this makes possible the same thing on the part of a substitute. Some schools maintain a policy of requiring daily lesson plans to be available in the event of unforeseen absence.

No set formula can be given for the preparation of lesson plans for all persons. Each teacher, as in other elements of methodology, will, with experience, develop his own scheme of committing his plans to paper. There may finally be no written plan at all. It is fairly sure, however, that good teachers will plan, and that most of them will continue through their careers to write out the essence of their plans.

A lesson plan to be most useful should contain certain elements regardless of the individual form it takes. It should refer clearly to the course objective, and this is usually indicated in the title of the plan. It should give the specific sub-portion of the course in which its subject matter falls, such as the name and number of the unit or chapter involved. It should be identified as to its place among other plans; this may be accomplished by a sequence of numbers, a set of dates or reference to other criteria covering the whole course. Each plan should have a concise and specific purpose to be translated into student achievement, such as "to help students understand the meaning of a federal system of government." The plan should list the references used by the teacher and the students, preferably as to page and figure. It should briefly indicate the type of procedure to be used in the presentation, with provision for any unusual equipment such as a globe or a slide projector.

Another aspect of planning has to do with the room environment and the actual arrangement of things. If the plan calls for use of a variety of materials, different books, maps, etc., these items should be listed in the plan prior to their use, placed in the proper sequence in a convenient place and made ready to use without delay or fumbling. Especially with younger pupils, no time can be lost in transition from one thing to another without danger of losing control of the situation.

The above items are mainly mechanical aids to memory or administration, but they are essential. The principal part of any lesson plan is a logically organized outline of the subject matter to be taught. This, of course, can have no set pattern. It should be as extensive as is needed by the individual teacher. This requirement will vary with the skill, preparation and experience of the teacher. It must be remembered that a lesson plan in its written form is primarily

TEACHING SECONDARY SCHOOL SOCIAL STUDIES

for the use of the teacher, and a mark of good planning may be that the students are unaware of it, only enjoying the results of a well organized and interesting lesson.

## Motivation

Planning, whether or not the particular plan contains a statement, must include a conscious effort at student motivation. Most often, at least for beginners, some concrete indication of the motivational device ought to appear in the written plan. There should be some specific way in which the teacher tries to arouse student interest in the topic even before launching into the specific content. Motivation, if done well, should tie the lesson together from beginning to end. An example of such a device, in connection with study of the Constitution, might be the teacher's reading to the class a news report of a recent Supreme Court application of one of the principles of the Constitution. At the end of the class discussion on the document, attention could again be directed to the initial item concerning modern application.

Prospective teachers should attempt several exercises in the preparation of lesson plans before they actually go into the job of handling a class. In summary, there must be a daily lesson plan designed to further the objective of education, of the particular year, month and week of a specific course. Preferably this should be committed to writing at least a week in advance. It should be detailed enough to have consequence, yet flexible enough to permit deferment, acceleration or fruitful digression. The problem of motivation should be considered in each plan.

## SAMPLE LESSON PLAN 1

United States History.

Unit II: The American Revolution and Founding of the Nation.

Topic E: United States Constitution.
Item 2: Federalism, powers and restrictions of the national and state governments.

Text for topic: Bruce Findlay, *Your Rugged Constitution* (Stanford University Press, 1950).

*Purpose of the lesson:* To help students understand the meaning of a federal system of government, and to encourage study of the Constitution. To specify powers granted or denied to the national and state governments by the Constitution and to relate the division of power to the federal system. *Procedure:* By means of lecture and question and answer, define federalism.

1. Delegated powers and residual powers (10th Amendment).
2. Hierarchy of laws (Article VI, clause 2).
3. Contrast Constitution and Articles of Confederation.
4. Contrast federal system with unitary system.
5. Attempt to develop certain concepts. Is federalism the "best" system? What are its advantages? Disadvantages? Under what conditions will it work best? What unique features of the United States contribute to the growth of federalism? Has the system adapted to the changes which have taken place in our country? Police power. Trade regulation. Franchise.
6. Have lists of state and national powers listed on the board in advance. Point out which ones have expanded with the increasing complexity of life.
7. Assign homework. Students are to discover the passages in the Constitution upon which are based the present state and national powers. Duplicate and hand out: beginning on page 64 of *Your Rugged Constitution*, look at the left hand pages for sections of the Constitution which grant or withhold powers. The explanation is on the facing right hand page. Make two lists of section and page numbers that (1) grant national powers (2) that grant state powers. Hand in tomorrow.

## SAMPLE LESSON PLAN 2

Subject:    United States History, Grade Eleven.
Unit:       Civil War.
Topic:      Prisons of the North and South.
Date:       December 8, 1959, 9:00 o'clock period.
Objective:  To acquaint students with the magnitude, destruction, and
            cruelty of the Civil War, with special reference to the prisons.

| Content | Procedure |
|---|---|
| Review last topic: British attitude toward Civil War. | Summarize why England did not intervene, why King Cotton failed to bring British support to the South. |
| Introduce new topic: Civil War prisons, their propaganda effect and what they contributed to the outcome of the war. | Read aloud to the class selections from *The Blue and the Gray* (p. 686 Danville). Could these conditions have been avoided? Stewards Hospital (p. 688), Andersonville (p. 690), and Northern prisons, Libby (p. 692), Point Lookout (p. 695), Fort Delaware (p. 698). |
|  | Which were worse, Northern or Southern prisons? |

Make assignment for homework: Write about a hundred words to bring to class for discussion tomorrow on the topic, "What did the prison system during the Civil War do toward determining the outcome of the war?"

References: *The Blue and the Gray,* edited by Henry Steele Commager (Bobbs-Merrill, Indianapolis, 1950).

Thomas Bailey, *A Diplomatic History of the American People* (Appleton-Century-Crofts, New York, 1958), rev. ed.

*Preliminary Checklist for Student and Beginning Teachers*

Things to do at the outset of student teaching or upon getting a new position:

I. General

Obtain policy statement of the school system, map of city, plan of school layout, names of principal system administrators, names and duties of administrative staff of the school.

II. Local Routine

Get acquainted with chairman and members of the department in which work is to be done.

Discover the location of facilities to be used: classrooms, workroom, library, offices, rest rooms, medical quarters.

Learn schedules and procedures for use of duplicating and audio-visual equipment, library use, procurement of books and supplies.

Get schedules of special principal's meetings, faculty meetings and extra duties of critic teacher. Attend those functions indicated.

Find out procedures for handling discipline cases, referrals to authority of serious cases, taking care of emergency medical situations and accidents.

Find out about fire and disaster drills and the procedures of evacuation—routes, areas, duties.

Procure overall class and activity schedule including regular assemblies and possible special assemblies.

Learn how attendance is taken and how bulletin announcements are made to both students and teachers.

Learn system of interstaff communication: bells, runners, etc.

Make every effort to discover regulations imposed at state, county, district and school levels. Avoid infringement of rules through ignorance of them.

III. The Students

Learn the individual characteristics of each child in class through observation, conversation with them, discussions with the teacher and by checking in the permanent school records for test scores—aptitude, achievement, personality—health records, behavior records, honors, athletic recognition, extra activities and home life.

Discuss the extraordinary cases with nurse, counselor, work experience officer, vice-principal.

Learn the names of every child in class.

IV. Curriculum and Cooperating Teacher's Methodology

Procure pertinent curriculum guides and get an overall view of the way education is conducted in the school. Study carefully the whole social studies program. Determine the specific part of instruction that your class is to encompass.

Observe your master teacher's performance and discuss methodology with him. Find out how he would like you to begin.

Volunteer services of a routine nature: checking assignments and preparing materials or helping in arrangement of the room, etc.

V. Planning Work

Three way conference among student teacher, cooperating teacher and supervisor.

Lay out an outline of material to be covered in the course.

Establish responsibility for your particular units of work.

Collect needed materials.

Write out daily lesson plans in advance of performance and submit them to cooperating teacher in time for approval or suggestion.

Try to assess the proper amount of work to attempt each day.

Be sure students know exactly what they are to do and that they are continually occupied.

Determine school's homework policy and abide by it.

Familiarize yourself with the students' materials: texts, workbooks, references, etc.

Ascertain evaluation policy and plan your own program of testing.

Ask advice on teaching procedures and know your subject.

### Discipline

Anticipation of discipline problems and what to do when they arise stands very high among the apprehensive thoughts of prospective teachers. The closer a candidate comes to the actuality of facing a class the more concerned he usually becomes about the vague apparition of "discipline." Few persons understand this matter until they have really taught classes in school. Much has been written about student discipline, but little really good advice can be given because there are no prescriptions with a specific result. Only one thing is certain. Good discipline always accompanies satisfactory learning in school. How this is achieved is a matter having to do with so many variables that no single statement can encompass them. On the whole, the best teachers do not have discipline problems; these do not arise when students are interested, know what they are doing and are kept to the task of doing it.

Throughout this book knowledge has been stressed as the basic and most important component of education and therefore of the schools, and if this philosophy is maintained, bad conduct among students will be at a minimum. Therefore discipline grows right along with the increase in knowledge of everyone concerned with the education process. If all teachers make sure from the outset that every student understands the nature of school work, that strict attention is not simply demanded but essential to the discharge of responsibility, then discipline problems will not arise and there will be no need for corrective measures.

There are a few simple procedures that may help to achieve the desired result: start each lesson promptly. Maintain dignity yet be friendly. Teach only when there is perfect attention. Insist on the completion of all assignments in the degree commensurate with each student's ability. Do not give more work or more difficult work than the students can do, but be sure that they do not have too little.

### Homework

In connection with the last point, and very important in establishing and maintaining good discipline, homework assignments must never be given as punishment. It is not punishment to learn, and if a negative value is placed on learning outside class the results can be devastating. To punish with extra work is as outmoded as ridiculing stupidity or using the device of the dunce cap.

At the secondary level, homework should be a regular part of the learning program. Every school and each teacher should participate in a coordinated program of outside assignments. The total amount of homework is a matter to be determined by the whole faculty in response to the philosophy of the school, but no teacher should usurp the complete time of students. All of the subjects are important, and they all have their place in the curriculum. The homework program should have no punitive aspect whatsoever, and it should not be considered as an encroachment on students' free time. It is simply an extension of the school learning situation into the everyday lives of the learners.

One of the best ways to handle this, and at the same time to promote the cause of good discipline and high morale, is to start each homework assignment in class. At the end of recitation periods a few minutes can be set aside for explanation of the assignment and some actual checking on the way in which individual students go about it. If the assignment requires reference books or a large variety of materials the teacher may profitably take the whole class to the library and see that they get started properly. A definite time for completion of assignments must be established and understood, and every bit of homework assigned must be evaluated by the teacher. If students know what is expected of them they will do better work, learn more and exhibit better behavior patterns.

### Internship

Under the pressure of teacher shortages throughout the United States other means of professional training have been explored. The programs that have proved successful and satisfactory are generally classifiable as internship—a form of apprenticeship in lieu of academic professional training or to supplement it. Two approaches are usually indentifiable: (1) waiving of all professional work, including student teaching, with the substitution of a year or more of actual teaching supervised by a member of the school staff or a college supervisor, and (2) substituting a year or more of partial responsibility for a classroom plus a limited amount of professional work either prior to or concurrently with the internship, for the normal year of professional course work and student teaching.

There are a number of such programs, representing both approaches, now in operation, especially in the areas of greatest congestion.[3] Some advocates of reform of teacher preparation espouse some form of internship as the desirable substitute for the present practice including student teaching. This is still a very debatable subject, but certainly internship holds a promise of accelerating the entry into critical fields of enough teachers, and it may very well attract some persons of high quality and attainment in academic fields who would not otherwise be interested in spending the necessary time in schools of professional education. In the social studies, for example, persons trained in economics, sociology or political science, but employed in non-teaching positions, might very well be attracted to the teaching profession if they could enter it without spending the time and money required for a year of resident study.

[3] One such program is conducted by the University of Southern California in conjunction with the Los Angeles City Schools. Their brochure describes, in part, the duties of the student in his first two years' study leading to a secondary credential and a master's degree. "These duties are specified in detail by the University and the District. Examples: assisting in demonstrations and experiments; administering and checking subject area examinations; developing and readying audio-visual equipment and materials; contributing specialized knowledge for enrichment purposes; checking on incomplete or omitted assignments; developing individualized assignments based upon individual students' abilities and interests; analyzing cumulative records; and performing certain routine tasks as required in language laboratories, etc." (Southern California High School Specialist-Teacher Program, U.S.C., 1960.)

In any case, an internship program must be designed to furnish the same degree of competence that is the aim of academic preparation, and for those entering the profession by this means everything pertinent to student teaching also applies.[4]

## 2. Professional Ethics

The moment a student teacher or intern enters the classroom of a public school he is no longer merely a college student. He is a teacher in the eyes of the children and their parents. He has the same professional ethical standards to meet that are demanded of fully accredited teachers. In return for the respect of the students and the cooperation of public school personnel and the use of their facilities, the student teacher must strive to understand and accept an ethical code by which he will have to live professionally.

### Ethics

Every person of integrity operates from day to day on the basis of some definable code of ethics. This is usually the product of his social status and whatever environment has done for him, including his educational experience. The professional teacher has an ethical feeling substantially in common with that of most other teachers. He will have developed a sense of social responsibility, a feeling of loyalty for friends, respect for American institutions. The social studies teacher will find many fields in which to exercise loyalty, tact, judgment and concern for others. For example, the social studies teacher may have emphasized the study of history in his preparation for teaching; this same teacher may get an initial position in a large social studies department whose chairman has concentrated on a study of sociology both during and after his preparatory period. Both persons must have mutual ethical regard for the integrity of intellectual interests and choices. Fortunately, in the case of the social studies there is a common purpose and definition for all participants regardless of their individual specialties of learning. On the whole, personal ethical considerations must be left up to the individual teacher to be resolved into a code of behavior. Incidentally, the best way to approach an intellectual grasp of the elements of a desirable ethical code is to study philosophy, a large part of which is devoted to that end.

The National Education Association has formulated a satisfactory

[4] See Paul Woodring, *A Fourth of A Nation* (McGraw-Hill, New York, 1957), p. 235 ff., for a description of an internship plan including a minimum of professional education courses.

code of ethics for teachers, stressing loyalty, honesty and intellectuality. It is a good basic guide to professional behavior for all teachers to follow. For social studies teachers, the obligation extends just a little farther: social studies teachers have a special burden of representing the school to the public and of interpreting society to the school and their colleagues. First of all, this requires tact. It requires humility on the part of the teacher (perhaps above all else because of the scope of the field). The social studies teacher must be scrupulously honest in his intellect, careful of the feelings of others and extremely judicious in his statements which may be misconstrued in a derogatory way. The worst pitfall of the social studies teacher is to be misquoted to the prejudice of someone else, either colleague or patron.

American values and ethical choices are continually the concern of the social studies teacher. He must sustain the values and retain his own integrity. We have been warned in jocular spirit, "Always to remember never to use such definitive words as *always* and *never*," but in this matter their use in admonition is justified: always remember never to do or say anything that will redound to the discredit of the teaching profession or to any member of it. This is not to say that everything done in the name of education is sacred or that our government, right or wrong, is always justified. It is part of the American system of democratic values to allow healthy and honest criticism of institutions and individuals. This right should be exercised with judicious care.

### Code of Ethics for Teachers

*WE THE MEMBERS* of the National Education Association of the United States, hold these truths to be self-evident—

That the primary purpose of education in the United States is to develop citizens who will safeguard, strengthen, and improve the democracy obtained through a representative government.

That the achievement of effective democracy in all aspects of American life and the maintenance of our national ideals depend upon making acceptable educational opportunities available to all.

That the quality of education reflects the ideals, motives, preparation, and conduct of the members of the teaching profession.

That whoever chooses teaching as a career assumes the obligation to conduct himself in accordance with the ideals of the profession.

The body of the Code sets out the teacher's responsibilities under the headings of five principles. First Principle deals with the primary obligation of teachers to guide children in the pursuit of suitable knowledge and skills for the purpose of achieving adequate citizenship. Second Principle indicates the school's cooperative responsibility with the home for children's welfare, intellectually and morally. Third Principle emphasizes the public trust that teachers hold, and the interaction of the school and community. Fourth Principle sets out the mutuality of employer-employee relationships and the teacher's part in entering into a contract of employment. Fifth Principle reminds teachers that they are members of a profession with widespread and mutual objectives to be met in a cooperative and constructive manner.

### 3. Suggested Further Reading

*Analytical Didactic of Comenius,* translated from the Latin and edited by Vladimir Jelinek (University of Chicago Press, 1953), originally published in the seventeenth century, presents an interesting perspective on modern teaching methods. Modern students can still learn from Comenius.

John G. Flowers, Allen D. Patterson, Florence D. Stratemeyer and Margaret Lindsay, *School and Community Laboratory Experiences in Teacher Education* (American Association of Teachers Colleges, 1948), presents a broad sampling of various ways in which student teaching has been conducted.

Paul R. Grim and John U. Michaelis, *The Student Teacher in the Secondary School* (Prentice-Hall, New York, 1953).

Lawrence O. Haaby, *How to Plan for Student Teaching* (Washington, D.C., 1954), is a handy little pamphlet giving general hints as to procedure.

Clarence D. Samford, "A Word to Beginning Student Teachers," *Social Education* (February, 1947), pp. 71–73.

Raleigh Schorling, *Student Teaching* (McGraw-Hill, New York, 1949).

Raymond Schultz, *Student Teaching in the Secondary Schools: A Guide to Effective Practice* (Harcourt, Brace, New York, 1959), is a recent, concise treatment of the subject based on much experience.

Edgar B. Wesley and Stanley P. Wronski, *Teaching Social Studies in High Schools* (Heath, Boston, 1958), 4th ed., Chapter 31, p. 599 ff.

### 4. Suggested Activities for Further Study

1. Make a list of the things you expect to result from a term of practice teaching. How does it compare with the list at the beginning of this chapter?

2. What is the responsibility of the principal of a school in regard to student teachers?

3. Prepare a checklist of the planning procedure, starting with a course outline.

4. From an actual situation, if possible, prepare a set of lesson plans to cover a week of instruction in some social studies course. Pay attention to form, sequence, coverage and motivational devices.

5. What would you do in case of a serious infraction of classroom discipline, such as unprovoked profanity or a personal attack of one student by another?

6. Write to the headquarters of the National Education Association and procure a copy of the Code of Ethics for Teachers. Can you improve on it?

# 16

# Professional improvement and professional references

The whole art of teaching is only the art of awakening the natural curiosity of young minds for the purpose of satisfying it afterwards.

From *The Daughter of Clémentine,*
ANATOLE FRANCE, 1844–1924

## 1. Further Training

*Professional Growth*

If teaching is primarily concerned with awakening natural curiosity, then both the teacher and the learner must share that curiosity. Among the features that distinguish the superior teacher one stands out above the rest. He learns and enjoys learning throughout a lifetime. He never ceases to be curious.

The good teacher is teachable himself. He continues to learn and grow throughout his professional life. If this is true of all teachers, it is particularly so in the case of the social studies teacher. As the specialized expert in social relations the social studies teacher is often called on to perform outside of school, to give speeches, and book reviews, to lead discussion groups and moderate panel discussions. He is expected to know about and keep abreast of local and state politics and to help the community interpret these things. Two important aspects of the social studies teacher's professional status are pointed up here. First, academic freedom must be guaranteed to him outside school as well as in the classroom. This depends on a combination of his own stature and the attitudes of the community, which in turn are dependent to a large degree upon his ability to interpret the school to the community and to express with impartiality, objectivity and tact, the content of the problems which he is supposed to discuss.

Second, steady professional growth in all of the aspects of teaching is requisite to successful dispatch of the varied tasks of the social studies teacher. In order to build and maintain a reputation for learned skill and satisfactory interpretation of the school to the public, every teacher must continue to improve his knowledge and to broaden his experience. There are several ways in which to accomplish this. Community service as indicated above is one very good way in which to amplify the teacher's experience. There is no substitute for participation in civic affairs as a learning device for the social studies teacher. Every new teacher should enter with a will into the life of his community and grow along with it.

Along with such participation it must be remembered that teachers are citizens and therefore have the rights and obligations of citizenship. They should vote, discuss civic and state problems and enter into a real and interested identification with the situation in which they live and work just as should all citizens. Teachers have a right to be and should be Republicans and Democrats, support or disavow public measures, know about and help in the public scrutiny of public servants (they themselves are public servants), and in general exercise the prerogatives of citizenship, political and otherwise. Although unheard of a few years ago, there are now cases where social studies teachers are members of state legislatures, city councils and boards of college trustees. This constitutes real academic freedom and also true professional growth.

A person who has prepared himself as a competent social studies teacher and who enters into the life of his community with a sense of balance and interest in the welfare of family and friends will undoubtedly fall into the classification of those who are teachable. He will learn through his experiences and he will apply that learning to his professional job of teaching young men and women. In addition, there are a number of specific ways in which he can keep alive his interest in his profession and improve and advance himself. One of the most common requirements of school districts in regard to their teachers is to ask them to attend school themselves periodically—to go back to college in summer sessions and keep abreast of the latest developments in their respective fields. As a rigid requirement this is probably to be deplored, because if it is forced there is little likelihood that much good will accrue from the process. On the other hand, alert social studies teachers, knowing that they have a tremendous field of knowledge for which they are responsible in some measure will probably want to increase their competence in some phase of it at rather regular intervals. College study during summers is desirable under such circumstances. Very often, high school teachers of social studies have a typical pattern of pre-service training which includes a bachelor's degree in social sciences or history and a year of professional education taken at the post-graduate level. In many cases some of the graduate work will have been applicable toward a master's degree and the prospective teacher after a short time in teaching will want to return to school, either during summers or during a year's leave, and finish the advanced degree, usually in the discipline in which he specialized as an undergraduate.

Reading as the primary tool of social studies teachers and students is the most universally available way in which to advance one's professional status. The successful social studies teacher will probably find that there are several categories of reading which will be essential to his growth: manuals and journals in the various fields of his specialty, journals and books devoted to professional education, and the great field of belletristic writing both past and present, especially novels which are unsurpassed in allowing insight into the social processes which are such a vital part of the social studies teacher's responsibility.

Every teacher, even before he enters professional service, will quite likely become a member of some professional organization. National, state and local education associations exist and comprise in their membership the vast majority of teachers. This is the professional mark of the bond among those who teach. Such organizations are essential to internal communication within the profession and for the extremely important task of making known to the public those aspects of education which make possible its public support and improvement. Parent-teacher associations exist in all schools, and their successful operation depends upon the participation and activity of both groups.

For social studies teachers, there is another specialized professional organization which is of utmost importance. The National Council for the Social Studies is a special professional organization that forms the bond among all of those persons who are continuing students of social relations. In the interests of exchanging ideas and maintaining a broad concept of the profession, it is highly desirable for all social studies teachers to join and support this group. Their journal, *Social Education,* is a forum for the interchange and discussion of ideas, techniques and subject matter in the teaching of social studies. In addition, there is a professional organization representing each of the discrete disciplines of knowledge which go to make up the social sciences. Most social studies teachers will want to affiliate with one of these groups, such as the American Historical Association or the American Geographical Society. There are many others.

Although often overlooked by teachers in public schools because of the normal heavy work load there is a fertile field for professional advancement in research and writing in the various segments of the social studies. Every social studies teacher should have some basic training in the methodology of research in his special social science or in professional education itself. There is no better qualified group of people in the world to do research in the teaching of social studies than the social studies teachers. Moreover, research and writing is a most desirable way in which to advance oneself professionally.

Professional growth is not all work. In order to survive as a social studies teacher one must relax now and then. It is possible to relax and enjoy a vacation spent in travel and still contribute almost unwittingly to the objective of professional growth. Social relations, the basis of social studies, may be observed by the traveling teacher in all parts of the world. And what better way is there to spend a summer vacation than taking a Caribbean cruise or a trip to Europe?

## 2. Technique and Intellectuality

### Technique

What has been said applies to all teachers minimally qualified to perform the tasks implicit in any secondary school social studies curriculum. In addition, some of the differences in training and outlook have been sketched which mark social studies teachers and teachers of other subjects. What is to be presented now has to do with the differences between ordinary teachers and good teachers of social studies. The teacher of the future, charged with the moral and intellectual well-being of our youth in preparation for and participation in competent citizenship, ought to be better than teachers of the past. This does not mean that all teachers in the past were poor in their craft—by no means; many great teachers have functioned in all times, the remote past and the immediate past. It does mean, however, that we, now, as present day teachers, have an advantage that no one in any period of the past has ever had. We have full potential for taking advantage of all of the cumulative heritage that humans possess which is greater now than ever before, therefore we can and ought to be better in application of the techniques of instruction simply because there is more experience for us to go on.

In the adoption and use of teaching methodology a cardinal principle should always remain uppermost: Do not be afraid to experiment with new techniques, but do not discard old ones simply because they are old. The converse is also true: Adopt new techniques only if they are fruitful and good, and discard old ones only if they are not producing the results that they should. This ought to be incorporated into a point of view, a way of looking at teaching problems. In line with a positive philosophy of education, the teaching-learning process is supposed to accomplish something, i.e., an alteration and reinforcement of ideals, attitudes, behavior; it should put students in possession of the basic elements of the common knowledge of our culture so that civilization can survive, and it should, above all, give students a way of thinking creatively and critically. It is assumed that these things will be done if enough people learn enough things and learn how to think with the things they learn. Techniques of instruction, methodologies of pedagogy, have no other purpose than furthering the aims of education based on a sound philosophy.

When and if a particular set of techniques fails to accomplish its end, then, as in a factory where the tools wear out, it is time to change techniques. The main difference here is that we cannot shut down the production line to re-tool. It is necessary to maintain constant vigilance, and as a technique fails in its function, before the product is damaged, replace it with another. Such an outlook forces continual evaluation of the results of instruction in terms of positive learning. It also makes imperative the teacher's never-ending search for new and better techniques of presentation. No teacher should ever rely on one tried and true method, simply because there is none. The good social studies teacher will not try to find the end-all in teaching methodology; he will constantly seek the best tool to do the job he has in hand because he knows what the job is. It is not preoccupation with polished technique or perfection of method; it is to make possible learning on the part of his students to the end of better citizenship.

With the increase in student enrollments that has taken place in the past forty years and the expectation of even greater increases in the future, it has become necessary to give up—even though with nostalgia —certain types of instruction because they no longer work. Scholarship and technology have produced new knowledge and new techniques for reaching the perceptive capacities of a much more heterogeneous group than was the case before World War I. More is now known about ability testing and grouping, about the processes of learning and the psychology of personal adjustment. There are highly complex and useful machines for producing sights and sounds that can furnish the stimuli needed for perception of the facts, relationships and concepts necessary to an understanding of social information. Social studies teachers would be wrong to overlook or ignore the possibilities offered as teaching aids in the great audio-visual field that has grown up and been tested in schools, industry and the government.

There is no single teaching device that can do the whole job of teaching. It requires a judicious combination of specific methods and devices which should be chosen carefully and adapted to the particular purposes of the individual teacher and his class at the moment. As an illustration, it has been popular for many years to ridicule the use of a lecture method in high school teaching (even though practically all college teaching is done in this manner), and to espouse the use of a discussion or socialized recitation method exclusively. Recently it has been shown empirically that the learning results of one method as over against the other are about the same. The real difference appears when a combination is used; then there is more interest, more chance of real influence being exerted in behavioral change and increased development of skills concomitant to the main objective of the particular course of instruction.[1]

### Intellectuality

Intelligence and intellectuality are not the same thing. The first may be thought of as native capacity to learn, to adjust quickly to new situations, to have a special aptitude for something. Intellectuality is a way of looking at things, a point of view, which may be exercised without much regard to actual intelligence, except as it affects the degree of intellectuality and the scope of its application. The intellectual, at whatever level, tends to attempt to solve his problems by means of mental processes. He does not kick the automobile that fails to function; he tries to find out why it refuses to run. If he cannot do this himself, he finds someone who can. The non-intellectual's approach to a problem is generally to assign its complexity and his inability to solve it to some exterior force, usually a superhuman one such as the weather or the juxtaposition of the stars. The anti-intellectual (one hopes this is a diminishing quantity) tends to believe that mental processes are worthless, that all worthwhile ends can be achieved through force or coercion, that problems yield to demolition

[1] Thomas F. Stovall, "Lecture vs. Discussion," *Social Education* (January, 1956), pp. 10–12.

more easily than to analysis. Violence is the watchword of anti-intellectualism as peaceful discussion is the hallmark of the intellectual.

Obviously, every successful social studies teacher *must* be an intellectual. As a student of social situations, the social scientist cannot advocate force. He may not succeed in solving his problems, and certainly he will never give the world a flawless method of permanent problem solution; but the intellectual believes that the world will be a better place in which to live if its problems are attacked with mental powers. The world's knowledge, its cultural heritage which is the province of education to preserve and enhance, is very largely the result of intellectual processes. Behavioral application of principles learned in an intellectual fashion is often of a non-intellectual character and done by habit; but the principles have been derived through mental effort, intellectualized and made available to human use.

Education is not wholly an intellectual matter because much of what people learn both in and out of school is of a tool using nature —automatic in some cases, and devoted to mere human survival. The basic, important part of education, however, and most particularly in the social studies, is intellectual. That is, it depends, not primarily upon capacity or intelligence, but upon the point of view that the mind will function in the interest of the individual and of mankind. Sir Thomas Vaux, in the sixteenth century gave the thought in verse:

> Companion none is like
> Unto the mind alone;
> For many have been harmed by speech,
> Through thinking, few or none.

Professional status for social studies teachers is achievable through the processes of recognizing the basic nature of man, his struggle from uncivilized state to highly organized society, man's "perfectability," his capacity to learn and the ways in which he does this. Education to help man survive and improve is a matter of gaining competency in the several aspects of citizenship; basically how and why we live together on a particular planet. The social studies teacher, as part of that educational effort, has a tremendous task. He must know as much as he can, and be able to put it together: to integrate knowledge for a purpose. To learn disciplined knowledge, teaching methodology and personal integrity—this is professionalization of the subject matter.

### 3. Selected Professional Journals and Curricular References

Some of the items suggested here are repetitious, but only for good cause. There are certain professional journals that appear again and again in any study of social relations as a school subject. The competent social studies teacher-citizen must know and use them. First of all there is the necessity to keep up with current affairs. To do this one should read one or more of the half dozen weekly news magazines and a local newspaper. It is superfluous to specify which ones. Next, every teacher should have a program of belletristic reading. Again, no suggestion in particular would be adequate or in order here. It is enough to say that it should be done.

### PROFESSIONAL JOURNALS

Social Studies and Education

*Social Education,* published each school month by the National Council for the Social Studies, is the primary journal for all social studies teachers. It contains articles of all kinds pertinent to the growing needs of the professional in this field. It covers the whole scope from elementary grades on up through junior college. A glance at the footnotes in this volume will attest to the importance of the magazine.

*Social Studies,* published each school month by McKinley Publishing Company, Philadelphia, is second only to *Social Education,* and only because it is mainly devoted to the needs of high school teachers. Its articles are about equally divided between pedagogical subjects and unique subject matter treatment of interest to the secondary level of social studies.

*High Points,* published each school month by the Board of Education, New York City, is not strictly a social studies journal. It is devoted to the problems of high school teaching in general, and in this field has no counterpart.

*Harvard Educational Review,* a quarterly, deals in scholarly fashion with topics of philosophic interest in education—not concerned much with methods and techniques.

*Journal of Educational Sociology,* published each school month by The Payne Educational Sociology Foundation, New York, deals with the specialized field of sociology as it relates to education—of particular interest to social studies.

Under the following headings have been listed a few suggestions (not exhaustive) of the best journals in the various social science fields.

Social Sciences General

*Annals of the American Academy of Political and Social Science,* published bimonthly by the Academy, deals issue by issue with pressing social problems of international significance. Each issue utilizes the various methods and knowledge of many different social science approaches to one topic.

*Pacific Affairs,* published quarterly by the Institute of Pacific Relations, Richmond, Virginia, is devoted to timely and scholarly articles dealing with the Pacific Ocean area; *Journal of Central European Affairs,* published quarterly by the University of Colorado, deals with the area indicated.

*Foreign Affairs,* published quarterly by the Council on Foreign Relations, New

York, contains descriptive articles dealing with all phases of foreign affairs— all three of these journals have in common an integrated social science approach making them extremely useful to the teacher of social studies.

*Southwestern Social Science Quarterly,* published quarterly by the Southwestern Social Science Association, covers results of findings in eight different fields as well as joint efforts in two or more social sciences. Its areal emphasis is on the American southwest.

Geography

*Geographical Review,* published quarterly by the American Geographical Society, New York, is the most significant journal in the field of geography and is therefore of interest to all social studies teachers. It is not only scholarly, but its format and content are lively and provocative.

*Journal of Geography,* published each school month by the National Council of Geography Teachers, Bloomington, Indiana, is particularly oriented toward the needs of geography teachers, containing articles dealing with both method and content.

Sociology and Anthropology

*American Anthropologist,* published quarterly by the American Anthropological Association, Evanston, Illinois, is the technical journal of anthropology and is therefore of value to the general social studies teacher even though anthropology is not a secondary subject; but by virtue of that reason it is doubly necessary for social studies teachers to make the necessary effort to become aware of the findings and trends in the field of anthropology in order to enrich their presentation of the complex subject of social studies.

*American Sociological Review,* published bimonthly by the American Sociological Society, Yale University, presents a wide variety of articles in general sociology. As well as being the outstanding professional outlet for scholars in sociology, it is of interest to social studies teachers because of the intimate and vital connection between their subject, social relations, and the scholarly findings of sociology.

*Sociology and Social Research,* published bimonthly at the University of Southern California, contains a large number of short articles on various aspects of social research most of which have implication for the teacher of social studies.

Political Science

*American Political Science Review,* published quarterly by the American Political Science Association, Duke University, carries articles dealing with the scholarly aspects of political affairs. It is the outstanding journal in the field.

*Western Political Quarterly,* published quarterly by the Western Political Science Association, Salt Lake City, belies its name in that it does not deal with only western subjects, but rather is the outlet for western political scientists.

Economics

*American Economic Review,* published five times a year by the American Economic Association, Washington, D.C., is the top journal of scholars in the field of economics, sometimes rather technical.

History

*American Historical Review,* published quarterly by the American Historical Association, Washington, D.C., carries two or three extensive articles presenting research findings in world history. The valuable asset of the journal for the social studies teacher is the extensive and careful book and article reviews which it contains.

*Mississippi Valley Historical Review,* published quarterly by the Mississippi Valley Historical Association, Tulane University, is devoted to American history with a large section of book reviews and a teachers' section in each issue. The space devoted to notes and documents alone would justify its use by social studies teachers.

In addition to the above journals in history there are approximately one hundred others, each devoted to a special aspect of history or to a regional phase. Some samples are *William and Mary Quarterly* (colonial), *Journal of the History of Ideas* (intellectual), *Journal of Negro History, Journal of Economic History, Pacific Historical Review, Pennsylvania Magazine of History and Biography* and many others.

Outstanding enough to be given special attention by all teachers of social studies is a relatively new magazine, *American Heritage,* published every two months in hard back book style. This book-magazine is an eminently successful compromise between journalism and scholarly history that is very useful at the secondary level of instruction. The articles are readable and authentic. They cover the whole range of interest to be found in any examination of American life and for the most part can be read by high school students as well as teachers. The same publishers have recently launched another magazine of the same format but dealing with matters of general cultural interest. *Horizon* does not have the same curricular application that its sister publication has, but for meeting the needs of the teacher in an intellectual and cultural way it is unsurpassed.

## CURRICULAR REFERENCES AND GUIDES

In a field as broad as the social studies and so important to the whole subject of education it is impossible to list all of the books that might be valuable or applicable. It would not even be desirable. The number of books is so great that only frustration would ensue. Here, as a recapitulation of representative items will be noted a few titles designed to give bearings in a sea of literature. The best starting point might be Edwin R. Carr, *Guide to Reading for Social Studies Teachers,* Bulletin 26, National Council for the Social Studies (Washington, D.C., 1951). This small book contains one selection of significant book and magazine titles for the beginning as well as for the experienced secondary teacher of social studies. Naturally one teacher will be more interested in certain subfields of social studies than in others, therefore the various social science disciplinary lines have been observed to some degree. That book, as this section, is devoted to the purpose of minimal guidance only, and in each case the selection reflects the tastes and training, the biases and blind spots of its author.

Education

American Council on Education, *Latin America in School and College Teaching Materials* (American Council on Education, New York, 1944), is as full a treatment of the subject as exists in any one place. See also Chapter 15 and the issue of *Social Education* (November, 1958) devoted to Latin America.

Association for Supervision and Curriculum Development, *Fostering Mental Health in Our Schools*, 1950 Yearbook, National Education Association (Washington, D.C., 1950), surveys the pertinent material in relationship to the vital problem of staying sane.

Jacques Barzun, *Teacher in America* (Little, Brown, Boston, 1945), is a stimulating attack on the foibles of educators and the ills of education, with some answers that may be thought provoking.

Howard K. Beale, *Are American Teachers Free?* (Scribner's, New York, 1936), says that practically every facet of the teacher's academic freedom has been abridged.

I. B. Berkson, *Education Faces the Future: An Appraisal of Contemporary Movements in Education* (Harper, New York, 1943), is an attempt to chart a philosophic course in the welter of modern educational thought. It is based in the liberal tradition. The same author's more recent book, *The Ideal and the Community* (Harper, New York, 1958), brings his thinking up to date and contains a thoroughly documented critique of pragmatism as a basis for education philosophy.

Francis J. Brown, *Educational Sociology* (Prentice-Hall, New York, 1947), is one of the rare textbooks in this essential field of study for the student of social relations. This book is a good summary of the content of the subject.

R. F. Butts, *A Cultural History of Education: Reassessing Our Educational Traditions* (McGraw-Hill, New York, 1947), is a fair summary of the growth of education, placing stress on the last fifty years of development in America.

James Bryant Conant, *Education in a Divided World: The Function of the Public Schools in Our Unique Society* (Harvard University Press, 1948), probes the matter of what our schools are really meant to do. Again, in his more recent work in evaluation of American high schools, Dr. Conant has attempted to ✓ point out some limits to the function of schools as they may affect citizenship and as education may be the responsibility of the public.

Lee J. Cronbach, *Educational Psychology* (Harcourt, Brace and World, New York, 1954), is a general text covering the principles of psychology as applied to the school learning situation.

Merle Curti, *The Social Ideas of American Educators* (Scribner's, New York, 1935), is an examination of the social role of American educators of the nineteenth century in molding educational practice into a conservative pattern. ✓

John Dewey, *How We Think* (Heath, Boston, 1933), treats the problem of critical thinking and how it can be taught.

Benjamin Fine, *Our Children Are Cheated: The Crisis in American Education* (Holt, New York, 1947), discusses the imperative nature of the need for more and better teacher training. An antidote to the idea that all Americans are educated and that all teachers in America are well qualified.

Arnold Gesell and Francis Ilg, *Child Development: An Introduction to the Study of Human Growth* (Harper, New York, 1949), is one of the series of studies that has come from the famous Gesell Institute at Yale.

Ernest R. Hilgard, *Theories of Learning* (Appleton-Century-Crofts, New York, 1948), is a scholarly exposition of the principal theories of learning, each identified historically.

*Encyclopedia of Educational Research,* edited by Walter S. Monroe (Macmillan, New York, rev. ed., 1950), is a concise guide to significant research.

Mark Van Doren, *Liberal Education* (Holt, New York, 1943), is one of the earliest statements of the current position held by advocates of the "great books" program of liberal education as the only answer to college education needs. Arthur Bestor, *The Restoration of Learning* (Knopf, New York, 1955), is perhaps the best documented and most comprehensive treatment of the same subject.

Paul Woodring, *A Fourth of A Nation* (McGraw-Hill, New York, 1957), is one of the most significant books yet written in the field of educational philosophy. It is an attempt to make a synthesis of the two opposing views in the current polemic concerning the purpose of education in America. Professor Woodring is especially concerned with the need of modern teachers to be learned, to understand their subject fields, and at the same time to be aware of and use the best methods of instruction which have emerged from the experience of professional education during the past fifty years.

## Social Studies

Since social studies as a separate field of endeavor is relatively new, only having come into existence in 1916, the literature is not nearly as extensive as in other teaching fields, and a great deal of it is not yet in book form. Much of the best current publication appears in the specialized social studies periodicals that have been mentioned elsewhere. General teaching methodology is in many ways applicable to social studies teaching, so in addition to the particular social studies books there will be included here a few titles under general teaching methods.

Important in the field are a number of serial publications sponsored by the National Council for the Social Studies. Among these are the Bulletins (the guide to reading mentioned above is a sample of them). Most of the Bulletins are devoted to various teaching materials that may be of use to the social studies instructor. The Curriculum Series is another sequence of publications devoted to arrangement of the subject matter in the most useful and appropriate ways. Many alternatives are suggested. Typical of this group are *Social Studies for Young Adolescents,* edited by Julian C. Aldrich, Curriculum Series, Number Six (Washington, D.C., 1951), and *The Future of the Social Studies,* edited by James A. Michener (Washington, D.C., 1939). The third series of particular interest to the social studies teacher is composed of the yearbooks of the Council. These are devoted primarily to the problems of special content and techniques of instruction designed to meet the needs of young people in the modern schools who are attempting to learn about social relations. Typical of these are *Improving the Teaching of World History,* edited by Edith West, Twentieth Yearbook of the National Council for the Social Studies (Washington, D.C., 1949), *Skills in Social Studies,* edited by Helen McCracken Carpenter, Twenty-fourth Yearbook of the National Council for the Social Studies (Washington, D.C., 1953), and *Interpreting and Teaching American History,* edited by William H. Cartwright and Richard L. Watson, Thirty-first Yearbook of the National Council for the Social Studies (Washington, D.C., 1961).

General Methods

Jean D. Grambs, William J. Iverson and Franklin K. Patterson, *Modern Methods in Secondary Education* (rev. ed., Holt, New York, 1958), presents a number of case studies and generalizations concerning teaching methodology specially applicable in the high school. The wide range of student ability is stressed.

Raymond E. Schultz, *Student Teaching in the Secondary Schools: A Guide to Effective Practice* (Harcourt, Brace and World, New York, 1959), is a particularly useful manual for the apprentice teacher. It describes most of the pitfalls and gives practical advice as to how to avoid them.

Kimball Wiles, *Supervision for Better Schools* (Prentice-Hall, New York, 1950), is a thoughtful analysis, based on much experience, of the position of the supervisory officer in relation to classroom teaching. Permissiveness is the keynote.

Social Studies Methodology

This category contains two major subdivisions, elementary and secondary. Among the elementary books only the most recent need be mentioned here. John Jarolimek, *Social Studies in Elementary Education* (Macmillan, New York, 1959), treats the basic elements of curricular content and the specialized methodology to be employed in presenting this material to grade school children. Geography plays an important part in this book.

Few books paying special attention to secondary social studies appeared before the thirties, and since that time only a few authors have joined the ranks. The following list contains some of the outstanding books in this field.

Arthur C. Bining and David H. Bining, *Teaching the Social Studies in Secondary Schools* (2nd ed., McGraw-Hill, New York, 1941), is a practical guide. A. C. Bining, W. H. Mohr and R. H. McFeely, *Organizing the Social Studies in Secondary Schools* (McGraw-Hill, New York, 1941), is a companion volume extending the curricular implications of the other book.

Ernest Horn, *Methods of Instruction in the Social Studies* (Scribner's, New York, 1937), has been a most useful book because of its penetration into the problems of teaching thinking and reading in the social studies.

Henry Johnson, *Teaching of History in Elementary and Secondary Schools with Applications to Allied Studies* (Macmillan, New York, 1940, rev. ed.), is one of the earliest efforts to organize teaching methodology around a discrete social studies field. Despite this, history is the principal concern of the author.

I. James Quillen and Lavone A. Hanna, *Education for Social Competence* (Scott, Foresman, Chicago, 1961), rev. ed. It is largely a report on the five-year study of social studies teaching conducted by Stanford University. It is very useful as a reference to determine actual practice and especially for social studies teachers' points of view regarding philosophies of methodology.

Edgar B. Wesley and Stanley Wronski, *Teaching Social Studies in High Schools* (4th ed., Heath, Boston, 1958), is perhaps the most widely used text in the field, having been revised a number of times. This book is comprehensive, even to the extent of being too diffuse. It is useful as a reference in the matter of applying theory.

Social Sciences

The final reminder that social science is the scholarly repository of vital formulations concerning the human component of world relationships is here given in a very short list of books by persons concerned with the problem of making those formulations available to the field of education. The student and teacher of social studies must put himself into the position of the social scientist from time to time if he is to remain as a coherent interpreter of social scientific findings at the level of the schools.

Charles A. Beard, *A Charter for the Social Sciences in the Schools* (Scribner's, New York, 1932), is a brief and brilliant statement of the relationship between the social sciences and their school outlet, the social studies.

Charles A. Beard, *The Nature of the Social Sciences* (Scribner's, New York, 1934), is the clearest available description of what social science really is, and the differences between social and natural science.

Stuart Chase, *The Proper Study of Mankind: An Inquiry into the Science of Human Relations* (Harper, New York, 1948), presents an insistent argument for the application of method borrowed from physical science to solve the problems of social science.

Leonard W. Doob, *Public Opinion and Propaganda* (Holt, New York, 1949), shows how individual psychology is involved in the mass influence that is so often exerted on societies to make them behave collectively in a certain way.

*Encyclopedia of the Social Sciences,* edited by Edwin R. A. Seligman, 8 vols. (Macmillan, New York, 1930–1935), is a comprehensive collection of individual articles which discuss most of the facets of social science, including the important definitions.

*The Science of Man in the World Crisis,* edited by Ralph Linton (Columbia University Press, 1945), is a symposium of thought on research in the various social sciences.

Robert S. Lynd, *Knowledge for What? The Place of Social Science in American Culture* (Princeton University Press, 1939), is an important book which is designed to cultivate a true integration in the social sciences for the purpose of investigating significant aspects of human behavior, not merely data gathering.

M. F. Ashley Montagu, *Anthropology and Human Nature* (Porter Sargent, Boston, 1957), gives a sharp insight into basic human nature as it is illustrated and highlighted by the comparative methods of anthropology.

Kurt Lewin, *Field Theory in Social Science* (Harper, New York, 1951), presents the principles of a method of inquiry that disregards the limiting boundaries of disciplined knowledge, rather assuming that each subject to be studied is a separate field around which study may be organized utilizing whatever techniques and materials are appropriate.

## Postword

Anyone entering the teaching profession, and most especially that part of it dealing with social relations—social studies—has taken on a burden of responsibility unmatched in today's world. He must, as well as embark on a new phase of professional endeavor, undertake a lifetime of learning and attention to the social needs of individuals and the demands of society. His life will be rewarding just in proportion to the effort he gives to the growing and continuing problem of understanding his society in a world that grows more closely knit, and actually greater in extent, almost hourly. The social studies teacher must be a lifelong student of all sorts of things; he must be sensitive, learned and patient at the same time that he is vigilant in the realms of ideas and affairs. He must be national in allegiance and at the same time cosmopolitan in outlook. We think the social studies field to be very important and the social studies teacher to be a most important part of that professional endeavor.

Arthur Schopenhauer once said that "every man takes the limits of his own field of vision for the limits of the world." It is the task of the social studies teacher to expand the limits, first in himself, then in the rest of mankind.

# Index